Victims and Victimization

Victims and Victimization

David Shichor

Professor Emeritus
California State University, San Bernardino

Stephen G. Tibbetts

California State University, San Bernardino

WAVELAND

PRESS, INC.

Prospect Heights, Illinois

For information about this book, contact:
Waveland Press, Inc.
P.O. Box 400
Prospect Heights, Illinois 60070
(847) 634-0081
www.waveland.com

Cover: *Corridor in the Asylum*, Vincent Van Gogh

Contents

v

Part III: Society and the Victim   261

Preface

Victimology is a relatively new field of study, strongly related to criminology. In the last thirty years it has developed a large volume of research and methodologies of data collection, and it has influenced public policy on different levels. Currently many consider it a subdiscipline of criminology; some even think of it as a separate discipline having its own audience, research agenda, organizations, conferences, journals, and professional literature. Increasing numbers of universities offer academic courses in victimology that focus on learning about the victims of crime, their victimization, the problems that they face socially and psychologically, the efforts to reduce the risk of victimization, and the ways social institutions and individuals relate to victims and their needs.

The interest in victims was dormant for a long time partially because of the criminal law that viewed offenses as violations against the state rather than violations against the individuals who were actually harmed. Since the 1930s and 1940s, a handful of lawyers and academics began to show interest in the victims' behavior as a part of the criminal event. Others observed that victimization is not a completely random phenomenon and tried to ascertain the personal and social factors that make certain people more vulnerable to becoming victims of crime. The focus of interest on victims and their victimization became sharper during the 1960s and 1970s when grassroots organizations, such as civil rights groups, women's liberation, and children's rights movements, made strong demands that society should pay attention to the plight of the victims and deal with their particular problems. As a result, such issues as child abuse, domestic violence, sexual assaults, sexual harassment, and hate crimes were defined as important social problems that had to be addressed by considering not only the crime but its impact on victims.

Eventually, many of these issues prompted legislative actions. In addition to new laws, government agencies, nonprofit organizations, and private for-profit groups emerged to handle the psychological, social, and financial problems experienced by crime victims. These organizations and agencies included shelters for battered women, rape hotlines, victim aid and advocacy programs, victim/witness programs, and various counseling services. One of the major developments of intensified interest in victims of crime was the establishment and standardization of official victimization surveys. In addition to their importance as a statistical basis for policy making, they facilitated a great volume of academic and policy-related research projects focusing on victims and victimization issues.

This volume of selected readings is intended to familiarize readers with the history of the study of victims, the relationship between victims and the criminal justice system, and the various aspects of research on victimization. Some of the articles focus on topics that have only recently caught the attention of victimologists. These include, among others, victims of white-collar crime, victimization by corporate crimes, victims of hate crimes, and the victimization of college students.

We believe that the interest in the study of victims and victimization will continue to grow, and research in this area will be able to contribute theoretical, empirical, and policy-oriented knowledge for the treatment of victims of crime and for the prevention of victimization. We hope this volume of readings will help the readers become familiar with many of the issues victimology confronts in seeking explanations and resolutions for victims of crime.

Introduction

Victimology—the study of victims—is a relatively new field of study for social scientists, primarily criminologists. While the beginnings of victimology as an academic discipline can be traced to the 1940s and 1950s, it became an established and recognized field of study in the late 1960s and early 1970s. Since then, books, articles, symposiums, research projects, and published reports addressed various aspects of victims and victimization. Governmental agencies and voluntary organizations were established to assist victims and to uphold their legal rights. On the federal level, these organizations include the National Organization of Victim Assistance (NOVA) and the Office for Victims of Crime (OVC) (part of the U.S. Department of Justice); victim compensation agencies, victim/witness programs, various hotlines, and shelters were established at the local level. In addition, the World Society of Victimology convenes a professional conference every three years, and several national and international workshops are organized periodically to further legislation on victim issues and to develop services for victims.

One of the pioneers of victimology was Benjamin Mendelsohn, who saw this discipline as "the science of the victim." It is important to trace the development of Mendelsohn's interest in the victims of crime. In criminal proceedings victims were almost superfluous; essentially they were assigned the passive role of being the object of the crime perpetrated against them. As a defense attorney in Rumania handling criminal cases during the 1930s, Mendelsohn inquired about the victim's behavior prior to and during the commission of the crime. In order to provide an effective legal defense to his clients, Mendelsohn thought it was important to know the contribution of the victim, if any, to the criminal act. Mendelsohn's interest in the victim's behavior and possible role in the criminal episode could be interpreted as casting the victim in a negative light (by questioning the presumption of the innocent bystander against whom a crime is committed), but it brought attention to the role of victim, which had been submerged in criminal procedures.

Mendelsohn continued to develop his ideas about victims of crime until he arrived at the theory of "General Victimology" (Hoffman, 1992). According to his later writings this was a new field of study, not a subfield of criminology. Its purpose was to help "victims of all kinds—including victims of

1

events beyond human control" (Hoffman, 1992: 90). In this effort Mendelsohn (1975: 25) developed the concept of "victimity," which he described as the "whole of the socio-bio-psychological characteristics, common to all victims in general, which society wishes to prevent and fight, no matter what their determinants are (criminal or others)."

Mendelsohn thus launched the study of victims and victimization. When he died in 1998 (at the age of 98) he had initiated intense interest in a burgeoning field. Some followed his approach of focusing on the effects of all types of victimization. For example, V. L. Dadrian suggested that victimology should be seen as "the study of the social processes through which individuals and groups are maltreated in such a way that social problems are created" (1976: 40). Others narrowed the area of concern. Following another pioneer in the field of victimology, Hans von Hentig, the majority of scholars, researchers, and professionals currently involved in the study of victims and the provision of victim services draw a clear connection between criminology and victimology.

Criminal Victimization

There are important underlying assumptions attached to the term *victim*. As noted, the traditional implication is that the victim is innocent and therefore has a moral claim for compassion, sympathy, and help from others (Ziegenhagen, 1977). On the other hand, the criminal justice system did not address victims as essential components of the criminal law. At the same time, the role of the state, sanctions against offenders, psychological and behavioral specifications concerning criminal acts, and juristic standards were defined in detail. Until the 1970s penal policies and procedures did not pay much attention to victims' experiences and viewpoints concerning their victimization. During much of the twentieth century, when rehabilitation was the major penal ideology, punishment was often applied "as a tool to influence the future behavior of the lawbreaker rather than as a device providing satisfaction for those individuals who are harmed through violation of the law" (Ziegenhagen, 1977: 3).

During the last quarter of the twentieth century, the situation changed with the decline of the rehabilitation ideal and the adoption of retribution, deterrence, and incapacitation-oriented punishment policies (Shichor, 2001). The major developments in legislation and criminal justice policies concerning victims' perspectives offered certain opportunities for the victims to participate in the justice process. The new approach was the result of the changing sociopolitical climate that demanded tougher treatment of criminals and the growing activism by grassroots groups fighting for victims' rights, such as the women's liberation movement, the children's rights movement, and, to a certain extent, the civil rights movement (for more details see Weed, 1995).

The Status of Victims in the Past

In ancient times, victims had a major role in social control. Because of insufficient social organization, there was no recourse for wrongs other than personal retribution. The individual "made the law, and he was the victim, the prosecutor, and the judge" (Schafer, 1977: 7). Victims sought revenge for the wrongdoings against them and/or demanded compensation from offenders.

When people began to live in larger family groups, social control was maintained by extended kinship units. In this context an offense against the individual was considered to be an offense against the entire group. The individual victim's position was generalized to the extended group. Offense and victimization was no longer an affair between individuals; it became an issue to be settled by kinship units.

The social arrangement of blood-revenge recognized that the major threat to the individual came from outside the kinship group; family members controlled interpersonal problems. In this sense the blood feud increased the cohesion of the group and served as a defense for the individual against outsiders. However, the acceptance of collective responsibility (meaning that the entire extended family was responsible for the actions of an individual member) led to a vicious cycle of blood feuds and a chain of endless violence. People slowly started to realize that this custom aggravated and prolonged conflicts rather than solving them. In addition, it did not bring any tangible help to the specific individual who was victimized.

With the gradual development of more stable economic systems and a higher level of material culture, the arrangement of compensation-restitution emerged. The historical sources of compensation can be found in several ancient cultures. One of the first known legal documents that mentioned compensation was the Code of Hammurabi (king of Babylon in eighteenth century, B.C.). Although better known as a source of retributive justice than of compensation, this famous code of law makes a clear reference to compensation.

> If the brigand has not been taken, the man plundered shall claim before God what he has lost; and the city and sheriff in whose land and boundary the theft has taken place shall restore him all that he has lost. If a life, the city and sheriff shall pay one mina of silver to his people. (Edwards, 1971: 31)

Similarly the Hittites who conquered Babylon and became the dominant power in the Middle East from about 1900 to 1200 B.C. had clear elements of proportionality in their law of compensation (Dorff and Rosett, 1988). Biblical law also contained compensation, mainly in property crimes, but also in certain cases of personal injuries (Schafer, 1977). Generally, ancient law was more a law of torts (civil law) than a law of crimes (Maine, 1887). For example, many offenses that modern societies consider to be criminal violations—such as theft, robbery, assault, trespassing, libel—were treated as torts in the Roman law (Meiners, 1978). Similarly, the laws in primitive societies contained evaluations for most offenses as compensation to be paid to victims and not as punishments for criminals (Laster, 1970). In his exploration of the criminal-victim relationship among the German tribes, the Roman historian Tacitus found that: "Even homicide is atoned by a certain fine in cattle and sheep; and the whole family accepts the satisfaction to the advantage of the public weal, since quarrels are most dangerous in a free state" (quoted in Schafer, 1977: 11).

Offenses that were liable to receive societal punishment in primitive and in early German and Anglo-Saxon law were transgressions considered to be mainly sins committed against a deity, such as incest, witchcraft, bestiality, and blasphemy. The main reason for this practice was that these types of crimes could not be restituted to an individual person or to a family unit (Laster, 1970).

During these times, victims occupied a major position in the administration of law and justice. Their behavior or their role in the offense was not questioned, they were assumed to be innocent and passive, and their major function in the justice process was to be compensated for the injuries and harms accrued to them. The seriousness of the crime and the compensation were determined not only by the nature of the harm caused but also by the social status of the victim and the offender.

The importance of the victim started to decline in Europe during the Middle Ages with the rise in political and economic power of kings, on the one hand, and the Roman Catholic church, on the other. These two major forces developed the modern concept of criminal law that considers an offense committed by one private party against another as an offense against the state, which is charged with keeping the peace. Thus, offenders were held responsible to the state rather than to the actual victim. Later, the victim's relation to the crime was viewed as a civil rather than a criminal matter, and he/she could find remedies only through prolonged civil legal procedures. These developments clearly indicated the decline of the victim in society in general and the criminal justice process in particular (Schafer, 1977).

Toward the middle of the twentieth century the interest in the fate of the victim gradually started to rise again. It became evident and increasingly important that violators of criminal law cause not only social harm but personal harm as well, often with very serious consequences for the individual victim. In this vein, Schafer observed that: "There has been renewed recognition during the past few decades that crime gives rise to legal, moral, ethical, and psychic ties not only between the violator and society, but also between the violator and his victim" (1977: 24). This recognition led to a growing interest in studying the relationship and interaction between criminals and their victims.

The Study of the Victim

The rediscovery of the victim as an integral part of the criminal event was related to the efforts of scholars and professionals to understand the etiology of criminal behavior. As previously mentioned, Mendelsohn wanted to know the whole "truth" about the criminal cases that he handled. Since he was interested in understanding the total criminal situation, it became important to examine whether victims contributed to the criminal event in any way.

Hans von Hentig also focused on the victim's identity and behavior in the analysis of criminal events. He suggested a list of personal and social weaknesses that make certain individuals easier prey for criminals than others. In fact, he accorded a major role to the victims as illustrated in one of his statements: "In a sense the victim shapes and molds the criminal. The poor and ignorant immigrant has bred a peculiar kind of fraud. Depressions and wars are responsible for new forms of crimes because new types of potential victims are brought into being" (von Hentig, 1948: 384). Since not every individual has the same risk to become a victim of a crime, certain types of people have a higher probability than others to become victims. Walter Reckless, a well-known criminologist, made a distinction between victims predisposed by personal or social attributes and victims who are victimized because of their behavior:

> Certain categories of persons, property, and valuables seem to attract doer behavior because of their weaknesses or availability, while other kinds of individuals . . . appear to instigate criminal deeds in the doer as a result of escalation in social interaction, such as an exchange of insults, jealous accusations, unjustified obstruction, and so forth. (Reckless, 1973: 93)

Several scholars also have examined the victim's behavior as a contributing factor in crime. Marvin Wolfgang, in his comprehensive *Patterns of Criminal Homicide* (1958) labeled one type of homicide as *victim precipitated-homicide* in which physical force or the threat of physical force was first used by the victim. His students also used this concept in their research involving other crimes such as robbery and rape. While *victim precipitation* seemed to be a useful analytical concept in the study of face-to-face violent crimes (most cases of homicide and assaults), many researchers question its validity for the analysis of property and sex crimes where it is much harder to define what constitutes *precipitation*. For example, in the case of rape the definition of *precipitation* was largely determined by the perpetrator using terms such as the victim "behaved provocatively" or "she acted seductively" (Amir, 1971).

More recently, researchers have looked at an individual's lifestyle as a predisposing factor in victimization (Hindelang, Gottfredson and Farafalo, 1978). The focus was on the pattern of routine involvements in vocational and leisure activities. The research tried to determine if work, recreation, and other everyday activities created differential exposure to victimization. These differences are also related to demographic factors such as race, gender, age, income, marital status, and place of residence. This line of study is closely related to the routine activities approach of analyzing crime and victimization (Cohen and Felson, 1979). According to this approach, crime and subsequently victimization is a function of a motivated offender, an attractive target, and the nature of guardianship. When the guardianship is reduced or the pool of motivated offenders grows, the opportunity for victimization increases.

Most of these studies implied (some of them quite strongly) that to various degrees victims share the responsibility for their own harm. As was seen, the study of victims and victimization from its beginning showed a negative tilt against victims. Asking the mere questions of "what was the role of the victim in the criminal event?" or "what did the victim do when the crime was committed?" indicated some doubt as to the complete innocence of the victim. In other words, it was assumed that in a large number of criminal events, victims bear some amount of responsibility. "Blaming the victim" was reinforced by the tendency of victims asking themselves the following question upon their victimization: "what have I done wrong?" Also, the popular belief in the "just world" concept that people get what they deserve leads to the idea that victims are at least partially responsible for the criminal event (Karmen, 2001).

The tendency to blame the victim led to the construction of several typologies of "shared responsibility" between the offender and the victim. Mendelsohn (1956) suggested the following victim types: (1) completely innocent; (2) having minor guilt; (3) as guilty as offender; (4) more guilty than offender; (5) most guilty; fully responsible; (6) simulating or imagining. In a similar approach Fattah (1967) distinguished among five major types of victims: (1) nonparticipating victims; (2) latent victims—those who have certain character dispositions to be victimized; (3) provocative victims; (4) participating victims; (5) false victims. Some of these typologies include personal attributes of victims. Karmen (1990) provided a combined table of some of these typologies based on the degrees of shared responsibility.

Related to the study of victims and victimization is the issue of fear of crime—a perception of the risk of becoming a victim of crime. This is an important link. The fear often influences everyday life; for example, people may be afraid to leave their homes or to walk in certain parts of a city. The media exacerbate such fears. News reports of acts of violence or television programs that portray violent crimes or movies filled with violent attacks fuel the notion that crime is pervasive and increase the level of public fear (see for instance Skogan and Maxfield, 1981). In some cases there is a negative relationship between fear of crime and actual victimization. For example, it is known that the elderly tend to have the highest level of fear of crime and the lowest level of actual victimization rates. This paradoxical situation is the outcome, to a large degree, of the measures taken by fearful seniors to avoid becoming a victim. As a result of these measures, many elderly citizens stay home after dark, keep guard dogs, install burglar alarms in their homes, and put bars on their windows. High levels of fear can be considered a form of psychological victimization impacting the everyday life of individuals ("victims").

Renewed interest in the victim was essential in the development of the National Crime Victimization Survey (NCVS)—the most comprehensive source on victims and victimization. The first national survey, based on

10,000 households, was conducted in 1966 as a part of the President's Commission on Law Enforcement and the Administration of Justice. The primary source of official statistics on crime and criminal activity at that time was the Uniform Crime Report (UCR) that publishes crimes known to law enforcement agencies. Reporting only crimes known to the police does not provide a completely accurate picture of the crime situation. Therefore, the original intent of victimization surveys was to receive more information about the real extent of crime by surveying a large random sample of people about crimes that may have been committed against them. Over time these surveys became methodologically sophisticated and are now routinely conducted by the Bureau of Justice Statistics, a research arm of the U.S. Department of Justice. The NCVS encouraged secondary analyses of the data sets containing the accumulated information on victims and victimization. These sophisticated research studies were instrumental in learning about the patterns of victimization and had policy implications for crime prevention.

The Victim and the Criminal Justice System

Victims are the most important persons in the criminal justice process. Without their participation the overwhelming majority of crimes would not be reported, most suspects would not be apprehended, and many court cases would not result in convictions. Nevertheless, a large number of victims feel that the system does not handle them well and often inflicts a "second wound" (the actual victimization being the "first wound").

Studies of crimes and victimization point out that the criminal justice system does not handle all cases uniformly. Historically, the identities of both the offender and the victim have been determining factors in justice procedures (Barnes and Teeters, 1959). To a degree, this is still true today at every stage of the criminal justice process. The victim's identity, character, and behavior may be a factor in the arrest of a suspect, in the prosecutorial decision, in the determination of guilt or innocence, and in the sentencing (Williams, 1976). One of the determining factors is the personal relationship between the victim and the offender. The likelihood that a case will be dismissed or dropped when there is a family or friendship relation between the victim and the defendant is much higher than in other cases.

Victims express dissatisfaction with law enforcement's failure to apprehend and arrest suspects, with the lack of adequate protection against intimidation from offenders, and with impersonal handling of their case by officers. On the other hand, victims can influence police proceedings. Researchers found that the attitude of the victim toward the offender and the crime played an important part in police decisions concerning the handling of a case. For example, Sellin and Wolfgang (1964) suggested that victim attitudes ranked immediately below the prior criminal record of the offender and the nature of the offense as the most important factors in police decisions.

The proliferation of victim/witness programs is another indication of the victim's importance in the criminal justice process. These programs were established to ensure the readiness of victims and witnesses to participate in the criminal justice proceedings. Despite their critical importance to the functioning of the system, many victims perceived that the rights of the offenders received much more attention than the rights of the victim witnesses. When a suspect was arrested and brought to trial, victims and witnesses often were subject to a great deal of inconvenience. They had to appear several times in the courtroom, sacrificing time from work or from family and submitting themselves to rigorous questioning on the witness stand by the defense attorney. Often, they had to wait for hours in the same waiting room with the offenders who had victimized them. Because of these unfavorable conditions, many victims and witnesses were not ready to report crimes and to cooperate with the criminal justice agencies.

Since the 1970s victim/witness programs have attempted to address the problem. Separate waiting rooms for victims and witnesses now exist; "on-call service" notifies victims and witnesses shortly before they have to appear to testify rather than having them wait for hours at the court; transportation is arranged if needed; and remuneration is provided for wages lost because of participation in the justice process.

Despite efforts to address concerns of victims, there are issues that can make the relationship between victims and the prosecution problematic. Victim/witness programs usually are operated by prosecutors. Many victims believe that the primary goal of the programs is to benefit the district attorney's office, which needs a high conviction rate to prove its effectiveness. Also, these programs mainly help victims who are considered essential in winning a case, and there is a perception that prosecutors do not care about other victims. This reinforces the victims' beliefs that their interests are only secondary to the prosecutor's interests.

The victim is represented in the proceedings by the district attorney—who is also the representative of the "people" in his/her entire jurisdiction. This fact means that issues other than the interest of the victim might influence the handling of a case. The prosecutor has the discretion to determine the priority of the cases. In contrast, the defense attorney has only one client—the defendant—and considers only what is in his/her client's interest. It is well known that the large majority of cases are settled through plea negotiations between the prosecution and the defense rather than by trial. Victims do not participate in these negotiations and are often frustrated by their results. Many victims criticize the plea-bargaining system as disrespectful of their suffering, treating them as mere pieces of evidence expected to testify but not to be informed of developments in their case (McCoy, 1998: 469).

Programs aimed at providing financial aid to victims of crime are another result of the upsurge of interest in victims. Victim compensation started in the 1960s in a few foreign countries and in several states in the United States as well. The intent was to provide public funds to the victims of violent crimes (and in some states to their relatives) to recoup some of their financial losses. Currently, almost all states have compensation programs, but the amounts and conditions of coverage differ. Also, many victims claim that the filing process is burdensome and payment substantially delayed. Restitution (payment by offenders to their victims) has become a regular part of sentences. In addition to the victim benefiting from the payment, restitution "may help criminals to appreciate the nature of the harm they inflict on others" (Geis, 1977: 162).

Various other victim assistance programs such as counseling and emergency services, rape hotlines, and shelters for abused children and for battered women have emerged over the years. Victim advocacy programs provide legal advice to victims and protect their rights and interests during legal proceedings. Other programs involve victims and offenders in a mediation process to achieve better understanding of each other, to reach agreement on restitution, and to bring closure to a painful episode for both parties.

Suggestions from researchers have also prompted changes. Wolfgang's (1979) recommendation that sentencing should be based on both the legal culpability of the offender *and* on the degree of harm caused to a particular victim was incorporated into criminal justice proceedings. Wolfgang (1979: 22) argued that "If varying the attributes of the victims and consequences to the victims alters the degree of harm, corresponding variations in the penalty can be justifiably argued, so long as degrees of harm define seriousness and seriousness commands sanction."

Since this suggestion was made, several laws have been enacted to enhance punishment for the victimization of certain specific population groups including children, the elderly, and the victims of hate crimes. Ever since allowing victim impact statements during the judicial proceedings, special consideration has been given to the particular harm done to individual victims. While these developments are generally beneficial for the victims, there have been controversial effects as well. For example, singling out certain victim groups and introducing individual harm considerations raise questions regarding the uniformity of justice. These changes reinforce claims that policies ostensibly designed for the support and benefit of victims are actually aimed at inflicting more severe punishments against offenders. In general, it is important for the maintenance of just penal policies that laws aimed at maintaining victims' rights do not automatically result in harsher punishments for offenders. Often, groups advocating law and order and the embracement of "tough on crime" policies are using the victims' cause to further their objectives of promoting more severe punishments.

Victimization and Organizations

Originally, victimology focused on individual victims of violent crimes committed by individual perpetrators. Gradually, victimological studies expanded to organizations and corporations as victims and victimizers.

Organizations are often easy targets for victimization, because many people who interact with them (employees, customers, clients, etc.) do not have much interest in the welfare of the organization. They see organizations as impersonal and able to absorb losses, not as victims. Organizations, thus, are vulnerable to crimes of low visibility such as employee theft, embezzlement, and bribery. Because of the low visibility of crimes committed against them and the public's lack of identification with them, organizations are "denied access to an important source of protection afforded the personal victim: the sympathy and conscience of the general population" (Smigel and Ross, 1970: 5). In addition, the belief that organizations are not really harmed by victimization because they carry comprehensive insurance and will be reimbursed for any loss that they may incur further decreases public concern and sympathy toward them as victims.

Lately there is a growing interest in the study of crimes committed by organizations and corporations (for example, see Ermann and Lundman, 2002) In spite of the fact that the number of people victimized by organizations/corporations is likely to be much larger than those victimized by individual offenders, there is less research on the victims of organizational crime, whether they are victims of business corporations or government organizations. One reason for the relative neglect of this type of victim is that their victimization is mostly nonviolent. Often victims are not aware that a victimization has occurred (for example, the health effects of illegal waste disposal may not surface for years), which compounds the underreporting of crimes. Another related reason is that usually the perpetrators of organizational and corporate crimes are socially and politically more influential and powerful than their victims.

This collection presents theoretical and empirical studies that focus on various kinds of victimization. Because research in this field is expanding rapidly, the articles included do not cover all areas of victimological interest. Nevertheless, we believe that this volume provides a good sample of works in this field and a valuable introduction to this relatively new and developing discipline.

REFERENCES

Amir, M. 1971. *Patterns of Forcible Rape.* Chicago: University of Chicago Press.

Barnes, H. E. and N. K. Teeters. 1959. *New Horizons in Criminology.* Englewood-Cliffs, NJ: Prentice Hall.

Cohen, L. and M. Felson. 1979. "Social change and crime rates trend: A routine activity approach." *American Sociological Review* 44: 588–607.

Dadrian, V. N. 1976. "An attempt at defining victimology." In E. C. Viano (editor), *Victims and Society.* Pp. 40–42. Washington, DC: Visage Press.

Dorff, E. N. and A. Rosett. 1988. *A Living Tree: The Roots and Growth of Jewish Law.* Albany: State University of New York Press.

Ermann, M. D. and R. J. Lundman (editors). 2002. *Corporate and Governmental Deviance.* New York: Oxford University Press (sixth edition).

Edwards, C. 1971. *The Hammurabi Code.* Port Washington, NY: Kennikat Press.

Fattah, E. 1967. "Towards a criminological classification of victims." *International Criminal Police Review* 209: 162–169.

Geis, G. 1977. "Restitution by criminal offenders: A summary and overview." In J. Hudson and B. Galaway (editors), *Restitutions in Criminal Justice*. Lexington, MA: D. C. Heath.

Hindelang, M. J., M. Gottfredson and J. Garofalo. 1978. *Victims of Personal Crime: An Empirical Foundation for a Theory of Personal Victimization*. Cambridge, MA: Ballinger.

Hoffman, J. 1992. "What did Mendelsohn really say?" In S. Ben David and G. F. Kirchhoff (editors), *International Faces of Victimology*. Pp. 89–104. Monchengladbach, Germany: WSV Publishing.

Karmen, A. 1990. *Crime Victims: An Introduction to Victimology*. Belmont, CA: Wadsworth (second edition).

Laser, R. E. 1970. "Criminal restitution: A survey of its past history and analysis of its present usefulness." *University of Richmond Law Review* 5: 71–98.

Maine, H. S. 1887. *Ancient Law*. John Murray.

McCoy, C. 1988. "Prosecution." In M. Tonry (editor), *The Handbook of Crime & Punishment*. Pp. 457–473. New York: Oxford University Press.

Meiners, R. E. 1978. *Victim Compensation: Economic, Legal, and Political Aspects*. Lexington, MA: D. C. Heath.

Mendelsohn, B. 1956. "Victimology." *Etudes Internationales de Psycho-Sociologie Criminelle* (July–September): 23–26.

Mendelsohn, B. 1975. "Victimology and the technical and social sciences: A call for the establishment of victimological clinics." In I. Drapkin and E. Viano (editors), *Theoretical Issues in Victimology*. Pp. 25–35. Lexington, MA: D. C. Heath.

Reckless, W. C. 1973. *The Crime Problem*. Englewood Cliffs, NJ: Prentice Hall (fifth edition).

Schafer, S. 1977. *Victimology: The Victim and His Criminal*. Reston, VA: Reston.

Sellin, T. and M. E. Wolfgang. 1964. *The Measurement of Delinquency*. New York: Wiley.

Shichor, D. 2001. "Penal policies at the threshold of the twenty-first century." *Criminal Justice Review* 25(1): 1–30.

Smigel, E. O. and H. L. Ross (editors). 1970. *Crimes Against Organizations*. New York: Van Nostrand Reinhold.

Skogan, W. G. and M. G. Maxfield. 1981. *Coping with Crime: Individual and Neighborhood Reactions*. Beverly Hills, CA: Sage.

von Hentig, H. 1948. *The Criminal and His Victim*. New Haven, CT: Yale University Press.

Weed, F. J. 1995. *Certainty of Justice: Reform in the Crime Victim Movement*. New York: Aldine de Gruyter.

Williams, K. M. 1976. "The effects of victim characteristics on the disposition of violent crime." In W. F. McDonald (editor), *Criminal Justice and the Victim*. Pp. 177–213. Beverly Hills, CA: Sage.

Wolfgang, M. E. 1958. *Patterns in Criminal Homicide*. Philadelphia: University of Pennsylvania Press.

Wolfgang, M. E. 1979. "Basic concepts in victimological theory." Keynote lecture, Third International Symposium on Victimology. Munster, Germany.

Ziegenhagen, E. A. 1977. *Victims, Crime and Social Control*. New York: Praeger.

PART I
Conceptual Issues

As discussed in the introduction, victimology is a relatively new discipline still in the process of theoretical development. Donald Cressey (1992) highlighted the ambiguous nature of developing fields when he complained that victimology hardly could be seen as a scientific discipline given the varied approaches, backgrounds, and attitudes of the people who considered themselves victimologists.

We can identify two major trends in victimology: one addresses the study of crime victims as a research-oriented, scientific enterprise; the other views it as a social service and help-oriented endeavor. While victimology as a separate and evolving discipline made great strides during the last few decades, it still needs theoretical and conceptual development. The first part of this volume includes readings that focus on the rediscovery of victims, the historical development of victimology as a separate discipline, the scientific approach to victimology, general concepts of this emerging field, and general theoretical issues.

Eminent criminologist Gilbert Geis provides an overview of victim-related issues in the first article. Geis addresses the general neglect of victims in the past, political reasons for the renewed interest in victims, the cost of victimization, hate crimes and their victims, compensation and restitution, mental anguish, and Good Samaritan laws.

In the second selection Ezzat Fattah focuses on conceptual issues, exposing and refuting misconceptions concerning victims and victimology. He discusses the important contributions of victimology to an awareness that a criminal act is the outcome of a process where several factors might be at work. Often crime is a response to external, environmental stimuli—a reaction to an event in which the victim may have been a contributing factor. According to Fattah, criminological theories often fail to provide a satisfactory explanation of crime because of their static nature and their inability to incorporate different factors into their explanatory scheme. The author also addresses blaming the victim and the concept of victim precipitation. Fattah emphasizes the importance of victimological research in revealing the factors that determine differences of vulnerability and exposure to victimization.

The next article applies the routine activities approach to the study of victimization by violent crime. The original "routine activities" theory of Lawrence Cohen and Marcus Felson suggested that to understand property crime, it is necessary to consider the distributions of both criminals and victims and their everyday (routine) activities across both space and time. Cohen and Felson (1979) identified three indispensable elements of victimization: (1) a motivated offender, (2) a suitable target, and (3) the absence of capable guardian. Richard B. Felson uses the routine activities approach to investigate the effects of active "night life" on the extent of involvement in interpersonal violence.

In the fourth selection, David Shichor explores the reasons for the neglect of white-collar victims and the effects of white-collar offenses. The focus of most victimology textbooks is almost entirely on the victims of violent street crimes, "abuse" crimes (involving children, spouses and the elderly), and sex crimes. Similarly, the professional literature rarely mentions white-collar crime victims and their experiences. Many believe that because white-collar offenses are primarily property or financial crimes, the harm caused is not too serious since losses are often recovered from insurance, out of court settlements, or civil court procedures. However, a growing volume of research indicates that certain white-collar offenses cause as much physical harm as violent crimes and/or extensive financial and psychological harm. The neglect of victims of white-collar crime, according to Shichor, hinders the full development of victimology, limiting its credibility as a serious academic discipline.

Victimology, similar to other relatively new and evolving disciplines, is in the process of delineating its focus of study, defining its key concepts, developing its theoretical approaches, refining its data-collection methods, and generally trying to establish itself as a legitimate and independent discipline. The readings selected for this section present some of the issues involved with the development of victimology as a field of academic study.

REFERENCES

Cohen, L. E. and M. Felson. 1979. "Social change and crime rate trends: A routine activity approach." *American Sociological Review* 44: 588–608.

Cressey, D. R. 1992. "Research implications of conflicting conceptions of victimology." In E. A. Fattah (editor), *Towards a Critical Victimology.* Pp. 57–73. New York: St. Martin's Press.

Chapter One

Victims

Gilbert Geis

The striking increase in attention to victims by the world's criminal justice systems may well be the most significant development in those systems during the second half of the twentieth century. In earlier times, crime victims were consigned to a peripheral position, much like spear-carriers in a grand opera. They were necessary as background players but of no true importance. Once their crime report and their testimony had been recorded, they typically were ignored.

Victims were raped, mugged, their homes invaded, their handbags or wallets stolen on the street. Then, if that were not enough, they were often "double victimized." Law enforcement personnel, frequently cynical from dealing with so many crimes for so long, sometimes inflicted the second insult. Frustrated by their inability to do much about offenses such as burglary and car theft—crimes rarely witnessed (meaning few leads about the perpetrator)—law enforcement agents tended to be abrupt and dismissive in the face of victims' despair. They often failed to understand that for most of us victimization is a unique and novel experience.

If the perpetrator was apprehended, very often the attorney for the accused and the prosecutor would reach a plea bargain, trading a guilty plea by the offender for a lesser sentence. Typically, nobody would bother to inform the victim. In those rare instances when a case went to trial, the victim would have to miss work (and often forfeit pay), suffer through any number of postponements, and endure a possibly humiliating grilling by the defense attorney. Frequently victims found themselves uncomfortably alone in a hallway or waiting room with the perpetrator. All the crime victim got for that effort was a story to tell friends and neighbors—often a story saturated with irritation and anger.

In the United States, neglect of crime victims changed dramatically from about 1960 onward. The change had two major components. The first was the establishment of programs for victim compensation and victim and witness

From *Encyclopedia of Crime and Justice*, by Joshua Dressier, Vol. 4 © Macmillan 2002. Reprinted by permission of The Gate Group.

assistance to ease the physical, financial, and emotional burdens that can accompany being victimized by a criminal act. Efforts were made to introduce victims more comprehensively into the conduct of criminal justice business and to deal directly with their anxieties and outrage. Concern about an apparently dwindling willingness of victims to report offenses and cooperate with law enforcement agencies provided a further impetus for establishment of the assistance programs. Cooperation was required before a victim could be compensated.

The second component involved efforts to assess more accurately the level of criminal activity by conducting interviews with representative samples of the American population. The surveys also sought to measure correlates of the victimization experience, such as fear of crime, curtailed activities, and the respondents' confidence in the law enforcement machinery.

There also emerged a comprehensive academic and agency research enterprise that dealt with the subject of crime victims. There now exists a very considerable scholarly literature on the likelihood and consequences of being a victim of particular kinds of crimes. We have learned, for instance, that rape victims tend to be more traumatized if the offender is an acquaintance rather than a stranger. Burglary victims, for their part, often see the crime as an invasion of their private space and feel dirtied.

Numerous self-defense strategies, some of them controversial, have been advanced to help victims to protect themselves. One intense debate centers around carrying a gun. Does this safeguard the owner because the weapon can be used to defend against a predator or does having a gun escalate violence and further endanger the gun-carrier by encouraging risky responses? Rape victims confront a similar dilemma: will forceful resistance cause a sexual aggressor to desist, or will it result in greater injury or in death? Other advice is less arguable. To protect against burglary, potential victims (all of us) have been advised that the best place to secrete valuables is in a child's room: experienced burglars will get in and out of the house very quickly, usually searching only the master bedroom, perhaps a desk, and the kitchen, seeking primarily cash, weapons, and jewelry (Wright and Decker, 1994).

Those professionally involved with crime victims formed an organization, now called the World Society of Victimology, which cooperates with the United Nations and the Council of Europe on issues related to crime victims. The Society directory notes that "its members from around the world brought together by their mutual concern for victims, include victim assistance practitioners, scientists, social workers, physicians, lawyers, university professors, and students." The group first met in Jerusalem in 1973 and ushered in the new century with its tenth meeting, held in Montreal in August 2000.

Distinguishing Victims and Offenders

A particularly important difference between offenders and victims is that criminals have actively done something against the law. To try to understand the roots of criminal behavior we can look at upbringing, values, school performance, and associates. We can have offenders undergo psychological tests to try to determine how they might differ from nonoffenders and how those who committed one type of offense might be distinguished from those who engaged in another kind of law-breaking.

Victims of crime, on the other hand, typically engage in no behavior that is designed to produce their victimization. Some may have been involved in actions correlated with criminal outcomes: drunkenness and aggressive verbal behavior in a bar that is considered "unsavory" is one of innumerable examples. But a large percentage of crime victims show no qualities or behavior that might allow a sensible anticipation of their fate. They can be passengers on an airplane that is hijacked or they can be customers in a grocery store shot during a holdup because the perpetrator wants to avoid being identified or they may be window-shopping pedestrians run over by a drunk driver. Any of us might readily be a crime victim (and many of us sooner or later will be), but most of us will not engage in behavior to which the victimization can be attributed.

Despite the fact that a considerable percentage of victims are virtually random recipients of injury and loss, there does exist a coterie of *chronic victims*, persons who suffer multiple victimizations, well beyond the number attributable to chance occurrence. A review of the four British Crime Surveys found that between 1.1 and 2.2 percent of victims of property crimes had experienced a loss at least five times in fifteen months. For crimes of violence the figure ran from 0.7 and 1.0 percent of the victim totals. People who were victims of five or more personal and property offenses in the stipulated time period represented between 24 and 38 percent of all such offenses.

The British (survey) found that 63 percent of all property crime victims had suffered at least one other such victimization during the fifteen-month study period. For personal crimes the figure rose to 77 percent. The researchers noted that massive crime reductions are available simply by the reduction of repeat victimization (Ellingsworth, Farrell, and Pease, 1995). The precise explanation for the multiple-victimization phenomenon is still largely unclear. The first victimization is said to become an important factor in predicting future victimization; multiple victimizations are related in a complex way to both household and area characteristics (Osborn, Ellingsworth, Hope, and Trickett, 1996).

When there are crimes, there almost invariably will be criminals—even if they sometimes are anthropomorphized institutions, such as corporations, that commit offenses such as antitrust violations. But there are many crimes in which there are hordes of unknowing victims or no victims at all. What theater patron with several dollars in change in the pocket of a coat checked in the cloakroom will be aware that the attendant has helped himself or herself to a few quarters? Who counts the number of rubber bands in a package that claims (incorrectly) to have one hundred, or who knows whether a gas station tank reading has been altered illegally? Drunken driving detected in a routine traffic stop is an example of a criminal offense without a victim. For some offenses, the state, under the presumption that its interests (that is, our interests) have been harmed or that it must protect its citizens from possible outcomes, adopts the role of victim for some so-called victimless offenses, such as the sale of proscribed drugs or prostitution.

Distinctions between actions that produce criminals and those that produce crime victims have contributed significantly to the study of victims—or *victimology*, to use the rather awkward term coined by Benjamin Mendelsohn in the early 1940s. Unable to "explain" victimization, those who specialize in its study tend to focus on its dimensions, its consequences, and the way that the social political system deals with it.

There is some sparse theoretical work bearing on the process of victimization. In an early study, sociologist Marvin Wolfgang noted that for about a quarter of homicides "the victim may be one of the major precipitating causes of his own demise" (Wolfgang, 1958:245). Wolfgang coined the phrase *victim-precipitation* to identify such situations:

> The victim-precipitated cases are those in which the victim was the first to show and use a deadly weapon, to strike a blow in an altercation—in short, the first to commence the interplay of recourse to physical violence (Wolfgang, 1958:252).

Almost forty years later, Kenneth Polk (1997) found essentially the same pattern and percentage of victim-precipitation that Wolfgang had documented in Philadelphia in a study of homicides in Melbourne, Australia. William E. Foote (1999), after a comprehensive review of studies using the concept, suggests that future attempts should divide subjects into relevant types. Among the more interesting incidents are those that Foote calls *intentional* victim-precipitated deaths, instances in which persons deliberately engage in episodes that they desire to have lethal consequences. Shooting at a police car would be an example of what Foote calls *suicide by cop*.

When Israeli criminologist Menachim Amir (1971) employed the concept of victim-precipitation with rape victims, scholars insisted, correctly, that it did not necessarily travel well from one kind of offense to another—that matters such as wearing "provocative" clothing differ significantly from starting a barroom brawl. William Ryan's classic *Blaming the Victim* satirizes the tendency to denigrate victims with a story of a senator fulminating in front of colleagues who are debating the origins of World War II. "What was Pearl Harbor doing there?" he asks (Ryan, 1976:153–154).

It is not an easy task to disentangle the diverse elements that energized the movement toward greater recognition of the role and importance of victims in criminal justice affairs. Their condition for centuries aroused little comment or interest. Once they were "discovered," it was baffling how their neglect could have gone without remedy for so long.

In the United States, it was national politics that first moved the subject of crime victims to center stage. In 1964, Barry Goldwater, the Republican candidate for president, thrust the issue of crime into his campaign. It was a false issue, in the sense that the federal government does not have jurisdiction over most of the kinds of criminal activity that concern the average citizen. Thus, there is little, except perhaps symbolically, that a president can do to make a notable impact on criminal behavior; such behavior is almost exclusively the concern of state, county, and municipal governments.

Goldwater, nonetheless, had touched a sensitive public nerve. His allegations that the Democrats were "soft on crime" resonated with citizens. The accusation was based on Democratic opposition to capital punishment, concern with the rights of defendants, and their unwillingness to endorse tougher punishment policies. Lyndon Johnson overwhelmed Goldwater in the election, but the issue of crime had beleaguered him during the campaign. He vowed that he would not be caught unprepared the next time (although the deteriorating situation in Vietnam would force him to abandon his 1968 Presidential aspirations).

Johnson chose a time-tested political strategy to defuse the crime issue. He appointed the President's Commission on Law Enforcement and Administration of Justice, with a sweeping mandate to examine and make recommendations about virtually all aspects of the crime problem (the death penalty was one of the exceptions). The Commission, very well funded, endorsed the fledgling victim compensation programs and launched a pioneering project to better measure the extent of traditional crime through an annual survey of the population. These surveys attempted to shed some light on what is known as the *dark figure* in crime, offenses that fail to come to the attention of the authorities.

National Crime Victimization Survey

In a variety of sizes and shapes, victimization surveys are conducted today in many of the major countries of the world. Since 1989, under the leadership of the Netherlands, many countries have collaborated on a standard survey technique that allows some comparative conclusions to be drawn. The lowest European crime rates were found in Northern Ireland, Switzerland, and England; Spain and the Netherlands had the highest (Dijk, Mayhew, and Killias, 1990). Three years later the results were essentially the same, although the English rate had escalated somewhat (Dijk and Mayhew, 1992).

In the United States, the Law Enforcement Assistance Administration initiated the National Crime Victimization Survey (NCVS) in 1972. A thoroughgoing revision of the survey instrument in 1992 makes it impossible to compare earlier results with surveys completed after that date. The new screening procedures introduced in 1992 included detailed cues to help respondents recall crime incidents. The new instrument produced a higher reported level of victimization, especially for assaults. The updated approach also focuses more heavily on offenses committed by family members against each other and by acquaintances. These are subjects that respondents often are reluctant to discuss without considerable prompting.

The victimization survey now is conducted annually by the Bureau of the Census under the auspices of the Bureau of Justice Statistics, housed in the U.S. Department of Justice. NCVS interviews are held every six months, using a national panel of approximately 49,000 households with a total of about 101,000 residents. Ninety-five percent of the persons asked to partici-pate in the survey agree to do so. In interviews that take about half an hour, a single household respondent details crime victimizations for all members of the household over the age of twelve. Each household is contacted for information seven times. The first and the fifth interviews are done face-to-face; the other five are conducted by telephone. If a household changes location, its members remain in the survey pool for the full period before being replaced on the panel. This approach minimizes *telescoping* (the tendency of persons to report victimizations that occurred before the time period of concern). To keep the data as time bound as possible, the results of the initial interview with a household are not included in the NCVS.

NCVS reports a good deal more criminal activity—more than twice as much—than does the annual Uniform Crime Reports (UCR) issued by the Federal Bureau of Investigation, which takes into account only offenses reported to the police.

Problems with the Victimization Survey

A shortcoming of the NCVS is that respondents may be inclined to report events that are not criminal, though they believe them to be. This has been particularly true in regard to minor assaults, which rarely capture the attention of law enforcement. Also, *series incidents*, matters such as spouse abuse, that often have no clear-cut beginning or end, frustrate the NCVS since the survey focuses only on discrete events. There also is the matter of bias inherent in the interview format. Persons may desist reporting if what they have to say involves too much of their time and becomes tedious, or they may feel compelled to play into what they interpret as an interviewer's desire to hear about a lot of criminal episodes, real or imagined. In addition, the respondent may not recall or be aware of all of the victimization experiences of other people living in the household. The NCVS fails to include the expe-riences of persons not anchored in fixed households, such as the homeless and transients.

The bias inherent in victim surveys is illustrated by the fact that persons with college degrees typically report more assaults than do persons with only an elementary school education (Gove, Hughes, and Geerken, 1985). Since it is likely that members of the latter group actually have been victimized by assaults at least as much and probably much more often than the col-lege-educated group, it is reasonable to believe that behaviors that are regarded as routine and inconsequential by persons in the less well-educated group are taken much more seriously by those with more schooling.

Finally, *reverse record checks* have revealed that persons who reported to the police that an acquaintance committed a crime against them often failed to inform a victimization interviewer of the event. The reverse record checks found that two-thirds of such offenses were not mentioned in crime victim surveys, while three-quarters of the crimes reported to the police and committed by strangers were disclosed.

The Bureau of Justice Statistics supplemented the NCVS survey with a telephone survey in 1999. A total of 800 households were contacted in twelve cities, using a method called random digital dialing. The survey found that from 20 to 48 percent of the respondents noted that they were "fearful" of crime, though in no city did more than 10 percent say that they were "very fearful." The highest levels of expressed fear were in Chicago and Washington, D.C. (48%) and the lowest in Madison, Wisconsin (20%) (Smith, Steadman, Minton, and Townsend, 1999).

The Incidence of Victimization

The NCVS shows that Americans experience more than thirty million victimizations each year. In any one year, a person has about a 3 percent chance of being a victim of a crime of violence. That figure is more than double for property offenses.

Teenage black males are the most likely victims of crimes of violence, followed by teenage black females. The next four highest victimization rates, in descending order, are for teenage white males, young adult black males, young adult black females, and teenage white females. The elderly—be they male, female, black, or white—have the lowest victimization rates from violence.

Persons most victimized by property crimes are teenage white males and adult black males. Least victimized are elderly black males and elderly black females. This somewhat counterintuitive finding may result from property offenders targeting affluent neighborhoods where the haul is more likely to be worth the risk.

The surveys pinpoint the considerable toll that crimes of violence take upon young black youths. The strikingly lower rate of victimization of elderly persons by both crimes of violence and property offenses in one respect challenges the rationality of the commonly reported high level of fear of crime found among the elderly. One explanation is that older persons often have the most to lose if they are victimized: they are less likely to be able to recover (or to survive) a violent crime, and they often have no way to recoup the financial loss inflicted by a burglary or other property offenses. In that regard, their fears can be seen as perfectly reasonable.

This finding of higher rates of fear of crime among the elderly, however, has been disputed by Kenneth Ferraro, who argues that too much has been made of answers to a single question on the NCVS survey and that failure to inquire about particular crimes rather than crime in general undercuts the adequacy of the responses to support the usual conclusion of a high level of fear of crime among the elderly. Ferraro's own work indicates that the only particular offense that the elderly fear more than persons in other age groups is panhandling, and that this fear is confined to older women.

Urban metropolitan areas, expectedly, show higher crime victimization rates than suburbs and rural areas. One victimization study found that about 31 percent of the robberies in which suburbanites were victims occurred while they were in a central city and only 6.2 percent occurred outside that city's boundaries (Dodge, 1985:2).

White-Collar Crime Victimization

The NCVS's focus on victimization by so-called *street crimes* (to the neglect of white-collar or *suite crimes*) reinforces the greater public attention accorded offenses generally committed by persons in the lower socioeconomic strata. Fraud and other white-collar crimes can visit severe economic and psychological hardships on their victims. Some white-collar crimes, such as medical malpractice and pollution, kill and maim large numbers of people. While the tally of street crimes dropped significantly during the last decade of the twentieth century, the number of white-collar crimes, enforcement officials believe, has increased greatly. Victim complaints to the Securities and Exchange Commission, for instance, jumped by 20 percent between 1996 and 1998.

Fraud has been labeled *assault with a fiscal weapon*. A newspaper report tells of a bogus scheme in which persons were persuaded that they were investing in ultra-safe securities backed by banks and real estate. In the end, the victims of the scam were bilked out of at least $20 million. Some lost their homes, many marriages were bruised, and retirements had to be postponed.

The National White-Collar Crime Center reported in mid-1999 that almost 40 percent of the persons in a nationwide sample said that they were victims of some type of fraud during the past year. Most complained of consumer rip-offs such as unnecessary auto repairs. Others of the 1,169 respondents said that they had lost money through Internet schemes, credit card fraud, and investment swindles. Victim help groups note that many persons who have been cheated prefer to suffer in silence rather than seek aid because they are embarrassed about their gullibility.

Senior citizens appear to be the most common victims of telemarketing schemes, while people in their 30s and 40s, often well-educated, fall prey most often to Internet swindles. A study of female victims of a telemarketing oil-well scam found that older women were likely to blame themselves, but those who were younger tended to take a *c'est la vie* attitude in shrugging off the loss (Sechrest et al., 1999).

Researchers have estimated the annual cost to victims in the United States of crimes against the person to be $105 billion (Miller, Cohen, and Wiersema, 1996). This figure includes medical costs, lost earnings, and the outlay for programs that provide victim assistance. Kennedy and Sacco

(1998) raise the loss figure to $426 billion for violent crimes and $24 billion for property crimes by adding in the price of pain and suffering, but they emphasize that these victim cost estimates have to be regarded as far from totally reliable figures.

Hate Crimes and Kindred Laws

Since time immemorial, there have been distinctions in the law based on the social position of the victim. Typically, criminal statutes offered greater protection for those with greater social status. In early English jurisprudence, for example, more stringent penalties were attached to the poisoning of husbands by their wives; wife poisoning was regarded as just another form of murder. The former called for burning at the stake; the latter for the more common punishment of hanging.

In recent years in the United States, there has been a proliferation of laws to protect potential crime victims from crimes committed because of a person's status. The additional victim security is premised on the belief that tougher penalties will prevent such crimes. Most notable in this category are *hate crimes*, proscribed acts that are judicially determined to be motivated by prejudice against a member of a specific ethnic or behavioral group. Beating a homosexual because he is a homosexual or torching the house of a rabbi will likely get the offender(s) a heavier penalty than would have been dealt out for an assault against a nonhomosexual or the arson burning of a house of a suburban mainstream family (Jacobs and Potter, 1998; Jenness and Broad, 1997).

This kind of special victim protection is extended to the elderly in some state laws. During the summer of 1999 witnesses testifying before the U.S. House of Representatives Committee on the Judiciary pled for inclusion of women as a group under hate crime statutes. The argument was that women are less able to protect themselves against male predatory behavior and that, particularly in regard to sexual assault, they are an especially vulnerable crime victim group.

This vulnerability of women was underlined by a report in May 1999 of a national survey showing that 17.6 percent of American women have been rape victims at least once during their lifetime, with an additional 14.8 percent being victimized by an attempted rape. Forty-three percent said that they had been slapped or hit at least once in their life, 21.2 percent had been hit with an object, 6.2 percent had been threatened with a gun, and 8.1 percent had been the victim of a stalking. All told more than half of the women surveyed had been victimized by rape, physical assault, and/or stalking.

Critics of hate crime and similar legislation see it as a political cozying-up to identifiable segments of the electorate and more of a symbolic gesture than a practical measure. They argue that the law should inquire only into behavior, not into subjective motives, and that present penalties are presumed to be sufficient to deter or, at least, adequately punish those who commit the acts. What good, some insist, is it to add the legal designation of hate crime to the murder of a black man by bigoted youths when there already exists a perfectly adequate penalty for murder? Cynics add that the lesson conveyed by the laws is that if you are going to be a sensible criminal, your least dangerous course of action is to victimize someone who shares your own background and beliefs.

Crime Victim Compensation

Victim compensation programs were the earliest manifestations of what was to become a comprehensive and very powerful victims' movement. The first programs were established in New Zealand in 1963 and in England in 1964; then victim compensation was adopted by California in 1965 and thereafter duplicated in other American states and throughout the world. A 1999 count showed that 29 countries now have programs to compensate crime victims. All but three offer benefits to foreign citizens who suffer crime-inflicted injuries while visiting the country. The U.S. programs by law must provide assistance to U.S. residents or their survivors who are injured or killed in a terrorist attack while visiting a foreign country. The state programs are partially supported by the federally subsidized Crime Victims Fund. They currently assist more than two million crime victims and survivors annually.

From the beginning, crime-victim compensation programs have faced questions about their existence. If they serve a legitimate government function, then why are there not also programs to compensate persons who suffer losses from natural disasters or from any other problems not of their own creation? One answer has been that prudent people ought to buy insurance to protect against such exigencies; but the same might be said of crime victims. The truth seems to be that aiding crime victims has a strong political component—sponsors could score points with the electorate—so this particular issue was singled out for legislative attention.

Programs providing compensation to crime victims owe their origin to the pioneering efforts of Margery Fry, an Englishwoman and a Quaker, who devoted her life to the cause of correctional reform. Ms. Fry ridiculed the inadequacy of restitution as a court-ordered method to allay the deprivation suffered by crime victims. She pointed out that the offender is often not apprehended or, if caught, is not convicted. Even if there is a conviction, most offenders are too impoverished to pay the cost of the victim's crime-associated expenses. For those offenders who can contribute something, those monies are often diverted from support of their families, who then might well have to be subsidized by welfare.

Problems with restitution and with tort remedies were highlighted in the sensational O. J. Simpson case. Survivors of the victims—Simpson's former wife's parents and the family of Ronald Goldman—together received a judgment of $8.5 million and were awarded punitive damages of $25 million. But they have obtained very little of that money, though Simpson lives lavishly on the $25,000 a month he receives from a judgment-proof $4.1 million pension fund.

Compassion Joins Compensation

After victim compensation efforts were established, an understanding soon developed that crime victims often suffer from difficulties beyond those that can be remedied by money alone. In a study of victim compensation in an eastern U.S. state, for instance, Robert Elias (1989) found that applicants to the program were more discontented than they would have been had the program not existed. The programs led victims to anticipate that they would be helped in an expeditious and kindly manner. When they encountered delays and bureaucratic barriers, they became further alienated from the system and hostile to it.

When it turned its attention to the subject of crime, the burgeoning women's movement picked up the cue that victims may need more than money to render them whole. Looking for a specific issue to which to devote their energies, feminist leaders initially took up the cause of prostitutes, seeing them as exploited victims of a patriarchal society. Difficulties arose when many prostitutes rejected this definition, insisting that they preferred what they were doing to the menial and low-paying office or sales jobs they might otherwise be able to obtain. They saw themselves as entrepreneurs rather than as victims, and they viewed feminist concern for their plight as condescension by middle-class women. Perhaps the major achievement here was a semantic one. It no longer is considered politically proper to employ the term *prostitute*: Women in the trade now are to be identified as *sex workers*.

The women's movement, after abandoning the issue of prostitution, turned its attention to victims of the crime of rape. Overwhelmingly rape offenders are men. Only 200 or so cases each year involve arrests of women for rape, usually as accomplices who, for instance, hold a gun on another woman while a male co-offender sexually assaults her.

Many rape victims suffered profound mental anguish that could only be relieved, if at all, by participation in treatment programs. Rape victims, like victims of other offenses, had a tendency to assume blame for what had happened to them. They would ask themselves why they had trusted the acquaintance who assaulted them. Why had they not attended to the obvious clues about this true character? Why had they gone out that night—and to that particular neighborhood? Why had they not fought back more forcefully or been able to talk their way out of the offense? Why had the man picked on them and not somebody else? What was there about them that made them vulnerable and "victimizable"?

The pioneering victim-support programs, often devoted exclusively to rape victims, stumbled along, generally understaffed (and usually depending largely on volunteers), until the passage of the Victims of Crime Act (VOCA) by Congress in 1984. VOCA provided subsidies not only to state victim compensation programs (35 percent of their costs) but to victim assistance efforts as well. In 1988, VOCA-supported programs were further authorized to aid victims of domestic violence and of drunken driving.

The embrace of victim-assistance programs primarily extends to victims of sexual and spousal abuse (including marital rape, a criminal offense newly defined in the 1960s) and child abuse, again offenses largely committed by men against women and children. Somewhat cynical onlookers point out that these offenses have always existed and that the intense limelight suddenly focused on them is based primarily on political and ideological maneuvering rather than on an increase in their number or seriousness. Deep concern with child abuse, it is claimed, is the result of efforts by medical doctors to aggrandize their own position (and increase their income) by creating the term *battered-child syndrome* and defining a social problem as a medical issue, one calling for greater recourse to x-rays and physician intervention. Attorneys also prosper by filing suits against alleged child abusers (Costin, Karger, and Stoesz, 1996). The movement against child abuse also gave rise to a number of well-publicized cases in which adults claimed to have recovered long-repressed memories of abuse, usually by their father. Similarly, there were a bevy of cases accusing child-care workers of sexual abuse of their young charges. In many of these situations strong evidence emerged that the child had been induced to give damning testimony by leading and suggestive questioning tactics (Ceci and Bruck, 1995).

The professional literature came to label the consequences of being a rape victim in medical terms, *rape trauma syndrome*. Diagnosis of such a condition—later extended to other forms of victimization and formalized in medical annals as PTSD, *post-traumatic stress disorder*—would come to play a significant role in some court cases. Defense attorneys might argue, for instance, that a person suffering from such a syndrome was no longer able to think rationally and therefore should not be held responsible for, say, the murder or maiming of the perpetrator, even if the retaliatory act came a considerable time after the original offense. A severely battered woman would stand a decent chance of avoiding charges or being declared not guilty even though she had killed her husband while he was asleep and many hours after she had been severely beaten. Opponents of such outcomes complained that however abhorrent the crime of wife-battering, it is not a death penalty offense.

Services to victims and witnesses customarily include crisis counseling (that is, short-term help with emotional difficulties), practical assistance (such as help in locating a new place to live, obtaining pregnancy tests and tests for venereal infections and AIDS, changing locks and repairing windows), and/or filing a criminal complaint. Referrals might be made to other social service agencies, such as welfare offices, and for psychiatric treatment. In addition, there has been a proliferation of shelters where women who are victims of abuse may find refuge and support. Some programs also will transport a victim to the courtroom where the hearing or trial regarding the assault will be held so that the victim becomes familiar with the setting beforehand. Some critics deplore the fact that defense witnesses do not usually have the same, but those aiding victims see it as a justified attempt to balance the procedural advantages enjoyed by defendants.

A recent survey in the United States found that nearly eight of ten persons reported that they were "very" or "somewhat" satisfied with the services they received from victim assistance programs. The major complaints involved slipshod operating methods and poor follow-through. A typical criticism was this: "They had me fill out forms and I never received any feedback. When I contacted them again they had me fill out the same old forms and nothing happened" (Davis, Lurigio, and Skogan, 1999:112).

The National Organization of Victim Assistance, headquartered in Washington, D.C, coordinates the network of victim service agencies. A federal agency, the National Center for Victims of Crime, provides a website detailing developments in the field and a computerized list of some 20,000 federal and state victim-related statutes. The center also has created a database of approximately 10,000 court decisions dealing with crime victims and a roster of attorneys who handle civil cases for victims. The center can be reached tollfree at (800) FYL-CALL.

In 1997, Congress passed a law permitting money in the Federal Crime Victims Fund to be allocated to pilot programs that help those injured by white-collar crimes, although the victims themselves cannot receive direct financial aid. Ironically, most of the money that goes into the fund is derived from fines paid by white-collar criminals.

Victim Responsibility

The victim movement has given rise to a complicated issue that fundamentally rests upon an irresolvable question: whether human beings have free will or whether their actions are determined by immutable forces. Mental health counselors understandably work to relieve victims—especially victims of sexual assaults—of their common belief that in some way they were responsible for what happened to them. There is some tension between the insistence that the perpetrator alone bears full responsibility for his behavior, while the victim never should indulge in bouts of self-blame. The difficulty becomes manifest when the offender adopts the same posture as the victim. He is not responsible either: it was an abusive father, faulty schooling, a slum upbringing, a brain malfunction, or some other predisposing factor beyond his control that led him to commit the crime. A 1999 *New Yorker* cartoon epitomized the situation: it shows a woman testifying in court: "I know he cheated on me because of his childhood abuse," she says, "but I shot him because of mine."

The most public manifestation of this issue came when Hillary Clinton tried to explain the matter of her husband's infidelity. Her husband had to learn to take responsibility for his sexual waywardness, she declared in an interview, but at the same time she said that his behavior was the result of "abuse" as a child, apparently "abuse" growing out of "terrible conflict" between his mother and grandmother. "He was so young, barely four, when he was scarred by abuse," Ms. Clinton said, adding that a psychiatrist had told her that being placed in the midst of conflict between two women "is the worst possible situation" for a boy because of his desire to please them both. Her husband's behavior, Ms. Clinton said, was a "sin of weakness" rather than one of "malice."

Criticism of Ms. Clinton's statement was widespread, indicating, perhaps, public saturation with the tendency to "justify" so much current waywardness by labeling it as an outcome of earlier victimization or deprivation. A *New York Times* columnist pointed out that Ms. Clinton had blamed her husband's sexual adventures on two deceased women who had adored him and who were no longer alive to defend themselves. The columnist also noted shrewdly that the president's wife had done precisely what she deplored, placed her husband in the middle of a conflict between defending her position and defending his mother and grandmother. The president, displaying the considerable talent for verbal gymnastics that had helped get him where he was, managed to agree publicly with what his wife said and at the same time exonerate his mother and grandmother for any role in his sexual waywardness.

Criminological Theory and Crime Victims

Two major criminological theories often are used to interpret crime victimization. Lifestyle theories postulate that certain work and leisure patterns are more highly associated with crime victimization than others. According to this viewpoint, three major considerations influence lifestyles: the social roles that people play, their position in the social structure, and decisions about desirable behaviors (Hindelang, Gottfredson, and Garafalo, 1978). Thus, a woman working a job that ends in the early hours of the day may have to use public transportation and walk several lonely blocks to her apartment because of her low income; she is more likely than a woman driven about town by a chauffeur to become a crime victim.

Routine activities concepts state that criminal offenses are related to the nature of everyday patterns of social existence. When most adults in a neighborhood are working, for instance, there is a greater likelihood that youngsters with increased freedom from adult supervision will get into trouble. So too houses unoccupied during the day make much more inviting targets than those with people at home or neighbors who make it their business to be aware of what is occurring on the street (Cohen and Felson, 1979).

Rescuing Victims: Good Samaritans

The blatant failure of persons to provide help for victims of crime when they might readily do so occasionally thrusts the issue of Good Samaritan laws into the headlines. Good Samaritan laws take their name from the Biblical parable (*Luke* 10:29–36), of a Samaritan (a member of a minority religious sect) who, on his way from Jerusalem to Jericho, came upon a man lying beside the desert road. The man had been set upon by robbers who stripped him, beat him, and went off, leaving him half-dead. Others had passed the wounded man. The Samaritan placed the man on a donkey and had him carried to an inn. He left money there to see to the stranger's care. "Look after him," he told the innkeeper, "and if you spend any more I will pay you on my way back."

Such laws, present in virtually all European countries (except England), mandate punishment for persons who, when they safely can, do not take action to assist a person being victimized. In the United States, only a handful of states have passed such laws. It would be no crime in any but a few states if an Olympic swimmer, sunning himself on the beach, feels too lazy to respond to the call for help from an infant drowning a few feet away. Nor does anyone need to warn a blind man if he walks by and unknowingly heads toward a steep cliff a few yards away (Geis, 1993).

An early New York appellate court decision, *Zelinko v. Gimbel Bros.* [158 Misc. 904], captures the nature of the U.S. approach to aiding victims in distress. A woman had collapsed in Gimbel's department store and was carried to the store infirmary and left there unattended for several hours. When she died, her heirs sued the store and recovered. The court noted that the store and its employees owed the woman "no duty at all" and "could have let her be and die." Had they done so, they would have avoided liability. Responsibility came into play only because of the store's "meddling in matters in which legally it had no concern."

The absence in the United States of Good Samaritan statutes is traced to our philosophy of individualism—that nobody should be responsible for anybody but himself or herself. But there are those who believe that such laws underline that all of us are intertwined and that we should be compelled to help crime victims when we can if for no other reason than we might need such assistance ourselves on some occasion.

Conclusion

At a reunion held in 1997 in the nation's capital to commemorate the thirtieth anniversary of the work of the President's Commission on Law Enforcement and Administration of Justice, James Vorenberg, the commission's director, said that the development that the group had most failed to anticipate was the surge of concern with crime victims.

Considerations that led to the striking increase in emphasis on crime victims include the broad campaign to empower those who were not being dealt with satisfactorily, including minorities, women, gays, and the disabled. In addition, support of victim initiatives carried a great number of political pluses. Few could oppose aiding victims, except in terms of cost, and those who did would appear cold-blooded and uncaring.

Once launched, the victim's movement inevitably built up a constituency that developed a strong vested interest in seeing its expansion: crisis center workers, victimology scholars, and, of course, victims and potential crime victims. The movement has provided benefits for a great number of people who otherwise might have gone neglected. It has influenced the operation of the criminal justice system, sometimes for the better, sometimes for the worse, with that judgment depending on the observer's political preferences. Most importantly, the renewed focus on crime victims has tilted the balance of the scales of justice more toward equity and fairness to all those who participate in and are affected by our system of administration of criminal justice.

BIBLIOGRAPHY

Amir, Menachem. 1971. *Patterns of Forcible Rape*. Chicago: University of Chicago Press.

Ceci, Stephen J., and Bruck, Maggie. 1995. *Jeopardy in the Courtroom: A Scientific Analysis of Children's Testimony*. Washington, DC: American Psychological Association.

Cohen, Lawrence E., and Felson, Marcus. 1979. A General Theory of Expropriate Crime: An Evolutionary Ecological Approach. *American Journal of Sociology* 94:465–501.

Costin, Lela B., Karger, Howard J., and Stoesz, David. 1996. *The Politics of Child Abuse in America*. New York: Oxford University Press.

Davis, Robert C., Lurigio, Arthur J., and Skogan, Wesley G. 1997. *Victims of Crime* 2nd ed. Thousand Oaks, CA: Sage.

Davis, Robert C., Lurigio, Arthur J., and Skogan, Wesley G. 1999. Services for Victims: Market Research Study. *International Review of Victimology* 6:101–115.

Dijk, Jan J. M. van, and Mayhew, Pat. 1992. *Crime Victimization in the Industrial World*. The Hague: Ministry of Justice.

Dijk, Jan J. M. van, Mayhew, Pat, and Killias, Martin. 1991. *Experiences of Crime Across the World: Key Findings of the 1989 International Crime Survey*. Boston: Kluwer.

Dodge, Richard. 1985. *Locating City, Suburban and Rural Crime*. Washington, DC: Bureau of Justice Statistics, U.S. Department of Justice.

Elias, Robert. 1983. *Victims of the System: Victims and the System in American Politics and Criminal Justice*. New Brunswick, NJ: Transaction.

Ellingsworth, Dan, Farrell, Graham, and Pease, Ken. 1995. A Victim Is a Victim Is a Victim? Chronic Victimization in Four Sweeps of the British Crime Survey. *British Journal of Criminology* 35:360–365.

Ferraro, Kenneth F. 1995. *Fear of Crime: Interpreting Victimization Risk*. Albany: State University of New York Press.

Foote, William E. 1999. Victim-Precipitated Homicide. Pp. 174–202 in Harold V. Hall, ed., *Lethal Violence: A Sourcebook on Fatal Domestic, Acquaintance and Stranger Violence*. Baton Rouge, LA: CRC Press.

Geis, Gilbert. 1993. Should I (Legally) Be My Brother's Keeper? Pp. 432–441 in Timothy Shiell, *Legal Philosophy: Selected Readings*. Orlando, FL: Harcourt Brace Jovanovich.

Gove, Walter R., Hughes, Michael, and Geerken, Michael. 1985. Are Uniform Crime Reports a Valid Indicator of the Index Crimes? An Affirmative Answer with Minor Qualifications. *Criminology* 23:451–501.

Hindelang, Michael J., Gottfredson, Michael, and Garofalo, James. 1978. *Victims of Personal Crime: An Empirical Foundation for a Theory of Personal Victimization*. Cambridge, MA: Ballinger.

Jacobs, James B., and Potter, Kimberly. 2000. *Hate Crimes: Criminal Law and Identity Politics.* New York: Oxford University Press.

Jenness, Valerie, and Broad, Kendal. 1997. *Hate Crimes: New Social Movements and the Politics of Violence.* New York: Aldine de Gruyter.

Karmen, Andrew. 1996. *Crime Victims: An Introduction to Victimology,* 3rd ed. Belmont, CA: Wadsworth.

Kennedy, Leslie W., and Sacco, Vincent F. 1998. *Crime Victims in Context.* Los Angeles: Roxbury.

Mawby, Rob I., and Walklate, Sandra. 1994. *Critical Victimology: International Perspectives.* London: Sage.

Miller, Ted R., Cohen, Mark A., and Wiersema, Brian. 1996. *Victim Costs and Consequences: A New Look.* Washington, DC: National Institute of Justice.

Osborn, Denise R., Ellingsworth, Dan, Hope, Tim, and Tickett, Alan. 1996. Are Reportedly Victimized Households Different? *Journal of Quantitative Criminology* 12:223–245.

Polk, Kenneth. 1997. A Reexamination of the Concept of Victim-Precipitated Homicide. *Homicide Studies* 1:141–168.

Roberts, Albert R. (ed.). 1990. *Helping Crime Victims: Research, Policy, and Practice.* Newbury Park, CA: Sage.

Ryan, William. 1976. *Blaming the Victim.* Rev. ed. New York: Vintage Books.

Sebba, Leslie. 1996. *Third Parties: Victims and the Criminal Justice System.* Columbus: Ohio State University Press.

Sechrest, Dale K., Shichor, David, Doocy, Jeffrey H., and Geis, Gilbert. 1998. Women's Responses to a Telemarketing Scam. *Women and Criminal Justice* 10:75–89.

Smith, Steven K., Steadman, Greg W., Minton Todd D., and Townsend, Meg. 1999. *Criminal Victimization and Perceptions of Community Safety in 12 Cities, 1998.* Washington, DC: Bureau of Justice Statistics, U.S. Department of Justice.

Wolfgang, Marvin E. 1958. *Patterns in Criminal Homicide.* Philadelphia: University of Pennsylvania Press.

Wright, Richard T., and Decker, Scott H. 1994. *Burglars on the Job: Streetlife and Residential Break-ins.* Boston: Northeastern University Press.

Chapter Two

Some Problematic Concepts, Unjustified Criticism and Popular Misconceptions

Ezzat A. Fattah

A Brief History of Victimology[1]

Early victimological notions were developed not by criminologists or sociologists but by poets, writers and novelists. These include Thomas DeQuincey, Khalil Gibran, Aldous Huxley, Marquis DeSade, Franz Werfel among others. The first systematic treatment of victims of crime appeared in 1948 in Hans von Hentig's book *The Criminal and his Victim*. In the fourth part of the book, under the provocative title "The Victim's Contribution to the Genesis of the Crime," von Hentig offered a new dynamic approach as a substitute for the static, unidimensional study of the offender which had dominated the discipline of criminology. Von Hentig had earlier treated the topic in a paper published in the *Journal of Criminal Law and Criminology* in 1940. In it von Hentig noted that:

> It is true, there are many criminal deeds with little or no contribution on the part of the injured individual.... On the other hand we can frequently observe a real mutuality in the connection of perpetrator and victim, killer and killed, duper and dupe. Although this reciprocal operation is one of the most curious phenomena of criminal life it has escaped the attention of socio-pathology.

In his book, von Hentig is critical of the legal distinction between offenders and victims and the criteria used by the criminal law to make such attributions.

From *International Debates of Victimology*, 1994, pp. 82–103, USV Publishing. Used with permission.

Most crimes are directed against a specific individual, his life or property, his sexual self-determination. For practical reasons, the final open manifestation of human motor force which precedes a socially undesirable result is designated as the criminal act, and the actor as the responsible criminal. The various degrees and levels of stimulation or response, the intricate play of interacting forces, is scarcely taken into consideration in our legal distinctions, which must be simple and workable.

Elsewhere in the book von Hentig points out that:

The law considers certain results and the final moves which lead to them. Here it makes a clear-cut distinction between the one who does and the one who suffers. Looking into the genesis of the situation, in a considerable number of cases, we meet a victim who consents tacitly, co-operates, conspires or provokes. The victim is one of the causative elements.

Von Hentig insisted that many crime victims contribute to their own victimization be it by inciting or provoking the criminal or by creating or fostering a situation likely to lead to the commission of the crime. Other pioneers in victimology, who firmly believed that victims may consciously or unconsciously play a causal role, outlined many of the forms this contribution can take: negligence, carelessness, recklessness, imprudence and so forth. They pointed out that the victim's role could be a motivational one[2] or a functional one.[3,4]

Von Hentig's book was followed by a number of theoretical studies, written by various criminologists, that dealt with victims types, victim-offender relationships and the role victims play in certain kinds of crime. The book also provided an impetus for several empirical studies which devoted special attention to the victims of specific offenses.

The term "victimology" was coined in 1949 by an American psychiatrist, Frederick Wertham, who used it for the first time in his book *The Show of Violence*. Wertham wrote:

The murder victim is the forgotten man. With sensational discussions on the abnormal psychology of the murderer, we have failed to emphasize the unprotectedness of the victim and the complacency of the authorities. One cannot understand the psychology of the murderer if one does not understand the sociology of the victim. What we need is a science of victimology.

What Is the Need for Victimology?

It is important to emphasize that victimology is neither a fad nor a fashion. It is a scientific reality that emerged at a specific stage of the historical evolution of criminology to meet scholarly and practical needs felt by researchers and professionals, to fill certain gaps in our theoretical knowledge about the phenomenon of crime, and to guide our social action to help and assist crime victims. At a certain point in the development of criminology it became clear that we need to collect information on the victims, their characteristics, their attitudes, their relationships, and interactions with the offenders, their behavior and the role they play in facilitating or precipitating the crime, as well as on their needs and their grievances.

The Classical School of Criminal Law[5] placed the emphasis on the criminal act. The Italian Positivist School[6] focused on the individual criminal. Since most traditional crimes[7] involve a criminal and a victim, it seems natural that the next stage was characterized by paying more attention to the victim.

Despite this, it took criminologists several decades to realize that criminological research would not be complete unless and until it included the other central protagonist in the crime drama, paid equal attention to the victim as to the criminal, and carefully examined and studied the party against whom the unlawful act is directed. Surprisingly, it was not until the late forties that criminologists came to the realization that a full understanding of the crime phenomenon requires a comprehensive, indepth study of both the victim and the crime situation. After all, in most cases, the criminal act is not an isolated gesture occurring on the sudden, out of the blue. Quite often, and this is particularly true of most crimes of violence and sexual offenses, the act is the outcome of a long or a brief interaction between the offender and the victim. It would, therefore, be impossible to understand it without analyzing the chain of interactions that led to its perpetration.

Traditional, mainstream criminology focused almost exclusively on the peculiarities and abnormalities of the offender. The search for the causes of crime was a search for those predispositional factors that render certain individuals prone to delinquency or make them inclined to commit crime. Whether the search is for genetic, biological, psychological, or social background variables, the underlying premise is that criminals are different from non-criminals. The central aim was to discover whatever innate qualities or acquired traits that create a special tendency or a particular inclination to violate the law, or the social conditions that may push certain individuals into delinquency and crime. This led to the formulation of a wide variety of biological, psychiatric, psychological, sociological, and cultural theories attempting to explain why some people commit crime and others do not. Although this approach is based on a doubtful premise,[8] despite the fact that it is essentially a static approach,[9] and although it has not been successful in offering a satisfactory theory of crime and delinquency, it has been quite popular and its main product[10] dominate[s] the majority of criminology textbooks. The popularity of this sterile approach can be directly traced to the comforting feeling it provides social scientists and the general public by categorizing those who commit crime as a unique and fundamentally different population, thus allowing us to distance ourselves from them and their actions and to view them as an inferior group of subhumans or "Unter-menschen."

To focus on the predispositional factors is to dissociate the criminal act from the dynamic forces that prepared, influenced, conditioned or determined it and from the motivational and situational processes that led to its commission.

Current theories of criminal and deviant behavior, whether trying to explain causation or association offer only static explanations. But criminal behavior, like other forms of human behavior, is dynamic behavior. As such it can only be explained through a dynamic approach, where the delinquent and the victim, their reciprocal attitudes, their interactions, their actions, reactions and counterreactions are inseparable elements of a total situation which culminates in the criminal act or the victimizing gesture.[11]

The traits approach which seeks the genesis of the behavior in the characteristics, attributes and attitudes of the offender is both simplistic and static. That is why etiological theories focusing on so-called offender abnormalities, peculiarities or aberrations fail to explain why other individuals sharing these same characteristics or growing up in identical or very similar social conditions to those of the offenders do not engage in delinquency or persist in a criminal career. They shed no light whatsoever on why the offender committed the crime in a particular situation, at a given moment, against a specific victim.

The traits approach, as popular as it may be, either completely ignores or deliberately minimizes the importance of situational and catalytic factors in actualizing human behavior. It overlooks the fact that the motives for criminal behavior do no develop in a vacuum. They emerge in the course of human interactions. Not infrequently, the future victim is involved consciously or unconsciously in the motivational process, as well as in the process of mental reasoning or rationalization in which the criminal engages prior to committing the crime. An examination of the victim's role in these previctimization processes is absolutely essential to understanding why the act was committed, why it was committed when it was, and why this particular target was chosen.

In other words, the commission of a crime is the outcome of a process where many factors[12] are at work. In many instances, crime is not an action but a reaction,[13] it is not something that simply emanates from within but is a response to external and environmental stimuli. Some of these stimuli emanate from the victim. The victim is an important part of the environment and the criminogenic situation that cannot be ignored or overlooked in any explanatory model or theory.

The need for a holistic approach to the explanation of crime, an approach encompassing the study of the victim, cannot be overemphasized. As the Swedish criminologist/psychiatrist Olof Kinberg[14] points out:

> It is not possible to regard certain facts or groups of facts as separate entities when analyzing the genesis of an action from a causal point of view. The logical intellectual process requires an overall view of the intricate web of factors that form a close causal chain of which the last link is the action in question.

The lack of success of current criminological theories and their failure to offer a satisfactory explanation of crime can be attributed in large part not only to their static nature but also to their inability to incorporate situational, catalytic, and triggering factors in their explanatory schemata.

Victimology, the study of crime victims, their characteristics, their relationship to, and their interactions with, their victimizers, their role and their actual contribution to the genesis of the crime, offers a great promise for transforming etiological criminology from the static, one-sided study of the traits and attributes of the offender into a dynamic, situational approach that views criminal behavior not as a unilateral action but as the outcome of dynamic processes of interaction. Victimology offers the prospect of a comprehensive model that integrates endogenous and exogenous factors, individual and situational variables, predisposing and catalytic forces, a model encompassing the perpetrator's motives and environmental temptations and opportunities, the victimizer's initiative and the victim's response, one party's action and the other party's reaction.

New and Old Misconceptions about Victimology

Misconceptions about victimology are by no means new! However, they seem to be reaching new heights and gaining new converts. In a[n] . . . issue of *Time* magazine[15] victimology is being given a new meaning. Quoting an unidentified article by John Taylor that appeared in *New York* magazine, the *Time* article talks about a double-barreled social phenomenon it claims is now threatening the real exercise of American civil liberties. The first of these two barrels, according to Taylor is "victimology." The second is what Amitai Etzioni chose to call the "rights industry." The authors of the *Time* article then go on to claim that:

> Under the corrosive influence of victimology, the principle of individual responsibility for one's own actions, once a vaunted American virtue, seems like a relic."[16]

As no reference or date is given for John Taylor's article, it was not possible to locate it. It is rather amusing, however, that victimology, which in the past has been blamed for all kinds of sins, is now being accused of contributing to the erosion of "the principle of individual responsibility for one's own actions" in American society.

As we all know, this is not the first time that unjustified or outright false accusations have been leveled at the discipline of victimology. This is slowly becoming a tradition. I need not remind you of the familiar and persistent accusation, the one that brands victimology[17] as the art of blaming the victim. As I point out elsewhere,[18] most of the criticism leveled at the concept of victim-precipitation can be traced to the failure of the critics to grasp the subtle distinction between exculpatory concepts and explanatory concepts. When correctly understood, victim-precipitation is nothing other than a legitimate effort to understand the motives of the crime, to analyze the dynamics of victim-offender interaction, and to explain the chain of events that ultimately led to the act of victimization. In such an explanatory model there is no place for normative or value judgements such as guilt or blame. Still, from the very beginning, critics of the concept of victim-precipitation did not accept it for what it really is and what it is meant to explain, but insisted that it was designed and used to blame the victim. Surprisingly, the feminists who led the campaign against victim-precipitation saw nothing wrong in using the abuse, battering, and maltreatment to which many women were subjected to explain, and even to justify, the violence that was finally used by a few women against abusive lovers and spouses. Cases of homicide, attempted murder, or assault were invariably explained by reference to the abusive behavior of the male victim. A new syndrome "the battered wife syndrome" became a popular defense in criminal cases in which a husband had been attacked, injured or killed by his female spouse.[19]

Some critics did not limit their attacks to the concept of victim-precipitation but extended their criticism to the entire discipline of victimology. Clark and Lewis,[20] for example, offered the following proposition:

> In the social sciences, victim blaming is becoming an increasingly popular rationalization for criminal and "deviant" behavior. Over the past few years, victim blaming has become institutionalized within the academic world under the guise of victimology. . . . The male researcher finds his escape in victimology. He seeks the problem's cause in the behavior of its victim, and goes on to persuade himself and the public at large that by changing that behavior, the problem can be controlled. In this way, the study of victimology becomes the art of victim blaming.[21]

The ideological and gender biases underlying this criticism are too obvious to require a rebuttal. If there is a problem with the concept of victim-precipitation, then the problem does not lie in the concept itself,[22] but in the way the concept was operationalized in some studies, particularly in Amir's study of forcible rape in Philadelphia.[23] Silverman[24] shares the view that most of the operationalizations of victim-precipitation leave much to be desired. He believes that with the exception of Wolfgang's definition of victim-precipitated homicide, there has been no adequate operational definition of the concept. The problem, as he sees it, is that the measures used have been highly unreliable from a methodological point of view because they are largely dependent on the researcher's interpretation rather than on fixed criteria. Yet, the fact that the concept has been defined too broadly or operationalized too loosely in one[25] is not a good reason to dismiss it altogether or to challenge its inherent validity and its potential utility, when correctly applied, to the explanation of the dynamics of criminal victimization.[26]

Wolfgang's definition of victim-precipitated homicide is a clear indication that it is not impossible to operationalize victim-precipitation using objective and unequivocal criteria that do not imply any attribution of guilt or assignment of blame.[27]

With a growing emphasis in criminology in recent years on the dynamics of criminal behavior, victim-offender interactions, situational and triggering variables, environmental stimuli and opportunities, differential risks of victimization, and repeat and multiple victimization, one would have expected the victim-precipitation debate to quietly come to an end. However, this is not the case. The debate seems to be regaining momentum with new critics emerging from the new political right. Surprisingly, victim advocates and spokespersons for the victim movement are being joined by some radical criminologists. Victim-precipitation, it seems, creates strange bed fellows![28]

Among . . . critics of victim-precipitation are Timmer and Norman[29] who claim that victim-precipitation functions as an ideology which blames the victim and diverts attention from the structural causes of crime. They argue that the "ideology of victim-precipitation," as expressed in both academic criminology and criminal justice practice, serves to legitimate existing criminogenic structural and institutional arrangements in American society. This, in turn, leads to more of the "ideology" of "victim-precipitation." Since structure is not responsible for crime, individuals must be. Once again we see here a good example of a widespread misconception, namely, that any attempt to explain the victimization at a micro level, by reference to the behavior of the victim, is an effort to blame the victim and to stress the individual rather than the structural causes of crime. The fallacy of this contention should by now be clear: victimology does not seek to explain crime but to explain victimization. It does not seek to explain why some people become criminals but why some people[30] become victims and others do not. This obviously cannot be adequately done without looking at the characteristics, the behavior, and the life-style of those who are victimized. To claim that by so doing attention is diverted from the structural causes of crime is ludicrous. Explaining the differential risks of victimization requires that we look not only at the individual characteristics of the victim, but also at the structural factors that enhance vulnerability and proneness such as age, gender, minority status, unemployment, and poverty. It sheds light on the role these structural factors play in the etiology of victimization. Such macro explanations need, however, to be supplemented by others capable of explaining victimization in individual cases, explaining why this particular victim was chosen, why the victimization occurred in this specific situation, at that specific time and place, and in the circumstances it did. Hence, the need for dynamic concepts such as victim-precipitation, victim-facilitation and victim-participation.[31] Continuing with their earlier critique Timmer and Norman[32] then claim that focusing on victim-offender interaction—on "situational variables" and "environmental opportunities" only—cannot go far to increasing our understanding of the etiology of crime. They add:[33]

> The ideology of victim precipitation blames neither the structure of society nor the individual offender for crime. Instead it blames the victim who precipitates crime.[34]

Finally, it is not true, as some critics[35] claim, that victim-precipitation reduces the offender to a passive actor who is set into action by the victim's behavior. What is true is that victim-precipitation, according to both its original definition[36] and its current definitions[37] is a form of overt, aggressive, and provocative behavior by the victim that triggers the action of the criminal. It is an actualizing factor, the stimulus that elicits the violent response. Thus, what may be considered, if viewed unilaterally, as an "action" would be regarded, when viewed in the dynamic, interactionist perspective of victim-precipitation, as a reaction, or more accurately an "overreaction." To establish victim-precipitation, then, is to demonstrate that had it not been for the precipitating actions of the victim, the victimization would not have occurred against that particular victim in that particular situation.[38]

Conclusion

This brief review of some of the problematic concepts in victimology, some of the unwarranted criticisms, and some of the popular misconceptions about this relatively new discipline, should not deflect attention from the achievements of victimology. Victimology, after all, is a very young discipline, much younger than its parent discipline: criminology. Victimology is less than ... [sixty] years old but it is neither a fad nor a fashion, it is a scientific reality that has imposed and affirmed itself. Its impact on, and its contribution to, criminology have been significant. Victimological research fills an enormous gap in our knowledge about the phenomenon of crime. It satisfies a need deeply felt by researchers and practitioners alike for factual and systematic information about crime victims.

The study and the understanding of the phenomenon of crime will never be complete unless the victims are included in the explanatory models. No valid theory of criminal behavior can afford to ignore the victim. To do so would be to try to explain a dynamic and interactionist form of human behavior in a unilateral, unidimensional and static manner. This is why the study of the victim is, and will always remain, an integral part of criminology. It is also why any attempt to separate victimology from criminology, or to treat it as an independent or autonomous discipline is bound to fail. We should not forget that what we are studying, that is crime and victimization, are not parallel phenomena but are one and the same phenomenon. As the study of the crime phenomenon would not be complete if it excluded the victims, so the study of victimization would not be whole if it did not include the victimizers. What we desperately need is a holistic approach, a comprehensive model where the theoretical tenets of criminology and victimology are incorporated and integrated.

This realization should, I hope, put to rest the current debate about the present and future status of victimology and whether it will become a separate discipline or remain as an integral part of criminology.

NOTES

[1] For a more detailed history of victimology see E. A. Fattah (1967) La Victimologie: Qu'est elle et quel est son avenir? *Revue Internationale de Criminologie et de Police Technique.* 1967 (21), no. 2, pp. 113–124 and no. 3 pp. 193–202; compare Kirchhoff, G. F. (1994).

[2] attracting, amusing, inducing, inciting . . .

[3] provoking, precipitating, triggering, facilitating, participating . . .

[4] Fattah, 1991.

[5] Beccaria, Bentham, Feuerbach, etc.

[6] Lombroso, Ferri, Garofalo, etc.

[7] homicide, rape, robbery, assault, theft, etc.

[8] criminals are fundamentally different from non-criminals.

[9] attempting to explain a dynamic phenomenon, criminal behavior.

[10] theories of crime causation.

[11] See Fattah, E. A., The Use of the Victim as an Agent of Self-Legitimization: Toward a Dynamic Explanation of Criminal Behavior. *Victimology: An International Journal*, 1976, Vol. 1, No. 1, pp. 29–53.

[12] other than predispositional ones.

[13] or an overreaction.

[14] 1960.

[15] August 12, 1991, p. 37.

[16] 1991:37.

[17] at least the part that examines the behavior of the victim as a situational variable or analyzes the victim's role and the victim's provoking, precipitating, facilitating or instigating conduct.

[18] Fattah, 1991.

[19] Fattah, 1991.

[20] Clark and Lewis 1977.

[21] Pp. 147, 148, 150.

[22] and has nothing to do with victim blaming.

[23] Amir, 1967, 1971.

[24] 1973.

[25] or several studies.

[26] Fattah, 1979.

[27] Fattah, 1991.

[28] Fattah, 1991.

[29] 1984.

[30] targets.

[31] Fattah, 1991.

[32] Timmer and Norman, 1984.

[33] Timmer and Norman, 1984.

[34] P. 66.

[35] Franklin II and Franklin, 1976.

[36] Wolfgang, 1958.

[37] Gobert, 1977.

[38] Fattah, 1991.

REFERENCES

Amir, M. (1971). Victim-precipitated Forcible Rape. *Journal of Criminal Law and Criminology*, vol. LVIII, no. 4, pp. 493–502.

Amir, M. (1971). *Patterns in Forcible Rape*. Chicago: University of Chicago Press.

Christie, N. (1977). Conflicts as Property. *British Journal of Criminology*, 17, no. 1, pp. 1–19.

Clark, L., and Lewis, D. (1977). *Rape: The Price of Coercive Sexuality*. Toronto: Women's Press.

Elias, R. (1986). *The Politics of Victimization Victims, Victimology, and Human Rights.* New York: Oxford University Press.

Fattah, E. A. (1967). La Victimologie: Qu'est-elle et Quel est son Avenir? *Revue Internationale de Criminologie et de Police Technique*, 21, no. 2, pp. 113–124 and no. 3, pp. 193–202.

Fattah, E. A. (1976). The Use of the Victim as an Agent of Self-Legitimization: Toward a Dynamic Explanation of Criminal Behavior. *Victimology: An International Journal*, no. 1, pp. 29–53.

Fattah, E. A. (1979). Some Recent Theoretical Developments in Victimology. *Victimology: An International Journal*, 4, no. 2, pp. 198–213.

Fattah, E. A., and Sacco, V. F. (1989). *Crime and Victimization of the Elderly.* New York: Springer Verlag.

Flynn, E. E. (1982). Theory Development in Victimology: An Assessment of Recent Progress and of Continuing Challenges. In H. J. Schneider (ed.), *The Victim in International Perspective.* Berlin: de Gruyter, pp. 96–104.

Franklin II, C. W., and Franklin, A. P. (1976). Victimology Revisited: A Critique and Suggestions for Future Direction. *Criminology*, 14, no. 1, pp. 177–214.

Gibbons, D. C. (1971). Observations on the Study of Crime Causation. *American Journal of Sociology*, 77, pp. 262–278.

Gobert, J. J. (1977). Victim-precipitation. *Columbia Law Review*, 77, no. 4, pp. 511–553.

Hentig, H. von (1948). *The Criminal and His Victim.* New Haven: Yale University Press.

Kennedy, L. W. (1990). *On the Borders of Crime: Conflict Management and Criminology.* New York: Longman.

Kinberg, O. (1960). *Les Problemes Fondamentaux de la Criminologie.* Paris: Cujas.

Kirchhoff, G. F. (1994). Victimology: History and Basic Concepts. In G. F. Kirchoff (ed.), *International Debates on Victimology.* Mönchengladbach: WSV Publishing, pp. 1–81.

Kirchoff, G. F., and Sessar, K. (eds.) (1980). *Das Verbrechensopfer: Ein Reader zur Viktimologie.* Bochum: Studienverlag Dr. Brockmeyer.

Quinney, R. (1972). Who Is the Victim? *Criminology*, 10, no. 3, pp. 314–323.

Silverman, R. (1973). Victim Precipitation: An Examination of the Concept. In I. Drapkin and E. Viano (eds.), *Victimology: A New Focus.* Vol 1. Lexington, MA: Lexington Books.

Timmer, D., and Norman, W. H. (1984). The Ideology of Victim Precipitation. *Criminal Justice Review*, 9, pp. 63–68.

Walklate, S. (1990). *Victimology: The Victim and the Criminal Justice Process.* London, Unwin Hyman.

Wertham, F. (1949). *The Show of Violence.* New York: Doubleday.

Wolfgang, M. E. (1958). *Patterns in Criminal Homicide.* Philadelphia: University of Pennsylvania Press.

Chapter Three

Routine Activities and Involvement in Violence as Actor, Witness, or Target

Richard B. Felson

According to the routine activity approach, crime occurs when there is a motivated offender and a suitable target in the absence of capable guardians (Cohen & Felson, 1979; Felson, 1994). Routine activities that bring motivated offenders and suitable targets in contact, isolated from the protection of third parties, lead to criminal activity.

Victimization data have provided key evidence for the routine activity approach. Research based on the National Crime Survey indicates that the risk of victimization for assault is greater if people live near the central city and low-income neighborhoods (Cohen, Kluegel, & Land, 1981). Those who frequently go out for nighttime entertainment are also more likely to be the victim of violent crimes (Clarke, Ekblom, Hough, & Mayhew, 1985; Miethe, Stafford, & Long, 1987). Evidence from the Canadian Urban Victim Survey shows that residents who patronize bars, who work or go to class, or who go out for a walk or drive at night are more likely to be victims of assault than those who do not engage in these activities (Kennedy & Forde, 1990; see also Lasley, 1989).

The assumption in these studies is that nighttime and other activities create opportunities for crime. However, there is an alternative interpretation of the relationship between risk-prone activities and criminal victimization. Perhaps people who go out often are different from people who stay at home. Those who like to take risks, who seek excitement, who are present-oriented, or who use more alcohol may have more active night lifes. Such people are also likely to be less inhibited in their social behavior. They may be more likely to engage in aggression, deviance, and other behaviors that others find offensive. Their provocative behavior may lead them to be the target of violence.

Those with active night lifes may also be at greater risk for engaging in violence themselves. Potential offenders who have an active night life are likely to be tempted more often than those who stay at home. However, any correlation observed between having an active night life and engaging in violence could be attributed to the individual differences just mentioned. For example, people who seek excitement may go out at night more frequently, and may commit more crime.

Another problematic issue in the literature on routine activities is the treatment of domestic violence (Miethe, Stafford, & Long, 1987). Some incidents of crime, particularly those involving violent disputes, target family members. The specific routine activities usually associated with domestic violence are not likely to be the same as those associated with street crime. Activities that draw people away from their home are not likely to increase violence in the home. If anything, they would have the opposite effect, because going out at night reduces the frequency of contact between family members. These complications may explain why daytime activities, such as working outside the home, predict victimization for property crimes but not for violent crimes (Miethe et al., 1987).

The Present Study

This article applies the routine activity approach to interpersonal violence. We examine whether persons who are involved in nighttime recreational activities outside the home are more likely to be involved in violence as actors and targets, and whether they are more likely to witness such events. To our knowledge, the effects of routine activities on witnessing violence have never been examined.

If routine activities produce opportunities for violence, then they should affect potential actors, targets, and witnesses similarly. Thus we predict that persons who go out at night for recreation are more likely to be involved in nondomestic violent encounters as actors, targets, and witnesses. If we find that routine activities predict violence or being the target of violence but not witnessing violence, it casts doubt on an opportunity explanation. It suggests that respondents who go out at night are getting involved in violent interactions because they are more likely to be provocative or violent themselves. On the other hand, if going out at night predicts all three dependent variables, it suggests that the result, is due, at least in part, to differential opportunity.

Personal characteristics may affect witnessing violence as well as offending: and victimization. Those who are risk-averse, for example, may witness violence less often if they avoid activities and places where violence occurs. Still, the effects of personal characteristics on witnessing must be mediated by activity patterns. In other words, the impact of night life on witnessing violence must involve some type of opportunity effect, unlike the impact of nightlife on offending and victimization. Therefore, an effect of night life on witnessing violence provides support for the routine activity approach.

Another method of testing whether the relationship between night life and violence is due to differences in opportunity is to examine effects on domestic violence. According to a routine activity approach, night life should have no effect on engaging in domestic violence, because going out does not increase opportunities for domestic conflict, and might even decrease it.[1] A positive relationship between night life and domestic violence cannot be attributed to differences in opportunity. Some personal characteristic associated with violent behavior and going out at night would be implicated.

In contrast to previous research on the effects of routine activities, we include a measure of alcohol consumption. Evidence shows that both criminal offenders and victims are frequently intoxicated (see Fagan, 1993, for a review). Alcohol use is clearly a situational risk factor for violence. However, the research literature is unclear about whether chronic use of alcohol—which is what is studied here—is associated with how often individuals engage in violence (Collins, 1991; see Fagan, 1993).

Alcohol consumption may mediate the effects of night life on involvement in violent interactions. People often consume alcohol when they go out at night for recreation, and it may be the alcohol and not the night activities that produces risk. Alcohol may increase the propensity to engage in violence or it may lead to behaviors that provoke others (Tedeschi & Felson, 1994). In addition, people who are intoxicated may take fewer precautions to avoid victimization, and they may appear more vulnerable to potential offenders. In one sense, drinking alcohol may be considered a type of routine activity because it creates opportunities for violence. However, the mediating process is psychological and behavioral, not spatial.

We also examine the role of routine activities in explaining the effects of family obligations on violence. According to a routine activity approach, people with family responsibilities go out less and therefore have fewer opportunities to be involved in crime. Family obligations keep people at home and reduce the opportunity to be either an offender, a victim, or a witness. In the language of control theory, involvement in conventional activities reduces the time available for criminal activity (Hirschi, 1969).

The routine activity approach may also help explain age effects on violent behavior. As people get older they go out less and have fewer opportunities to engage in violent behavior outside their families. Also, as people enter adulthood, family obligations increase and keep them at home. As they age further, and their children "leave the nest," family obligations are likely to decline, and the risk of violent behavior may increase. The result of their extra leisure activity could be an increase in the risk of nondomestic violence. Such an effect could suppress a portion of the linear negative effect of age on violence.

Methods

The analyses are based on interviews in Albany County, New York with persons aged 18 to 65. The data were collected in 1980 as part of a larger study of situational factors in violence. A representative sample of the general population ($N = 245$) was obtained through multistage sampling. Random samples of streets in each census tract and then the dwellings on those streets were randomly sampled. Male and female respondents were then chosen in equal number.

People may go out more or less frequently than they did in 1980, but such a change would affect the likelihood of violence, not the relationship between going out and the likelihood of violence. However, the strength of the effect of night life on the risk of violence is likely to depend on the violent crime rate at a particular time and location. According to data from the National Crime Survey, the assault rate in the early 1990s is similar to what it was in 1980, when these data were collected (Bureau of Justice Statistics, 1994). Albany County ranked eighth out of 62 counties in New York State in terms of its violent crime rate, according to statistics obtained from police reports (Criminal Justice Services, 1993). It ranked 23rd in terms of its rate of hospitalizations due to assault in 1992 (New York State Department of Health, 1994). Thus, the risk of going out at night in Albany County is higher than the risk in most counties in New York.

Respondents were asked about various acts against their children, their spouse, other family or relatives, other people they knew, and strangers. The questions were "How many times in the last year have you pushed or shoved or slapped _____?" and "How many times in the last year have you hit with your fist or an object _____?" The response categories were: "never; 1 or 2 times a year; 3 or 4 times a year; twice a month; monthly; weekly." Responses were coded 0 through 5 and summed. Two-item scales were created for violence against children (ranging from 0 to 9) and violence against spouse (ranging from 0 to 5). Nondomestic violence was based on four items, two involving other people they knew, and two involving strangers. For males, the summated scale ranged from 0 to 10. The item could not be analyzed for females, because only three females (out of 115 or 2.6% of the sample) reported engaging in such an attack. Note that minor forms of violence occur with much higher frequency and therefore dominate these scales.

In order to measure being the target of violence; respondents were asked how often in the past year someone "pushed or shoved or slapped you?"; "hit you with a fist or an object?"; "threatened you with or hurt you with a gun or knife?" In order to measure witnessing violence, respondents were asked how many times in the last year they had seen other people "hit each other" or "threaten to use or actually use a knife or gun on each other?" The same response categories were used for these variables as before. The summated scales ranged from 0 to 11, and 0 to 10, respectively.

Unfortunately, information on the respondent's relationship with the antagonist is not available for items involving witnessing and being a target of violence. Some of these incidents could involve domestic violence. To the extent that domestic incidents are counted, the relationships between night life and these variables should be weakened. In other words, measurement error should result in a bias against our hypothesis. This issue will be discussed further later in terms of its relevance for gender differences in effects.

Responses to two items were added together to measure night life. Respondents were asked: "On the average how many evenings a week do you go out at night for fun and recreation?" and "On the average how many times a week do you go to a bar or tavern?" Note that most but not all visits to bars occur at night. Thus, to a large extent, the latter activity is a subcategory of the former activity.

Obviously, some locations are more likely to expose people to risk than others. For example, going to a movie or a bar that caters to an older clientele is likely to entail less risk than going to a hockey game or a bar catering to young people. General activity items—which are typically found in the literature—are rough measures of exposure to risk.

Other variables include alcohol use, education, race, age, marital status, and whether there was a preteen at home. Alcohol use is based on the product of measures of frequency and quantity (measured in ounces). The items involved were "On the average how many times a week do you drink alcoholic beverages?" and "About how much do you drink at a time?"

Age is coded as a continuous variable. Marital status is a dichotomy based on whether respondents are married or not. Respondents who are divorced, widowed, or single are excluded from analyses involving violence against spouses, and the variable is coded as married or separated. Preteen children is a dichotomy based on whether a child under age 13 is living in the respondent's home.

Education and race are included as control variables. Education is measured in terms of years of education. Nonwhite is coded as a dichotomous variable. The nonwhites included seven Puerto Ricans and two persons classified by interviewers as "other." The results were almost identical when these persons were omitted from analyses, and blacks were compared with whites.

Results

Because preliminary analyses revealed gender differences in the effects of night life, analyses are presented separately for males and females. Zero-order correlations, means, and standard deviations are presented in table 1. Regression coefficients for males are presented in table 2, and regression coefficients for females in table 3.[2] A one-tailed test is used in evaluating the statistical significance of regression coefficients when the relationship was predicted.

Analyses in which night life is the dependent variable are presented in the first column of tables 2 and 3. In general, the results are similar for males and females. Respondents who are older, who are married, and who have a preteen living in the home, tend to go out less than their counterparts. The results show that older people and those with family obligations are less likely to go out at night for recreation. There is also a tendency for white females to go out more often than nonwhite females.

Effects on measures of violence are presented in the remaining columns. For males, the pattern of findings clearly supports the routine activity approach. Males who go out at night are more likely to witness violence, experience victimization, and engage in violence against people outside their families. On the other hand, males with an active night life are no more likely to engage in violence against family members. In fact, the coefficients for family violence are negative in sign.[3]

For females, night life does not affect either victimization or witnessing violence (see table 3). The coefficients are positive, as predicted, but small and statistically insignificant.[4] Night life is negatively related to violence against children, but the effect is not statistically significant.

One reason night life might not be associated with either witnessing or victimization for females is that the experience of females with violence is primarily within the family. This explanation is supported by evidence that the witness and target variables are influenced by domestic violence for female respondents. First, the correlation between the victimization measure and the measure of violence against spouses is quite strong for females ($r = .69$ for females vs. $r = .17$ for males; see table 1). The strength of this correlation suggests that attacks and counterattacks by spouses are influencing the target measure for females. Second, evidence from table 3 shows that females who have preteens living in, home are more likely to witness violence and be the target of violence. Although the effects are not quite statistically significant, they suggest that mothers are targeted by their children and that some of the violence they witness is their children fighting with each other. Past research suggests that children frequently fight with their siblings (Felson & Russo, 1988).

Alcohol consumption is also associated with the violence measures. For both males and females, the greater the consumption of alcohol the higher the risk of victimization. Presumably, people who drink a lot are more likely to engage in behaviors that provoke others. Alcohol consumption is also related to engaging in nondomestic violence for males, and witnessing violence for females. It is unrelated to domestic violence for either males or females.[5]

Other results should be mentioned. Age is negatively associated with all measures of violence, although not all effects are statistically significant. Years of education has small negative relationships with most measures of violent behavior; all but one is statistically insignificant. The effects of race are slight and statistically insignificant, with one exception: nonwhite males are more likely to witness violence. Finally, respondents are more likely to engage in violence against children if a child under 13 shares the household.

TABLE 1. Means Standard Deviation, and Zero-Order Correlat

	1	2	3	4	5	6	7	8	9	10
1. Marital status	—	45	53	06	-13	-27	-51	-43	-16	-23
2. Preteen children	18	—	-07	09	01	-13	-28	-14	07	03
3. Age	20	-51	—	-28	-01	-10	-42	-40	-27	-29
4. Education	16	06	-03	—	-30	-31	-01	-12	-09	-10
5. Nonwhite	-23	18	-14	-18	—	-10	07	29	-11	02
6. Alcohol use	-19	-03	02	-23	-09	—	41	24	32	33
7. Nightlife	-44	-13	-29	08	-12	26	—	52	29	37
8. Witness	-15	22	-26	-09	05	23	15	—	39	57
9. Target	-07	25	-25	-16	-02	31	16	26	—	71
10. Nonfamily violence	-10	15	-11	-09	04	08	06	04	03	—
11. Violence against spouse	08	08	-16	-15	-09	02	07	04	69	09
12. Violence against child	10	50	-51	02	05	-08	-08	09	01	18
X̄	.69	.52	37.92	12.82	.11	1.08	1.62	.88	.50	.04
SD	.47	.50	14.60	2.70	.32	2.55	1.66	1.45	1.50	.28

Note. Data for males is above the diagonal, data for females below (decimal points omitted from correlat

TABLE 2. Regression Coefficients and Standard Errors for Ma

	Nightlife		Witness		Target		Respondent's V Nonfamily		
	b	beta	b	beta	b	beta	beta	b	b
Marital status	-1.19* (.56)	-.24	-.37 (.51)	-.08	.10 (.36)	.04	-.00	-.00 (.43)	.1 (.1)
Preteen children	-1.01* (.51)	-.19	-.08 (.47)	-.02	.41 (.33)	.13	.11	.44 (.40)	-.10 (.1)
Age	-.05* (.02)	-.33	-.05* (.02)	-.23	-.02* (.01)	0.22	-.19	-.02 (.01)	-.0 (.0)
Education	-.05 (.07)	-.07	-.07 (.06)	-.09	.07* (.05)	-.15	0.10	-.05 (.05)	-.00 (.0)
Nonwhite	.10 (.51)	.02	1.45* (.49)	.23	-.57 (.34)	-.15	-.01	-.03 (.41)	-.10 (.1)
Alcohol use	—	—	.02 (.04)	.05	.06* (.03)	.19	.20	.07* (.04)	.00 (.0)
Night life	—	—	.32* (.09)	.34	.11* (.06)	.18	.23	.16* (.08)	-.02 (.0)
R^2	.32		.40		.17		.22		
N	125		125		125		125		

Note. b = unstandardized coefficient with standard error in parentheses; beta = standardized coefficient.
*$p < .05$ (one-tailed where predicted).

TABLE 3. Regression Coefficients and Standard Errors for Female

	Nightlife		Witness		Target		Respondent's V	
							Spo	
	b	beta	b	beta	b	beta	b	b
Marital status	-1.44* (.32)	-.41	.04 (.10)	-.09	.07 (.34)	.02	.73 (.50)	
Preteen children	-.64* (.33)	-.20	.54 (.34)	.19	.66 (.33)	.22	.04 (.31)	
Age	-.04* (.01)	-.33	-.01 (.01)	-.13	-.01 (.01)	-.13	-.02 (.01)	
Education	.07 (.05)	.11	-.03 (.05)	-.05	.08 (.05)	-.14	-.08* (.04)	
Nonwhite	-1.03* (.45)	-.20	-.04 (.45)	-.01	-.33 (.45)	-.07	-.43 (.45)	
Alcohol use	—	—	.11* (.06)	.19	.15* (.06)	.25	.00 (.05)	
Night life	—	—	.04 (.10)	.05	.09 (.10)	.10	.08 (.11)	
R^2	.33		.14		.20			
N	115		115		115			

Note. b = unstandardized coefficient with standard error in parentheses; beta = standardized coefficient.

*p <.05 (one-tailed where predicted).

Discussion

These results support the hypothesis that an active night life has a causal effect on the opportunity to be involved (as a victim, offender, or witness) in nondomestic violence. Two findings suggest that the relationship between routine activities and violence is due, at least in part, to differential opportunity. First, for males, night life is associated with witnessing violence as well as offending and victimization. The witness variable is more suitable for measuring the spatial and temporal effects of routine activities because it depends on visual contact, not on the behavior of the offender or victim.

Second, the routine activities that lead to violence against persons outside the family do not lead to domestic violence. If the people who go out at night have personal characteristics that cause them to be more provocative or violent, they would also engage in more domestic violence. However, the relationships between night life and the measures of domestic violence are negative and insignificant. These findings are therefore consistent with a routine activities explanation, and inconsistent with the explanation that personal characteristics are affecting behavior, independent of opportunity factors.

VIOLENCE INVOLVING WOMEN

There was no evidence that going out at night was a risk factor for women. The failure to find an effect may be due to fact that females are much less likely than men to attack or be attacked by people outside their family. When they are involved in violence (as a witness, offender, or victim), a domestic situation is usually involved. Thus, the witness and target variables for females were dominated by incidents of domestic violence.

There is another reason why an active night life is not likely to be as risky for women as for men. When females go out at night, they are more likely to go to places where the risk of being the target of violence or witnessing violence is low. Evidence shows that females are more risk-averse than males and have a greater fear of crime (Block, 1993; Warr,1984). They are less likely than men to walk alone at night. They may be more likely than males to avoid rough bars and other dangerous locations. Future research should examine in more detail the types of places men and women frequent when they go out at night.

SOCIAL-DEMOGRAPHIC FACTORS

This research demonstrates the role of routine activities in explaining social-demographic variation in involvement in violence. It shows that routine activities can help explain why young, single men are at the greatest risk for violent offending and victimization. Thus, the results show that as people get older they have a less active night life. Staying at home reduces the risk of nondomestic violence, at least for males. Family obligations also affect night life. Those who are married and those with pre-teenage children at home are less likely to go out at night. For males, these activities reduce the risk of their involvement in nondomestic violence.[6]

Age and family obligations do not operate independently, however. As people age they are more likely to marry, which leads to a further reduction in night life. Age also has a nonlinear effect on whether they are responsible for preteen children. In these data, the presence of preteen children was highest in the late 20s for females and early 30s for males. As children get older, their parents are able to go out more frequently, increasing their risk of involvement in nondomestic violence. This pattern offsets the negative linear effect of age on involvement in violent activity.

THE ROLE OF ALCOHOL

Alcohol consumption was associated with male violence outside the family, but not with domestic violence. It may be that unless individuals are intoxicated, they are unlikely to become embroiled in violent disputes outside the family. Conflicts with strangers and acquaintances are likely to be less frequent, and less intense, and less likely to culminate in violence unless the antagonists are disinhibited due to alcohol. Domestic disputes, on the other hand, are more likely to be more frequent and intense, and therefore less likely to require intoxication to become violent. In addition, many parents use violence routinely to discipline their children; the role of alcohol is likely to be less significant.

Alcohol consumption was also associated with victimization. Those who consumed high levels of alcohol were more likely to be the target of violence. It may be that the disinhibitory effect of alcohol leads people to engage in impolite or otherwise offensive behaviors. The resulting conflict may culminate in violent attacks from others. In other words, alcohol interferes with performance, and individuals who perform poorly are more likely to be the target of grievances and violence. A similar argument has been used to explain why the experience of stressful life events is more highly correlated with violent victimization than with engaging in violence (Felson, 1992).

Alcohol consumption may mediate some of the effect of night life on the frequency of nondomestic violence.[7] People may drink more if they go out at night, particularly if they go to parties or drinking establishments. Drinking may then increase the likelihood of violence outside the home.

POSSIBLE LIMITATIONS

The results from this study are based on a relatively small sample from one city at one point in time. Because the risks of going out at night are likely to be greater in some cities than in others, estimates of the size of effects are not generalizable across time and space. (In a national sample, these risks are simply averaged out across difference locations.) However, our interest is in whether night life affects witnessing, victimization, and offending inside and outside the family. It is the pattern of effects that allow us to examine the causal process involved.

There are also some measurement problems in this research. As indicated earlier, the target and witness variables may have included some incidents of domestic violence that are not affected by an individual's night life. This measurement problem may explain why we found no effects of night life for women. In addition, the night life measure is only a rough indicator of opportunity. The risk of going out is likely to depend on the places males frequent and the activities they engage in at these locations. For example, a key predictor of the frequency of violence in bars is the age of the clientele (Felson, Baccaglini, & Gmelch, 1984). Men who frequent bars with a young clientele therefore put themselves at a greater risk of witnessing or being involved in violence than those who go to bars with an older clientele.

These measurement problems are likely to produce random rather than systematic error. The coefficients might have been stronger if only violence outside the family was measured and if a more refined measure of opportunities was used. It is noteworthy that we found substantial effects of night life for males, particularly on witnessing violence, given the limitation of our measures.

Another potential limitation involves the issue of displacement. Perhaps men with a propensity to violence are more likely to attack strangers if they go out, and attack family members if they stay home. Routine activities affect whom they target but not how often they engage in violence.

We think displacement is likely to have minimal impact on dispute-related violence, which is primarily what is studied in this data set (Felson, 1982). Situational factors are critical in motivating people to commit dispute-related violence. Even individuals with a propensity toward violence are not violent in most situations. In addition, targets are not as substitutable in dispute-related violence as they, are in predatory crime. Offenders are usually interested in one target—the person with whom they are in conflict (Felson, 1993).

In sum, the evidence suggests that the routine activities of males affect their risk of involvement in violence outside the family. When males go out at night for recreation, their chances of observing and becoming involved in violent disputes increase. These opportunities help explain social-demographic differences in nondomestic violent behavior. The tendency to go out at night is one reason for the higher levels of violence among young single men.

NOTES

[1] It is possible that going out at night creates conflict with spouses and thus leads to domestic violence.

[2] The normality assumption of ordinary least squares (OLS) is violated in varying degrees in our dependent variables. To address this issue, we reanalyzed the data using Poisson regression, a technique more appropriate for count variables with non-normal distributions (Beck & Tolnay, 1995). The results were quite similar. We present the OLS results because the technique is more familiar and the results are easier to interpret.

[3] For males, the measure of violence against spouses is highly skewed, because most respondents did not report engaging in violence against their spouse. We dichotomized this variable, coding respondent "1" if they had engaged in violence against

a spouse, and zero otherwise. The pattern of results from logistic regressions using this coding procedure was the same as the pattern of results presented in table 2.

[4] We reanalyzed the results treating the two measures of night life as separate variables. For males, going out at night was a better predictor of being a witness and engaging in violence than going to bars. Going to bars was a stronger factor in predicting being the target of violence. Neither bar frequency not going out at night predicted the violence measures for females.

[5] We also examined statistical interactions between night life and alcohol consumption. Significant statistical interactions were observed using OLS for male aggression against nonfamily and female victimization. However, this pattern was not observed when we analyzed the data using Poisson regression. We conclude that the effects of night life and alcohol consumption are probably additive.

[6] Marital status and preteen children have negative but nonsignificant effects on witnessing and engaging in nondomestic violence, when night life is omitted from the equation. Apparently, the indirect effects of family obligations on involvement in violence are not strong enough to be observed in these equations.

[7] Alcohol consumption and night life are correlated for both males ($r = .41$) and females ($r = .21$). We do not know to what extent the relationship is causal or spurious, because those who desire to drink tend to drink more and they tend to go to bars to purchase alcohol.

REFERENCES

Beck, E. M., & Tolnay, S. E. (1995). Analyzing historical count data: Poisson and negative binomial regression models. *Historical Methods, 28L*, 125–131.

Black, D. (1983). Crime as social control. *American Sociological Review, 48*, 34–35.

Block, J. (1983). Differential premises arising from differential socialization of the sexes: Some conjectures. *Child Development, 54*, 1335–1354.

Bureau of Justice Statistics. (1994). Criminal victimization in the United States: 1973–1992 trends. U.S. Department of Justice. Washington, DC: U.S. Government Printing Office.

Clarke, R., Ekblom, P., Hough, M., & Mayhew, P. (1980). Elderly victims of crime and exposure to risk. *The Howard Journal, 24*, 1–9:

Cohen, L. E., & Felson, M. (1979). Social change and crime rate trends: A routine activity approach. *American Sociological Review, 44*, 588–608.

Cohen, L., Kluegel, J., & Land, K. C. (1981). Social inequality and predatory criminal victimization: An exposition and a test of a formal theory. *American Sociological Review, 46*, 505–524.

Collins, J. J. Jr. (1991). Drinking and violations of the criminal law. In D. J. Pittman & H. R. White, (Eds.), *Society, culture and drinking patterns re-examined* (pp. 650–660). New Brunswick, NJ: Rutgers Center of Alcohol Studies.

Criminal Justice Services. (1993). *Crime and justice annual report*. Albany, NY: Division of Criminal Justice Services.

Fagan, J. (1993). Set and setting revisited: Influences of alcohol and illicit drugs on the social context of violent events. In S. E. Martin (Ed.), *Alcohol-related violence: Fostering interdisciplinary perspectives*. Rockville, MD: U.S. Department of Health and Human Services.

Felson, M. (1994). *Crime and everyday life: Insights and implications for society*. Thousand Oaks, CA: Pine Forge.

Felson, M. (1987). Routine activities and crime prevention in the developing metropolis. *Criminology, 25,* 911–931.

Felson, M. (1986). Linking criminal choices, routine activities, informal control, and criminal outcomes. In D. B. Cornish & R. V. Clarke (Eds.), *The reasoning criminal: Rational choice perspectives on offending* (pp. 119–128). Berlin: Springer-Verlag.

Felson, R. B. (1982). Impression management and the escalation of aggression and violence. *Social Psychology Quarterly, 45,* 245–254.

Felson, R. B. (1992). Kick 'em when they're down: Explanations of the relationship between stress and interpersonal aggression and violence. *Sociological Quarterly, 33,* 1–16.

Felson, R. B. (1993). Predatory and dispute-related violence: A social interactionist approach. In R. V. Clarke & M. Felson (Eds.), *Advances in criminological theory, 5,* 189–235.

Felson, R. B., Baccaglini, W. & Gmelch, G. (1986). Bar-room brawls: Aggression and violence in Irish and American bars. In A. Campbell & J. J. Gibbs, *Violent transactions* (pp. 153–166). Oxford, England: Basil Blackwell.

Felson, R. B., & Russo, N. (1988). Parental punishment and sibling aggression. *Social Psychology Quarterly, 51,* 11–18.

Hirschi, T. 1969. *Causes of delinquency.* Berkeley, CA: University of California Press.

Kennedy, L. W., & D. R. Forde. (1990). Routine activities and crime: An analysis of victimization in Canada: *Criminology, 28,* 137–152.

Lasley, J. R. (1989). Drinking routines/lifestyles and predatory victimization: A causal analysis. *Justice Quarterly, 6,* 529–42.

Miethe, T. D., Stafford, M. C., & Long, J. S. (1987). Social differentiation in criminal victimization: A test of routine activities/lifestyle theories. *American Sociological Review, 52,* 184–194.

New York State Department of Health. (1994). Injury facts for New York State. Unpublished.

Tedeschi, J. T., & Felson, R. B. (1994). Violence, aggression, and coercive actions. Washington, DC: American Psychological Association.

Warr, M. (1984). Fear of victimization: Why are women and the elderly more afraid. *Social Science Quarterly, 65,* 681–702.

Chapter Four

Corporate Deviance and Corporate Victimization
A Review and Some Elaborations

David Shichor

Introduction

White-collar crime is an ambiguous concept. Sutherland, who introduced this term, defined it as "a crime committed by a person of respectability and high social status in the course of his occupation" (Sutherland, 1949:2). This definition is a very broad one and includes everything from embezzlement to bribery. Sutherland focused mainly on offenses connected with business (Coleman, 1985). Clinard and Yaeger (1980:17) claim that:

> The concept of white-collar crime was developed to distinguish a body of criminal acts that involve monetary offenses not ordinarily associated with criminality.

According to them, white-collar crime can be divided into two types: occupational and corporate. Occupational crime is usually committed by individuals or small groups of people in connection with their occupational activities (Clinard and Quinney, 1973). Corporate crime, on, the other hand, is:

> organizational crime occurring in the context of complex relationships and expectations among board of directors, executives, and managers, on the one hand, and among parent corporations, corporate divisions, and subsidiaries on the other. (Clinard and Yaeger, 1980:17)[1]

There is much less research conducted on white-collar crime in general, and upon corporate crime in particular, than on street crime. Some of the

From *International Review of Victimology*, 1(1) (1989): 67–88. Used with permission.

reasons for this are mentioned in the literature: (1) many corporate violations are defined in the civil and administrative codes rather than in the criminal law;[2] (2) white-collar crimes (including corporate violations) are less visible than street crimes (Geis, 1984); they usually are not open for first-hand observation and their effects are not clearly seen; (3) the defendants often plead "nolo contendere," thereby avoiding detailed transcripts which would shed light on these offenses (Geis and Meier, 1977); (4) even when white-collar (economic) crime is being prosecuted they tend to be those cases in which the defendant is an individual and the victim is an organization (Neff-Gurney, 1985); (5) there is relatively little information available about the victims of these crimes though victimology had developed considerably during the 1970s and 1980s.[3]

This article analyzes the major characteristics of corporate deviance (crime), the types of victims, and the patterns of victimization they involve.

Corporate Deviance[4]

Corporate deviance is organizational deviance, committed by individuals during their normal activities as employees or representatives of the corporation and is meant to achieve organizational goals (Edelhertz, 1970; Clinard and Quinney, 1973; Conklin, 1977; Schrager and Short, 1978; Shover, 1978; Sherman, 1978; Finney and Lesieur, 1982). The corporation is considered to be the violator, not the individual (Kramer, 1981). Clinard and Yaeger (1980:16) expand this definition by stating that "a corporate crime is any act committed by corporations that is punished by the state, regardless of whether it is punished under administrative, civil, or criminal law."[5] This violation "is committed on behalf of the organization; it occurs in the course of participating or working in it" (Finney and Lesieur, 1982:264).

To understand better the nature of corporate deviance there is a need to analyze its organizational context. Corporations generate occasions for deviance because: (a) the complex and impersonal nature of transactions allows for misleading advertisement, and consumers are unable to test the product; (b) organizations are subject to special norms which can be easily broken, thus resulting in illegality and deviance, for instance anti-trust laws, etc. (Shapiro, 1980).[6] Corporations are legal entities, having legal rights, separate and distinct from those who own or manage them or are employed by them (Bequai, 1978; Coleman, 1974). Legally they are conceived as intangible persons (Little, 1983). Their major goal according to the classical market model, is the maximization of profit (Jacoby, 1973). Capitalist ideology stipulates that this goal should be achieved through free competition.

The profit maximization thesis has been criticized by several authors. For instance, Stone (1975:38–39) cites various economists who suggest that corporations are more likely to seek a "satisfactory level of profits" to satisfy their stockholders than maximum profits. Bozeman and Straussman (1983) argue that corporations seek stable growth, which is less risky, in preference to rapid growth and profit maximization. Nevertheless, by nature, private enterprise "breeds a materialistic preoccupation, a competitive drive to get ahead, and individuality" (Chamberlain, 1973:189). Since organizations are formally rational, following the bureaucratic model, the congruence between their procedures and their substantive goals is closer than that of most other social groups (Sutton and Wild, 1978:189).

Maximization of profit and free competition—two elements of the capitalist ethos[7] are often incompatible (Conklin, 1977). The profit motive has achieved its fullest acceptance in America, although it is followed in other capitalist societies as well (see, for instance, Yokoyama, 1984). It has become so prevalent that it has often been used to justify questionable business practices, since corporate interest is narrower and more relentlessly pursued than private interest (Scott, 1981). The embracement of the "caveat emptor" principle in the business world has contributed to this process. In pre-capitalist society the protection of customers had a high priority. Fraudulent practices were perceived as harmful to the whole community and were punished accordingly. In the late eighteenth century, commerce expanded greatly and the political power of merchants increased with it. Mercantile interests sought to rid themselves of feudal supervision (Hamilton, 1931). This process reached its peak in the Industrial Revolution when "the doctrine of caveat emptor unilaterally determined the buyer's rights" (Rothchild and Throne, 1976:666). The situation has changed considerably during the twentieth century, with the development of consumerism and the establishment of consumer protection agencies,[8] but the commitment to the doctrine of *caveat emptor* still has strong roots in the capitalist ethos.

The principle of free competition is the other cornerstone of this ideology.[9] The classical economist Adam Smith (1937) maintained that only free competition would bring about maximum productivity. This goal was to be accompanied by reduction of the authority of the state; in other words by adopting the *laissez-faire* doctrine of political power. Following Smith's ideas, artificial legal restraints would increase white-collar crime (Jesilow, 1982).

A corporation can increase its profit by limiting free competition (see, Conklin, 1977; Vaughan, 1980). Antitrust violations are aimed at diminishing "the negative impact of the demand constraint on the pursuit of corporate objectives" (Barnett, 1981:5). Sutherland (1956:90) pointed out that "big business does not like competition, and it makes careful arrangements to reduce it and even eliminate it." He quotes Walter Lippman, who noted that "competition has survived only where men have been unable to abolish it."[10] In fact, according to Arnold (1937) antitrust legislation is only a symbol, without much practical consequence. In several "basic" industries, there are only a handful of large companies which dominate the domestic market. Even without illegal price-fixing, or other methods of "conspiracy," certain kinds of accommodations and "market sharing" among these companies are likely to develop (Moore, 1962). Thus an "oligopoly" emerges with considerable discretion to set prices (Galbraith, 1958).

Blau and Scott (1962:218) have observed that: "If a few organizations become dominant in a market, symbiosis comes to replace competition."

Braithwaite (1984) in his research in the pharmaceutical industry disputes that the maximization of profit is the major motive for corporate deviance. Nevertheless, the general corporate atmosphere is basically criminogenic since it encourages corporations to increase their profits, even if this does involve the violation of laws and regulations. There are several other factors which facilitate corporate misconduct: (a) the occurrence of a corporate crime is not readily apparent (Braithwaite and Geis, 1982); (b) to prove guilt is difficult in corporate crime cases (Braithwaite and Geis, 1982); (c) the usual legal sanction for corporate crime is a fine, and whilst the size of the fines is increasing, they are still in most cases not proportional to the illegal gains of the corporations,[11] (d) usually, there is a lack of vigorous rule-enforcement in cases of corporate deviance (Clinard and Quinney, 1973); (e) relatively little public condemnation is aroused by corporate misconduct (Geis and Meier, 1977). Using the concept of the "hedonistic calculus," Barnett (1981) notes that a corporation is more likely to engage in violations when the expected cost of the crime is low in relation to the expected gains. Therefore, the fear of legal sanctions "is apt to be far less of an item than other things" that concern the corporation's business (Stone, 1975:40).

The organizational climate[12] of corporations also facilitates violations. Corporations are large complex organizations with a maximum division of labor. This requires a wide-scale delegation of responsibility and decentralization, i.e., the establishment of elaborate hierarchies based on authority, duties, and specializations (Clinard and Yaeger, 1980). "Decentralization dilutes the power structure" (Thompson, 1967:129) and division of labor and specialization often provides only limited information and responsibility to individuals. This can produce a situation where "no individual has been deviant but the combinations of their work-related actions produces deviance" (Ermann and Lundman, 1982a:7). March (1981) shows that in large organizations individuals often act with limited information about possible choices and their possible outcomes. This can lead to violations. The corporate climate also allows the abdication of a large degree of personal responsibility (Clinard and Yaeger, 1980). This applies to all levels of the hierarchy, since by delegation of authority and decentralization of decision making responsibility is diffused (Kramer, 1982). Thus top executives can claim that violations were made without their knowledge (Clinard and Yaeger, 1980) even though they are setting the general ethical standards of the corporation (Clinard, 1983a). They can also "indirectly initiate deviant actions by establishing particular norms, rewards, and punishments for people occupying lower-level positions" (Ermann and Lundman, 1982a:7). Meyer (1972) notes that executives frequently find that violation of laws or norms are the best way for profit maximization and can be attained by policy directives carried out by lower-echelon workers and mid-level managers. Similarly, in Clinard's (1983a) study many middle managers claimed that financially-oriented top managers, as opposed to the professionally-oriented ones, were primarily concerned with short-term profits and were more inclined to resort to deviance. For instance, General Electric's performance criteria for evaluation of managers could influence lower management behavior. The order of priorities was as follows: (1) Profitability, (2) Market position, (3) Productivity, or the effective utilization of human and material resources, (4) Product-leadership, (5) Personnel development, (6) Employee attitudes, (7) Public responsibility, (8) Balance between short-range and long-range goals (Conklin, 1977:42). This list sends the message that public responsibility is far behind profitability; thus much less concern should be given to it.[13]

Furthermore, group support of deviance among corporate officials exists within the same organization and across organizations. There is a "differential association" among executives in reinforcing attitudes favorable for the violations of business laws and regulations (Lane, 1953). Often these executives are "ambitious, shrewd and possessed of a nondemanding moral code" (Gross, 1978:71). Also, there is a tendency to shield executives from external scrutiny and their "deviance" is often covered up (Katz, 1977). This "peer group" supports also the "neutralization of guilt" of the executives (Hills, 1987), using reasoning similar to the "techniques of neutralization" (Sykes and Matza, 1957). Using Levi's terminology of "verbalization" this executive subculture reinforces the executives' claims that they are committing their violations for their corporations and not for individual gain (Levi, 1985). Additional factors conducive to corporate crime include: a seemingly lacking public and official condemnation,[14] and a perception that executives who deviate in the name of the corporation do it because of their loyalty to the organization rather than to further their own interest.[15] Furthermore, the legal system is designed to punish the legal violator, namely the corporation. Therefore, the corporation is fined, has to compensate, or is being restricted in its activities, not the officials who make the decisions. Thus, the decision makers usually do not experience the direct consequences of their infractions, which may encourage them to take risks on behalf of the corporation to increase profits (Donaldson, 1982).[16]

Corporate deviance may be influenced also by "conditions of distance in space, time, and social class between the decision makers and the potential victims" which can result in "a lack of empathy for the victims of harmful organizational decisions" (Monahan and Novaco, 1980:19). The financial situation of the corporation may also have an impact. The likelihood of law-breaking is higher in organizations which are in financial trouble (Simpson, 1986) or fiscally-marginal (Coleman, 1985).

Monahan and Novaco (1980) suggest that huge corporations may have the most tolerance for the harm caused by their decisions although there are some opposing views; for instance Steiner (1975) claims that as corporations become larger their standards of ethics rise because of greater public exposure.

In summary, the internal structure of the corporation is such that it raises the possibility that in order to attain goals the corporation may violate "societal laws of organizational behavior" (Gross, 1978:72).

Types of Corporate Violations

There are several possible classifications of corporate offenses. Clinard and Yaeger (1980) list six major types of corporate violations:

1. Administrative Violations—which involve noncompliance with regulations;
2. Environmental Violations—such as air and water pollution;
3. Financial Violations—illegal payments (bribery), securities violations (e.g., false public statements, etc.), tax fraud, accounting malpractices, etc.;
4. Labor Violations—employment discrimination, occupational safety and health violations, unfair labor practices, etc.;
5. Manufacturing Violations—which involve violations of standards and regulations set by government agencies;
6. Unfair Trade Practices—such as: price-fixing, bid-rigging, false and misleading advertising, credit violations, etc.

Blau and Scott (1962) suggest using the *cui bono* (who benefits?) principle which states that four groups have socially defined rights to benefit from the activities of an organization: the owners, employees, customers, and the public-at-large. Corporations have a connection with all of these groups. They have to produce a satisfactory profit for the owners, they should provide their employees with "reasonable wages, safe working conditions, and secure retirement benefits," they are supposed to sell to their customers competitively-priced and safe products, and are obligated to minimize pollution and toxic waste that might be injurious to the public-at-large (Ermann and Lundman, 1982b:240). When corporations fail in respect of one or more of these groups, they can be considered as deviant. Accordingly, this approach suggests four categories of corporate violations: (1) against owners—e.g., various ways of defrauding the stockholders; (2) against employees—e.g., violations of the safety laws; the minimum wage laws; the regulations of pension and retirement benefits; (3) against customers—e.g., consumer fraud, price fixing, the production and sale of faulty goods, deceptive advertising; and (4) against the public-at-large—e.g., air and water pollution, faulty disposal of toxic waste, etc.

Victimological Aspects of Corporate Deviance

There is a paucity of systematic research regarding the victimological aspects of corporate deviance. It is likely that "by definition, certain kinds of white-collar crime insist upon certain kinds of victims" (Geis, 1975:90). Thus, there is a need to differentiate among the victims and the types of victimization of corporate violations. The most comprehensive classification of corporate violations is the one suggested by Clinard and Yaeger (1980). The following analysis is to a large degree based on their categorization. However, in an attempt to systematize the various works in this field, and to deal more fully with this subject, some additional concepts are introduced as well. Clinard (1983b) points out that the various classifications of corporate violations, victims and harms are based on dissimilar criteria and purposes, therefore trying to summarize them in one framework is confusing. Nevertheless, I do believe that there are several similar underlying assumptions that can be related to the different classifications, and by suggesting conceptual linkages among them the study of corporate deviance and victimization can be furthered.

For purposes of analysis a distinction is made between direct and indirect victims.[17] Direct victims are the ones against whom the crimes are committed, the indirect victims are those who suffer from the violation even though they are not the ones against whom the offense was initially perpetrated (see, Karmen, 1984).

From a different perspective victimization can be viewed as primary, secondary or tertiary victimization. (a) Primary Victimization—involves a personalized victim. (b) Secondary Victimization—the victim is impersonal (commercial establishments, churches, etc.), but not so diffusive as to include the community at large. (c) Tertiary Victimization—is a diffuse victimization that extends to the community at large and includes offenses against the public order, social harmony, or the administration of government, regulatory offenses and violations of city ordinances (Sellin and Wolfgang, 1964:156).[18]

Using the Clinard and Yaeger (1980:113–116) classification the following categories of corporate violations are suggested: (1) *Administrative Violations*—"involve non-compliance with the requirements of an agency or court" (p. 113). The direct victim is the government, since its authority is diminished because of the lack of adherence to laws, rules and regulations. The failure to comply with rules and regulations usually results in the indirect victimization of the customers. It may also "victimize" the competitors of the corporation who go according to the book, since the violator usually gets a financial edge over the complier.[19] In certain cases, it can result in the victimization of the public-at-large, when the noncompliance involves regulations designed to protect the public. Most administrative violations result in tertiary victimization, but there is a possibility for secondary victimization when another organization is victimized. (2) *Environmental Violations*—are violations in which the major victim is the physical environment. In this case, the direct victim is the public-at-large, the indirect victims are competitors who comply with the environment regulations and are therefore in less advantageous financial positions than the violator. It is mainly tertiary victimization, but there is also secondary victimization involved. (3) *Financial Violations* include several subcategories. These subcategories involve different kinds of victims: (a) Payoffs—in these cases the direct victim is the government since its officials are the target of the violation. The indirect victims are: the "public-at-large"—since the officials who should work for the public are bribed and they often act against the public interest; competitors—

because the objective of the payoffs is to receive preferential treatment from public officials for the payee (Gardiner and Lyman, 1978), thus jeopardizing the interest of the competitors. (b) Securities' violations—often involve the shareholders (owners) as the direct victims (primary victimization) who are buying shares on the basis of misrepresentation (Shapiro, 1984). Indirectly, the competitors and the government (insurer of financial institutions) are also victimized. As a consequence, primary, secondary and tertiary victimization can take place. (c) Transaction violations—the direct victims are usually consumers and suppliers (individuals and/or organizations) which can be considered to be primary or secondary victimization. This category would include the check kiting scheme of E. F. Hutton which victimized several banks, "long firm fraud" against creditors (Levi, 1981) as well as various banking violations (Leroux, 1984). Indirect victimization in these cases usually involves the government. However, the government can also be the direct victim as in cases of overcharge by defense contractors, by Medicare providers (Vaughan, 1983), or by suppliers to government agencies. (d) Tax violations—again the direct victim is the government, and the indirect one is the "public-at-large," since social programs and other benefits might be cut because of shortage of funds, and competitors who pay their "fair" tax are in a disadvantageous financial situation vis-à-vis the violators. These violations tend to entail tertiary and secondary victimization. (e) Accounting violations—often victimize directly the shareholders through the concealment of questionable payments and kickbacks (Mautz et al., 1980), or various "creative accounting" schemes. The government can be a direct victim of these violations when they involve tax concealment. The above mentioned overcharges of government by various contractors can include accounting violations such as billing a program for private expenses, etc. Potential competitors, the public-at-large, and consumers who have to pay higher prices than otherwise can be considered as the indirect victims. Thus, these violations are mainly primary (e.g., shareholders), but can involve secondary (e.g., competing corporations), and tertiary (e.g., government, public-at-large) victimization. (4) *Labor Violations* victimize individuals working and their families, and the indirect victims are potential competitors who do follow the labor laws and regulations, because the violators tend to obtain undue advantages over the competitors. Regulatory agencies and labor unions can also be seen as indirect victims because their regulations and contracts are broken by the violators. These are mainly primary victimizations with a possibility for secondary victimization as well.[20] (5) *Manufacturing Violations*—usually involve consumer fraud and defective products.[21] In these cases the direct victims are the customers (primary victimization), while the indirect victims are the competitors (providing that they are not violators themselves) who are at a disadvantage because their competitive efficiency is curtailed by their adherence to the rules (secondary victimization). (6) *Unfair Trade Practices*—include violations such as industrial espionage, in which the direct victims are the competitors. In this type of cases, the

Table 1
Corporate Deviance—Types of Victims, Harms and Victimization

Corporate Deviance	Victims of Corporate Deviance* (Direct)	Types of Harm	Type of Victimization
Administrative	Government	Collective; Moral Climate	Tertiary; Secondary
Environmental	Public	Collective; Physical	Tertiary; Secondary
Financial			
(a) Payoffs & Kickbacks	Government; Competitors	Collective; Financial	Primary; Secondary
(b) Transactions	Consumers; Business Partners	Individual; Financial	Primary; Secondary
(c) Securities	Shareholders; Consumers	Individual; Financial	Primary
(d) Tax	Government; Public	Collective; Financial	Tertiary
(e) Accounting	Shareholders	Individual; Financial	Primary
Labor			
(a) Discrimination	Public; Employees	Individual; Financial & Moral Climate	Primary
(b) Occupational Safety	Employees	Individual; Physical	Primary
(c) Unfair Labor Practices	Employees	Individual; Financial	Primary; Secondary
(d) Wage	Employees	Individual; Financial	Primary
Manufacturing	Consumers	Individual; Collective; Physical & Financial	Primary; Secondary
Unfair Trade	Competitors; Business Partners	Individual; Collective; Financial & Moral Climate	Primary; Secondary

*In this table only the direct victims are indicated. Because of the large number of possible indirect victims they cannot be included in this table.

aim is to secure a larger share of the market, or to acquire valuable information regarding other companies' products. Another kind of violation in this category is using false and misleading advertising. Usually it involves primary victimization, with a possibility for secondary victimization. Price-fixing or anti-trust violations also belong to this category. As a rule, the direct victims are the consumers who have to pay higher prices because of the lack of free competition. In this sense it is primary victimization. There are also indirect victims, such as potential competitors who are not a part of the price-fixing scheme and may lose business because of it (secondary victimization).[22]

Some Further Victimological Considerations

Cullen et al. (1982) divided white-collar offenses into six categories, five of which are applicable to corporate deviance as well: (1) violent white-collar offenses—manufacturing of products which might be physically dangerous, i.e., producing harmful drugs, or faulty cars which might cause death or serious injury; (2) crime against a business organization—e.g. embezzlement. This is not applicable directly to corporate crime since it is an offense not by, but against the corporation; (3) government corruption—involves bribes to officials in order to obtain favorable treatment for the corporation; (4) corporate price-fixing; (5) defrauding consumers; and (6) income tax fraud.

These categories can be combined with the Clinard-Yaeger (1980) classification. (a) Violent offenses can fit into the administrative, labor, and manufacturing violations categories; usually the direct victims are the consumers (primary victimization). (b) Government corruption falls into the financial violations category: the direct victim is the public-at-large and the possible indirect victims are competitors who are treated less favorably than the corporation paying the bribe and consumers who are less protected if the bribe involves violation of production standards or results in higher prices for covering the expense of the bribe (primary, secondary, tertiary victimization). (c) Corporate price-fixing fits into the category of unfair trade practices, the direct victims are the customers and the indirect victims are the competitors who are not a part of the scheme (primary and secondary victimization). (d) Defrauding consumers can be placed in the category of financial violations. The direct victims are the consumers, while indirect victims are the competitors (primary and secondary victimization). (e) Income tax fraud is included in the category of financial violations. The direct victims are the government and the public-at-large which is deprived of tax revenues. Indirect victims are the competitors who are in a disadvantageous position since their expenses are higher (tertiary and secondary victimization).

There are several works which deal with the nature of harm caused by corporate violations. Simon and Eitzen (1982) suggest a dichotomy of individual and collective jeopardy. Individual jeopardy relates to hazards that people face as individuals, such as dangerous products, contaminated food, hazardous working conditions, etc. Collective jeopardy relates to "problems society faces from various corporate activities—the waste of natural resources and ecological contamination" (p. 97). Meier and Short (1982) suggest that three major kinds of harms can occur as a consequence of white-collar crime (these hold for corporate crime as well): financial harm, physical harm, and damage to the moral climate. Financial and physical harm are self-explanatory. Damage to the moral climate relates to the harm caused by the loss of trust in social institutions when high-status persons and/or powerful corporations violate laws and norms.

Other researchers concern themselves with the types of corporate victims. For example, Schrager and Short (1978) depict employees, consumers, and the general public as possible victims of corporate deviance. This classification basically concurs with the conceptual framework used by Ermann and Lundman (1982b) mentioned earlier. Geis (1975) refers to consumers, authorities, competitors, and the general public as possible victims of white-collar (corporate) crime. Epstein (1969) claims that the corporation owes responsibility to the community, consumers, employees, stockholders, and society. When this responsibility is violated, these entities can become victims. Delord-Raynal (1982) suggests the following types of victims: the state, citizens, shareholders, employees, consumers, and competitors. Box (1983) considers five categories of corporate victims: competitors, state, employees, consumers, and the public. Tomlin (1982) mentions individuals, corporate enterprises, government institutions, the international order, and society as corporate victims. He also considers the international order as a victim of violations of multinational corporations. Excepting this last type, the other victims mentioned can be part of our framework of discussion. Barnett (1981) considers corporate victims as labour, consumers, investors, taxpayers, and other corporations. And finally Elias (1986) includes among the possible victims of corporate crimes consumers, the economic system, the environment, labour, government, and the public. On the basis of these studies of corporate victimization the following victim categories are suggested for further study in this field: (a) government (federal, state, or local), (b) public-at-large (includes the environment), (c) consumers, (d) shareholders (owners), (e) employees, (f) competitors, (g) business partners (creditors, suppliers, investment partners). The only category suggested here which is not included in most other works is "business partners."

Additional Victimological Concerns

The general opinion that there is no strong public condemnation against corporate crime seems to be overstated (see for instance, Cullen et al., 1982). Nevertheless it is true that physical harm arouses much stronger public reaction than economic harm. This reaction is parallel to the reaction to street crimes, yet the results of white-collar (including corporate) victimization, are not much different from the result of street crimes (Moore, 1980).

There is an increased need to include the nature of the victim in the analysis of corporate victimization. As is known, the identity of the victim, and whether substantial segments of the public can identify with the victim, have an impact on public opinion.[23] Similarly, the victim's identity may influence criminal justice proceedings. Swigert and Farrell (1980–81:181), analyzing the Pinto case, show that by personalization of the harm and by using the vocabulary of deviance there was a transformation of a consumer problem into a crime: "At issue was no bad-faith to consumers, but reckless violence against individuals for corporate profit."

However, there are increasing numbers of cases where large corporations not only victimize small and powerless individuals (customers, employees, etc.) but harm public organizations and other corporations (Dinitz, 1982). In these cases, criminal justice reaction is usually subdued. For instance when REVCO, through Medicaid fraud, harmed the Ohio Department of Public Welfare, the case was settled by the resignation of two executives and a negotiated plea by REVCO. The company paid a $500,000 restitution, while the two executives paid a $2,000 fine each.

In the case of E. F. Hutton which defrauded about 400 banks, the corporation settled to repay the money and to pay $2.75 million in fines and court costs. No individuals were sentenced (Alexander, 1985). The victims (the banks) were not interested in a long criminal procedure generating much publicity, since a drawn out case could be harmful to the entire corporate community, including the victims themselves. Besides, there is probably some empathy among the executives of the victim corporation toward the executives of the offending corporation, since all of them are a part of the corporate subculture.

Exploring Future Avenues

There is a large volume of work analyzing various approaches to the control of corporate violations (see for instance, Fisse, 1971; 1981; Braithwaite, 1984; Frank, 1984; Stone, 1980; Lynxwiler et al. 1984; Kadish, 1963). This issue can be addressed from a victimological perspective as well.

The victims' role in the criminal justice process is an important one (McDonald, 1976). Wolfgang (1982:48) suggests that:

> A variety of victim attributes and characteristics relative to the harm inflicted on the victim might be taken into account not only in scientific research but in statutory provisions and in the adjudication and offender sentencing process.

This suggestion is different from the prevailing practice of looking at crime in terms of the nature of the act rather than in terms of the degree of harm, with the exception of certain crimes against the person. While there is some recognition of the differential effects of harm on different victims, for instance in the case of elderly or very young victims, there is little legislative recognition of this issue.

Nevertheless, in some instances victim characteristics are a factor in the determination of penalty; for example, the murder of a police officer usually draws a more severe sentence than the murder of another individual. Similarly, sexual relations with a female under 16 years of age is considered an offense regardless of her consent. Keeping all this in mind, Kruttschmitt's (1985:226) point should be taken into consideration, namely that the "analysis of victim attributes in the study of deviance processing decisions is long overdue."

Another important factor to consider is the nature of harm inflicted upon the victim. For instance, individual harm usually has more serious effects than collective harm, and similarly physical harms have more severe consequences than financial or "moral climate" harms. In the same vein, primary victimization seems to have a more serious impact on the victim than secondary and tertiary victimizations, and usually direct victimizations have more dire consequences than indirect ones. All these should be considered in the victimological analysis of corporate deviance.

There are additional factors mentioned by Wolfgang (1982) that facilitate the individualization of victims. Age and sex of the victim and the emotional trauma caused by the victimization may have a relevance when individual victims such as consumers, employees, and to a lesser degree, shareholders are concerned. Another factor is the duration of victimization; its effects may be different if it is a short episode than if it continues for a longer period of time. In the case of corporate victimization it can be asked whether it is a one-time occurrence or a continuous ongoing process endured by the victim(s).

Severity of harm is obviously a major issue. As noted, even though the public does not consider corporate crime as a severe violation, it is seen as serious when it results in physical harm (see for instance, Cullen et al. 1982). Emotional traumas caused by victimization are usually a factor in cases of labor-related deviance, particularly occupational safety violations, or in manufacturing violations when a faulty product causes serious physical harm, such as injury by the exploding gas tank of a Pinto, or a birth defect by thalidomide (Braithwaite, 1984). Emotional trauma may also occur when individual shareholders or business partners lose their investments due to financial corporate deviance. These are also related to economic loss, which is another element in the individualization of victims as suggested by Wolfgang. Economic loss as a detrimental outcome of corporate victimization occurs when the victims are other corporations such as competitors or business partners, especially when they are relatively small in comparison to the deviant corporation. In fact, economic loss can be an important factor in victimization of government and public as well.

The victim-offender relationship is one of the major concerns of victimology. In the analysis of victimization of individuals by individuals, factors such as family relationship, position of trust or fiduciary relationship, and other kinds of interpersonal relationships are taken into account in the determination of the nature and degree of victimization. Similar considerations can be introduced in corporate victimization as well. For instance, whether the victim is in a dependent position vis-à-vis the corporation, e.g., an employee or a subsidiary organization, should be considered. Also whether there is an implied relationship of trust between the victim and the corporation (e.g., shareholders, business partners) should be a part of the analysis. Similarly, power relations between the victim and the victimizer should be analyzed etc. Finally, the multiple-victim-variability-factor, which is basically the interaction of two or more variables mentioned above, should be considered (Wolfgang, 1982).

This approach to the individualization of the victim is related to the prevailing penal philosophy of retribution (Wolfgang, 1982). When the major objective is to sanction the offender according to the gravity of offense perpetrated, then the seriousness of crime can be defined also by the degree of harm inflicted upon the victim. According to this approach it is not the individualization of the offender (which has come under criticism lately) but the individualization of the victim which becomes the major factor in punishment, a practice that could enhance the idea of "just deserts."

This suggestion is in line with the idea mentioned earlier of personalization of the harm, and may lead to a more severe handling of corporate crime. Personalization of the harm and individualization of the victim facilitate the ability of the public to identify with the victims of corporate deviance and to recognize the seriousness of corporate violations. The personalization of harm and individualization of corporate victims correspond with the corporate accounts and justifications of deviance which, according to Lundman (1984), are strikingly similar to the ways individuals excuse or justify their own actions.[24] Thus, both the victimization and the justification of corporate deviance can be personalized and individualized to a large degree.

There are several avenues for future research that can be followed which utilize concepts developed in the study of individual victimization. Various victim categories depicting the nature of interaction between the offender and the victim should be examined (e.g., Wolfgang and Singer, 1978; Sheley, 1979; Fattah, 1967, etc.). These explorations may contribute to the clarification of issues related to societal response to corporate deviancy (corporate *vs.* individual responsibility).

Discussion and Conclusions

The review of the professional literature on corporate crime, deviance, and victimization indicates that these areas of criminological study, although having received increased attention recently, are still much less researched than "street crimes." Therefore, there is a need to clarify definitions and to develop concepts which could further theoretical and empirical research in this area.

To this end an attempt has been made here to compare and combine several works dealing with corporate violations, corporate harms, corporate victimizations, and corporate victims. Some of the suggestions that can be derived from this review are the following: (a) various kinds of corporate victimizations cause different kinds of harms and hurt different kinds of victims to different degrees; (b) in the analysis of corporate deviance more attention should be paid to the nature of the harm and the identity of the victims; (c) in most corporate victimization cases there are multiple victims, i.e., besides direct victimization indirect victimization also takes place; (d) there is a widespread interorganizational victimization among corporations. The corporate victims more often than not are indirect victims. For a notable exception, see Vaughan, 1980.)

In addition, this summary of classification schemes may have a practical value in policy making aimed at curbing corporate deviance. The fact that the effects of corporate violations in terms of victimization and harm are very widespread (indirect, secondary and tertiary victimization) could spur renewed efforts for educating the public about the extent and the consequences of corporate crime. The need for changing public opinion toward corporate violations as a means of social control has been suggested by several scholars (e.g., Braithwaite and Geis 1982); one suggested way to do so is through widescale publicity (Fisse, 1971; 1981; Fisse and Braithwaite, 1983), by "personalization of the harm"; (Swigert and Farrell, 1980–81), "individualization of the victim" (Wolfgang, 1982), or by the personalization of the offender (see, for instance, Parisi, 1984). One of the further goals in this direction would be to demonstrate to the public and to corporate executives that many corporate actions and business practices are often more harmful than street crimes (Moore, 1980), victimize a large number of people, undermine public trust in social institutions and deviate from social and legal norms.

NOTES

[1] Another definition suggests that white-collar crime is against business, while corporate crime is by business (Smith, 1982).

[2] The importance of this factor is stressed by Blum-West and Carter (1983) who have claimed that there is no difference between the criminal and civil law in the manner liability is being determined.

[3] There are a few exceptions in this regard; see for instance, Ermann and Lundman, 1978, 1982b; Geis, 1975; Nader, 1973; Schrager and Short, 1978; Vaughan, 1980; Walsh and Schram, 1980.

[4] Following Sherman (1978) and Ermann and Lundman (1982a, b), I use the inclusive term of deviance to depict organizational behavior which deviates from societal norms and laws, rather than the more narrow concept of crime which is restricted to the violation of legal statutes.

[5] One of the most detailed definitions of corporate crime was suggested by Kramer (1984:18) who states that corporate crimes are:

> criminal acts (of omission or commission) which are the result of deliberate decision-making by persons who occupy structural positions within the organization as corporate executives or managers (or culpable negligence on their part). These decisions are organizational in that they are organizationally based—made in accordance with the operative goals (primarily corporate profit), standard operating procedures, and cultural norms of the organization—and are intended to benefit the corporation itself.

[6] Shapiro (1980) mentions more organizational factors conducive to illegal behavior such as the victimization of organizations by others, using the organizational con-

text exclusively for individual gain, e.g., indealing, etc., or cover-up abilities for organizations which were established for the purpose of illegal activities. These issues are not covered in this article because they are beyond the concept of corporate deviance as used here.

[7] As Weber (1958:17) states: "capitalism is identical with the pursuit of profit, and forever renewed profit, by means of continuous, rational, capitalistic enterprise."

[8] In her research, Appleton (1983) found that basically these agencies have abandoned their preventative activities and their main function today is only mediation with business violators.

[9] The long legal history of this principle is reviewed by Jones (1926).

[10] In an early work, Lloyd has shown how oil production in the U.S. was controlled by large oil companies which were in unlawful collusion to control the market. He demonstrated how big business has "the will and the power to control markets, livelihoods, and liberties" (Lloyd, 1894:6).

[11] For instance, E. F. Hutton paid 2 million dollars in fines for using about 10 billion dollars without interest through check kiting. Geis (1984) calculated that the fines in the famous heavy electric equipment case were equivalent to a $3 penalty for an individual who has a $175,000 annual income. Recently new approaches for determining fines against corporate violators, such as equity fines and day-fines, have been suggested (see the review in Schlegel, 1988).

[12] Here organizational climate is defined as:

> a relatively enduring quality of the internal environment of an organization that (a) is experienced by its members, (b) influences their behavior, and (c) can be described in terms of the values of a particular set of characteristics (or attributes) of the organization. (Tagiuri and Litwin, 1968:27)

[13] A similar situation is illustrated by Leonard and Weber (1970) in their description of the criminogenic pressures applied by automakers or dealers and mechanics to violate the law.

[14] However, there are indications that corporate crimes which have physical consequences do concern the public; thus, the impression of an almost complete lack of condemnation might be overstated (Schrager and Short, 1980, and Cullen et al., 1982).

[15] See for instance some examples mentioned by Orland (1980), who illustrates this approach by the criminal justice system. Obviously, there is an oversight in this perception since "organizational success" does benefit the personal careers of executives and rewards them economically.

[16] To a large degree this category is similar to the one suggested by Edethertz (1970) under the title of: "Crimes incidental to and in furtherance of business operations, but not the central purpose of the business."

[17] Vaughan (1980) uses the terms of "direct" and "indirect" victims, although she does not define these concepts in detail; Wolfgang and Singer (1978) mention "Victims of Crime by Indirection," a category corresponding to "indirect" victims.

[18] Sellin and Wolfgang discuss also Mutual Victimization—in which the participants engage in mutually consensual acts that are violations of the law (e.g., fornication, adultery, statutory rape). In the present analysis this category is not used.

[19] Delord-Raynal (1982) mentions competitors as possible victims of white-collar crime for similar reasons. She claims also that competitors can be victimized through the use of the "dominant market position" by large corporations.

[20] Donnelly (1978), in his analysis of the Occupational Safety and Health Act

(OSHA) regulations, claims that these regulations were strongly influenced by corporate interests.

[21] For examples in the automobile industry see the Pinto case (Kramer, 1982; Cullen et al., 1987; Dowie, 1979), or the Corvair case (DeLorean and Wright, 1980; Nader, 1972).

[22] The contradiction in the case of this kind of violations is illuminating. Corporations which are constantly demanding the abolition or at least the minimization of trade regulations as obstacles of "free trade" are involved themselves in curbing free trade through elimination of competition.

[23] That is one reason why the public is not overly concerned with crimes against organizations (Smigel and Ross, 1970).

[24] This claim is only partially supported by Waegel et al. (1981), who point out that while some organizational accounts which justify and excuse corporate actions are similar to those of individuals, others are unique to organizations, e.g., restricting public access to potentially discrediting information, etc.

REFERENCES

Alexander, C. P. (1985). Crime in the Suites, *Time*, 125, 3, 56–67.

Appleton, L. M. (1983). Equifinality and Implementation: Consumer Protection in the American States. Paper presented at the Annual Meeting of the American Sociological Association, Detroit.

Arnold, T. W. (1937). *The Folklore of Capitalism*. New Haven: Yale University Press.

Barnett, H. C. (1981). Corporate Capitalism, Corporate Crime. *Crime and Delinquency* (January), 4–23.

Bequai, A. (1978). *White-Collar Crime: A 20th Century Crisis*. Lexington, MA: D. C. Heath.

Blau, P. M., and Scott, W. R. (1962). *Formal Organizations*. San Francisco: Chandler.

Blum-West, S., and Carter, T. J. (1983). Bringing White-Collar Crime Back in An Examination of Crimes and Torts. *Social Problems*, 30/5:545–554.

Bozeman, B., and Straussman, J. D. (1983). "Publicness" and Resource Management Strategy. In *Organizational Theory and Public Policy* (R. H. Hall and R. E. Quinn, eds.). Beverly Hills, CA: Sage.

Box, S. (1983). *Power, Crime and Mystification*. London: Tavistock.

Braithwaite, J. (1984). *Corporate Crime in the Pharmaceutical Industry*. London: Routledge & Kegan Paul.

Braithwaite, J., and Geis, G. (1982). On Theory and Action for Corporate Crime Control. *Crime and Delinquency* (April), 292–314.

Chamberlain, N. W. (1973). *The Place of Business in America's Future*. New York: Basic Books.

Clinard, M. B. (1983a). *Corporate Ethics and Crime*. Beverly Hills, CA: Sage.

Clinard, M. B. (1983b). *Discussion—White Collar Crime Section*. Annual Meeting of the American Society of Criminology, Denver.

Clinard, M. B. and Yeager, P. C. (1980). *Corporate Crime*. New York: The Free Press.

Clinard, M. B. and Quinney, R. (1973). *Criminal Behavior Systems: A Typology*. New York: Holt, Rinehart and Winston.

Coleman, J. S. (1974). *Power and the Structure of Society*. New York: Norton.

Coleman, J. W. (1985). *The Criminal Elite: The Sociology of White Collar Crime*. New York: St. Martin's Press.

Conklin, J. E. (1977). *Illegal But Not Criminal: Business Crime in America*. Englewood Cliffs, NJ: Prentice Hall.

Cullen, F. T., Link, B. G., and Polanzi, C. W. (1982). The Seriousness of Crime Revisited: Have Attitudes Toward White-Collar Crime Changed? *Criminology*, 20/1, 83–102.

Cullen, F. T., Maakestand, W. J., and Cavender, G. (1987). *Corporate Crime Under Attack*. Cincinnati, OH: Anderson.

Delord-Raynal, Yvette (1982). Victims of White Collar Crimes. In *The Victim in International Perspective* (H. J. Schneider, ed.). Berlin: Walter de Gruyter.

De Lorean, J. Z., and Wright, J. P. (1980). A Look Inside GM. In *The Big Business Reader* (M. Green and R. Massie, Jr., eds.). New York: The Pilgrim Press.

Dinitz, S. (1982). Multidisciplinary Approaches to White-Collar Crime. *In White-Collar Crime: An Agenda for Research*, (H. Edelhertz and T. D. Overcast, eds.). Lexington, MA: D.C. Heath.

Donaldson, T. (1982). *Corporations & Morality*. Englewood Cliffs, NJ: Prentice Hall.

Donnelly, P. G. (1978). A Sociological Analysis of Occupational Safety and Health Regulations. Paper presented at the Annual Meeting of the Society for the Study of Social Problems, San Francisco.

Dowie, M. (1979). Pinto Madness. In *Crisis in American Institutions* (J. H. Skolnick and E. C. Curie, eds.), Fourth Edition. Boston: Little, Brown.

Edelhertz, H. (1970). *The Nature, Impact and Prosecution of White-Collar Crime*. Washington, DC: U.S. Department of Justice, LEAA.

Elias, R. (1986). *The Politics of Victimization*. New York: Oxford University Press.

Epstein, E. M. (1969). *The Corporation in American Politics*. Englewood Cliffs, NJ: Prentice Hall.

Ermann, M. D., and Lundman, R. J. (eds.) (1982). *Corporate and Governmental Deviance* (Second Edition). New York: Oxford University Press.

Ermann, M. D., and Lundman, R. J. (1982b). *Corporate Deviance*. New York: Holt, Rinehart and Winston.

Ermann, M. D., and Lundman, R. J. (1978). Deviant Acts by Complex Organizations: Deviance and Social Control at the Organizational Level of Analysis. *The Sociological Quarterly*, 19, 55–67.

Fattah, E. F. (1967). Vers une Typologie Criminologique des Victimes. *Revue Internationale de Police Criminelle*, 209, 162–169.

Finney, H. C., and Lesieur, H. R. (1982). A Contingency Theory of Organizational Crime. In *Research in the Sociology of Organizations* (S. B. Bacharach, ed.), Greenwich, CT: JAI Press.

Fisse, B. (1981). New Penal Sanctions Against Corporations. Paper presented at the Annual Meeting of the Pacific Sociological Association, Portland.

Fisse, B., and Braithwaite, J. (1983). *The Impact of Publicity on Corporate Offenders*. State University of New York Press: NY: Albany.

Fisse, B. W. (1971). The Use of Publicity as a Criminal Sanction Against Business Corporations. *Melbourne University Law Review*, 8, 250–279.

Frank, N. (1984). Policing Corporate Crime: A Typology of Enforcement Styles. *Justice Quarterly*, 1, 2, 235–251.

Galbraith, J. K. (1958). *The Affluent Society*. Boston: Houghton-Mifflin.

Gardiner, J. A., and Lyman, T. R. (1978). *Decisions for Sale: Corruption and Reform in Land-Use and Building Regulation*. New York: Praeger.

Geis, G. (1984). White-Collar Crime. In *Major Forms of Crime* (R. F. Meier, ed.). Beverly Hills: Sage.

Geis, G. (1975). Victimization Patterns in White-Collar Crime. In *Victimology: A New Focus* (I. Dropkin and E. Viano, eds.), 5, 89–105.

Geis, G., and Meier, R. F. (1977). *White-Collar Crime*. New York: The Free Press.

Gross, E. (1978). Organizational Crime: A Theoretical Perspective. In *Studies in Symbolic Interaction* (N. Denzin, ed.). Greenwood, CT: JAI Press.

Hamilton, W. H. (1931). The Ancient Maxim Caveat Emptor. *Yale Law Journal*, XL/8, 1133–1187.

Hills, S. L. (ed.) (1987). *Corporate Violence*. Totowa, NJ: Rowman and Littlefield.

Jacoby, N. H. (1973). *Corporate Power and Social Responsibility*. New York: Macmillan.

Jesilow, P. (1982). Adam Smith and White-Collar Crime. *Criminology*, 20/34 (November), 314–328.

Jones, F. D. (1926). Historical Development of the Law of Business Competition. *Yale Law Journal*, XXXV/8, 905–938.

Kadish, S. H. (1963). Some Observations on the Use of Criminal Sanctions in Enforcing Economic Regulations. *University of Chicago Law Review*, 30, 423–449.

Karmen, A. (1984). *Crime Victims: An Introduction to Victimology*. Monterey, CA: Brooks/Cole.

Katz, J. (1977). Cover-up and Collective Integrity: On the Natural Antagonisms of Authority Internal and External to Organizations. *Social Problems*, 25/1, 3–17.

Kramer, R. C. (1982). Corporate Crime: An Organizational Perspective. In *White Collar Crime and Economic Crime* (P. Wickman and T. Dailey, eds.). Lexington, MA: D.C. Heath.

Kramer, R. C. (1984). Corporate Criminality: The Development of an Idea. In *Corporations as Criminals* (E. Hockstedler, ed.) Beverly Hills: Sage.

Kruttschmitt, C. (1985). Are Businesses Treated Differently? A Comparison of the Individual Victim and the Corporate Victim in the Criminal Courtroom. *Sociological Inquiry*, 55, 3, 225–238.

Lane, R. E. (1953). Why Businessmen Violate the Law. *Journal of Criminal Law, Criminology and Police Science*, 44/2, 151–165.

Leonard, W. N., and Weber, M. G. (1970). Automakers and Dealers: A Study of Criminogenic Market. *Law and Society Review*, 4/3, 407–424.

Lernoux, P. (1984). *In Banks We Trust*. Garden City, NY: Anchor/Doubleday.

Levi, M. (1981). *The Phantom Capitalists*. London: Heinemann.

Levi, M. (1985). A Criminological and Sociological Approach to Theories of and Research Into Economic Crime. In *Economic Crime—Programs for Future Research* (D. Magnusson, ed.). Stockholm: The National Council for Crime Prevention.

Little, C. B. (1983). *Understanding Deviance and Control: Theory, Research and Social Policy*. Itasca, IL: Peacock.

Lloyd, H. D. (1984). *Wealth Against Commonwealth*. New York: Harper and Brothers.

Lundman, R. J. (1984). Accounts of Corporate Deviance. Paper presented at the Annual Meeting of the American Sociological Association, San Antonio.

Lynxwiler, J., Shover, N., and Clelland, D. (1984). Determinants of Sanction Severity in a Regulatory Bureaucracy. In *Corporations as Criminals* (E. Hochstedler, ed.). Beverly Hills: Sage.

March, J. G. (1981). Decision Making Perspective. In *Perspectives on Organizational Design and Behaviour* (A. Van de Ven and W. Joyce, eds.). New York: Wiley.

Mautz, R. K., Kell, W. G., Maher, M. W., Merten, A. G., Reilly, R. R., Severence, D. G., and White, B. J. (1980). *Internal Control in U.S. Corporations: The State of the Art*. New York: Financial Executives Research Foundation.

McDonald, W. F. (ed.) (1976). *Criminal Justice and the Victim*. Beverly Hills: Sage.

Meier, R. F., and Short, J. F., Jr. (1982). The Consequences of White-Collar Crime. In *White-Collar Crime: An Agenda for Research* (H. Edelhertz and T. D. Overcast, eds.). Lexington, MA: D.C. Heath.

Meyer, J. C., Jr. (1972). An Action-Orientation Approach to the Study of Occupational Crime. *Australian and New Zealand Journal of Criminology*, 5, 35–48.

Monahan, J., and Novaco, R. W. (1980). Corporate Violence: A Psychological Analysis. In *New Directions in Psycholegal Research*, (D. P. Lipsitt and B. D. Sales, eds.). New York: Van Nostrand Reinhold Co.

Moore, M. H. (1980). Notes Toward a National Strategy to Deal with White-Collar Crime. In *A National Strategy for Containing White-Collar Crime* (H. Edelhertz and C. Rogovin, eds.). Lexington, MA: D.C. Heath.

Moore, W. E. (1962). *The Conduct of the Corporation*. New York: Vintage Books.

Nader, R. (1972). *Unsafe at Any Speed: The Designed-In Dangers of the American Automobile*. New York: Bantam.

Nader, R. (ed.) (1973). *The Consumer and Corporate Accountability*. New York: Harcourt, Brace, Jovanovich.

Neff-Gurney, J. (1985). Factors Influencing the Decision to Prosecute Economic Crime. *Criminology*, 23, 4, 609–628.

Orland, L. (1980). Reflections on Corporate Crime: Law in Search of Theory and Scholarship. *American Criminal Law in Review*, 17, 501–520.

Parisi, N. (1984). Theories of Corporate Liability. In *Corporations as Criminals* (E. Hochstedler, ed.). Beverly Hills: Sage.

Rothschild, D. P., and Throne, B. C. (1976). Criminal Consumer Fraud: A Victim-Oriented Analysis. *Michigan Law Review*, 74/66, 661–707.

Schlegel, K. (1988). Fining Corporations: Practices, Problems and Alternatives. Paper presented at the Annual Meeting of the Academy of Criminal Justice Sciences, San Francisco, April.

Schrager, L. S., and Short, J. F., Jr. (1978). Toward a Sociology of Organizational Crime. *Social Problems*, 25/4, 407–419.

Schrager, L. S. and Short, J. F. Jr. (1980). How Serious a Crime? Perceptions of Organizational and Common Crimes. In *White Collar Crime: Theory and Research* (G. Geis and E. Stotland, eds.). Beverly Hills: Sage.

Scott, W. R. (1981). *Organizations: Rational, Natural, and Open Systems*. Englewood Cliffs, NJ: Prentice Hall.

Sellin, T., and Wolfgang, M. E. (1964). *The Measurement of Delinquency*. New York: Wiley.

Shapiro, S. P. (1984). *Wayward Capitalists*. New Haven, CT: Yale University Press.

Shapiro, S. P. (1980). *Thinking About White Collar Crime: Matters of Conceptualization and Research*. Washington, DC: U.S. Department of Justice.

Shelly, J. F. (1979). *Understanding Crime: Concepts, Issues, Decisions*. Belmont, CA: Wadsworth.

Sherman, L. W. (1978). *Scandal and Reform: Controlling Police Corruption*. Berkeley: University of California Press.

Shover, N. (1978). Defining Organizational Crime. In *Corporate and Governmental Deviance: Problems of Organizational Behavior in Contemporary Society* (M. D. Ermann and R. Lundman, eds.). New York: Oxford University Press.

Simon, D. R., and Eitzen, D. S. (1982). *Elite Deviance*. Boston: Allyn and Bacon.

Simpson, S. S. (1986). The Decomposition of Anti Trust. *American Sociological Review*, 51, 6, 859–875.

Smigel, E. O., and Ross, H. L. (1970). *Crimes Against Bureaucracy*. New York: Van Nostrand Reinhold.

Smith, A. (1937). *Inquire into the Nature and Causes of Wealth of Nations*. New York: The Modern Library.

Smith, D. C. (1982). White-Collar Crime, Organized Crime and Business Establishment: Resolving a Crisis in Criminological Theory. In *White-Collar and Economic Crime* (P. Wickman and T. Dailey, eds.), Lexington, MA: Lexington Books.

Steiner, G. A. (1975). *Business and Society* (2nd Edition). Random House: New York.

Stone, C. D. (1980). The Place of Enterprise Liability in the Control of Corporate Conduct. *Yale Law Journal*, 90, 1–77.

Stone, D. C. (1975). *Where the Law Ends: The Social Control of Corporate Behavior*. New York: Harper and Row.

Sutherland, E. H. (1961). *White Collar Crime*. New York: Holt, Rinehart and Winston.

Sutherland, E. H. (1956). Crime of Corporations. In *The Sutherland Papers* (A. Cohen, A. Lindesmith and K. Schessler, eds.). Bloomington: Indiana University Press.

Sutton, A., and Wild, R. (1978). Corporate Crime and Social Structure. In *Two Faces of Deviance: Crimes of the Powerless and the Powerful* (P. R. Wilson and J. Braithwaite, eds.). Queensland, Australia: University of Queensland Press.

Swigert, V. L., and Farrell, R. A. (1980–81). Corporate Homicide: Definitional Processes in the Creation of Deviance. *Law and Society Review*, 15, 1, 161–182.

Sykes, G. M., and Matza, D. (1957). Techniques of Neutralization: A Theory of Delinquency. *American Sociological Review*, 22, 664–670.

Taguiri, R., and Litwin, G. H. (1968). *Organizational Climate: Exploration of a Concept*. Boston: Harvard University.

Thompson, J. D. (1967). *Organizations in Action*. New York: McGraw-Hill.

Tomlin, J. W. (1982). Victims of White-Collar Crimes. In *The Victim in International Perspective* (H. J. Schneider, ed.). Berlin: Walter de Gruyter.

Vaughan, D. (1983). *Controlling Unlawful Organizational Behavior*. Chicago: University of Chicago Press.

Vaughan, D. (1980). Crime Between Organization: Implications for Victimology. In *White-Collar Crime: Theory and Research* (G. Geis and E. Stotland, eds.). Beverly Hills: Sage.

Waegel, W. B., Ermann, M. D., and Horowitz, A. M. (1981). Organizational Responses to Imputations of Deviance. *The Sociological Quarterly*, 22, 1, 43–55.

Walsh, M. E., and Schram, D. D. (1980). The Victim of White-Collar: Accuser or Accused? In *White-Collar Crime: Theory and Research* (G. Geis and E. Stotland, eds.). Beverly Hills: Sage.

Weber, M. (1958). *The Protestant Ethic and the Spirit of Capitalism*. New York: Scribner.

Wolfgang, M. E. (1982). Basic Concepts in Victimological Theory: Individualization of the Victim. In *The Victim in International Perspective* (H. J. Schneider, ed.). Berlin: Walter de Gruyter.

Wolfgang, M. E., and Singer, S. I. (1978). Victim Categories of Crime. *The Journal of Criminal Law and Criminology*, 69, 3, 379–394.

Yokoyama, M. (1984). Crimes of Private Corporations in Japan. Paper presented at the meeting of the Sociology and Deviance and Social Control. International Sociological Association, San Jose, Costa Rica.

PART II
Types of Victims

The wide variety of criminal activity creates a corresponding broad range of types of victims. Although all victims of crime are affected by the actions of criminals, some victims are particularly impacted by such experiences. This section includes articles that examine the more notable categories of victims. These victims often suffer from significant long-term damage, whether physical, psychological, or financial. It is important to understand the prevalence and experiences of some of these categories.

The most victimized group in our society is children. It is interesting to note that the most respected national measure of victimization, the National Crime Victimization Survey (NCVS), does not collect information from individuals under the age of twelve. However, most experts agree and empirical studies have clearly shown that our youngest individuals are the most frequent targets, and higher rates of victimization extend into the teenage years. Given the pronounced rate at which young persons are victimized, we have included two articles that deal specifically with offenses against youth.

Article 5, the first selection in this section, is a Department of Justice monograph from the Office for Victims of Crime (OVC) that considers the prevalence and impact of children witnessing violence. After reviewing various characteristics of children's services and the legal system that children find particularly stressful, the report provides specific recommendations on how best to interact with young victims at all stages of the justice system. The article concludes with a discussion of a number of successful programs that incorporate these guidelines, such as multidisciplinary teams and child advocacy centers.

The next article examines the newest context for child victimization: the Internet. Millions of children are currently using the Internet, and that number is growing exponentially. As discussed in the report issued by the Office for Victims of Crime, the Internet poses particular difficulties because it is anonymous, inexpensive, and far-reaching. Perhaps most problematic is that predators no longer have to abduct their victims from public places; rather, they can select young victims who are in their own homes on the family computer, often with their nonsuspecting parents down the hall. This article highlights some of the major challenges authorities face in addressing Internet crimes against children and provides tips on how best to respond to such challenges and the needs of these victims.

Another common location for both property and violent victimization, contrary to idyllic characterizations, is the college campus. Many recent studies have shown that institutions of higher learning are predisposed to criminal activity due to the relaxed atmosphere on most college campuses combined with the large population of young adults. There are many vulnerable targets and, conversely, many candidates to commit offenses. Bonnie Fisher, John Sloan, Francis Cullen and Chunmeng Lu conducted an extensive survey of thousands of randomly selected students at 12 different institutions of higher learning. The authors report that large percentages of the respondents were victimized on campus during a one-year academic period. Not surprisingly, the findings also revealed that the most important factors that predicted campus victimization were related to lifestyle (e.g., partying). These determinants continue to be relevant throughout the life span; decisions regarding one's behavior contribute to the overall likelihood of being victimized. Fisher et al. provide an excellent foundation for the impact of these issues.

Traditionally, the criminal justice system has not treated partner violence as a serious problem. However, domestic violence increasingly demands special attention. It is important to understand the experiences and consequences of domestic violence and how such cases are handled by the justice system. In their article, Melanie O'Neill and Patricia Kerig examine the (mal)adjustment of battered women, with special emphasis on their self-blaming attributions. Based on data collected from 160 battered women, findings revealed that perceived control was lowest and self-blame was highest among women who were still currently involved in a violent relationship; these two factors moderate battered women's psychological adjustment or lack thereof. O'Neill and Kerig expose the causal mechanisms involved in the cognitive attributions and adjustment of battered women, a necessary step toward identifying effective programs to help victims of domestic violence.

Sherry Hamby and Bernadette Gray-Little provide another important, albeit controversial, domestic violence study in the ninth article. They sampled 78 women who experienced at least one physical assault in their current relationship. They emphasize situational factors that are likely to have significant effects on labeling propensities. Hamby and Gray-Little use this information to advise prevention and intervention programs to include more contextual characteristics.

In the tenth selection in this section, Scott Decker (1996) examines differences between two motives of homicide across varying victim-offender relationships. The author focuses on homicides that are "deviant"—they do not fit the usual framework of expressive motives for intimate-relationship homicides and instrumental motives for stranger-relationship homicides. Using homicide data from St. Louis, Decker explores the incidence of deviant homicides in light of demographic characteristics of killers and their victims (e.g., age, race), as well as situational characteristics (e.g., type of weapon, drug-related, etc.). The study reveals that expectations regarding motives of homicide given particular victim-offender relationships are not as clear-cut as other studies suggest.

Some property crimes, such as burglary and vehicle theft, have long been considered an important area for study. Even occupational crimes, such as embezzlement, have received attention. As mentioned in the introduction to Part I, the victims of corporate (i.e., organizational) crimes have largely been ignored until recently. In article 11, our first selected study on corporate victimization, David Shichor clarifies the scope and categories of damage from organizational deviance to both persons and property. One unique aspect of this study is that it explores the possibilities of personalizing the corporate offenders, as well as the harms that they do. Of particular value to policymakers is Shichor's summary of classification schemes, which outlines the vital issues in devising strategies to curb corporate crime.

The next selection is a study of investment fraud. David Shichor, Dale Sechrest, and Jeffrey Doocy survey victims of a telecommunications scam that promised lucrative oil and gas partnerships. This scam pulled in approximately 7,500 people (possibly more), and the damages reached almost $200 million. Telemarketing schemes target the elderly, who are more vulnerable and more impacted by the crimes against them. This article details the perceptions about victims of investment fraud by the public and the criminal justice system and the feelings of the victims involved.

Many people in our society, as well as most of our elected legislators, have concluded that crimes against others (or against property in the forms of graffiti, vandalism, and arson) are considered more serious if motivated by hatred. Hate crimes have been charged when victims are targeted because of race, sex, and ethnicity. The events of September 11, 2001, were horrifying evidence of the most extreme effects of crimes inspired by hate. Brian Levin provides a thorough review of hate-crime data collection and research on the impact of hate crime on victims. Such crimes are more likely to inflict emotional harm on victims, to cause retaliatory crimes, and to trigger social instability.

The final article in this section reviews a wide range of issues and recommendations and provides practical advice for practitioners who deal with victims of crime. The report by the Office for Victims of Crime reviews and synthesizes guidelines for dealing with special types of victims: the elderly, children, victims of sexual assault, victims of domestic violence, and survivors of homicide attempts. We hope that these guidelines will increase awareness of the wide variety of victims and the most sensitive procedures for dealing with specific problems.

Space does not permit this section to include all types of victims; other categories of victims are equally important. We have selected these groups because they represent some of the most vulnerable and defenseless victims in our society. Our intent is for readers to recognize the problems experienced by victims and to extrapolate from these specifics to an informed concern for the impact of crime against any individual or group.

Chapter Five

Children as
Victims and Witnesses

Office for Victims of Crime

"In all the wide-ranging discussions about crime over the last few years, there is an important fact that is not often recognized or talked about: Children and youth are substantially more vulnerable to crime victimization in general than are adults. Not just more likely to be offenders, young people are also more likely, much more likely, to be victims."[1] Young people, particularly teens, commit about 18 percent of crime but make up about 25 percent of victims. Annually, an estimated 1 million violent crimes involving child victims are reported to the police, and another 1.1 million cases of child abuse are substantiated by child protection agencies. As many as half a million children may be encountered by police during domestic violence arrests. Of the nation's 22.3 million adolescents aged 12 to 17, approximately 1.8 million reported having been victims of a serious sexual assault, 3.9 million reported having been victims of a serious physical assault, and almost 9 million reported having witnessed serious violence during their lifetimes.[2]

Prevalence

It appears that all children, regardless of race or social class, are victimized at higher rates than adults in both urban and rural areas. Children are more vulnerable because of their size, age, and dependency status. Children have little or no control over who lives in their home or who associates with members of the household. Certain children are targeted more frequently, including those labeled "bad kids"; shy, lonely, and compliant children; preverbal and very young children; and emotionally disturbed or "needy" ado-

---

Source: Office for Victims of Crime (NCJ 176983).

81

lescents. Children with physical, emotional, or developmental disabilities are particularly vulnerable to victimization.

Children are victimized in multiple ways—sexual and physical assaults, sexual exploitation (such as forcing a child or teenager into prostitution or posing for pornography), neglect, homicide, and abduction. Their assailants are frequently their parents but may be other family members, friends, acquaintances, caretakers, and strangers. The closer the relationship of the child to the offender, the stronger the feelings of betrayal, particularly as time goes by. The longer the abuse continues, the more difficult it is for the victim to recover.

Invisible Victims: Children Who Witness Violence

In this country, children witness violent crimes on a daily basis, including homicide, rape, assault, and domestic violence. Even when child witnesses do not suffer physical injury, the emotional consequences of viewing or hearing violent acts are severe and long-lasting. In fact, children who witness violence often experience many of the same symptoms and lasting effects as children who are victims of violence themselves, including post-traumatic stress disorder (PTSD).

Although child witnesses to violent crimes are often on the scene when police respond, investigators may overlook both the child's ability to provide information and the child's trauma from witnessing the violence. Adults often minimize or deny the presence of children at the scene while crimes are occurring. However, when children are questioned later about events they witnessed or heard, they are able to provide, depending on their stage of development, a detailed description of the events.[3] It is not uncommon for adults—even some mental health professionals—to minimize the impact on children of witnessing violence and fail to provide appropriate intervention. Caretakers may mistakenly believe that young children will "forget" about the violent event if they are "left alone" and not reminded of it. On the contrary, children need to talk about what they saw and their perceptions of the consequences. Further, child victims and witnesses need to be free from intimidation and persuasion aimed at pressuring them to change their description of events.

While exact numbers are not available, it is clear that each year hundreds of thousands, if not millions, of children witness domestic violence and are present in many domestic violence incidents to which police agencies respond. It is estimated that physical abuse of children occurs in between a third and half of domestic violence situations involving abuse of the mother. Children who are present during domestic violence are at an increased risk for being murdered or physically injured. Children who are exposed to domestic violence experience feelings of terror, isolation, guilt, helplessness, and grief. Many children exhibit psychosomatic complaints such as headaches, stomach problems, and other medical problems. Children can experience problems with depression, anxiety, embarrassment, and, if exposed to violence for an extended period of time, ambivalence. Children act out what they see; their demonstration of violent behavior can be a manifestation of their exposure to domestic violence.[4]

Approximately 34 percent of rapes are estimated to occur in the victim's home where children are likely to be present to see or hear the sexual assault of their mothers or caretakers. Depending on the age of the children and their knowledge of sexual activity, their perceptions of the assault and their reactions will vary significantly. Children who are present during a sexual assault are at significant risk for developing post-traumatic stress disorder. Children may have recurrent and intrusive thoughts about the sexual assault and may reenact the event in repetitive play. Feeling a loss of control and the inability to protect their mothers may leave children feeling anxious, depressed, vulnerable, and angry. After witnessing a sexual assault, children may become more concerned with their own safety and may exhibit more anger and irritability than prior to the assault.[5]

Children witness many different types of homicide. They may witness the death of a sibling, parent, another relative, a friend, or a stranger. When a child witnesses the fatal abuse of a sibling or parent, it is highly probable that the child knows the perpetrator intimately as a parent or other family member. A child who witnesses a homicide is likely to be traumatized and may experience a range of grief responses. The child may have recurrent and intrusive thoughts about the homicide, traumatic or anxiety-provoking dreams, other sleep disturbances, and a diminished interest in activities.

Long-Term Impact of Victimization and Witnessing Violence

Exposure to violence as a victim or witness poses a serious threat to American children. In 1992, the National Institute of Justice released a report, "The Cycle of Violence," by Cathy Spatz Widom, University of Albany, New York. The reported study revealed a significant link between victimization in childhood and later involvement in violent crimes, revealing a cycle of violence. Those who had been abused or neglected as children were more likely to be arrested as juveniles and as adults for violent crimes. On average, abused and neglected children begin committing crimes at younger ages, they commit nearly twice as many offenses as nonabused children, and they are arrested more frequently. Widom also interviewed a large number of people 20 years after their childhood victimization. Findings from this follow-up study suggest that the long-term consequences of childhood victimization may also include mental health problems, educational difficulties, alcohol and drug abuse, and employment problems.

Saunders and Kilpatrick found that approximately 2 million adolescents, ages 12–17, appear to have suffered from post-traumatic stress disorder (PTSD)—a long-term mental health condition characterized by depression, anxiety, flashbacks, nightmares, and other behavioral and physiological symptoms. A significant number of these adolescents abuse alcohol and drugs as a method of coping with PTSD. Estimates are that 25 percent of disabled adults were disabled as a result of physical or sexual victimization. In younger children, victimization and PTSD can derail normal mental, emotional, and physical development.

Since trauma in children may not be revealed for months or years, caretakers, service providers, and support persons should not postpone reporting abuse or providing assistance in the form of support or therapy because they feel the child is "too young" to understand, appears to be unaffected, or suffered the victimization years ago. While a child's traumatic reaction to victimization cannot be prevented, it can be minimized when assistance is provided quickly.

Children who are victims of or witnesses to violence need to be identified quickly and their continued safety ensured. They need to be able to communicate what happened and to have the reality of their experience validated. Child victims and witnesses need emotional support from nonoffending family members, their caretakers, the school, and the professionals involved in any investigation or civil or criminal case. Child victims need age-appropriate therapeutic services from mental health professionals who have training and experience working with violent victimization and traumatized children.

Not all children who are exposed to violence develop symptoms associated with the trauma. Many children, supported by nonoffending family members and other support systems, can be very resilient. The criminal justice response can be a critical turning point in defining how experiencing violence will impact a child's life.

Child Victims and Witnesses in the Criminal Justice System

Child victims and witnesses face some difficult issues that may impact their ability to participate effectively in the criminal justice process. First, children are just that—children. The way they understand, communicate, and participate is determined by their developmental status. The adult professionals working with children must be able and willing to adjust their approach to the child's developmental level. Since most law enforcement officers and prosecutors are not child development specialists, it becomes critical to do two things—to involve other professionals who can provide advice and assistance in dealing with children and to give police and prosecutors enough training to provide them a basic understanding of child development.

If the perpetrator is a family member, child protective services and the dependency court are likely to become involved. Disclosure of abuse or violence can result in total upheaval of the child's life. Caregivers and parents often initially disbelieve the child, minimize the acts, or withdraw affection. The suspected abuser may be arrested, causing havoc in the family, including loss of financial support and recriminations from family members. The child may be removed from the home and placed in foster care. Social service and legal system responses may feel like punishment to the child, prompting the child to recant the disclosure. A child victim may have tried to report previously but the report was not documented. The child may have been threatened with personal harm, harm to a loved one, or public embarrassment.

Children are more likely than adult victims to blame themselves, particularly when they have a close bond with the abuser. Perpetrators often tell their child victims that the abuse or violence was the child's fault. Since adults are powerful authority figures, the child is likely to accept that explanation. In a child's mind, it is easier for the child to believe he or she was somehow to blame for the abuse than to recognize and accept that an adult who was supposed to protect the child instead intentionally harmed the child.

Like adults, children find it upsetting to talk about traumatic events. As they talk about it, children may "re-live" the abuse and feel the associated emotions again. This is particularly true of younger children. Professionals should be sensitive to the potential impact of this "re-emergence" into the details of the crime. This "re-living" of the abuse may intensify the victim's trauma and generate behavior that poses additional barriers to successful investigation and prosecution.

Most children do not make up stories of abuse. False allegations are the exception. Professionals should not let the possibility of a false report prevent a thorough investigation. They should know that it is far more likely a child will lie to conceal abuse to protect the abuser.

Children disclose abuse and facts regarding traumatic events over time. The more comfortable a child becomes with an adult, the more likely he or she is to provide additional information. This dynamic can present particular problems for police and prosecutors who may face challenges to the child's credibility because the child did not present complete information at the initial interview.

A System Designed for Adults

The criminal justice system is not designed to accommodate the special developmental needs of children. Many police officers, attorneys, judges, and other criminal justice professionals find it difficult to work with children. Many children find the criminal justice system intimidating, particularly the courtroom experience. Under these circumstances, the child can be a poor witness, providing weak testimony and contributing less information than needed to make or win the case. Also, the lengthy process of navigating the formal and adversarial criminal and civil justice systems can affect the child's psychological development in significant and long-lasting ways. Listed below are a number of court-related factors that have been identified as stressful for child victims and witnesses:

- Multiple interviews and not using developmentally appropriate language
- Delays and continuances
- Testifying more than once
- Lack of communication between professionals
- Fear of public exposure
- Lack of understanding of complex legal procedures
- Face-to-face contact with the defendant

- Practices that are insensitive to developmental needs
- Harsh cross-examination
- Lack of adequate support and victims services
- Sequestration of witnesses who may be supportive to the child
- Placement that exposes the child to intimidation, pressure, or continued abuse
- Inadequate preparation for testifying
- Lack of evidence other than the testimony of the child[6]

It is clearly in the best interest of the child and criminal justice system to handle child victims and witnesses in the most effective and sensitive manner possible. A number of studies have found the following: reducing the number of interviews of children can minimize psychological harm to child victims (Tedesco and Schnell, 1987); testifying is not necessarily harmful to children if adequate preparation is conducted (Goodman et al., 1992; Oates et al., 1995; Whitcomb, Goodman, Runyon, and Hoak, 1994); and, having a trusted person help the child prepare for court and be with the child when he or she testified reduced the anxiety of the child (Henry, 1997).

To ensure children receive special assistance, all professionals working with child victims and witnesses must be willing to learn the basics of child development, to tailor their methods of practice to children, and to take advantage of the skills and services of allied professionals such as victim-witness advocates and child interview specialists. Studies indicate that the participation of victim-witness advocates in child sexual abuse cases appears to increase the percentage of guilty verdicts. One study found the conviction rate for child sexual abuse cases almost doubled (38 percent to 72 percent) after offices implemented child victim-witness advocacy programs. The proportion of offenders receiving prison sentences also almost doubled, from 25 percent to 48 percent. Over the same period, prison sentences increased from 9.24 years to 16.48 years (Dible and Teske, 1993). Research consistently suggests that prepared and relaxed child victims and witnesses are more credible, enabling prosecutors to present stronger cases and win more convictions.

Working effectively with child victims is emotionally demanding. While some adults have a natural ability to relate comfortably to children, many do not, especially to children whose lives and experiences are different from their own. With training and guidance, however, all professionals can develop skills that improve their ability to work with young victims and witnesses.

What Works: Innovative Practices and Programs

During the past 15 years, the criminal justice system has seen a huge increase in the number of cases involving child victims and witnesses. Over time and with experience, many individuals and agencies have developed programs and practices that enhance the ability of criminal justice professionals to handle these cases more effectively and to prevent unnecessary system-related trauma for children. These programs include multidisciplinary initiatives that do a number of things: they coordinate the responses of the various agencies involved with the child victims; they enhance support and representation for child victims in the criminal justice and juvenile court system; and, they access treatment programs to help children recover and to help prevent future revictimization. Ultimately, improving practice with child victims benefits both the child victims and the cause of justice. Some helpful strategies are listed below:

- Apply "child friendly" practices when working with children.
- Use personnel trained in interviewing children to meet with the children as soon as possible after the event. Use standard interviewing protocols for child victims and witnesses.
- Involve victim advocates and clinicians in the early stages to help manage these cases and ensure that assistance is provided to child victims on a continuing basis.
- Prepare children for court in a manner that is developmentally appropriate and sensitive to the child's mental health needs. In many cases, it may be necessary to have a clinician assess the psychological capability of the child to testify in court.
- Use a multidisciplinary, team approach when handling cases involving child victims and witnesses. Maintain good communication with representatives from other agencies involved with the child.

SPECIALIZATION AND TRAINING OF CRIMINAL JUSTICE PROFESSIONALS

Police officers need to be trained to recognize the situations in which children may be victims and witnesses. Both prosecutors and police officers need information and training on how to interview children. Police also need information on how to appropriately handle children on crime scenes.

Law enforcement agencies and chief prosecutors should designate specialists or create special units to handle child victims and witnesses. Officers and prosecutors assigned to child cases need to have a basic understanding of normal child development and limitations for children of different ages. Cases involving child victims and witnesses require more time and resources than do most other types of cases. A national survey of prosecutors found that of all cases, child abuse and adult sexual assault required the most time and resources.[7] To be effective, professionals handling these cases should have reasonable case loads and access to victim assistance professionals who also have special training for working with child victims.

Criminal justice agencies should provide a "child friendly," developmentally appropriate place to work with children. Many police departments and prosecutors' offices set aside a room designed to be comfortable and appropriate for interviewing or preparing children. Other agencies use existing facilities created for these purposes, which may be housed in children's hospitals or children's advocacy centers.

Dallas Crimes against Children Unit, Dallas, Texas

The Dallas Police Department Investigations Unit has developed four specialty areas for crimes against children:

- The Child Abuse Unit works with four other partner agencies at the Dallas Children's Advocacy Center to conduct investigations in a child friendly environment in cases of physical, sexual, and fatal child abuse and neglect.
- The Child Exploitation Unit investigates child sexual offenses and exploitation involving nonfamily members.
- The Internet Crimes Against Children Unit handles Internet child pornography cases.
- The Sex Offender Apprehension Program (SOAP) was developed in response to the Sex Offender Registration Law. By strictly enforcing compliance with the law, the SOAP arrested 600 registered sex offenders within its first 2 years of operation and won the Weber-Seavey Award for innovative law enforcement.

USE OF CHILD INTERVIEW SPECIALISTS

Conducting a forensic interview with a child about traumatic events the child experienced or witnessed can be difficult. If done incorrectly, it can jeopardize a case. To obtain reliable information from a child, the interviewer must assess the developmental level of the child and adapt the interview accordingly. Professionals conducting forensic interviews should use consistent methods and should follow a tested protocol. To be effective and legally defensible, any forensic interviewing protocol should include techniques based on updated research.

It is extremely important that professionals who interview child victims have adequate training. Cases involving very young children (under age 6), severely abused children, children who have witnessed extreme violence, and children with developmental disabilities require experienced, highly trained interviewers. Children's Advocacy Centers and hospital-based child protection teams are frequently good sources for finding experienced interviewers and receiving training. Interview training is also offered at many regional and national child abuse conferences and on-site through organizations funded by the Department of Justice. (See the section at the end of this monograph for training and informational resources.)

The environment in which the child is interviewed is also very important. Many jurisdictions now have facilities that allow observation through a two-way mirror, by closed-circuit television, or by videotaping the interview. The American Professional Society on the Abuse of Children (APSAC) has developed a series of practice guidelines for professionals on a variety of issues, including use of anatomical dolls, videotaping of child interviews, and medical evaluations of suspected child abuse victims. (For information on how to contact APSAC, see the resource section of this article.)

District of Columbia U.S. Attorney's Office

When prosecutors in the U.S. Attorney's Office in the District of Columbia must work on a murder case involving a young child as the only witness or if they must prosecute a case in which children were the victims of violent crime, they can go down the hall for help. Working and closely with the prosecutors to conduct forensic interviews in the Children's Advocacy Center and to meet with children to prepare for trial are Child Interview Specialists—Licensed Clinical Social Workers with extensive experience working with children and knowledge of child development. By building relationships with the traumatized children, the specialists are often able to get clear statements, bolster the children's confidence, and make it far more likely that child witnesses will be credible in court. Equally important, the children have the opportunity to have their experience validated, to receive help understanding and verbalizing their feelings about the crime they experienced, and to be linked to community resources for help with recovery from their ordeal. This demonstration project, funded by the Office for Victims of Crime, is being replicated in other U.S. Attorneys' offices throughout the country.

INTERACTING WITH CHILDREN WHO WITNESS DOMESTIC VIOLENCE

Children often see or hear domestic assaults. Children may become injured when they attempt to intervene and protect the victim parent, or they may be intended targets of the assault along with the victim parent. When police arrive on the scene, children may not be in plain view. Police officers responding to the crime should not assume that the children did not hear or see the violence. It is important for the police officers to ascertain what the children saw or heard, while taking care not to interview the children in the presence of the perpetrator. In some states, committing domestic violence in the presence of children may result in child endangerment charges or enhanced sentences. In most cases, prosecutors should avoid using children as witnesses against the perpetrating parent since doing so may cause additional trauma to the child.

Prosecutors may encounter cases involving severe violence where a child may be the only witness or may be able to provide crucial testimony. Criminal justice officials should take special care to let the child know that the trial and the outcome are not the child's responsibility, but the direct result of the violent parent's behavior. In some circumstances, children may be empowered by testifying—particularly if the perpetrator is not a natural parent or if the child witness feels very negatively about the perpetrator. Children who witness domestic violence need support, as does their battered parent; both will need counseling and education about domestic violence.

Children who witness violence against a sibling should not be ignored. Many of the same issues found in domestic violence cases occur when the victim is another child. Children may feel responsible for the violence or for not protecting the victim. Children who witness the homicide of another family member will need special support services, including mental health services, from professionals trained to work with highly traumatized children.

The San Diego Children's Hospital Family Violence Program, San Diego, California
The San Diego Children's Hospital Family Violence Program assists battered mothers in their efforts to establish a safe environment for their chil-

dren and themselves. Serving 120 women and 350 children each year, the program pairs battered women and their children with a two-person team of advocate and therapist. Mother and child receive free intensive advocacy, legal consultation, and mental health services. The children are often treated for PTSD and receive a range of preventive and therapeutic interventions, including age appropriate play therapy and teen groups. At intake, 88 percent of the program participants report physical assault. At the six-month follow-up, the level of physical violence the women experience has decreased to 10 percent. The proportion of children exposed to family violence decreased from 85 percent to 20 percent.

MULTIDISCIPLINARY INITIATIVES

Cases involving child victims tend to involve multiple agencies and professionals from various disciplines. In such cases, both the professionals and the child victims benefit from effective communication and collaboration. Experience indicates that coordinated responses to child victim cases can:

- Reduce the number of interviews a child undergoes
- Minimize the number of people involved in a case
- Enhance the quality of evidence discovered for criminal prosecution or civil litigation
- Provide information essential to family and child protection service agencies
- Minimize the likelihood of conflicts among agencies with different philosophies and mandates[8]

Cases involving child witnesses also involve complex medical issues and family relationships. These cases often involve a number of people and systems, including family members, police, clergy, hospital staff, prosecutors, guardians ad litem, civil attorneys, criminal defense attorneys, child protection agencies, family courts, and therapeutic clinicians. Prosecutors and victim advocates have to be particularly diligent in managing the case to monitor and provide for the well-being of the child witness.

Many communities have some form of multidisciplinary team (MDT) to effectively manage child abuse cases that involve several agencies. The purpose of multidisciplinary child abuse teams is to reduce duplication of agency procedures and the number of child interviews and to coordinate intervention and services. Apparent inconsistencies in young victims' statements are often caused by the phrasing of questions and differences in the way individuals interpret answers. Jointly conducted or monitored interviews can reduce inconsistencies and improve the quality of information.

Sharing information, expertise, and experiences with other professionals can improve the quality and outcome of child victim cases. Law enforcement officers and prosecutors with limited knowledge of child development stages should consult social workers and therapists who have studied and are experienced with troubled children. They should also meet with pediatricians and medical examiners. Social workers and medical providers may consult with police officers who can provide guidance on investigation and evidentiary issues.

Many states have laws requiring joint investigations and cooperation between law enforcement and child protection agencies in child abuse cases. Other states have laws authorizing creation of multidisciplinary and multi-agency child protection teams. Many more states have informal information-sharing arrangements. A formal MDT is not necessary for effective collaboration and information sharing, but the interagency relationships do need to be developed and institutionalized through written policies or memoranda of understanding.

CHILDREN'S ADVOCACY CENTERS

One of the best examples of a team approach to handling child victim cases is children's advocacy centers. More than 350 communities have established or are in the process of developing children's advocacy center programs. These centers allow law enforcement officers, child protection workers, prosecutors, victim advocates, medical professionals, and therapists to coordinate the investigation, prosecution, and treatment of the child victim. A single or limited number of investigatory interviews are conducted in "child friendly" settings rather than multiple interviews in intimidating environments. The children's advocacy center approach makes it easier for a team of professionals with varied expertise to work together to ensure that maltreatment of children is responded to in the most appropriate way with the least amount of additional trauma to child victims during the various stages of criminal justice intervention. Some centers are affiliated with medical centers and/or have facilities for medical examinations. Many are equipped with one-way mirrors and have videotaping capacity. All children's advocacy centers are furnished with young children in mind. The coordinated approach and team decision-making processes also improve the quality of information and increase the number of successful prosecutions. The Office of Juvenile Justice and Delinquency Prevention (OJJDP) in the U.S. Department of Justice provides funds to communities seeking to establish or strengthen children's advocacy centers. The funds are administered by the National Children's Alliance, which maintains a directory of existing centers (see the resource section of this article).

CHILD DEATH REVIEW TEAMS

Homicide is the leading cause of nonillness death of children under age five. More than half of these child victims are under age two. A significant number of these deaths are initially misidentified as SIDS or accidental deaths. Until recently, the death of a child as a result of chronic child abuse or severe neglect was not recognized under most state laws as an intentional homicide, nor prosecuted as first-degree murder. Today, more than 23 states and the District of Columbia have adopted "homicide by abuse" laws that do not require proof of specific intent to kill when a child's death results from abuse, thus allowing stiffer sentences, sanctions, and penalties. Child death review teams, first initiated in Los Angeles County in 1978, now exist in all 50 states and the District of Columbia and are charged with examining the circumstances surrounding certain child deaths known or suspected to be preventable or the result of child abuse or neglect. Child death review teams try to correctly determine when children have died from abuse or neglect, identifying risk factors and systemic problems in hopes of preventing future deaths. Most teams consist of representatives from law enforcement, the prosecutor, child protective services, the medical examiner or coroner's office, public health agencies, and emergency medical personnel and pediatricians.

The ICAN National Center on Child Fatality Review was launched by the Interagency Council on Child Abuse and Neglect in 1996 with support from the Los Angeles Times Mirror Foundation, the U.S. Department of Justice, and others. The center provides technical assistance and information to communities seeking to develop or enhance a child death review team. The center also facilitates the exchange of information among teams across the country. The center's repository of information from case reviews provides a valuable resource for teams to identify and to prevent future child fatalities, serious abuse and neglect, and accidental injuries and death.

CHILD DEVELOPMENT-COMMUNITY POLICING

The New Haven Department of Police Services and the Child Study Center at the Yale University School of Medicine, New Haven, Connecticut, have developed a unique collaborative program to address the psychological impact of family and community violence on children and families. The Child Development-Community Policing (CD-CP) program brings together police officers and mental health professionals to provide each other with training and consultation and to provide direct interdisciplinary intervention for children who are victims, witnesses, or perpetrators of violent crime. Police officers can call for support from a mental health clinician at the scene of a crime 24 hours a day. Clinicians respond immediately to work with traumatized children; if needed, they continue to work with the child and the family in a clinic or school setting. Families who become involved in the CD-CP program can receive ongoing intervention and support coordinated by a multidisciplinary case-conferencing team.

CD-CP Addresses Gang Violence and Domestic Violence

Through the Community Outreach Police in Schools (COPS) program, police officers and mental health professionals offer school-based support groups in the New Haven schools most affected by gang violence. These groups help fifth and sixth graders learn about themselves, understand their reactions to the violence around them, verbalize their fears, and learn to solve problems. Children who have participated in this program show a marked change in their relationships with their community police officers.

Focusing on the neighborhood of Fair Haven, the CD-CP program is implementing an approach to intervention in domestic violence cases where children are present that combines: (1) external authority to interrupt the violence, (2) concrete support for mothers' and children's safety through legal advocacy and linkages to other social services, and (3) acute and follow-up counseling services for women and their children. This approach is based on the assumption that the best help for battered women and their children is achieved by increasing their safety through the arrest of the perpetrator, heightened police presence, and realistic safety planning.

LEGAL REPRESENTATION FOR CHILD VICTIMS

For children who are the subject of protection proceedings in juvenile or family court, the Child Abuse Prevention and Treatment Act requires states to provide child victims with independent representation. In some communities, children are represented in such cases by an attorney appointed to act as guardian ad litem. Courts in hundreds of communities are also using volunteer court-appointed special advocates who perform independent assessments of the children's circumstances and file their own reports with the court. The National Court-Appointed Special Advocate Association is funded by OJJDP to help courts establish a volunteer program and to standardize training for volunteer advocates. The American Bar Association has developed standards and practices for lawyers representing children in abuse and neglect cases. While most of these programs are available only in family or juvenile courts, there has been an increase in the use of independent legal advocacy for child victims in criminal court proceedings.

REFORM OF JUVENILE/FAMILY COURT HANDLING OF CHILD ABUSE AND NEGLECT CASES

In recent years, several important developments are helping improve the ability of juvenile and family courts to work with greater effectiveness and speed in cases involving maltreated children. State court systems in 48 states received funding from the Children's Bureau at the U.S. Department of Health and Human Services to evaluate and improve operations in child abuse and neglect-related proceedings. Based upon administrative reforms undertaken by the Hamilton County, Ohio, Juvenile and Family Court, the National Council of Juvenile and Family Court Judges in 1995 developed and published a document entitled "Resource Guidelines: Improving Court Practice in Child Abuse and Neglect Cases." This publication sets forth the essential elements of properly conducted court hearings and describes how courts can more efficiently manage their work to ensure each child receives a fair, thorough, and speedy court process.

Using the "Resource Guidelines" as a blueprint, the Child Victims Model Courts Project of the National Council of Juvenile and Family Court Judges and the OJJPD focus on improving how courts handle child abuse and neglect cases. Since 1995, eighteen courts have adopted the model court practices developed in Hamilton County, Ohio. The model courts practices are characterized by the use of alternative dispute resolution; community-based services; multidisciplinary, court-led meetings and training; court calendar improvements; assignment of a single magistrate for the life of the case; more substantive preliminary hearings; and, increased representation for families and children.

Criminal courts can learn from the example of the juvenile and family court innovations to improve system responses to children. Children who are crime victims or witnesses may be involved in both juvenile and criminal courts and benefit from close coordination between the two systems.

Model Children's Court, El Paso, Texas

The Honorable Patricia Macias, lead judge for the El Paso Children's Court, guides that community's effort to improve the court's response to abused and neglected children. In all cases requiring foster care placement for abused or neglected children, the court involves local networks of professionals to provide "front-loaded" services to increase the likelihood of safe permanent homes. A new assessment foster home project has been established to provide a nurturing home environment where the child's special needs can be immediately identified. To ensure that the child's support system is fully involved in the proceedings, the court provides simultaneous language interpretation for all non-English-speaking court participants, and foster parents testify at each hearing and participate in permanency transition teams. Through such innovations, the court has streamlined court procedures and reduced the length of time children spend in foster care.

USE OF VICTIM ASSISTANCE PROFESSIONALS

Numerous victim assistance programs provide special support services for child victims who are involved in criminal justice system cases. Research indicates that participation of a victim-witness advocate appears to increase guilty verdicts in sexual abuse cases, suggesting that better prepared and more relaxed child victims and child witnesses are more credible at trial (Dible and Teske, 1993). Advocates working with child victims and child witnesses should have specialized training and experience with abused and traumatized children. A child advocate or a child interview specialist may provide a great deal of assistance, including the following: interview or help interview child victims or child witnesses; assess safety issues; assess the mental condition and developmental level of the child; as necessary, refer the child for more in-depth psychological assessment; participate in support groups or individual counseling; explain the legal process to the child and the nonoffending caretaker; make crisis intervention and social services referrals; conduct court preparation; provide logistical support for the child victim and family, including transportation and assistance with medical and therapy appointments; and, support the victim during trial, including accompanying the child to court when he or she testifies. Advocates can also help the victim and/or caretaker complete victim impact statements for sentencing, if desired. Victim advocates can help monitor the child's situation and alert prosecutors when the child is not supported, when stay-away orders are violated, or when the child is threatened or coerced into recanting. Many police departments and prosecutors' offices have their own victim assistance units and advocates who work closely with officers and prosecutors.

PREPARING CHILDREN FOR COURT: COURT SCHOOL PROGRAMS

Every witness needs some preparation prior to testifying. To bring a child into the complex and often stressful process of testifying in court without careful preparation is unthinkable. A child who knows what to expect and is prepared for his or her role will provide more credible testimony. Child victims and witnesses require extra time and special effort to prepare for court. There are two primary methods of preparing a child—individual preparation by the prosecuting attorney or through a group process that focuses on general orientation programs, such as court school. Individual preparation is best handled by the case prosecutor and a victim advocate. It should be tailored to the specific age and needs of the child. Specific case issues are covered in this type of preparation. Many prosecutors will take the child witness to an empty courtroom to familiarize the child with the setting.

Court school programs are designed to orient the child victim and child witness to the court process and to the role of the witness. These programs are usually facilitated by victim advocates and prosecutors and include a group of children scheduled to testify in the near future. Most programs include role-playing, a courtroom tour, and opportunities to practice answering questions in the courtroom. Individual cases are never discussed, and the program is designed to avoid jeopardizing the child's testimony in any way. Court school programs may use props, such as puppets, child-sized judges robes, coloring/activity books about court, and a wooden model of a courtroom with moveable figures. Court school programs help reduce anxiety in children and normalize what may have been a strange and frightening process. Many programs include a concurrent session for nonoffending parents and caretakers to provide information about the court process and how they can support their children.

Kids' Court, King County, Seattle, Washington

In King County, Washington, Kids' Court and Teen Court empower child crime victims and their parents through education about the legal process. In the five-hour Saturday court school, children meet with a judge and prosecutor and participate in activities that help them understand the roles of court personnel, discuss their concerns about testifying in court, and feel comfortable in the courtroom. Judges and prosecutors lead discussions about the importance of telling the truth and answer children's questions about the upcoming trial. Children and their parents learn stress reduction techniques to help them through the trial. Kids' Court has developed a comprehensive curriculum and has served over 1,200 children in the last 9 years. It is being replicated in several cities throughout the United States and abroad.

SPECIAL COURTROOM ACCOMMODATIONS

Judges should make efforts to ensure that the trial process and courtroom atmosphere help the child witnesses provide true and accurate information without unnecessary revictimization. Judges need to know and understand the special developmental needs of children. Judges can do many things to prevent trauma to children in court, such as making sure all objections are argued outside the hearing or presence of the child, requiring that all attorneys use developmentally appropriate language when questioning child witnesses, and arranging the courtroom to be less intimidating for the child witness. A simple example of how to arrange the courtroom to avoid intimidating the child witness would be to allow the child to sit in a child-sized chair or to allow the child to sit next to a support person. Continuances should be limited unless it is in the best interest of the particular child or in the cause of justice. Speedy resolution of child victim cases should be encouraged. In federal cases, when a child will be called to give testimony, judges can designate the case as being of special public importance which gives the case precedence over all others on the judge's calendar (18 U.S.C. 3509(j)). Safe and separate waiting areas should be available to prevent the child from encountering the defendant and the defendant's family. If a separate waiting area is impossible, a victim-witness advocate should remain with the child and caretaker to monitor the situation. Children should be allowed to have a support person in court with them. Judges should take care to ensure that the defense attorney does not unnecessarily subpoena support persons.

Courts should consider alternatives to live testimony. If the child would be too traumatized by seeing the defendant in the courtroom, prosecutors should consider making a motion for him or her to testify via closed circuit television. The use of closed circuit television has advantages and disadvantages. It may help reduce trauma and enable the child to testify more effectively, but it may be less compelling than a child's live presence in the courtroom. Prosecuting attorneys should weigh the advantages and disadvantages of testimony via closed circuit television on a case-by-case basis, always keeping in mind the level of trauma to the child. The federal courts and many states allow videotaped testimony of children under special circumstances; some states include tapes of original forensic interviews with children. These videotapes may be particularly useful when child victims recant their testimony.

Los Angeles County Children's Court, Los Angeles, California

Children's Court in Los Angeles County, California, was built with the 550 children who come to court each day in mind. Courtrooms have child-size proportions, a lower judge's bench, no jury box, and limited seating. Children who await hearings are protected from contact with offenders through private waiting rooms and seating areas that carry the Disney Channel and other children's programming. During the inevitable delays, an arts program and play rooms safely occupy the children. On site, immediate services and personnel, including school system personnel, mental health providers, and victim advocates are available for planning and consultation with children and families. Dependency Court administrators insist that more important than the new child-friendly facility is the court's philosophy that supports children's involvement in a secure court environment in all court proceedings affecting them.

VICTIM IMPACT STATEMENTS: IN A CHILD'S WORDS

A victim impact statement (VIS) from a child can be a powerful evidentiary tool, bringing the full impact of the crime home to the judge or jury in a potent way. Clearly, child victims should not be forced to make a VIS nor be made uncomfortable or fearful while making one. The process of making the VIS actually becomes an important step in the healing process for many children.

In most states and the District of Columbia, children have the right to present a VIS at the time of sentencing or to have an adult present a statement on their behalf. Since most children need help preparing a VIS, a victim advocate can work with the child to develop one that is accurate and age-appropriate. Knowledgeable professionals should assess the substantial body of research documenting the initial and long-term psychological effects of abuse on children and be sure to present this evidence as part of the VIS.

In most cases, the primary impact of abuse is psychological, not financial. However, the treatment of medical and psychological damage resulting from the abuse will often have a significant financial impact on the victim and the victim's family. Therefore, the financial impact portion of the victim impact statement should cover expenditures for medical treatment and psychological counseling expenditures. A restitution order should be requested for these expenditures, with contingencies for possible future medical and psychological expenses related to the crime.

While most VIS are technical documents unlikely to be reviewed directly by children, many children understand and like the idea of writing a letter to the judge describing what happened and how they were affected. Very young children can be encouraged to draw pictures of how they feel about the crime, themselves, or the defendant. Victim-witness advocates may wish to ask the child questions and transcribe the answers. Some courts allow audiotapes or videotapes of children making statements during an interview. Oral statements by the child at sentencing can be effective in helping judges understand the crime's impact. If a severely traumatized or injured child cannot provide a statement or drawing, the caretaker, physician, or therapist should prepare the primary statement and present it as part of an information package. Copies of research articles that document the short- and long-term impact of victimization on children can be attached. Nonoffending parents are usually good sources of information on how the abuse affected the child, the siblings, and the entire family. Siblings are often forgotten secondary victims and should be allowed to participate in the process or make their own VIS. Older children should be encouraged to write a letter to the judge expressing their feelings about the crime and the defendant. Some adolescent victims express their feelings and thoughts related to their abusive experience by keeping journals, writing poetry, or creating artwork. Copies of these can be presented as part of their VIS.

Recommendations for
Improving the Response to Children Exposed to Violence

RECOMMENDATIONS FOR ALL CRIMINAL JUSTICE PROFESSIONALS

1. To ensure the earliest possible recognition and reporting of crimes against children, all criminal justice professionals who come in contact with children should be trained to identify children who are exposed to violence as victims or witnesses and should be informed of the impact of victimization.

2. Criminal justice professionals assigned to handle cases involving child victims should have more in-depth training in forensic interviewing, child development, identification of abuse-related injuries, the emotional and psychological impact of abuse, and legal issues related to child victims and witnesses.

3. Children who witness violence should be provided the same level of victim assistance and special protections within the criminal and juvenile justice systems as child victims.

4. Criminal justice agencies handling cases involving children as victims and witnesses should work in collaboration with other agencies having responsibility for at-risk children, such as family and juvenile courts, social services agencies, medical and mental health providers, and victim services agencies. When multiple agencies are involved in a child's life, communication among professionals is critical to ensure complete and accurate information is available to decision makers to ensure the child is adequately protected.

5. Criminal justice professionals should adapt their practice to recognize the developmental stages and needs of child victims and witnesses to ensure they are sensitively treated throughout the investigative and trial process.

SPECIFIC RECOMMENDATIONS FOR LAW ENFORCEMENT AGENCIES

1. All officers should have at least basic training in recognizing and responding to children who are abused, neglected, or exposed to violence.

2. Agency heads should specially assign officers to handle cases involving child victims and witnesses, ensuring these officers receive in-depth training in interviewing children, identifying injury, child development, and understanding the impact of victimization and witnessing violence on children.

3. Police agencies should have written child abuse policies that provide sufficient guidance for making important decisions, such as whether to arrest a suspected perpetrator, whether to place a child in protective custody, and how to deal with unusual or difficult situations.

4. Law enforcement investigators should work in collaboration with medical and mental health providers, child protective services agencies, and victim assistance providers.

SPECIFIC RECOMMENDATIONS FOR PROSECUTORS' OFFICES

1. Chief prosecutors should ensure that cases involving child victims and witnesses receive priority and are handled as expeditiously as possible, minimizing unnecessary delays. They should ensure that child victims and witnesses receive support services as they go through the criminal justice process.

2. Prosecutors should be specially assigned to handle cases involving child victims and witnesses, receiving in-depth training on issues related to victimization of children, including medical and legal issues.

3. Prosecutors should ensure that child victims and witnesses are adequately and appropriately prepared for the court process and testifying.

4. Prosecutors should work in collaboration with medical and mental health providers, child protective services agencies, and victim assistance providers.

SPECIFIC RECOMMENDATIONS FOR CRIMINAL COURT JUDGES AND ADMINISTRATORS

1. Judges should ensure that cases involving children as victims and witnesses receive high priority and are handled as expeditiously as possible, minimizing unnecessary delays and continuances.

2. Judges who handle cases involving child victimization should receive adequate training in the dynamics of child maltreatment as well as the impact of victimization and witnessing violence on children and child development.

3. Judges and court administrators should ensure that the developmental needs of children are recognized and accommodated in the arrangement of the courtroom. Separate and safe waiting areas should be provided for child victims and witnesses.

4. Judges should ensure that the developmental stages and needs of children are recognized and addressed throughout the court process by requiring that all attorneys use age-appropriate language, by timing hearings and testimony to meet the attention span and physical needs of the child, and by allowing the use of testimonial aids when necessary to facilitate the ability of the child to testify.

5. Children should be presumed to be competent to testify.

6. Judges should be flexible in allowing the child to have a support person present while testifying and should guard against unnecessary sequestration of support persons.

7. Judges should ensure that child victims and witnesses, or their support persons, have an opportunity to present victim impact information. Judges should allow the victim impact information to be presented in a format consistent with the child's age and developmental level.

Conclusion

We ask a great deal of children who have been victims or witnesses to crime when we ask them to participate in the criminal justice system. It is a system designed for adults, not for children. We expect young children to take part in a process that many adults find complex, confusing, and intimidating. We want children to answer detailed questions about terrifying events in the presence of strangers and the defendant. If an investigation and a trial are a search for the truth, then we must do everything we can to enable children to tell what happened to them as clearly and completely as possible. Just as the criminal justice system makes accommodations for victims and witnesses who do not speak English or who have physical handicaps, it must also make accommodations for children. It is important that criminal justice professionals adapt their practice to the special needs of child victims and witnesses. If children cannot participate effectively in the criminal justice system, it may be impossible to protect them from future victimization and to hold the offenders accountable for their actions.

NOTES

[1] Finkelhor, D., "Children as Victims of Crime and Violence," Congressional Briefing, July 14, 1998.

[2] Kilpatrick, D., and Saunders, B., "Prevalence and Consequences of Child Victimization," Crime Victims Research and Treatment Center, Medical University of South Carolina, Research in Brief, National Institute of Justice, 1997.

[3] Christianson, S. A., "Emotional Stress and Eyewitness Memory: A Critical Review," *Psychological Bulletin*, vol. 112, 1992.

[4] Rhea, M. H., Chafey, K. H., Dohner, V. A., and Terragno, R., "The Silent Victims of Domestic Violence—Who Will Speak?" *Journal of Child and Adolescent Psychiatric Nursing*, vol. 9, no. 3, 1996.

[5] Pynoos, R. S. and Nader, K., "Children Who Witness the Sexual Assaults of Their Mothers," *Journal of the American Academy of Child and Adolescent Psychiatry*, vol. 27, 1988.

[6] Lipovsky, J., and Stern, P., "Preparing Children for Court: An Interdisciplinary View," *Child Maltreatment*, vol. 2, no. 2, May 1997.

[7] National Assessment Program: 1994 Survey Results, National Institute of Justice, U.S. Department of Justice, Washington, DC.

[8] Joint Investigations of Child Abuse: Report of a Symposium, National Institute of Justice, U.S. Department of Justice (p. 3), July 1993.

REFERENCES

Alexander, E., Chapter on Child Victimization, *National Victim Assistance Academy Manual*, Office for Victims of Crime, U.S. Department of Justice, 1996.

Benson, K., "From the Mouths of Babes," *Police*, (pp. 36–41), October 1993.

Berliner, L., "The Child Witness: The Progress and Emerging Limitations," *University of Miami Law Review*, 40:167, 1985.

Berliner, L. and J. Conte, "The Process of Victimization: The Victim's Perspective," *Child Abuse and Neglect*, 29, 1990.

Berliner, L. and Conte, J., "The Effects of Disclosure and Intervention on Sexually Abused Children," *Child Abuse and Neglect*, 19:371–384, 1995.

Briere, J., "Child Abuse Trauma: Theory and Treatment of the Lasting Effects," Sage Publications, Newbury Park, CA, 1992.

Bottoms, B. and G. Goodman, editors, *International Perspectives on Child Abuse and Children's Testimony*, Newbury Park, CA: Sage Publications, 1996.

"Child Victim Witness Investigative Pilot Projects: Research and Evaluation Final Report," Attorney General's Office, State of California, 1994.

"Child Victim-Witness Protocol," San Diego Regional Child Victim-Witness Task Force, June 1991.

"Child Witnesses in Criminal Court: A Protocol for Action," Prepared for the State Justice Institute by the Crime Victims Research and Treatment Center, Medical University of South Carolina, December, 1990.

Deblinger, E., "Diagnosis of Post-Traumatic Stress Disorder in Childhood," *Violence Update*, 2(4), 1991.

Dible, D. and R. H. C. Teske, Jr., "An Analysis of the Prosecutory Effects of a Child Sexual Abuse Victim-Witness Program," *Journal of Criminal Justice*, 21:79–85, 1993.

Dixon, S. and M. Stein, *Encounters with Children: Pediatric Behavior and Development*, St. Louis: Mosby-Year Book, 1992.

Dziech, B. and C. Schudson, *On Trial: America's Courts and Their Treatment of Sexually Abused Children*, Boston: Beacon Press, 1991.

Finkelhor, D. and A. Browne, "The Traumatic Impact of Child Sexual Abuse: A Conceptualization," *American Journal of Orthopsychiatry*, 23:215–218, 1984.

Flin, R., "Child Witnesses in Criminal Courts," *Children & Society*, 4(3): 264–283, 1990.

Gray, E., *Unequal Justice: The Prosecution of Child Sexual Abuse*, New York: The Free Press, 1993.

Goodman, G. and B. Bottoms, editors, *Child Victims, Child Witnesses: Understanding and Improving Testimony*, New York: The Guilford Press, 1993.

Henry, J., "System Intervention Trauma to Child Sexual Abuse Victims Following Disclosure," *Journal of Interpersonal Violence*, 12(4): 499–512, August 1997.

Herman, J., *Trauma and Recovery*, Basic Books, 1992.

"Investigation and Prosecution of Parental Abduction," American Prosecutors Research Institute, 1995.

Jones, D., *Interviewing the Sexually Abused Child: Investigation of Suspected Abuse*, Royal College of Psychiatrists, London, 1992.

Kilpatrick, D., and B. Saunders, *Prevalence and Consequences of Child Victimization*, Crime Victims Research and Treatment Center, Medical University of South Carolina, Research in Brief, National Institute of Justice, 1997.

King, N., W. Hunter, and D. Runyan, "Going to Court: The Experience of Child Victims of Intrafamilial Sexual Abuse," *Journal of Health Politics, Policy and Law*, 13:1–17, Winter 1988.

Lanning, K., "Criminal Investigation of Suspected Child Abuse; Criminal Investigation of Sexual Victimization of Children," J. Briere, L. Berliner, J. A. Bulkley, C. Jenny, and T. Reid, editors, *The APSAC Handbook on Child Maltreatment* (pp. 246–264), Sage Publications, 1996.

Lipovsky, J. and P. Stern, "Preparing Children for Court: An Interdisciplinary View," *Child Maltreatment*, 2(2): 150–163, May 1997.

Morgan, M., "How to Interview Sexual Abuse Victims: Including the Use of Anatomical Dolls," Newbury Park, CA: Sage Publications, 1995.

McGough, L. and A. Warren, "The All-Important Investigative Interview," *Juvenile and Family Court Journal*, 45(4): 13–29, 1994.

Myers, J. E. B., "Legal Issues in Child Abuse and Neglect," Newbury Park, CA: Sage Publications, 1992.

Myers, J. E. B., "Paint the Child Into Your Corner: Examining the Young Witness," *Family Advocate*, Vol. 42, Winter 1988.

Myers, J. E. B., "The Child Witness: Techniques for Direct Examination, Cross-Examination, and Impeachment," *Pacific Law Journal* (pp. 804–942), April 1987.

"A New Approach to Interviewing Children: A Test of Its Effectiveness," National Institute of Justice, U.S. Department of Justice, Research in Brief, 1992.

Oates, R., D. Lynch, A. Stern, B. O'Toole, and G. Cooney, "The Criminal Justice System and the Sexually Abused Child," *Medical Journal of Australia*, 162 (pp. 647–653), 1995.

Pence, D. and C. Wilson, *Team Investigation of Child Sexual Abuse: The Uneasy Alliance*, Newbury Park, CA: Sage Publications, 1994.

Perry, N. and L. Wrightsman, *The Child Witness: Legal Issues and Dilemmas*, Newbury Park, CA: Sage Publications, 1991.

Portable Guides to Investigating Child Abuse, Office of Juvenile Justice and Delinquency Prevention, U.S. Department of Justice, 1996:
> Battered Child Syndrome: Investigating Physical Abuse and Homicide
> Child Neglect and Munchausen Syndrome by Proxy
> Diagnostic Imaging of Child Abuse
> Interviewing Child Witnesses and Victims of Sexual Abuse
> Photo-Documentation in the Investigation of Child Abuse
> Recognizing When a Child's Injury or Illness Is Caused by Abuse
> Sexually Transmitted Diseases and Child Sexual Abuse
> Burn Injuries

Reviere, S., *Memory of Childhood Trauma: A Clinician's Guide to the Literature*, New York: The Guilford Press, 1996.

Saywitz, K., "Questioning Child Witnesses," *Violence Update*, March 1994.

Saywitz, K., "Preparing Children for the Investigative and Judicial Process: Improving Communication, Memory and Emotional Resiliency," Final Report to the National Center on Child Abuse and Neglect, U.S. Department of Health and Human Services by UCLA School of Medicine, Department of Psychiatry, 1993.

Saywitz, K., "Methods to Increase Developmental Sensitivity: Matching Form of Question to the Child's Language Level," Unpublished lecture materials.

Saywitz, K., "Bullying Children Won't Work: Interviewing Techniques That Will," *Family Advocate*, 10(3): 16–20, 1988.

Saywitz, K., "Children's Conceptions of the Legal System: Court Is a Place to Play Basketball, in *Perspectives on Children's Testimony*, Ceci et al., editors, Springer-Verlag, 1989.

Whitcomb, D., "Use of Innovative Techniques to Assist Child Witnesses," (Research Brief), Newton, MA: Educational Development Center, 1992.

Whitcomb, D., *When the Victim Is a Child*, (second edition), Issues and Practices Series, National Institute of Justice, U.S. Department of Justice, 1992.

Widom, C. S., "Cycle of Violence" (Research in Brief), National Institute of Justice, U.S. Department of Justice, 1992.

Zaragoza, M., et al., editors, *Memory and Testimony in the Child Witness*, Newbury Park, CA: Sage Publications, 1995.

Chapter Six

Internet Crimes against Children

Office for Victims of Crime

The growth of technology has changed our lives dramatically. Computers were viewed as a luxury or even an extravagance 30 years ago. We relied on television, newspapers, and radio as primary sources of news and information. Cables, modems, and online services were virtually nonexistent.

Today, computers are prevalent in businesses, homes, schools, libraries, and even airports. The World Wide Web provides instant access to news, reference information, shopping, banking, stock trading, auctions, and travel information and reservations. People routinely use the Internet to take college courses, play games, listen to music, and view videos. Chat rooms and e-mails are now replacing telephones as our favorite means of long-distance communication.

The proliferation of computer technology obviously has enhanced our lives in many ways, such as enabling improved productivity and efficiency at work, school, and home. Anyone with access to a computer and modem now has unparalleled recreational and educational opportunities.

Unfortunately, criminals are also using modern technology—to prey on innocent victims. Computers and the Internet have made the predator's job easier. Historically, child predators found their victims in public places where children tend to gather—schoolyards, playgrounds, and shopping malls. Today, with so many children online, the Internet provides predators a new place—cyberspace—to target children for criminal acts. This approach eliminates many of the risks predators face when making contact in person.

Scope of the Problem

The sheer number of young people using computers today makes our concern for them well founded. Recent years have seen a great increase in

Source: Office for Victims of Crime, May 2001 (NCJ 184931)

access to and use of the Internet. By the end of 1998, more than 40 percent of all American homes had computers, and 25 percent had Internet access.[1] This trend is expected to continue. Children and teenagers are one of the fastest growing groups of Internet users. An estimated 10 million kids are online today. By the year 2002, this figure is expected to increase to 45 million, and by 2005 to 77 million.[2] With so many youth online and vulnerable to predators, it is extremely important for parents, law enforcement officials, prosecutors, and victim service providers to know as much as possible about Internet crimes against children so they can prevent victimization and prosecute offenders.

Children as Targets of Internet Crimes— Who Is Vulnerable?

Traditionally, both intrafamilial offenders and strangers have found that young children and teenagers are perfect targets for criminal acts because they are often trusting, naive, curious, adventuresome, and eager for attention and affection. However, the most attractive factor to predators is that children and teenagers historically have not been viewed as credible witnesses. Today, the danger to children is even greater because the Internet provides predators anonymity. Whether the victimization occurs in person or over the Internet, the process is the same—the perpetrator uses information to target a child victim. For example, the predator may initiate an online friendship with a young person, sharing hobbies and interests. This may lead to the exchange of gifts and pictures. Just like the traditional predator who targets children in person, the online predator usually is willing to spend considerable time befriending and grooming a child. The predator wants to build the child's trust, which will allow the predator to get what he or she ultimately wants from the child.

Although no family is immune to the possibility that their child may be exploited and harassed on the Internet, a few factors make some children more vulnerable than others. Older children tend to be at greater risk because they often use the computer unsupervised and are more likely to engage in online discussions of a personal nature. Some victims become unwitting participants as they actively participate in chat rooms, trade e-mail messages, and send pictures online. Troubled or rebellious teens who are seeking emancipation from parental authority can be susceptible to Internet predators. The risk of victimization is greater for emotionally vulnerable youth who may be dealing with issues of sexual identity. These young people may be willing to engage in conversation that is both titillating and exciting but appears innocent and harmless. Unfortunately, Internet interactions that initially appear innocent can gradually lead to sexually explicit conduct.[3]

Types of Internet Victimization

Internet crimes are often thought of as victimless. Nothing could be further from the truth. Children and teenagers can and do become victims of Internet crimes. Predators contact teenagers and children over the Internet and victimize them by

- Enticing them through online contact for the purpose of engaging them in sexual acts
- Using the Internet for the production, manufacture, and distribution of child pornography
- Using the Internet to expose youth to child pornography and encourage them to exchange pornography
- Enticing and exploiting children for the purpose of sexual tourism (travel with the intent to engage in sexual behavior) for commercial gain and/or personal gratification.

Unique Characteristics of Cybercrimes

Several characteristics distinguish Internet crimes from other crimes committed against children:

Physical contact between the child and the perpetrator does not need to occur for a child to become a victim or for a crime to be committed. Innocent pictures or images of children can be digitally transformed into pornographic material and distributed across the Internet without the victims' knowledge.

The Internet provides a source for repeated, long-term victimization of a child that can last for years, often without the victim's knowledge. Once a child's picture is displayed on the Internet, it can remain there forever. Images can stay on the Internet indefinitely without damage to the quality of the image.

These crimes transcend jurisdictional boundaries, often involving multiple victims from different communities, states, and countries. The geographic location of a child is not a primary concern for perpetrators who target victims over the Internet. Often, perpetrators travel hundreds of miles to different states and countries to engage in sexual acts with children they met over the Internet. Many of these cases involve local, state, federal, and international law enforcement entities in multiple jurisdictions.

Many victims of Internet crimes do not disclose their victimization or even realize that they have been victims of a crime. Whereas children who experience physical or sexual abuse may disclose the abuse to a friend, teacher, or parent, many victims of Internet crimes remain anonymous until pictures or images are discovered by law enforcement during an investigation. The presumed anonymity of Internet activities often provides a false sense of security and secrecy for both the perpetrator and the victim.

Youth Internet Safety Survey

Although it was clear that young people are using the Internet in ever-increasing numbers, no research existed on how many youth encounter unwanted sexual solicitations and exposure to sexual material and harassment online. To obtain a clearer picture of the scope of the problem, the National Center for Missing & Exploited Children (NCMEC) provided funding to Dr. David Finkelhor, Director of the Crimes Against Children Research Center at the University of New Hampshire, to conduct a research survey in 1999 on Internet victimization of youth. His research provides the best profile of this problem to date.

Crimes Against Children Research Center staff interviewed a nationally representative sample of 1,501 youth, aged 10 to 17, who used the Internet regularly. "Regular use" was defined as using the Internet at least once a month for the past 6 months on a computer at home, at school, in a library, at someone else's home, or in some other place.

SURVEY AREAS

The survey looked at four types of online victimization of youth, which Finkelhor[4] defined as

- Sexual solicitation and approaches: Requests to engage in sexual activities or sexual talk or to give personal sexual information that were unwanted or, whether wanted or not, made by an adult
- Aggressive sexual solicitation: Sexual solicitations involving offline contact with the perpetrator through mail, by telephone, or in person, or attempts or requests for offline contact
- Unwanted exposure to sexual material: When online, opening e-mail, or opening e-mail links, and not seeking or expecting sexual material, being exposed to pictures of naked people or people having sex
- Harassment: Threats or other offensive content (not sexual solicitation) sent online to the youth or posted online for others to see

The survey also explored Internet safety practices used by youth and their families, what factors may put some youth more at risk for victimization than others, and the families' knowledge of how to report online solicitations and harassment.

STATISTICAL FINDINGS

The survey results offered the following statistical highlights:[5]

- One in 5 youth received a sexual approach or solicitation over the Internet in the past year.
- One in 33 youth received an aggressive sexual solicitation in the past year. This means a predator asked a young person to meet somewhere, called a young person on the phone, and/or sent the young person correspondence, money, or gifts through the U.S. Postal Service.

- One in 4 youth had an unwanted exposure in the past year to pictures of naked people or people having sex.
- One in 17 youth was threatened or harassed in the past year.
- Most young people who reported these incidents were not very disturbed about them, but a few found them distressing.
- Only a fraction of all episodes was reported to authorities such as the police, an Internet service provider, or a hotline.
- About 25 percent of the youth who encountered a sexual approach or solicitation told a parent. Almost 40 percent of those reporting an unwanted exposure to sexual material told a parent.
- Only 17 percent of youth and 11 percent of parents could name a specific authority, such as the Federal Bureau of Investigation (FBI), CyberTipline, or an Internet service provider, to which they could report an Internet crime, although more indicated they were vaguely aware of such authorities.
- In households with home Internet access, one-third of parents said they had filtering or blocking software on their computers.

OTHER FINDINGS

The survey results confirm what is already known: although the Internet is a wonderfully fun and educational tool, it can also be very dangerous. According to the survey, one in five youth who regularly use the Internet received sexual solicitations or approaches during a one-year period. The survey also found that offenses and offenders are more diverse than previously thought. In addition to pedophiles, other predators use the Internet. Nearly half (48 percent) of the offenders were other youth, and one-fourth of the aggressive episodes were initiated by females. Further, 77 percent of targeted youth were age 14 or older—not an age characteristically targeted by pedophiles. Although the youth stopped most solicitations by leaving the Web site, logging off, or blocking the sender, the survey confirmed current thinking that some youth are particularly vulnerable to online advances.

Most youth reported not being distressed by sexual exposures online. However, a significant 23 percent reported being very or extremely upset, 20 percent reported being very or extremely embarrassed, and 20 percent reported at least one symptom of stress. These findings point to the need for more research on the effects on youth of unwanted exposure to sexual materials and the indicators of potentially exploitative adult-youth relationships.

The large number of solicitations that went unreported by youth and families was of particular interest. This underreporting is attributed to feelings of embarrassment or guilt, ignorance that the incident was a reportable act, ignorance of how to report it, and perhaps resignation to a certain level of inappropriate behavior in the world.

Possibly due to the nature and small sample size of the survey, there were no reported incidences of traveler cases.[6] The survey also revealed no incidences of completed Internet seduction or sexual exploitation, including trafficking of child pornography. Despite the findings of this survey, law enforcement agencies report increasing incidents of Internet crimes against children.

RECOMMENDATIONS

Among the many findings of Finkelhor's survey, the most significant is that we are only beginning to realize the extent of the complex and increasingly prevalent phenomenon of Internet-based crimes against children. We have much to learn about the magnitude of the problem, the characteristics of its victims and perpetrators, its impact on children, and strategies for prevention and intervention.

Information and Intervention Resources

NATIONAL CENTER FOR MISSING & EXPLOITED CHILDREN

The National Center for Missing & Exploited Children is a comprehensive resource for families, victim service practitioners, and law enforcement personnel. NCMEC is supported by the U.S. Department of Justice's Office of Juvenile Justice and Delinquency Prevention (OJJDP) and functions as a clearinghouse and resource center for collecting and distributing information about missing, runaway, and sexually exploited children, including exploitation resulting from Internet solicitations. In partnership with the U.S. Postal Inspection Service, U.S. Customs Service, and FBI, NCMEC operates the CyberTipline, an online form for reporting suspected child sexual exploitation (www.missingkids.com/cybertip), and the Child Pornography Tipline (1-800-843-5678). Through the CyberTipline and the telephone hotline, NCMEC

- Receives reports 24 hours a day, 7 days a week, of child sexual exploitation and the production and distribution of pornography on the Internet. Calls to the toll-free Child Pornography Tipline can be received from the United States, Canada, Mexico, and the United Kingdom.
- Receives reports of offenses such as child pornography, child sex tourism, online enticement of children for sexual acts, and child sexual molestation (outside the family). Analysts review each report and provide information to investigating law enforcement agencies.
- Provides leads on child exploitation cases to appropriate law enforcement authorities and agencies.

NCMEC case managers work directly with law enforcement personnel, offering technical assistance, resources, information, and advice on child sexual exploitation. NCMEC also has developed specialized training programs, materials, and curricula designed for law enforcement personnel. Training is available at little or no cost to local jurisdictions through OJJDP. For more information on current programs, call 1-800-843-5678.

INTERNET CRIMES AGAINST CHILDREN TASK FORCE PROGRAM

In 1998, the Missing Children's Program of OJJDP initiated its Internet Crimes Against Children (ICAC) task force program, a national effort to combat the threat of offenders who use the Internet to sexually exploit children. Through this program, state and local law enforcement agencies can acquire the skills, equipment, and personnel resources to respond effectively to ICAC offenses. The program encourages law enforcement agencies to develop specialized multijurisdictional, multiagency responses to prevent, interdict, investigate, and prosecute Internet crimes against children. As of mid-2000, 30 ICAC task forces were participating in the ICAC task force program. Each task force is composed of federal, state, and local law enforcement personnel; federal and local prosecution officials; local educators; and service providers such as mental health professionals. These task forces serve as valuable regional resources for assistance to parents, educators, prosecutors, law enforcement personnel, and others who work on child victimization issues. You can obtain more information on this and other law enforcement programs from the OJJDP Web site at ojjdp.ncjrs.org/programs/programs.html.

FEDERAL BUREAU OF INVESTIGATION

The FBI has established the Innocent Images program to focus specifically on computer-facilitated child sexual exploitation. Each FBI Field Division has designated two Crimes Against Children Coordinators to work with state and local law enforcement officials to investigate and prosecute cases that cross jurisdictional boundaries. OVC has placed a victim witness coordinator in the Innocent Images program to focus greater attention on the needs of child victims.

U.S. POSTAL INSPECTION SERVICE

The U.S. Postal Inspection Service protects children online by monitoring the transmission of child pornography through the mail. Increased amounts of pornography are being sent through U.S. mail as more illicit Web sites emerge advertising child pornographic material for sale. In response, the U.S. Postal Inspection Service is tracking down these materials. In addition, the U.S. Customs Service Cyber Smuggling Center monitors the illegal generation, importation, and proliferation of child pornography.

The Future

The future holds many challenges for those fighting Internet crimes against young people. Cases involving Internet crimes against children are complex and labor intensive for both the police and prosecutors. The time between victimization and arrest can be lengthy. These cases are usually multijurisdictional, which presents challenges in the investigation and prosecution of a case and can present problems for the criminal justice system, the child victim, and the family in terms of resources, travel, and court appearances.

CHALLENGES

Child victimization on the Internet is a complex matter. The full impact of such victimization on children is not completely understood. Family dynamics often play a significant role in children's denial of a crime and their willingness to participate in the investigation and prosecution. A child's ability to acknowledge and accept the crime can be linked to family values, peer pressure, and feelings of guilt, shame, and embarrassment. Denial and recantation can be common among children who unwittingly participated in the crime. Because of these issues, the greatest challenges facing law enforcement and victim service professionals are to identify the victims, protect their privacy, and serve them without further victimization.

Until more knowledge is gathered about Internet crime and its effects on victims, law enforcement and victim service professionals will continue working on Internet child exploitation using the tactics and standard approaches that have proved effective for working with other types of child victims. These tactics and approaches are discussed below.

FOR CHILDREN

- Ensure that the interview is conducted with developmentally appropriate language. A child's ability to relate to concepts and receive messages varies depending on his or her stage of development. The interviewer must assess the child's developmental level and adapt the interview accordingly.
- Ensure that the interview is conducted in a culturally sensitive manner with culturally appropriate language. Determine which words the child is comfortable with. Is an interpreter needed? If so, use a professional interpreter and not a family member. Family members inadvertently may interject their interpretations into the translation and may prejudice the child's account.
- Be patient with victims. At first, many victims will deny their involvement. However, with continued support and encouragement, the child victim usually will divulge and discuss the victimization.
- Avoid duplicative interviews when possible. Multiple interviewers and interviews tend to confuse and intimidate children, especially younger ones, and may revictimize the child and produce inconsistent victim statements. Joint or taped interviews minimize the number of interviews required and maintain consistent phrasing of questions.
- If the victim is from another jurisdiction, work with victim witness staff in that community to ensure that victim services are provided.
- Do not show surprise or shock. Remember, the youth is probably already feeling guilt, shame, or embarrassment about what occurred.
- Be honest with the child about what he or she can expect from the investigation and prosecution of the case and about any future contact he or she may have with the perpetrator.
- Talk to the child victim about a victim impact statement and restitution if the case will be prosecuted and if it is developmentally appropriate. Regardless of the child's age, find ways to give him or her a sense of control over the situation—provide choices, no matter how small, and

help him or her prepare for the court process. Consider requesting a guardian ad litem to represent and support the child throughout the legal process. Make the child familiar with the courtroom environment. A properly prepared child may find active involvement in the case empowering.

FOR THE FAMILY

- Internet crimes against children impact the entire family. Family members may feel guilty for not protecting their child more effectively. They also may feel anger or shame about their child's involvement in the crime. Family members are secondary victims and need to be offered support and information to help them understand the nature of these crimes and know how to better handle their often conflicting feelings.
- Assist families victimized by Internet crime who require travel and lodging arrangements related to the legal proceedings, such as depositions and hearings.
- Prepare the family for media and press coverage. Be sensitive to the privacy needs of the victim and family. Will the victim's name appear in any public documents? If so, can these documents be sealed if the family so desires?
- Help the family understand what their child is experiencing so they can help the child and feel some sense of control over the situation.[7]

NOTES

[1] *Falling Through the Net: Defining the Digital Divide*, July 8, 1999, National Telecommunications and Information Administration, U.S. Department of Commerce.

[2] CyberStats, Federation of American Scientists Web site, www.fas.org/cp/netstats.htm.

[3] Magid, Lawrence, 1992, *Child Safety on the Information Highway* (pamphlet), National Center for Missing & Exploited Children.

[4] Finkelhor, David, Kimberly J. Mitchell, and Janis Wolak, 2000, *Online Victimization: A Report on the Nation's Youth*, Arlington, VA: National Center for Missing & Exploited Children.

[5] Ibid.

[6] A traveler case is when an adult travels to meet and have sex with a youth he or she met on the Internet.

[7] Turman, K. M., and K. L. Poyer, 1998, *Child Victims and Witnesses: A Handbook for Criminal Justice Professionals*, Washington, DC: Office for Victims of Crime, U.S. Department of Justice.

Chapter Seven

Crime in the Ivory Tower
The Level and Sources of Student Victimization

Bonnie S. Fisher
John J. Sloan
Francis T. Cullen
Chunmeng Lu

Claims of increased crime against college students have successfully converged to define on-campus student victimization as violent and as a widespread social problem in need of institutional and governmental intervention (General Accounting Office, 1997; Reaves and Goldberg, 1996). *The Chronicle of Higher Education* and other respected popular news outlets, including *The Washington Post*, *The New York Times*, and *The Chicago Tribune*, have routinely spotlighted heinous crimes on or near campuses and have made claims of rising violence on campus (Lively, 1997). Such stories have led some educators to dub college and university campuses as "armed camps" (Matthews, 1993) and as "dangerous places" (Smith and Fossey, 1995).

Grassroots efforts by campus crime victims and their parents and lobbying efforts by Security-On-Campus Incorporated, an advocacy organization started by parents of a slain student, have prompted the U.S. Congress and 16 state legislatures to approve laws addressing the disclosure of student victimization (Fisher, 1995; Griffaton, 1995). In 1990, Congress passed the Student Right-to-Know and Campus Security Act (20 USC 1092), which requires colleges and universities that participate in federal financial aid programs to publish statistics for specific on-campus FBI Index offenses, liquor and drug violations, and weapon possession. The law also mandates that institutions make available their respective crime prevention and security policies and procedures. Interest in claims of increased on-campus crime continues to hold the attention of Con-

From *Criminology*, 36(3) (1998): 671–710. Used with permission.

gress. The Senate currently is considering passage of the Campus Crime Disclosure Act of 1998, which expands the definition of campus, the categories of crime that must be reported, and provides for a fine for schools violating campus security disclosure laws (http://www.soconline.org/LEGIS/newindex.html#1, 1998). The Accuracy in Campus Crime Reporting Act of 1997 is still sitting in the House. The Act of 1997 would revise the security reporting provisions to achieve a more thorough, timely, and accurate disclosure of crime reports and statistics and would require specific methods of enforcement of campus security provisions (http://www. soconline.org/LEGIS/newindex.html1#1, 1998).

While these "claims makers" have been successful in socially constructing on-campus college student victimization as violent and as a widespread social problem, little is actually known about the nature, extent, or causes of student victimization on campus for several reasons. First, in some respects, the research into student victimization is still in the infancy stages of scholarly development and thus has many theoretical and empirical gaps. Very few, if any, broad-based studies of student victimization have been published in professional journals (for an exception, see Sloan et al., 1997). Much of the published research on student victimization, for example, has relied heavily on anecdotal evidence, on case studies, or on official crime statistics to describe the incidence and rates of on-campus crime. These works have overlooked two areas of research: broad-based measures of both on-campus and off-campus student victimization (Bromley, 1992; Fernandez and Lizotte, 1995; Fisher et al., 1995; Schwartz and Pitts, 1995; Sigler and Koehler, 1993; Sloan 1992, 1994). Second, the few large-scale victimization studies that have been conducted have narrowly focused on a single category of victimization (e.g., violence), a single type of crime (e.g., sexual assault), or a limited range of victimizations (e.g., only some forms of violence, such as assault, robbery, and date rape) (see Koss et al., 1987; Siegel and Raymond, 1992). These studies typically provide little insight into the patterns of student victimization, in part because researchers collect little information about the actual incident (e.g., if the incident occurred on or off campus or the lifestyle of the victim). Finally, a major shortcoming of the previous research has been a consistent lack of theoretical grounding (for an exception, see Schwartz and Pitts, 1995).

Our goals are to fill these voids in the current state of the student victimization research by contributing to the understanding of on-campus and off-campus student victimization and to the broader understanding of factors relating to students' risk of on-campus victimization. To these ends, we measured a wide range of victimization experiences from a large representative sample of four-year college students nationwide during the 1993–94 academic year. Using a structured telephone interview modeled after the redesigned National Crime Victimization Survey (NCVS), we collected extensive data on criminal victimizations experienced by the students both on and off campus during our reference period—since the school year began in fall 1993. Beyond describing the nature and extent of student victimization, we also compared on-campus student victimization rates to off-campus rates. Further, we explored variations in the extent and nature of student victimization. Accordingly, we examined how a range of both individual-level and contextual-level factors are related to on-campus violent and theft victimization. This analysis is informed by theory and research from the lifestyle-routine activity approach to explaining crime victimization. As a prelude to our empirical analyses, therefore, we review below how characteristics of students and the context of their environment might shape their risk of victimization.

Opportunities for On-Campus Student Victimization: Demographic and Lifestyle-Routine Activities Characteristics

Several theories of victimization—lifestyle-exposure, routine activities, criminal opportunity, and structural-choice—highlight the importance of the convergence in time and space of proximity to offenders, exposure to high-risk environments, target attractiveness, and the absence of capable guardians as key factors in predicting victimization (Cohen and Felson, 1979; Hindelang et al., 1978). Mixed support has been found for these theories, but in general, researchers have consistently shown that some individuals run a greater risk of victimization than others. Their findings support the notion that certain individual-level demographic and lifestyle routine activities characteristics are significantly related to the risk of criminal victimization (see Miethe and Meier, 1994).

There is reason to believe that the demographics of students and their on-campus lifestyle and routine activities can create opportunities for victimization, especially for violence and theft. We now turn to a general discussion of the research that has examined the relationship between Victimization, demographic characteristics, and lifestyle-routine activities. Throughout this discussion, we use the findings from recent studies to show how the demographic characteristics and lifestyle-routine activities of college students may potentially enhance their risk of experiencing an on-campus victimization, in particular an act of violence or theft.

DEMOGRAPHIC CHARACTERISTICS AND VICTIMIZATION

Independent of lifestyle-routine activities, demographic differences in victimization risks have been reported in several studies that have tested different theories of victimization (Miethe and Meier, 1994; Sampson and Lauritsen, 1990). Several demographic characteristics of victims are evident. One defining characteristic of victims is youthfulness. Results from the 1993 NCVS showed that members of younger age categories had among the highest rates of personal victimization (violence and theft) compared with other age categories. For example, 16–19-year-olds had the second highest violent victimization rate, followed by 20–24-year-olds and then by 25–34-year-olds

(12–15-year-olds had the highest rate). Results of the 1992 NCVS revealed that 20–24-year-olds had the highest rates of theft victimization, followed by 16–19-year-olds and 25–34-year-olds (Bureau of Justice Statistics, 1994).[1] Victims generally described offenders as someone close to their own age group. The 1993 NCVS reported that victims aged 20–34 perceived the age of the offender to be between 21 and 29 years of age in 44% of the single-offender victimizations and 30 years of age or older in over 40% of the victimizations (Bureau of Justice Statistics, 1996).

The victimization research has consistently supported these national-level statistics; violence and theft are a young person's game, especially among males. Researchers have also reported that unmarried and low-income individuals are at a higher risk of violent victimization than their married and middle-income to high-income counterparts (Kennedy and Forde, 1990; Miethe and Meier, 1994; Sampson and Lauritsen, 1990; Sampson and Wooldredge, 1987). Unmarried individuals and females are more at risk for theft than married individuals and males (Sampson, 1987).

Members of the college population have characteristics that researchers have reported make certain members of the general public favorable to victimization. First, the college population is youthful. In the fall of 1993, those less than 18 to 24 years old made up 62% of the undergraduate student population, and those 25 to 34 years old made up 46% of the graduate student population. Second, a large proportion of the undergraduate student body—nearly 75%—is either not married or separated. Third, the sheer number of college students—nearly 15 million enrolled during the 1993–94 academic year, of which a little less than one-half were males (U.S. Department of Education, 1995)—creates a sizable pool of potential victims and would-be offenders. Student enrollment continues to increase annually, thus adding to the number of attractive targets and would-be offenders.

Although members of the student population have demographic characteristics that research suggests would heighten their chances of victimization, for several reasons it is not clear which demographic characteristics, if any, put some students more (or less) at risk than their demographic counterparts in society or others within the student population. This is partly due to shortcomings in the body of student victimization research that do not allow for such analysis. Few, if any, published studies have examined the relationship between individual-level student demographics and student victimization either on or off campus. In general, student demographics have been measured at the aggregate-level, as have on-campus crime rates, or violence has been narrowly defined in terms of date rape or sexual assault (Belknap and Erez, 1995; Fernandez and Lizotte, 1995; Schwartz and Pitts, 1995; Sloan, 1992, 1994). As a result, little is known about the relationship between demographic characteristics and student victimization. A few studies have concentrated on the relationships between specific offenses (e.g., rape or sexual assault) and student demographic characteristics, but as previously noted, these are the exception (see Bromley and Sellers, 1996; Belknap and Erez,

1995; Koss et al., 1987). Students' demographic characteristics, however, are only one component to understanding the risks for on-campus violent and theft victimization. We now consider students' lifestyles-routine activities as factors for increasing or decreasing the risk of students' victimization.

LIFESTYLE-ROUTINE ACTIVITIES OF STUDENTS

Four main concepts are central to general explanations of victimization: (1) proximity to crime—physical closeness to a large number of offenders; (2) exposure to crime—one's visibility and accessibility to crime; (3) target attractiveness—having symbolic or economic value to the offender; and (4) lack of capable guardianship—ability of persons or objects to prevent the occurrence of crime (Cohen and Felson, 1979; Hindelang et al., 1978; Miethe and Meier, 1994). Researchers have tested hypotheses concerning the relationship between each of these constructs and different types of victimization in an attempt to understand what types of lifestyle-routine activities are conducive to victimization. For each of the four main concepts noted above, we highlight the major arguments and findings from victimization studies. We then relate the results to the on-campus lifestyle-routine activities of students and their potential risk of victimization.

Proximity to Crime

Physical proximity to crime can be maximized when targets—people or property—and potential offenders converge in time and space. Scholars have long argued that spending time in an area plagued by high crime increases the likelihood of frequent contact with potential offenders and thus increases one's risk of victimization (Hindelang et al., 1978; Miethe and Meier, 1994). High-crime areas where people live, work, or seek entertainment could place them in close contact to potential offenders (Lynch, 1987). For example, the work of Sampson and his colleagues suggests that certain socioeconomic characteristics of a community increase the likelihood of victimization (Sampson, 1985, 1987; Sampson and Lauritsen, 1990; Sampson and Wooldredge, 1987) (see the discussion of contextual factors below).

Another possible situation in which physical proximity to crime is maximized is people coming into routine contact with relatively unknown persons or living in buildings or complexes where there are many unknown residents. Cohen and associates (1981) argued that persons related by primary group ties will be more likely to have a mutual interest in each other's welfare; coming into contact with many people or living alone may not facilitate such interest. These situations may actually increase the odds of victimization. Indeed, research results support the notion that type of housing influences the risk of personal and property victimization (Sampson and Wooldredge, 1987). Risk of violent victimization is higher for those who reside in a multiunit dwelling (Miethe and Meier, 1994), while type of housing (e.g., single dwelling or apartment) and the number of stories of the residence are significantly related to the risk of property crime (Massey et al., 1989).

When students are on campus, they come in contact with many other students in a variety of situations such as in classes, in the library, and in the student center. In light of the NCVS victimization and offender patterns, students may be in close proximity to crime while on campus. Research results shed some light on this speculation. First, Siegel and Raymond (1992) reported that close to 80% of victimizations committed against students were by fellow students. Second, Rickgarn (1989) reported that violence in residence halls is neither unknown nor uncommon; rather it appears to be far more pervasive than most administrators or students would care to admit. And third, many studies have documented the high frequency of date rape and acquaintance rape among college women while on campus (Belknap and Erez, 1995; Koss et al., 1987).

Students' proximity to crime can also happen in on-campus living arrangements. Students living on campus typically reside in multiunit, high-density residence halls or dormitories. Smith and Fossey (1995) argued that when students live in a dormitory, they and their possessions are physically present on the campus 24 hours a day for many months. Not only is the proximity to likely offenders potentially much closer than someone who does not live on campus, but the amount of property that an offender could steal is also abundant. In large residence halls, exposure to victimization may be enhanced due to the lack of mutual interest for other students or their property. Further, because of the evidence that males are more likely to be victims than females, students living in an all-male dorm or a coed dorm may be more at risk of victimization than those who live in an all-female dorm. Whether the dormitory type (same sex or coed) and size of the dormitory contribute to student victimization are questions that college student victimization research has yet to address.

Finally, another proximity-to-crime situation could be that full-time students or students who spend several days and/or nights per week on campus may face higher exposure to would-be offenders than part-time students or those who spend less time on campus. Not all students who live on campus are there seven days and nights; some may work off campus and/or spend time with family or friends. Even full-time students may only be on campus four or five days or nights a week. Exposure and proximity to potential offenders for many students is a reality they may face while on campus.

Exposure to Crime

In addition to proximity to offenders being central to the risk of victimization, exposure to certain types of situations may also play a role (Cohen and Felson, 1979; Hindelang et al., 1978). Persons are exposed to higher risks of victimization when, according to Miethe and Meier (1994:48), "routine activities and lifestyles place them in risky or vulnerable situations at particular times, under particular circumstances, and with particular kinds of persons." Jensen and Brownfield (1986) and Sampson and Lauritsen (1990) also argued that many activities that involve the recreational and social pursuit of fun increase victimization risk, especially for violence.

Several studies have consistently found that the most vulnerable groups for violent victimization are those who engage in public activities at night, such as frequenting bars or going to movies (Felson, 1997; Kennedy and Forde, 1990; Miethe and Meier, 1994; Sampson and Lauritsen, 1990; Sampson and Wooldredge, 1987). Sampson and Lauritsen (1990) reported that a "deviant lifestyle"—minor forms of illegal behavior, such as marijuana use, DUI, or theft of services—is a significant predictor of violent victimization. Additionally, Miethe and Meier (1990) reported that a composite of night activity—the average number of nights spent outside the home in leisure and social activities and the average number of hours spent walking alone outside the home—was significantly related to the odds of personal theft and assault. Such lifestyles may lead to situations in which different factors coincide to reduce guardianship and thus to increase the risk for victimization (Sampson and Lauritsen, 1990).

Powell and associates (1994) and Smith and Fossey (1995) have characterized the college student lifestyle, in general, as providing opportunities that often lead to acts of violence and theft. For example, students join school-sponsored groups, such as fraternities or sororities and athletic teams, that engage in routine social activities. There is some evidence that belonging to these groups may be associated with a greater risk of victimization. Siegel and Raymond (1992) reported that membership in a fraternity or a sorority was a significant variable in constructing an at-risk profile for students likely to be victimized. Bausell et al. (1991) found that athletes were more likely than nonathletes to be victims of fights and thefts.

Additionally, the college years are notorious for recreational use of, and experimentation with, alcohol and drugs (Schwartz and Pitts, 1995; Smith and Fossey, 1995). National estimates indicate that in 1992, college students spent $5.5 billion on alcohol alone—more than the amount nationally budgeted for alcohol and other substance abuse research (Rivinus and Larimer, 1993). Regardless of whether they have reached the legal drinking age, students often couple on-campus and off-campus parties and activities with alcohol and/or drug use. Despite the fact that alcohol possession and consumption are illegal for most undergraduates, several studies have shown that heavy drinking and binge drinking are common among college students (Engs and Hanson, 1994; Rivinus and Larimer, 1993; Siegel and Raymond, 1992; Wechsler et al., 1994).

Several researchers have also reported that student drinking behavior, as well as the amount of drinking by the student body as a whole, plays an important role in predicting physical and sexual victimization (Belknap and Erez, 1995). Wechsler et al. (1994) reported that those who are not binge drinkers at schools with high binge rates are more likely than students at schools with lower binge rates to experience problems, including being hit, pushed, or assaulted, and to experience unwanted sexual advances. Schwartz and Pitts (1995) found that women who were sexually victimized since enrolling in college were more likely to go out drinking than other women and that they were more likely to drink more on the occasions when they went out.

Further, Rickgarn (1989) reported that 81% of violent acts against persons or property in residential halls were alcohol related. It thus appears that alcohol and drug use puts students at risk for becoming victims of violence.

Target Attractiveness

Victimization theories assume that certain targets are selected because they have symbolic or economic utility to the offender (Cohen and Felson, 1979). Targets can also be selected because they are easy to transport or because there is little resistance should they be taken (Miethe and Meier, 1994).

The research results offer mixed support for the importance of target attractiveness to increasing the risk of certain types of victimization (Miethe and Meier, 1994). For example, Miethe and Meier (1990) reported that the amount of cash a person carried in public did not significantly predict personal theft but did significantly predict assault. Those who carried large amounts of cash in public were significantly more likely to be assaulted than those who did not. The large student body and the volume of property they bring with them provide an ample supply of suitable targets for would-be offenders. The number of targets also changes every term, especially in the fall of each year, when a sizable new supply of suitable targets arrive on campus with spending money in hand.

Capable Guardianship

Victimization theories involve the ability of persons or objects to prevent the occurrence of crime by social (interpersonal) and/or physical (target-hardening devices) means (Cohen and Felson, 1979; Miethe and Meier, 1994). The research results are mixed with respect to the deterrent effect of social or physical guardianship on individual victimization. Several studies have reported that lower victimization rates are associated with social and physical guardianship, while other studies did not find such associations (Miethe and Meier, 1994; Rosenbaum, 1987; Skogan and Maxfield, 1981). Even within a single study, researchers have reported that physical and social guardianship have differential effects on different types of crime. Miethe and Meier (1994), for example, found little evidence for the deterrent effect of physical or social guardianship on individuals' risk of assault and robbery, but did find some deterrent effect on burglary. Further, they reported that higher levels of social guardianship were related to significantly higher risks of property victimization.

The lack of capable guardianship may also be a factor in explaining on-campus student victimization. In the context of the college campus, research has shown that students are poor guardians of themselves and their property, despite the fact that many schools require freshmen and transfer students to participate in a general crime prevention awareness program or in a program devoted to a specific topic, such as rape awareness (Fisher et al., 1997; 20 USC 1092). Walking away from their belongings or leaving the door to a dormitory room open, an office door unlocked, or the door to a building propped open are common for students. Research reveals that students, in general, routinely fail to engage in simple guardianship activities that could reduce their risk of becoming victims of theft (see Fisher et al., 1997). Sloan et al. (1995), for example, found that one-half of the students in their case study reported leaving their property unattended while on campus, thus making them ripe for theft victimization. It may be that students are not knowledgeable as to crime prevention measures or practices or do not seek out this information from their schools.

Guardianship may further be increased or reduced for students living on campus. If a student has a roommate or suite mate, he or she may act as a potential guardian. However, a roommate or suite mate may also be a potential offender and thereby increase the proximity to an offender. Although there is an ever-increasing literature on residence hall violence (see Rickgarn, 1989), to our knowledge no published work has examined the effects of living alone on campus on the risk of on-campus violence or theft victimization.

The unique lifestyle and routine activity characteristics of the students create an environment in which different types of victimization may frequently occur at different places on campus or at the same place—"hot spots of crime"—at any hour of the day or the evening by a variety of perpetrators. Given college students' lifestyle and routine activities while on campus, there are reasons to believe that they may have higher victimization rates while on campus than while off campus and have higher victimization rates than a similar age cohort since they are among mostly other young people when on campus. There are also reasons to believe that college students' lifestyle and routine activities are mainly a function of their youth, and thus that they are equally likely to be victimized on campus as off campus and when compared to a similar age cohort. To date, however, these speculations have not been tested empirically.

Opportunities for On-Campus Student Victimization: Contextual Factors

Research results suggest that victimization depends not only on individual-level demographics or lifestyle-routine activities but also on where the activity takes place and the characteristics of that place (Lynch, 1987). As the discussion below suggests, the characteristics of campuses and their adjacent neighborhoods might enhance their attractiveness as criminogenic environments ripe for different types of on-campus victimization.

The importance of contextual factors, especially proximity to crime, in influencing victimization risks independent of lifestyle is well supported in the victimization research (Miethe and Meier, 1994; Sampson, 1985, 1987; Sampson and Lauritsen, 1990; Sampson and Wooldredge, 1987). For example, Sampson and Wooldredge (1987) reported that the percent unemployed in a community increased the risk of personal theft within a 15-minute walk of the victim's residence. Sampson and Lauritsen (1990) found that the rate of violent victimization in an area significantly predicts violent victimization.

Different measures or proximity to crime predict different types of victimization. Sampson (1987) reported that the percent of single-adult households and residential mobility had significant positive effects on violent victimization, while urbanization had a significant positive effect on theft victimization. Similarly, research using official data suggests that the institutional-level characteristics of colleges and universities are significant predictors of campus crime rates. Sloan (1992, 1994), in a study of crime at over 500 four-year colleges and universities nationwide, found that the proportion of part-time students enrolled, the proportion of transfer students, and the proportion of enrolled students who were under age 25 were inversely related to on-campus theft rates. On the other hand, total enrollment, the number of national-level sororities and fraternities on campus, and the total number of faculty and students on campus were directly related to on-campus theft rates. Finally, Sloan (1992, 1994) found that, the percent of students who were minorities was directly related to on-campus rates of violence, while difficulty in admission, the proportion of students returning for their second year, and the proportion of faculty at the institution having a doctorate were inversely related to on-campus rates of violence. Other studies have found similar relationships, and the relationships were generally in the same direction as those described by Sloan (see Bromley, 1994; Fernandez and Lizotte, 1995; Fox and Hellman, 1985; McPheters, 1978). All of these studies, however, used official crime statistics and not data from victimization surveys. Accordingly, they could not examine whether contextual variables had the same effect when individuals were the unit of analysis.

We are aware of only two studies that have examined how the characteristics of areas surrounding college campuses affect campus crime rates. Each of these studies suggests that the characteristics of these areas have little impact on campus crime rates. Fox and Hellman (1985) reported that the location of the campus (urban or rural), the unemployment rate in the school's SMSA, and the population size of the community in which the campus was located were not significantly correlated with campus crime rates. More recently, Fernandez and Lizotte (1995) found that crime rates for the community in which the campus was located had little impact on campus crime rates. Their results suggested, however, that higher rates of motor vehicle theft and robbery on campus were associated with higher rates in the community. Other community-level characteristics, including the proportion of 18–20-year-olds in the population, percent African American, percent Hispanic, and average household income, did not significantly predict campus crime rates.

To summarize, despite a large body of theoretically informed work on the dynamics of victimization (e.g., lifestyle theory, routine activities theory, criminal opportunity, or structural-choice theories of victimization) (see Miethe and Meier, 1994), researchers examining student victimization have generally failed to include a theoretical component to their research (for an exception, see Schwartz and Pitts, 1995). Even recent efforts by researchers to explore the utility of multilevel models of victimization (Miethe and

Meier, 1994; Sampson and Lauritsen, 1990; Sampson and Wooldredge, 1987), which examine the role of individual-level and contextual-level variables in criminal victimization, have not been employed by researchers examining on-campus college student victimization. Accordingly, informed by previous research, we develop and test a multilevel theoretical model to explain on-campus violent and theft victimization of students.

Methods

This study attempts to overcome several of the methodological limitations of previous studies by (1) using a nationally representative sample of students; (2) measuring a broad range of victimizations that happened to students on campus and off campus since school began in the fall term of the current academic year (1993–94); (3) using a data collection process and instruments modeled after the redesigned NCVS; and (4) collecting contextual-level information. Below we detail our research process.

SAMPLING DESIGN

A list of all four-year institutions ($N = 2,142$) appearing in the Department of Education's *State Higher Education Profiles* (1993) defined our population. Total enrollment at these schools during the 1992–93 academic year was 8,707,053. Nearly all were enrolled as full-time students (90%), and slightly more women than males were enrolled (53% compared with 47%) (U.S. Department of Education, 1995).

We stratified all the schools on two variables: total enrollment (1,000–2,499; 2,500–9,999; 10,000–19,999; 20,000 or more)[2] and school location (urban, suburban, and small town/rural).[3] Using this 4×3 matrix, we randomly selected one school from each stratum. Once we selected the schools, we contracted with the American Student List Company, which directly buys currently enrolled students' names, addresses, and telephone numbers from the respective school throughout the year, to pull a random sample containing the names and school telephone numbers of undergraduate and graduate students from each school. A total of 3,472 students were ultimately interviewed across our 12 schools.

SAMPLE CHARACTERISTICS

Our overall response rate was 71%. Our sample consisted of 3,472 undergraduate and graduate students enrolled as full-time or part-time students at the selected school when classes began in the fall of 1993. The sample had the following characteristics: 88% were full-time students; seniors comprised the largest class (25%), followed by freshman (21%), juniors (20%), sophomores (18%), graduate students (15%), and certification program students (2%). A majority of the sample was female (56%). The racial composition of the sample was white-Caucasian (76%), black or African American (13%),

Asian-Pacific Islander (8%), and Native Americans (1%); 3% of sample members refused to report their race. Just less than one-third (31%) of the students were between 17 and 20 years old. Fraternity or sorority members made up close to 15% of the sample, and 10% of the students were members of athletic teams. Forty percent of the sample members lived on campus.[4]

PRIMARY DATA

Data from Student Respondents

We developed and administered an individual-level survey and an incident-level survey to randomly selected students during the spring of 1994. These surveys were used to measure the extent and nature of student victimization and to collect other necessary information, such as demographics. The individual-level and incident-level instruments were modeled after NCVS Redesign Phase III. Each student was asked a set of screen questions to determine eligibility. Two types of students were not eligible to participate in the survey: (1) those who were currently enrolled as a student and who also worked full-time for the respective school and (2) those who had enrolled after January 1994.

Each eligible student was then asked a series of victimization screen questions. If the respondent said yes to any of the screen questions, the interviewer completed an incident report for each yes response. We collected information about the following types of victimization: violence (rape, sexual assault, robbery, aggravated and simple assaults), theft (larceny with and without contact, and motor vehicle-related thefts), living-quarter crimes (burglary and living-quarters larceny), vandalism, threats, and harassment (verbal and telephone).[5] Among the goals of the incident-level survey were: (1) to identify the time and location of the incident (e.g., on campus or off campus, and specifically where) and (2) to assess the nature of the incident (e.g., what actually happened, what was tried, or what was threatened). Regardless of whether they had been victimized, all respondents were asked a series of questions relating to their lifestyles and demographics.

Data from Campus Officials

We mailed a brief survey to appropriate campus officials at the selected schools (e.g., chiefs of police, directors of campus security, or vice presidents for administration) that sought information on security personnel and on-campus security and crime prevention efforts. The response rate was 100%.

SECONDARY DATA

In addition to the primary data that we collected and analyzed, we collected and analyzed secondary institutional-level and community-level data. Institutional-level demographic information was used for two reasons. First, victimization theories detail the importance of the characteristics of place in determining victimization (e.g., Miethe and Meier, 1994). Second, prior campus crime research supports the importance of institutional factors in predicting campus crime rates (Fox and Hellman, 1985; McPheters, 1978; Sloan, 1992, 1994).

Two sources of secondary data were used to obtain institutional-level and adjacent community-level data. First, the *Peterson's Guide to Four-Year Colleges and Universities* (Peterson's Guide, 1994) was used to collect information about the characteristics of the schools. The data obtained included percent of undergraduate male students, the percent of African-American students, percent of students who live on campus, and the total number of national fraternities and sororities registered on campus. Second, we collected socioeconomic (SES) and demographic characteristics data from the U.S. Census for the census tract in which the respective school was located and for all the adjacent tracts.[6]

DEPENDENT VARIABLES

Two victimization measures were used in the multivariate analyses that explored the potential sources of on-campus victimization: violence and theft (see the appendix for a summary of all the variables and their descriptive statistics). These two measures were used for several reasons: (1) both have been the focus of previous research studies (see Miethe and Meier, 1994); (2) the media, Congress, and state legislatures have given on-campus violence much attention (see Fisher, 1995); and (3) previous campus-level studies have reported that the largest percentage of crimes on campus were thefts/larcenies (Sloan, 1992, 1994).

We decided to model on-campus victimization for reasons related to measurement and causality. Lynch (1987) has argued that domain-specific models of victimization are needed to improve the fit between theoretical concepts in lifestyle-based victimization theories and available data. His findings suggest that victimization may be dependent on the context in which the routine activity takes place. By focusing solely on victimizations that occurred on campus, we were able to take into account not only the demographics and the lifestyle-routine activities of students but also the characteristics of the campus and of the adjacent communities. In this respect, our work potentially improves on past ecological studies. Although many of these studies have examined community-level characteristics as predictors of victimization, they typically lack information about where the victimization took place; it may or may not have occurred within the boundaries of the residential community for which the researcher has theoretically relevant measures (for an exception, see Sampson and Wooldredge, 1987: table VI). In this case, for theoretical and logical reasons, community-level measures should not be used as predictors of victimizations that occur outside the residential boundaries. By pure chance, the community-level measures could be statistically significant. However, because our data tell us where the victimization occurred—on campus or off campus—we can use institutional-level measures and adjacent community-level measures to predict on-campus victimization and validly test hypotheses concerning their effects. Unfortunately, we were unable to, model off-campus victimizations because they could have occurred anywhere, from across the street from a campus to locations far from campus (e.g., another community or state), and we were not able to measure the characteristics of those domains.

We estimated two on-campus models, one for violence and one for theft. In estimating our multilevel logit model, we were constrained by the number of institutional-level and community-level variables (hereafter macro-level variables) that we could use in our model and estimate. Since we have 12 schools, the most macro-level variables we could estimate were 11 ($n - 1$). Theory and previous research guided us in our decision as to which independent variables were included in the reported models.[7]

INDEPENDENT VARIABLES

Below we describe how we operationalized and measured each of the four main constructs—proximity to crime, exposure to crime, target attractiveness, and guardianship—using responses from our victimization survey and secondary data. We were able to construct measures at three levels: individual, institution, and adjacent community.

Demographics

Following in the tradition of past victimization research (Miethe and Meier, 1987; Sampson and Lauritsen, 1990; Sampson and Wooldredge, 1987), we included the following demographic characteristics in our multilevel model: sex, age, race, and marital status. Sex was measured male or female. A dichotomous variable for age (aged 17 to 20 and all others) was created to measure those who were under the legal drinking age for alcoholic beverages. We made this distinction because of the research that suggests a positive relationship between alcohol consumption and frequenting bars and victimization (Kennedy and Forde, 1990). We realize that our age measure does not capture the magnitude of frequenting bars or alcohol consumption, but those over 21 years old do have the legal right to drink alcohol.

Two dummy variables for race—black and nonblack, and Asian and non-Asian—were created because both black students and Asian students made up a sizable proportion of our sample. Marital status was measured as married or not married (e.g., single, separated, divorced, or widowed).

Proximity to Crime

To capture the idea of a person being in physical proximity to potential offenders, we employed five individual-level measures of proximity to offenders that represent not only closeness to potential student offenders but also the number and sex of such offenders. Three of the measures were living in an on-campus, all-male dormitory; living in a coed dormitory; and the size of the dormitory (i.e., the total number of students living in the respective residence hall). Two interaction terms were created from these variables to capture the relationship between the sex of the student (i.e., all male or coed residence hall) and the size of the dormitory (the total number of students living in the respective on-campus residence) where he or she lived on campus.

We employed three other proximity-to-crime measures: the average number of days (7:00 a.m. to 6:00 p.m.) on campus since school began in fall 1993; the average number of nights (6:00 p.m. to midnight) on campus since school began in fall 1993; and standing as a student (part time or full time). The three measures capture the amount of time spent near other students, that is, potential offenders.

Following in the tradition of prior research that used macro-level indicators of crime proximity (see Miethe and Meier, 1994), we developed two sets of proximity-to-crime measures: institutional-level and community-level. First, similar to a measure used by Sampson and Lauritsen (1990), who aggregated individual-level data to area-level data, we constructed an area violence rate as a macro-level indicator of crime proximity. Having 300 students, on average, across each of our 12 schools, we aggregated types of victimization within each school and created two crime rates, violence and theft, per 1,000 students at each school. Each was used to estimate the respective victimization model.

The other proximity-to-crime measures at the institutional-level included measures that prior campus crime research has shown to be significant predictors of high campus crime rates: percent of students who live on campus, percent of male students, percent of African-American students, and the rate per 1,000 students of the number of Greek social organizations on campus (see, e.g., Sloan, 1992, 1994). All four measures were used in both models.

We also created two proximity-to-crime measures at the adjacent community level that were similar to measures used in previous research (see, e.g., Miethe and Meier, 1994; Sampson, 1985; Sampson and Wooldredge 1987). The first, an SES measure, included percent below the poverty line, percent black, percent less than a high school degree, and percent unemployed (standardized Cronbach's alpha = .90). A standardized SES scale was created by adding these four variables in their standardized form and then standardizing the summed variable. A second measure, percent of people aged 16–19 years, was also used in estimating both models.

Exposure to Crime

To measure exposure to crime, we measured the level and nature of non-household activity. Researchers have included measures of the individual's primary daily activity (e.g., going to school) and levels of nighttime activity (e.g., number of nights going to bars, number of nights out for leisure) as measures of exposure to crime (Felson, 1997; Massey et al., 1989; Miethe and Meier, 1994; Miethe et al., 1987; Sampson, 1987; Sampson and Wooldredge, 1987). Following the lead from this research, we employed six measures of exposure to crime in terms of risky and dangerous situations that were derived from the number of nights spent partying on campus since school began in fall 1993, the number of nights spent partying near campus (off campus, but close to it) since school began in fall 1993, the likelihood of regularly drinking three or more alcoholic beverages, the likelihood of regularly taking recreational drugs (e.g., marijuana, hashish, cocaine), being a member of a fraternity or sorority, and being a member of an athletic team.

Target Attractiveness

A variety of economic measures of target attractiveness have been used in previous studies, including the possession of cash or jewelry in public and family income (see Miethe and Meier, 1990,1994; Sampson and Wooldredge, 1987). We chose to use a measure of the possession of cash and not family income, for three substantive reasons. First, many students might not know their family's household income, and as a result the measure would be potentially plagued with measurement error. Second, studies such as the National Longitudinal Survey of Youth that measure students' family income use a substantial number of variables to create a constructed measure (Center for Human Resources, 1995). Our purpose in developing our survey was not to measure family income solely. And third, there may not be a high correlation between family income and a person's socioeconomic status as a student. A student from a wealthy family may not have such wealth as a student because his or her parents do not financially support the student. For these reasons, we asked students a question about the average amount of money spent on nonessentials (e.g., entertainment, recreation, or going to restaurants) each week while in school. We used this as our measure of target attractiveness.

Guardianship

Two forms of guardianship, social and physical, have routinely been used in prior research (see, e.g., Miethe and Meier, 1994). Social guardianship has included indicators of the concept of people's ability to prevent the occurrence of crime, such as measures of the number of household members, the amount of social integration and informal social control exercised with neighbors, and having any good friends or relatives living on his or her block. Extending the underlying concept of the previous work for the context of our study, we used three measures of social guardianship: living alone on campus (i.e., no roommates or suite mates), attending a nonmandatory crime prevention or crime awareness program, and the frequency of asking someone to watch personal property while it was left unattended (used only in the theft model). We created two measures of institutional-level guardianship using responses from the campus security survey. First, a measure of guardianship was created using the number of full-time security personnel (sworn officers and security guards) per 1,000 full-time students at each school. Second, a three-point index was created to measure institutional-level crime prevention education that included whether a school had the following: mandatory participation for students in rape awareness programs, mandatory participation for students in alcohol awareness programs, and mandatory participation for students in drug awareness programs (standardized Cronbach's alpha = .84). These items were used because they included the notion of being required by all students at least once in their tenure (e.g., during freshman or transfer-student orientation) and there was variation among the schools.[8]

DATA ANALYTIC TECHNIQUES

We used two data analytic techniques to describe and explain the victimization of college students. Below, we present a simple descriptive analysis of the on-campus and off-campus victimization rates of students. Following this, we present the results of multilevel logit models for explaining students' on-campus violent and theft victimizations.

Results

THE NATURE AND EXTENT OF STUDENT VICTIMIZATION

Overall Victimization

Table 1 presents the rate at which college students fall prey to criminal victimization. Overall, 37% of the students had experienced at least one type of victimization since the beginning of the 1993–94 academic year. Nearly one-fourth (23.7%) of the respondents had been victimized at least once on campus during this reference period, whereas a little less than one-fifth (19%) of the respondents had been victimized at least once off-campus during the same period (results not shown in table 1).[9]

Among crimes of violence, assault, especially simple assaults, was the most common type of victimization. Note, however, that sexual assaults were also comparatively prevalent. Among property offenses, personal larceny without contact was the most frequent victimization per 1,000 students; indeed, it was the most frequent victimization across all offenses in this survey. Motor vehicle theft was rare, but burglary of vehicles occurred more frequently. Burglary was the most widespread form of living-quarters victimization. Rates of vandalism were comparatively high. Harassment, which included harassing comments made face-to-face ("verbal") and over the telephone, was fairly widespread.

On-Campus versus Off-Campus Victimization

The important question of whether college students are at a higher risk of criminal victimization on campus or off campus remains unanswered by previous research. Our results suggest that the answer is not a simple one. As can be seen in the second and third columns of table 1, the on-campus personal victimization rate in our sample was 1.2 times higher than the off-campus personal victimization rate. A closer look at the results reveals that some on-campus crime rates are higher than the off-campus rates while others are slightly lower. For example, the violent crime off-campus 1.2 times higher than the on-campus rate, and the rate of theft crime on campus was 2.1 times higher than the off-campus rate.

A mixed pattern emerges within crimes of violence. The on-campus rape rate is similar to the off-campus rate, but the on-campus sexual assault rate is 1.4 times higher than the off-campus rate. Further, compared to the on-campus rate, the aggravated assault rate off campus was 4.5 times higher. The simple assault rate, however, was less than twice as high (1.5) as the on-campus rate.

Students were more likely to experience a theft on campus; the rate was 2.1 times higher than the off-campus rate. Other on-campus and off-campus

Table 1

On-Campus and Off-Campus Victimization Rates per 1,000 Students and Victimization Counts by Sector and Type of Crime

	VICTIMIZATION RATE PER 1,000 STUDENTS		
TYPE OF CRIME	OVERALL	ON-CAMPUS	OFF-CAMPUS
All Crimes	601.1	324.3	276.8
	(2,087)	(1,126)	(961)
Personal Sector	266.1	146.3	119.8
	(924)	(508)	(416)
Crimes of Violence	77.5	31.7	45.8
	(259)	(110)	(159)
Completed	46.7	21.3	25.4
	(162)	(74)	(88)
Attempted/Threatened	30.8	10.4	20.5
	(107)	(36)	(71)
Rape and Sexual Assault	30.0	16.7	13.3
	(104)	(58)	(46)
Rape	8.3	4.0	4.3
	(29)	(14)	(15)
Completed	3.4	1.4	2.0
	(12)	(5)	(7)
Attempted	4.9	2.6	2.3
	(17)	(9)	(8)
Sexual Assault	21.6	12.7	8.9
	(75)	(44)	(31)
Completed	16.4	10.4	6.0
	(57)	(36)	(21)
Attempted	5.2	2.3	2.9
	(18)	(8)	(10)
Robbery	2.9	0.3	2.6
	(10)	(1)	(9)
Assault	44.6	14.7	30.0
	(155)	(51)	(104)
Aggravated Assault	14.4	2.6	11.8
	(50)	(9)	(41)
Simple Assault	30.2	12.1	18.1
	(105)	(42)	(63)
Crimes of Theft[a]	169.9	114.6	55.3
	(590)	(398)	(192)
Completed	163.1	111.5	51.6
	(566)	(387)	(179)
Attempted	6.9	3.2	3.7
	(24)	(11)	(13)
Personal Larceny with Contact	11.2	5.2	6.0
	(39)	(18)	(21)
Completed	7.4	3.7	3.7
	(26)	(13)	(13)
Attempted	3.7	1.4	2.3
	(13)	(5)	(8)
Personal Larceny Without Contact	158.8	109.5	49.3
	(551)	(380)	(171)
Completed	155.5	107.7	47.8
	(540)	(374)	(166)

(continued on next page)

Table 1   *(continued)*

TYPE OF CRIME	VICTIMIZATION RATE PER 1,000 STUDENTS		
	OVERALL	ON-CAMPUS	OFF-CAMPUS
Attempted	3.1	1.7	1.4
	(11)	(6)	(5)
Motor Vehicle Theft	0.9	0.6	0.3
	(3)	(2)	(1)
Motor Vehicle Burglary[b]	23.3	4.9	18.4
	(81)	(17)	(64)
Living-Quarters Sector	78.7	41.5	37.2
	(273)	(144)	(129)
Completed	69.1	36.6	32.5
	(240)	(127)	(113)
Attempted	9.5	4.9	4.6
	(33)	(17)	(16)
Burglary	64.8	37.2	27.6
	(225)	(129)	(96)
Living-Quarters Larceny	13.8	4.3	9.5
	(48)	(15)	(33)
Vandalism Sector	113.2	54.4	58.8
	(393)	(189)	(204)
Threat Sector[c]	28.6	10.7	17.9
	(99)	(37)	(62)
Harassment Sector	109.2	66.0	43.2
	(379)	(229)	(150)
Face-to-Face	65.4	38.3	27.1
	(227)	(133)	(94)
Telephone Call	43.8	27.6	16.1
	(152)	(96)	(56)

NOTE: The number of victimizations is given in parentheses.
[a] The 1992 NCVS definitions for crimes of theft were used. Motor vehicle theft and burglary are not defined as an individual-level crime in the NCVS; they are defined as a house-hold-level crime.
[b] Includes motor vehicle forced or attempted entry and attempted motor vehicle burglary.
[c] Includes general threats of physical assault that we could not determine if they were simple or aggravated assaults, robbery, and vandalism.

victimization rates varied by type of crime. Two types of crime had higher on-campus rates: The crime rate for the living-quarter sector was 1.1 times higher than the off-campus rate, and the harassment rate was 1.5 times higher than the off-campus rate. Two types of crime had slightly higher off-campus rates: The vandalism rate was 1.1 times higher than the on-campus rate, and the threat rate was 1.7 times higher than the on-campus rate.

SOURCES OF VIOLENT OR THEFT VICTIMIZATION WHILE ON CAMPUS

Examining who is most at risk of an on-campus violent victimization and an on-campus theft victimization using individual-level characteristics, lifestyle measures, and institutional-level and community-level measures is central to addressing the shortcomings in the current state of campus crime research and, therefore, in bridging the gap between the student victimization research and routine-lifestyle activity research. Table 2 reports the results of the two multilevel logit models that estimated the probability of experiencing either an on-campus act of violence or theft.

Risk of Violent Victimization

Examining the results in the first column in table 2, three significant findings emerge. First, supportive of prior research, the chance of violent victimization was significantly heightened for students who engaged in a risky and dangerous "deviant" lifestyle. Students who spent several nights on campus partying and those who reported that they were quite likely to take recreational drugs regularly during the year faced an increased risk of experiencing an act of violence while on campus. Second, our results mirror the overall pattern found in other studies concerning the success of guardianship activities—mixed results. The only measure of guardianship that significantly decreased the risk of experiencing a violent victimization was attending a nonmandatory crime prevention or awareness meeting during the school term. Third, unlike other studies that have tested theories of criminal victimization or student victimization studies, we did not or find that any of our individual-level measures of proximity to crime or target attractiveness had a significant effect on the risk of experiencing an act of violence. Similarly, the contextual-level measures of proximity to a high-crime area and of guardianship did not have a significant effect.

Risk of Theft Victimization

Examining the results in column 3 in table 2, a different pattern of significant factors predicts theft victimization than those presented for the on-campus violence model. First, two of the five demographic characteristics significantly predict theft victimization. Supportive of other research, we found that the risk of theft was related to sex and age; males and those aged 17 to 20 years old had an increased risk of experiencing a theft.

Second, six of the eight individual-level proximity-to-crime variables significantly predicted the probability of on-campus theft victimization. The type of on-campus residence hall that the student lived in increased the probability of experiencing a theft; those who lived in an all-male dormitory or those who lived in a coed dormitory were more likely to experience a theft than those who lived in an all-female dorm. Size of the dorm mattered for those who lived in an all-male dorm; specifically, males who lived in an all-male dormitory with a large number of students were less likely to experience a theft than those who did not. Students who spent many nights on campus per week and full-time students were more likely to experience a theft than those students who did not spend as many nights on campus and part-time students.

Table 2

Results from Multilevel Logit Models Predicting the Probability of Experiencing a Violent Victimization and a Theft Victimization

INDIVIDUAL-LEVEL VARIABLES	VIOLENT VICTIMIZATION B COEFFICIENT (S.E.)	THEFT VICTIMIZATION B COEFFICIENT (S.E.)
Constant	−4.08 (2.34)*	−4.27 (1.49)***
Demographic Characteristics		
Sex	−.25 (.25)	.33 (.13)***
Age Dummy	.36 (.25)	.38 (.14)***
Black	.39 (.42)	.33 (.23)
Asian	.24 (.45)	.24 (.22)
Marital Status	−.37 (.64)	.31 (.22)
Proximity to Crime		
All-Male Dorm	.39 (.59)	1.17 (.41)***
Coed Dorm	.33 (.37)	.50 (.22)**
Size of Dorm	−.0003 (.002)	.0004 (.0008)
Interaction Term: All-Male Dorm × Size of Dorm	.0014 (.002)	−.005 (.002)**
Interaction Term: Coed Dorm × Size of Dorm	.0007 (.002)	−.0002 (.0008)
Average Number of Days on Campus	.002 (.12)	.04 (.06)
Average Number of Nights on Campus	.03 (.08)	.09 (.04)**
Academic Standing	−.30 (.64)	−.47 (.28)*
Target Attractiveness		
Average Amount of Money Spent Per Week on Non-Essential Items	.0015 (.004)	.004 (.002)*
Exposure to Crime		
Number of Nights Spent Partying on Campus	.20 (.09)**	−.06 (.06)
Number of Nights Spent Partying Near Campus	.09 (.10)	−.03 (.06)
Likelihood of Regularly Taking Recreational Drugs During the Year	.10 (.04)**	−.02 (.03)
Likelihood of Regularly Drinking 3 or More Alcoholic Beverages During the Year	.002 (.04)	.009 (.02)
Member of Fraternity or Sorority	.47 (.33)	−.58 (.21)***
Member of Athletic Team	.13 (.29)	.43 (.17)**

Table 2   *(continued)*

INDIVIDUAL-LEVEL VARIABLES	VIOLENT VICTIMIZATION B COEFFICIENT (S.E.)	THEFT VICTIMIZATION B COEFFICIENT (S.E.)
Guardianship		
Live Alone on Campus	−.19	.18
	(.31)	(.19)
Attending a Non-Mandatory Crime Prevention or Crime Prevention Awareness Program	−.41 (.16)***	−.12 (.11)
Asking Someone to Watch Property While Left Unattended		−.22 (.06)***
CONTEXTUAL LEVEL: INSTITUTIONAL-LEVEL VARIABLES		
Proximity to High-Crime Area		
Campus Theft Rate		.04
		(.01)**
Campus Violence Rate	.03	
	(.03)	
Percent of Students Who Live on Campus	−.93 (4.28)	−3.36 (1.34)***
Percent Male Students	.01	.0004
	(.03)	(.02)
Percent of African-American Students	−.01	−.02
	(.05)	(.01)
Greek Presence on Campus	.03	.20
	(.17)	(.16)
Guardianship		
Crime Programs Index	−.37	
	(.71)	
Existence of a Campus-Wide Crime Watch		.13 (.23)
Total Security Personnel Per 1,000 Students	.03 (.17)	−.02 (.09)
CONTEXTUAL LEVEL: CENSUS-TRACT LEVEL VARIABLES		
Proximity to High-Crime Area		
SES Scale	.50	.31
	(.81)	(.27)
Percent 16–19 Years Old	−1.72	−7.46
	(9.08)	(4.60)
Chi-Square Statistic	97.59	144.72
DF	31	32
Significance	.0000	.0000

   * $p \le .10$
   ** $p \le .05$
   *** $p \le .01$

Third, consistent with prior tests of criminal victimization theories, higher levels of target attractiveness increased the risk of on-campus theft for students. Those students who spent large sums of money per week on nonessential items had a higher risk of being an on-campus theft victim than those who did not.

Fourth, only two individual-level exposure-to-crime measures significantly predicted the probability of an on-campus theft. Contrary to the previous research, being a member of a fraternity or sorority lessened one's probability of experiencing a theft. Being a member of an athletic team, however, increased the risk of experiencing an on-campus theft.

Fifth, in partial accordance with our theoretical framework outlined above, our results suggest that one form of guardianship—asking someone to watch your property while it was left unattended—significantly reduced the risk of experiencing an on-campus theft.

And last, contrary to the results of previous multilevel models of theft victimization, only two of the nine contextual-level variables had a significant effect on the risk of theft. The campus theft rate significantly increased the probability of experiencing an on-campus theft, whereas the percent of students who live on campus significantly decreased this probability.[10]

Discussion

Two major concerns within two distinctive bodies of research guided our efforts. First, within the college student crime research, we wanted to provide an assessment of the nature of and extent to which students are victimized. Second, we wanted to explore, within a lifestyle-routine activities perspective, the factors that may increase or decrease the risk of victimization within a specific domain, namely on campus. We comment on each of these issues below.

LEVEL OF STUDENT VICTIMIZATION

Like the general population, college students, overall, are not sheltered from experiencing victimization; some types of crime are experienced at a higher rate than other types and some types of students are at higher risk than others. College campuses do not appear to be "hot spots" for predatory offenses—places, as portrayed in the media, that are "armed camps" and in which heinous crimes are a regular occurrence. Still, campuses also are not "ivory towers" that insulate students from the harsh realities of life. Instead, campuses are places that expose students to risks of victimization that, depending on the type of crime, may be lower than, rival, or surpass the risks experienced in other sectors of society. Further, college students as a group are not immune from crime. As noted, 37% of the sample had experienced some victimization during the 1993–94 academic year.

The results reported here suggest that students seem particularly at risk for having their property stolen. Completed larceny without contact was the most common form of victimization reported by the respondents. In part, the prevalence of larceny on campus may be part of the broader pattern of crime victimization in which theft crimes are widespread and comprise a large proportion of the offenses committed in society (see, e.g., Bureau of Justice Statistics, 1994, 1996, 1997). Even so, theft victimization against students, especially those on college campuses, may also reflect the general perception among students that they are not at risk for victimization and their failure frequently to take rudimentary steps to protect their property—such as locking the door to their room or asking another student to "keep an eye on" their property (Fisher et al., 1997). It also may depend on the nature of being a college student: Students usually have no office on campus and thus must carry their property (e.g., books, backpacks, purses, wallets, computers, CD players and disks) with them—from building to building on campus, from place to place off campus. Accordingly, the risk of their leaving their property unguarded in the presence of a potential thief is high. Even for those who live on campus, their property is highly concentrated in their living quarters—a place where guardianship may be low and proximity to crime may be high.

Previous research has suggested that college women are at risk for rape and sexual assault (Belknap and Erez, 1995; Koss, 1996; Koss et al., 1987). Our findings lend further, albeit tentative, support to this conclusion. We should note that the absolute level of sexual victimization may not appear pronounced in the sample (3.73% of the women). This result undoubtedly reflects the limited bounding period covered by the survey (6 to 9 months). Further, the NCVS—the model for our survey—may not use a range of detailed questions sensitive to this form of victimization (Koss, 1996). Even so, a revealing finding is that the rates of sexual victimization reported in our sample may well be higher than those for the general population and for a comparable age group. The nature of college-student life, which involves the close daily interaction of females and males in a range of social situations, would lead us to predict that college women would have a heightened risk of sexual victimization compared to the general population of women, including women in the same age cohort. Assessing this proposition, however, will require a systematic study of women attending and not attending college. Nonetheless, we attempted to obtain preliminary insight on this issue by comparing for 1993 and 1994 the rates of sexual victimization (rape and sexual assault) for our respondents and the NCVS rates for those aged 20 to 24. These comparisons may be confounded by methodological artifacts, but they are, in the absence of other data on this issue, suggestive.[11]

Compared to the overall rate per 1,000 persons aged 20 to 24, the students' rates for on-campus rape/sexual assault were 3.3 and 3.1 times higher for 1993 and 1994, respectively (that is, rape/sexual assault was 33.9 in our sample versus 5.7 and 5.0 for persons 20 to 24). Again, these results must be viewed with caution, although three considerations suggest that they may reflect an important reality: The size of the difference in the victimization rates between college students and the NCVS sample is not easily explained; similar differences did not occur when other violent crimes were analyzed in a similar fashion; and the reference period for our sample was shorter (6 to 9 months versus 12 months) than for the NCVS sample, which, if anything, might lead our data to underestimate the comparative victimization rates for our respondents.

Our analysis also showed the importance of distinguishing between victimization on and off campus. Often, researchers have grouped these offense categories together since they both happen to college students. However, *campus* crime arguably should be limited to those offenses occurring within the boundaries of the college or university. In any case, we found that the rate of on-campus victimization was higher than the off-campus rate. This result suggests that students were not victimized just when they traveled outside the safe haven of the campus, but that they were at risk on campus as well. It does appear that predatory crimes such as robbery, assaults and threats were more likely to occur off campus. Even so, the risk of rapes and sexual assaults, thefts, and harassments were more pronounced on campus.

SOURCES OF STUDENT VICTIMIZATION

In line with previous studies of lifestyle-routine activities, we also tested multilevel models that explored which factors placed students at greater risk for on-campus violent and theft victimization. Researchers have shown that certain lifestyle and routine-activities characteristics of individuals and contextual variables significantly predict an individual's risk for victimization. As we previously noted, little work has been done that either examines on-campus student victimizations in this context (for an exception, see Schwartz and Pitts, 1995) or examines victimization in a specific context (Lynch, 1987). Our analyses show the value of the lifestyle-routine activities approach to explaining victimization and show that the correlates of property and violent victimization are not the same (see, e.g., Kennedy and Forde, 1990; Miethe and Meier, 1994; Sampson and Wooldredge, 1987).

The value of lifestyle-routine activities theory is that it provides a conceptual framework for identifying and classifying factors that might predict victimization. In the model for property offenses, a number of variables derived from this perspective had significant effects. Most noteworthy, with the exception of two variables related to size of dorm, the remaining proximity-to-crime measures were all significantly related to property victimization (as measured by personal larceny with and without contact). Thus, those who lived in an all-male dorm or a coed dorm were more at risk of experiencing a theft on campus than those who lived off campus or in an all-female dorm. One interpretation is that those who reside in dorms with males potentially are in close proximity to "motivated offenders." A twist is that our results suggest that males who live in an all-male dorm with a large number of people are less at risk than those who live in a smaller dorm. A threshold may well exist above which male students realize that their property is among a group of faceless residents who do not share a mutual respect for others' property. It may be at this point that those students take precautions to protect their property from theft. Those who spent long periods of time on campus—full-time students and students who spent many nights on campus—also increased their risk of theft. Given their time commitments on campus, both types of students may find themselves in proximity to motivated offenders for periods of time and, hence, expose themselves to an increased risk of theft.

Also consistent with routine activities theory and previous research, target attractiveness increased victimization. Thus, students who spent more money on nonessential items were likely targets for theft. Similarly, property victimization was related to exposure-to-crime measures. Group membership in a fraternity or sorority reduced the likelihood of experiencing an on-campus theft. This might be a function of the members of such organizations serving as "guardians" for their fellow members' property while the members are away from their property; hence, exposure to crime is low. However, members of athletic groups did not enjoy reduced risks as fraternity and sorority members did; rather their risks were increased.

Contextual variables suggested by the lifestyle-routine activities approach, however, had only limited effects in predicting property victimization—a finding that was obtained for violent victimization as well. None of these factors was related to violent victimization and only two were related to property victimization. First, individual property victimization was higher among those who attended schools with a "climate" of theft (i.e., high overall theft rates). Second, such victimization was lower for those at schools where a larger percentage of students lived on campus. This latter finding might reflect more social integration and thus informal social control on campuses where students live and know one another. Another possibility is that on such campuses less property is available in public places to steal because students leave their belongings in their rooms on campus rather than carrying them around campus as "commuter" students must do.

It is possible that context would make more of a difference if our sample had included a greater number of institutions and thus had a wider variation in contextual measures. It may also be that the kind of contextual variables included in the analysis are not those most closely tied to preventing crime. Recent research by Sampson et al. (1997:918), for example, found that "collective self-efficacy" in neighborhoods—"defined as social cohesion among neighbors combined with their willingness to intervene on behalf on the common good"—was a significant predictor of criminal victimization. We do not measure at the contextual level this kind of informal social control. An alternative possibility, however, is that contextual variables simply are not as important as individual-level variables in predicting victimization on college campuses. Research by Fernandez and Lizotte (1995), for example, found that, with the exception of motor vehicle theft rates, community-level characteristics did not significantly predict campus crime rates (i.e., rape, assault, robbery, and larceny).

Further, beyond possible methodological issues (e.g., the inclusion of a wider range of variables), the failure of census tract variables (SES, age composition) to predict on-campus victimization might well indicate that college campuses are, to a degree, "ivory towers." Thus, the effects of wider contextual variables might be mitigated by the distinct boundaries that often separate college campuses from the community (e.g., gate houses, fences, hedges, and distinct buildings). In large part, contextual variables measure proximity to motivated offenders. As Bottoms (1994:608, 614) notes, however, offenders have "cognitive maps" of their environment; they know some parts of the city well but are more unfamiliar with other parts. Campuses are likely to be places that potential offenders do not "habitually use" and thus are not well integrated into their cognitive maps (see also Brantingham and Brantingham, 1981). Traveling onto a campus to commit a crime—especially if offenders "stand out" socially—may prove too uncomfortable to be practiced regularly. In short, as geographically and socially distinctive space, campuses may insulate themselves from the larger context by erecting both physical and social-psychological barriers to potential offenders.

Two demographics characteristics—age and sex—also influenced the probability of property victimization. Younger students and males appear to be more at risk than their older and female counterparts. These patterns are similar to those found in the NCVS (Bureau of Justice Statistics, 1994). It may be that younger and male students are less vigilant in guarding their property and/or place themselves in situations where they are more exposed to "motivated offenders."

In contrast to property victimization, few of the measures assessing lifestyle-routine activities concepts were related to the risk of being a victim of violent crime. It is possible that similar to other studies (see, e.g., Miethe and Meier, 1994; Sampson and Wooldredge, 1987), the relative infrequency of violent victimization make its prediction more difficult. In our study, for example, only 3% of the respondents experienced violent victimizations on campus. Further, the results may have differed if we could have conducted crime-specific analyses of the violent offenses. Again, this analysis was not possible given the small number of cases for specific types of violent victimizations.

Nonetheless, the lifestyle-routine activities approach was supported by the finding, consistent with past research (see, e.g., Cohen and Felson, 1979; Felson, 1997; Hindelang et al., 1978; Kennedy and Forde, 1990; Miethe and Meier, 1994; Sampson and Lauritsen, 1990), that students who led "risky" lifestyles—that is, who partied on campus several nights per week and were more likely to take recreational drugs—were more likely to be a victim of on-campus violent crime. Students who routinely party on campus at night and take drugs may so increase their exposure to victimization that a violent victimization—which is a relatively rare event—becomes more probable. There is also the possibility that these students contribute to their own victimization by engaging in conduct that precipitates a victimization. Clarifying this issue, however, is beyond the scope of this study.

Further, the data revealed that violent victimization was lower among students who attended a nonmandatory crime prevention program. It is possible, of course, that students more sensitive to victimization, and thus less likely to take more risks, were drawn to these seminars. Even so, it is also plausible that these crime prevention programs have educational value; they furnish students with strategies to avoid victimization on campus.

Conclusion

In closing, this study took seriously Lynch's (1987) suggestion on the importance of studying victimization within delimited social domains. Given the sheer number of people on the nation's campuses and the continuing political salience of crime against college students, investigating victimization in this domain seems an important endeavor. Again, our analysis indicates that college campuses should not be reduced to naive stereotypes—whether that is to portray them as ivory towers or locations for heinous crimes—but instead should be studied to see what kinds of victimization are more or less characteristic of this domain. Further, studying college-student victimization presented an opportunity to undertake a fairly complete test of the lifestyle-routine activities theories of victimization. Our results showed the value of this approach in explaining variations in risks of property victimization and, to a lesser extent, in accounting for the risk of being a victim of violence.

Finally, although beyond the scope of this study, we anticipate that our findings have implications for making college campuses safer. For example, we found that violent victimization was reduced by attending a crime prevention seminar and increased by involvement in nighttime partying on campus and by taking recreational drugs. The simple task of asking someone to watch one's property reduced the risk of being a theft victim. In contrast, the total number of security personnel was unrelated to victimization. Each of these results—and others in the study—is suggestive of strategies that might diminish the risk of victimization (e.g., making efforts to remind students to watch each other's property). More basic and applied research is needed, of course, to solidify knowledge of how best to protect students on the nation's campuses (see, e.g., Fernandez and Lizotte, 1995; Fisher et al., 1997).

NOTES

[1] In the 1993 NCVS results, property crime included thefts. These are now considered household-level crimes and not individual-level crimes, and as a result, are reported as rates per 1,000 households and not rates per 1,000 individuals. In the 1992 NCVS, thefts were considered individual-level crimes, and rates per 1,000 individuals were reported.

[2] We excluded schools with enrollments of less than 1,000 students because almost all of these schools were religious schools (e.g., Bible colleges or Yeshivas), or were specialty medical schools. We wanted to include more typical schools in our study. Additionally, though schools enrolling less than 1,000 students represent about 39% of all four-year colleges and universities in this country, only 6% of post-secondary students in the United States are enrolled in these schools (U.S. Department of Education, 1992). Because students were our main focus, we decided not to include students from these small schools in the study.

[3] These location categories were found in *Peterson's Guide to Four-Year Colleges and Universities* (1993). This was done because the U.S. Department of Education does not col-

lect a location measure similar to what we needed; they compile city, state, and zip-code information but no measure we could use in our proposed stratification design.

[4] We could not compare any individual-level characteristics of those students who completed interviews to those who did [not], for two reasons. First, it was cost prohibitive to purchase any demographic information beyond names and telephone numbers from ASLC. Second, to fulfill the conditions of the Human Subjective Review Committee at the University of Cincinnati, our survey firm was not allowed to give us the names or telephone numbers of the students who completed surveys and those who did not.

[5] We used the 1992 and 1993 NCVS's definition to define the types of crime. Crimes of violence, theft, and against the living quarters include completed and attempted acts.

[6] We used U.S. Census tract-level maps or talked with campus or city planners of the respective school or city to determine which census tracts bordered the boundaries of the campus.

[7] Because of this statistical constraint, we estimated several different models that included individual-level, institutional-level, and community-level measures of our four constructs. We found that the reported estimates of the multilevel logit models are robust. Any changes in the measures did not change the sign, magnitude, or significance level of the results reported in table 2.

[8] We asked several other institutional-level crime education questions, such as having rape awareness programs or having crime prevention programs available for students. These other questions were not used to construct the index because there was no variation across the schools—all claimed to have all the other programs we asked about on the survey. The only variation across schools was in the questions that asked about mandatory participation and self-defense classes.

[9] The on-campus and off-campus percentages will not sum to 37% because a respondent could have experienced one on-campus victimization and two off-campus ones. In this scenario, the student is counted as two victims—once for the calculation of the on-campus percentage and once for the calculation of the off-campus percentage.

[10] One reviewer suggested that we include an off-campus victimization variable in the on-campus violence model so that we could test if off-campus violent victimization predicts on-campus violent victimization (i.e., to "possibly reveal some interesting situational effects on risk that are now hidden by the inherent violence proneness of the person"). We created two dichotomous (victim or not victim) off-campus victimization variables: violence and theft. We reestimated both our models with these variables in the respective on-campus model. Neither variable was significant (off-campus violent victimization, $b = -56$ [s.e. $= .44$] and off-campus theft victimization, $b = .26$ [s.e. $= .32$]), and our initial estimates did not change.

[11] Note that this 20- to 24-year-old group was the only NCVS age category that could be compared with our data either because we did not have comparable groups (e.g., 16 to 19 years old) or because the number of victimizations for our sample age group was too small to make reliable comparisons (e.g., 25 to 34 years old). In any case, the comparison for the 20 to 24 age group covers the majority of students in our sample; 57% of the respondents fall into this category.

REFERENCES

Bausell, Carol, Barker Bausell, and Dorothy Siegel. (1991). *The Links Among Drugs, Alcohol, and Campus Crime*. Towson, MD: Campus Violence Prevention Center. Towson State University.

Belknap, Joanne and Edna Erez. (1995). The victimization of women on college campuses: Courtship violence, date rape and sexual harassment. In Bonnie S. Fisher and John J. Sloan (eds.), *Campus Crime: Legal, Social, and Policy Perspectives.* Springfield, IL: Charles C. Thomas.

Bottoms, Anthony E. (1994). Environmental criminology. In Mike Maguire, Rod Morgan, and Robert Reiner (eds.), *The Oxford Handbook of Criminology.* Oxford: Clarendon Press.

Brantingham, Paul J., and Patricia L. Brantingham. (1981). *Environmental Criminology.* Beverly Hills, CA: Sage.

Bromley, Max L. (1992). Campus and community crime rate comparisons: A statewide study. *Journal of Security Administration* 15:49–64.

———. (1994). Correlates of campus crime: A nationwide exploratory study of large universities. *Journal of Security Administration* 17:37–52.

Bromley, Max L., and Christine S. Sellers. (1996). Violent behavior in college student dating relationships: Implications for campus service providers. *Journal of Contemporary Criminal Justice* 12:1–27.

Bureau of Justice Statistics. (1994). *Criminal Victimization in the United States, 1992.* Washington, DC: Bureau of Justice Statistics.

———. (1996). *Criminal Victimization in the United States, 1993.* Washington, DC: Bureau of Justice Statistics.

———. (1997). *Criminal Victimization in the United States, 1994.* Washington, DC: Bureau of Justice Statistics.

Center for Human Resources. (1995). *National Longitudinal Survey User's Guide 1995.* Columbus: The Ohio State University.

Cohen, Lawrence, and Marcus Felson. (1979). Social change and crime rate trends: A routine activity approach. *American Sociological Review* 44:588–608.

Cohen, Lawrence, James R. Kluegel, and Kenneth C. Land. (1981). Social inequality and predatory criminal victimization: An exposition and formal test of a theory. *American Sociological Review* 46:505–524.

Engs, Ruth C., and David J. Hanson. (1994). Boozing and brawling on campus: A national study of violent problems associated with drinking over the past decade. *Journal of Criminal Justice* 22:171–180.

Felson, Richard B. (1997). Routine activities and involvement in violence as actor, witness, or target. *Violence and Victims* 12:209–221.

Fernandez, Adriana, and Alan J. Lizotte. (1995). An analysis of the relationship between campus crime and community crime: Reciprocal effects? In Bonnie S. Fisher and John J. Sloan (eds.), *Campus Crime: Legal, Social, and Policy Perspectives.* Springfield, IL: Charles C Thomas.

Fisher, Bonnie S. (1995). Crime and fear on campus. *American Academy of Political and Social Science,* May, 85–101.

Fisher, Bonnie S., John J. Sloan, Francis T. Cullen, and Chunmeng Lu. (1997). The on-campus victimization patterns of students: Implications for crime prevention by students and post-secondary institutions. In Steven P. Lab (ed.), *Crime Prevention at a Crossroads.* Cincinnati: Anderson.

Fisher, Bonnie S., John J. Sloan, and Deborah L. Wilkins. (1995). Fear of crime and perceived risk of victimization on an urban university campus: A test of multiple models. In Bonnie S. Fisher and John J. Sloan (eds.), *Campus Crime: Legal, Social, and Policy Perspectives.* Springfield, IL: Charles C Thomas.

Fox, James A., and Daryl A. Hellman. (1985). Location and other correlates of campus crime. *Journal of Criminal Justice* 13:429–444.

General Accounting Office. (1997). *Campus Crime: Difficulties Meeting Federal Reporting Requirement*. Washington, DC: General Accounting Office.

Griffaton, Michael C. (1995). State-level initiatives and campus crime. In Bonnie S. Fisher and John J Sloan (eds.), *Campus Crime: Legal, Social, and Policy Perspectives*. Spring field, IL: Charles C. Thomas.

Hindelang, Michael S., Michael Gottfredson, and James Garofalo. (1978). *Victims of Personal Crime*. Cambridge, MA: Ballinger.

Jensen, Gary F., and David M. Brownfield. (1986). Gender, lifestyles, and victimization: Beyond routine activity theory. *Violence and Victims* 1:85–99.

Kennedy, Leslie W. and David R. Forde. (1990). Routine activities and crime: An analysis of victimization in Canada. *Criminology* 28:137–152.

Koss, Mary P. (1996). The measurement of rape victimization in crime surveys. *Criminal Justice and Behavior* 23:55–69.

Koss, Mary P., Christine A. Gidycz, and Nancy J. Wisniewski. (1987). The scope of rape: Incidence and prevalence of sexual aggression and victimization in a national sample of higher education students. *Journal of Consulting and Clinical Psychology* 55:162–170.

Lively, Kit. (1997). Many murders on campuses involve neither students nor faculty members. *The Chronicle of Higher Education*, June 9:A46.

Lynch, James P. (1987). Routine activity and victimization at work. *Journal of Quantitative Criminology* 3:283–300.

Massey, James L., Marvin D. Krohn, and Lisa M. Bonati. (1989). Property crime and the routine activities of individuals. *Journal of Research in Crime and Delinquency* 26:378–400.

Matthews, Anne D. (1993). The ivory tower becomes an armed camp. *The New York Times Sunday Magazine*, March 7:38–47.

McPheters, Lee R. (1978). Econometric analysis of factors influencing crime on the campus. *Journal of Criminal Justice* 6:47–51.

Miethe, Terance D., Mark C. Stafford, and J. Scott Long. (1987). Social differentiation in criminal victimization: A test of routine activities/lifestyle theories. *American Sociological Review* 52:184–194.

Miethe, Terance D., and Robert F. Meier. (1990). Opportunity, choice, and criminal victimization: A test of a theoretical model. *Journal of Research in Crime and Delinquency* 27:243–266.

———. (1994). *Crime and Its Social Context: Toward an Integrated Theory of Offenders, Victims, and Situations*. Albany: State University of New York.

Peterson's Guide. (1993). *Peterson's Guide to Four Year Colleges and Universities*, 1994. Princeton, NJ: Peterson's Guide.

Powell, John W., Michael S. Pander, and Robert C. Nielsen. (1994). *Campus Security and Law Enforcement*. 2d ed. Boston: Butterworth-Heinemann.

Reaves, Brian and Andrew L. Goldberg. (1996). *Campus Law Enforcement Agencies, 1995*. Washington DC: Bureau of Justice Statistics.

Rickgarn, Ralph L. (1989). Violence in the residence halls: Campus domestic violence. In Jan M. Sherrill and Dorothy G. Siegel (eds.), *Responding to Violence on Campus*. San Francisco: Jossey-Bass.

Rivinus, Timothy M. and Mary E. Larimer. (1993). Violence, alcohol, other drugs, and the college student. In Jeffrey W. Pollard and Leighton C. Whitaker (eds.), *Campus Violence: Kinds, Causes, and Cures*. New York: Haworth Press.

Rosenbaum, Dennis P. (1987). Community crime prevention: A review and synthesis of the literature. *Justice Quarterly* 5:323–395.

Sampson, Robert J. (1985). Neighborhood and crime: The structural determinants of personal victimization. *Journal of Research in Crime and Delinquency* 22:7–40.

———. (1987). Personal violence by strangers: An extension and test of the opportunity model of predatory victimization. *Journal of Criminal Law and Criminology* 78:327–356.

Sampson, Robert J., and Janet L. Lauritsen. (1990). Deviant lifestyles, proximity to crime, and the offender-victim link in personal violence. *Journal of Research in Crime and Delinquency* 27:110–139.

Sampson, Robert J., Stephen W. Raundenbush, and Felton Earls. (1997). Neighborhoods and violent crime: A multilevel study of collective efficacy. *Science* 277:918–924.

Sampson, Robert J., and John Wooldredge. (1987). Linking the micro- and macro-level dimensions of lifestyle-routine activity and opportunity models of predatory victimization. *Journal of Quantitative Criminology* 3:371–393.

Schwartz, Martin D., and Victoria L. Pitts. (1995). Exploring a feminist routine activities approach to explaining sexual assault. *Justice Quarterly* 12:9–31.

Siegel, Dorothy G., and Carlinda H. Raymond. (1992). An ecological approach to violent crime on campus. *Journal of Security Administration* 15:19–27.

Sigler, Robert T., and Nancy M. Koehler. (1993). Victimization and crime on campus. *International Review of Victimology* 2:331–343.

Skogan, Wesley S., and Michael G. Maxfield. (1981). *Coping with Crime: Individual and Neighborhood Differences.* Beverly Hills, CA: Sage.

Sloan, John J. (1992). Campus crime and campus communities: An analysis of crimes known to campus police and security. *Journal of Security Administration* 15:31–46.

———. (1994) The correlates of campus crime: An analysis of reported crimes on college and university campuses. *Journal of Criminal Justice* 22:51–61.

Sloan, John J., Bonnie S. Fisher, and Francis T. Cullen. (1997). Assessing the Student Right-to-Know and Campus Security Act of 1990: An analysis of the victim reporting practices of college and university students. *Crime and Delinquency* 43:148–168.

Sloan, John J., Bonnie S. Fisher, and Deborah L. Wilkins. (1995). *Crime, Fear of Crime, and Related Issues on the U.A.B. Campus: Final Report.* Birmingham: University of Alabama at Birmingham.

Smith, Michael C., and Richard Fossey. (1995). *Crime on Campus: Legal Issues and Campus Administration.* Phoenix, AZ: The Oryx Press.

U.S. Department of Education. (1992). *State Higher Education Profiles,* 3d ed. Washington, DC: U.S. Department of Education.

———. (1993). *State Higher Education Profiles,* 4th ed. Washington, DC: U.S. Department of Education.

———. (1995). *Digest of Education Statistics,* 1995. Washington, DC: U.S. Department of Education.

Wechsler, Henry, Andrea Davenport, George Dowdall, Barbara Moeykens, and Sonia Castillo. (1994). Health and behavioral consequences of binge drinking in college: A national survey of students at 140 campuses. *Journal of the American Medical Association* 272:1672–1677.

Chapter Eight

Attributions of Self-Blame and Perceived Control as Moderators of Adjustment in Battered Women

Melanie L. O'Neill
Patricia K. Kerig

Although the negative effects of battering have been clearly documented, some women are able to be resilient despite exposure to such extreme stress. Understanding the factors that promote resilience is important for the development of effective interventions. By targeting those specific factors that allow women to psychologically survive abuse, interventions can effectively foster coping efficacy in victims of domestic violence. It was the purpose of the present study to investigate the role of one potential source of resiliency: the attributions women make about their experience of battering in intimate relationships.

Battered women's cognitive appraisals of their victimization play an important role in their psychological adjustment (see Weaver & Clum, 1995). Appraisals influence many aspects of the violent experience including the degree to which the violence is experienced as stressful, interpretations of the cause, of the violence, and the meaning of one's experience with violence; subsequent attributions are central in the management of emotional and psychological reactions (Lazarus & Folkman, 1984; Taylor, 1983). In particular, attributions of self-blame and perceived control have been identified as important moderators to the process of adjustment to stress and trauma, including the stress of physical abuse (Folkman, 1984; Janoff-Bulman, 1992; Tennen & Affleck, 1990).

Perceived control is the belief in one's ability to influence events in one's life or control one's own outcome. According to Skinner (1992), every individual has an inherent need to feel capable of producing desired events and avoiding

From *Journal of Interpersonal Violence*, 15(10): 1036–1049, copyright © 2000 by Sage Publications, Inc. Reprinted by permission of Sage Publications, Inc.

the undesired. This need provides perceived control with its capacity to regulate behavior and emotion under conditions of stress. Greater levels of perceived control can positively impact psychological adjustment across a variety of negative life events (Frazier & Schauben, 1994; Taylor, Lichtman, & Wood, 1984).

Perceived control over abuse can moderate the degree of psychological symptoms in battered women (Follingstad, Brennan, Hause, Polek, & Rutledge, 1991). The experience of emotional and physical violence by one's intimate partner can engender uncertainty, loss of control, and feelings of helplessness. Taylor (1983) suggested that generating beliefs of personal control over an acute stressor, its resultant effects, and life in general, can be one way to counteract feelings of vulnerability and helplessness. In addition, the perceived controllability of stressful events may impact the extent to which one attempts to alter a stressful environment, as opposed to just tolerating or adjusting to the adverse environment (Compas, Banez, Malcarne, & Worsham, 1991). Clearly, the role of perceived control in the psychological adjustment of battered women warrants further investigation.

Many individuals assume blame or personal responsibility following the experience of a traumatic event. Consequently, the attribution of self-blame has stimulated a considerable amount of research in the victimization literature (e.g., Abramson, Seligman, & Teasdale, 1978; Brewin, 1986, 1990; Brown & Siegel, 1988). Whereas self-blame is generally characterized as a maladaptive attributional response predictive of poor adjustment, Janoff-Bulman (1979) contended that self-blame may enhance the perception of future event avoidability. Furthermore, Porter (1983) suggested that the perception of future events as modifiable may be preferable to the admission that life experiences occur haphazardly. Taken together, these points suggest that a battered woman may challenge and overcome feelings of helplessness by assuming some degree of personal responsibility. However, research findings are mixed, and the adaptivity of self-blame as a coping mechanism continues to be controversial.

Janoff-Bulman's (1979) distinction between behavioral and characterological dimensions of self-blame challenges the previously untested assumption that self-blame is globally maladaptive. Behavioral self-blame involves attribution to a controllable or modifiable aspect of the self, such as one's actions or conduct, whereas characterological self-blame involves attributions to uncontrollable aspects of the self, such as one's character or disposition. Janoff-Bulman (1979) theorized that behavioral self-blame may be beneficial if it increases perceived control. This assumption should be reexamined in relation to the sense of control it gives to women involved in a violent relationship.

The clinical implications of the theory are important because the idea that self-blame is an adaptive attribution is inconsistent with current counseling strategies (Moss, 1991). Treatment strategies typically emphasize the elimination of self-blame and an increase in the focus on external factors (Frazier, 1990). If behavioral self-blame is associated with increased perceived control and better adjustment then counselors would need to reevaluate this approach to treatment. However, it is important to first determine whether the impact on adjustment is a function of behavioral self-blame or perceived control.

First, we hypothesized that women involved in abusive relationships would show a greater tendency toward self-blame compared with women who had left their abuser. We also expected that women who left the relationship would display higher levels of perceived control than women who remained with their abusive partner. The association between self-blame and perceived control with psychological adjustment will also be assessed. Second, we predicted that women who display higher levels of behavioral self-blame and perceived control would have lower ratings of symptomatology. Third, we hypothesized that the effect of battering on psychological symptoms would be moderated by attributions of self-blame and perceived control. We expected women who display characterological self-blame to show greater distress.

Method

PARTICIPANTS

A total of 160 women were recruited from battered women's shelters ($n = 128$) and support groups ($n = 13$) as well as through advertisements placed in community and campus newspapers ($n = 19$) in the province of British Columbia. Of this total, 78 women were currently involved in an abusive relationship, whereas 82 women had left the relationship.

Demographic data collected from the women indicated that participants were 76% White, 13% Native, 4% African Canadian, and 4% Hispanic. Thirty-five percent of the women had a high school education whereas 36% had some vocational school or college. Demographic variables did not significantly differ by recruitment source or relationship status.

PROCEDURE

Transition homes and support groups were initially contacted by telephone. The agencies that decided to participate either agreed to have the researcher personally distribute the questionnaire or, in the interest of location security, distribute the questionnaire themselves. The remainders were completed through transition house visits or phone interviews recruited through newspaper ads.

MEASURES

Extent of abuse

The frequency and severity of male physical violence were measured using the Conflict Tactics Scale (CTS) (Straus, 1979). The 18-item CTS consists of three subscales that assess Reasoning, Verbal Aggression, and Physical Violence. The extent of physical abuse was assessed using the 8-item Physical Violence subscale. This subscale ranges in severity from "threw something at the other one" to "used a knife or gun." Participants rated the frequency (0 = *from never occurred* to 6 = *occurred more than 20 times*) of their partner's abusive behavior during the past year. The CTS is scored by summing the frequency ratings over the 8 items, allowing a range of possible scores from 0 to 48. The reliability of the CTS ranges from .79 on the Verbal Aggression scale to .82 on the Physical Violence scale (Straus, 1979). The alpha coefficient for the Physical Violence subscale in this sample was .89.

Psychological symptoms

The type and severity of psychological symptoms were measured using the short form of the Hopkins Symptom Checklist (HSCL) (Derogatis, Lipman, Rickels, Uhlenhuth, & Covi, 1974). The HSCL is a self-report symptom-rating inventory that is widely used in a number of different clinical settings. The questionnaire includes measures of somatization, interpersonal sensitivity, obsessive compulsivity, and depression. Because depression has been implicated as one of the most severe and serious consequences of battering, the remaining 10 items from the 58-item long form of the HSCL were added to the questionnaire. Participants were asked how much this problem has bothered them in the past week. Each item on the inventory is rated on a 4-point scale of distress, ranging from *not at all* to *a lot*. The HSCL General Feelings of Distress (GFD) score is calculated by summing the frequency ratings over the 31 items, allowing a range of possible scores from 31 to 124. This measure demonstrates good psychometric properties and has high internal consistency (Green, Walkey, McCormick, & Taylor, 1988). The alpha coefficients for the four subscales ranged from .70 to .89 in this sample. The alpha for the GFD score was .94.

Behavioral and characterological self-blame. The levels of behavioral and characterological self-blame were measured by a questionnaire developed by the researchers specifically for the purposes of this study. The questionnaire consists of six questions for each dimension of blame. Examples of characterological self-blame are items stating the belief that one is to blame for the abuse because of physical appearance or personality traits. Examples of behavioral self-blame are items stating the belief that one is to blame for the abuse because of nagging or failure to remove oneself from the abusive situation. Each item on the questionnaire is rated on a 6-point scale, ranging from *strongly disagree* to *strongly agree*. The questionnaire is scored by summing the ratings for each dimension of self-blame across each of the six items, allowing a range of possible scores from 6 to 36. The internal consistency coefficients for this measure were adequate with alpha's of .71 and .78 for behavioral and characterological self-blame, respectively.

Perceived control

Beliefs about personal control were assessed using an adapted version of the Pearlin and Schooler's Self-Mastery Scale (Pearlin & Schooler, 1978). The questionnaire consisted of six items taken from the seven-item scale. One item was deleted from the scale due to poor internal consistency. Examples of the perceived control items are statements about the belief that one has little control over the future or over the events in life. Each item on the scale is rated on a 6-point scale, ranging from *strongly disagree* to *strongly agree*. The Self-Mastery Scale is scored by summing the ratings over the six items, allowing a range of possible scores from 6 to 36. The alpha coefficient for this measure was .80.

Results

ABUSE CHARACTERISTICS

Percentages, means, and standard deviations for abuse characteristics are presented in table 1. Fifty-seven percent of the women reported being beaten by their partners within the past year and 20% reported being beaten up more than 20 times in the past year. Fifteen percent of the women reported a knife or gun being used against them in the past year, whereas 3% of the women reported a knife or gun being used against them more than 20 times in the past year.

RELATIONSHIP BETWEEN STATUS, SELF-BLAME, AND PERCEIVED CONTROL

t tests assessed whether women who were currently involved or not involved in an abusive relationship differed in their attributions for the abuse. As shown in table 2, women still involved in the abusive relationship were higher in both behavioral and characterological self-blame when compared with women who had left the relationship. In contrast, women who had left their abuser displayed higher levels of perceived control in comparison with women still involved in the situation.

RELATIONSHIP BETWEEN SELF-BLAME, PERCEIVED CONTROL, AND PSYCHOLOGICAL ADJUSTMENT

Correlations were calculated among the attributional measures of characterological self-blame, behavioral self-blame, perceived control, and the outcome measure of psychological symptoms. As shown in table 3, both characterological and behavioral self-blame were positively correlated with psychological symptoms. However, perceived control was negatively correlated with psychological symptoms with the exception of somatization.

Table 1
Means, Standard Deviations, and Percentages for
Conflict Tactics Scale Physical Violence Subscale Items

Item	M	SD	Experienced in Past Year (%)
Threw something at the other one	2.61	2.42	64.4
Pushed, grabbed, or shoved	3.96	2.21	85.6
Slapped	2.81	2.51	63.7
Kicked, bit, or hit with a fist	2.73	2.50	65.0
Hit or tried to hit with something	2.59	2.45	65.6
Beat up	2.11	2.34	56.9
Threatened with a knife or gun	1.08	1.75	39.4
Used a knife or gun	0.38	1.19	15.0

NOTE: N = 160

Table 2
t Tests for Differences between Women Involved and Women Not Involved in the Abusive Relationship on Self-Blame and Perceived Control

Variable	Involved (*n* = 78)	Not Involved (*n* = 82)	t (df)
Characterological self-blame			3.57 (156.06)***
M	18.78	15.29	
SD	6.36	5.98	
Behavioral self-blame			4.15 (157.96)***
M	21.83	16.62	
SD	7.80	8.07	
Perceived control			−4.51 (148.98)***
M	23.06	26.83	
SD	5.76	4.72	

***$p < .001$

Table 3
Pearson Product-Moment Correlations between Self-Blame, Perceived Control, and Psychological Adjustment

Symptom	Characterological Self-Blame	Behavioral Self-Blame	Perceived Control
Depression	.36***	.41***	−.32***
Interpersonal sensitivity	.37***	.41***	−.30***
Obsessive compulsivity	.21**	.23**	−.17*
Somatization	.12	.13	.09

*$p < .05$
**$p < .01$
***$p < .001$

To compare the impact of involvement in an abusive relationship, both dimensions of self-blame and perceived control were correlated with psychological symptoms. The calculations were performed separately for women involved and for women not involved in the relationship. Perceived control emerged as a variable that significantly differentiated the two groups. For women currently involved in the abusive relationship, perceived control was correlated with depression ($r = -.32, p < .001$) and interpersonal sensitivity ($r = -.27, p < .01$). For women not involved in the abusive relationship, perceived control was not associated with higher levels of psychological symptoms. For women currently involved in the relationship, both dimensions of blame were associated with higher psychological symptoms ($p < .001$). For women not involved in an abusive relationship, behavioral self-blame was associated with higher psychological symptoms ($r = .25, p < .05$).

MODERATIONAL EFFECTS OF SELF-BLAME
AND PERCEIVED CONTROL ON PSYCHOLOGICAL ADJUSTMENT

Using the method recommended by Baron and Kenny (1986), a series of hierarchical multiple regressions assessed whether characterological self-blame, behavioral self-blame, or perceived control moderated the relationship between physical violence and psychological symptoms. The subscales of interpersonal sensitivity, obsessive compulsivity, depression, and somatization were highly intercorrelated ($r = .52$ to $.80$, all $p < .001$) and, therefore, were combined into one total symptom score.

As shown in table 4, results of the multiple regressions revealed that characterological self-blame, behavioral self-blame, and perceived control predicted the relationship between physical violence and psychological symptoms. Higher levels of characterological self-blame increased symptom levels, especially when the relationship was severely abusive. As the level of behavioral self-blame increased, symptoms were significantly increased across all levels of physical violence. Perceived control decreased symptoms at all levels of the physically abusive relationship but had a particularly strong effect when the relationship was moderately abusive.

Discussion

This study examined the role of characterological self-blame, behavioral self-blame, and perceived control in the psychological adjustment of battered women. The results of this study demonstrated that characterological and behavioral self-blame were associated with negative adjustment whereas perceived control was associated with positive adjustment.

The first objective of this study examined the hypothesis that levels of self-blame and perceived control would differ as a function of relationship status. As hypothesized, women currently involved in the abusive relationship were significantly higher on both dimensions of self-blame and significantly lower in perceived control. The higher self-blame found in women currently involved in an abusive relationship is consistent with previous findings, suggesting that the need for attributions is intensified when one is exposed to an uncontrollable event (Barnett, Martinez, & Keyson, 1996; Brewin, 1990). Attributions may enable women to maintain the belief that the stressors experienced are predictable and, therefore, controllable. The higher levels of perceived control found in women not involved in the abusive relationship suggests that the perception of control may have a significant impact on a woman's decision to leave the abusive situation. Furthermore, perceived control may be an effective mechanism that enables women to be resilient in the face of intimate violence. This may be a particularly useful tool for counselors working with women still involved in abusive relationships. Increasing the perception of control may act as a catalyst for the decision to leave.

Table 4
Hierarchical Multiple Regressions: Appraisals as Moderators of the Relationship between Spousal Violence and Symptoms

Variable	B	SE B	β	R^2	$R^2\Delta$
Violence	0.11	.04	.22	.05	.05*
Characterological self-blame	1.06	.25	.32	.15	.10***
Violence × Characterological	−0.01	.01	−.19	.16	.01*
Violence	0.11	.04	.22	.05	.05**
Behavioral self-blame	0.96	.19	.38	.19	.14***
Violence × Behavioral	−0.01	.00	−.37	.21	.02*
Violence	0.11	.04	.22	.05	.05*
Perceived control	−0.66	.31	−.24	.12	.07*
Violence × Perceived Control	−0.02	.01	−.79	.17	.05*

Note: $N = 160$
* $p < .05$
** $p < .01$
*** $p < .001$

The second objective of the study examined the relationships among attributions of characterological self-blame, behavioral self-blame, perceived control, and adjustment in battered women. As expected, characterological self-blame was associated with higher depression, interpersonal sensitivity, and obsessive compulsive symptoms. Unexpectedly, behavioral self-blame was also associated with higher symptom levels. This finding is consistent with Frazier (1990), who found that both types of self-blame were significantly associated with increased depression in victims of rape. In contrast, and as hypothesized, perceived control was found to be negatively associated with psychological symptoms. This result supports Cohen and Edwards's (1989) conclusion that feelings of control consistently relate to better adjustment across a variety of stressful life events.

Contrary to Janoff-Bulman's (1979) hypothesis, both behavioral and characterological self-blame negatively impacted psychological adjustment. The apparent maladaptiveness of behavioral self-blame could be due to several reasons. First, the distinctions between behavioral self-blame and characterological self-blame in Janoff-Bulman's (1979) model may not be made by victims of domestic violence. Consistent with Frazier and Schauben's (1994) findings with victims of rape, the correlations between both types of self-blame indicate that it may be hard to blame one's behavior without also blaming one's character.

Second, behavioral self-blame may derive from a false belief. In other words, as Janoff-Bulman suggested, although the attribution of behavioral self-blame may enhance perceived control, the belief that a battered woman can stop the abuse through her own behavior may be erroneous. As Taylor et al. (1984) stated, it is necessary to focus on the actual physical benefits of attributions and not just the psychological ones. Thus, whereas behavioral self-blame may increase the perception of control and encourage women to continue in the abusive relationship, the physical consequences of remaining may have a negative impact on adjustment.

Furthermore, the attribution of behavioral self-blame may be complicated by the repeated nature of domestic violence. Taylor et al. (1984) emphasize that distinguishing between events that are ongoing versus those that are not may distinguish when attributions do or do not have functional consequences. Janoff-Bulman's (1979) study focused on the attributions of rape victims. Consequently, these findings may not be generalizable to a population where the violence is ongoing. The majority of women who participated in the study experienced physical violence on a regular basis.

The third main objective of this study examined the extent to which characterological self-blame, behavioral self-blame, and perceived control moderated the effects of violence on battered women's reported level of psychological symptoms. Both characterological and behavioral self-blame moderated the relationship between physical violence and adjustment. As hypothesized, an increase in characterological self-blame was associated with higher symptom levels. Unexpectedly, an increase in behavioral self-blame was also associated with higher symptom levels. It may be that self-blame, whether characterological or behavioral, is not an adaptive mechanism for adjustment. In contrast, and as expected, perceived control moderated the relationship between physical violence and adjustment. An increase in perceived control was related to lower symptom levels. Consistent with Frazier's (1990) findings with victims of rape, perceived control was found to be beneficial but not when linked to the construct of self-blame.

These findings have important clinical applications. Women with abusive male partners must use certain coping mechanisms to comprehend and deal with the battering. Follingstad, Neckerman, and Vormbrock (1988) concluded that by serving basic psychological needs, self-blame may be superficially adaptive for battered women. However, these beliefs may give the woman an illusion of control over the abusive situation and ultimately encourage her continuation of the relationship. In this study, the finding that women who were involved in the relationship had higher levels of blame corresponds with this conclusion. Generally, as the length of the relationship increases so too does the severity of abuse (Cascardi & O'Leary, 1992). Increasing perceived control may be one mechanism for counselors to use before the abuse reaches critical and potentially fatal levels. Furthermore, the findings that both types of self-blame are maladaptive support the approach taken by most counselors (Katz & Mazur, 1979). The findings of this study suggest that the elimination of self-blame for battered women is important for better adjustment.

There are some methodological limitations to be taken into consideration when interpreting these results. First, a significant proportion of the participants described abusive situations, both physical and psychological, that were not addressed by the CTS. Women described events such as "sexual assault" or "strangulation" and "the slaying of pet animals." Future researchers should consider expanding the measure to include other abusive events that frequently occur. Second, the experimenter-designed measure of self-blame has no established psychometric data. And, third, there are the usual limitations involved with retrospective self-report measures gathered from a nonrandomly selected sample that need to be considered. Demand characteristics may have played a role in this study. The majority of the participants were recruited from battered women's shelters and support groups. Counseling efforts with battered women focus heavily on the elimination of beliefs about self-blame. Consequently, counseling efforts may have affected the reported levels of self-blame.

Longitudinal studies are needed to assess lifetime prevalence rates and to differentiate the effects between one-time violence and the cumulative effects of trauma. Furthermore, differentiation of life events could significantly increase our understanding of attributions and adjustment. For example, behavioral self-blame was associated with better outcomes for certain victim groups (Turnquist, Harvey, & Andersen, 1988). It would also be useful to include a control group of women who have never been abused to determine the exact extent of the effects of abuse on women's functioning. And finally, the effect of emotional abuse in relation to self-blame should also be considered.

The results of this study demonstrate that perceived control positively impacts the resiliency of battered women. Taylor et al. (1984) concluded that the strong relationship between perceived control and adjustment emphasizes the import of research examining attributions of control. The results of this study confirm this statement and suggest that counseling efforts with battered women intended to increase perceived control will have a positive impact on psychological adjustment.

REFERENCES

Abramson, L. Y, Seligman, M. E., & Teasdale, J. P. (1978). Learned helplessness in humans: Critique and reformulation. *Journal of Abnormal Psychology, 87,* 49–74.

Barnett, O. W., Martinez, T. E., & Keyson, M. (1996). The relationship between violence, social support, and self-blame in battered women. *Journal of Interpersonal Violence, 11*(2), 221–233.

Baron, R. M., & Kenny, D. A. (1986). The moderator-mediator variable distinction in social psychological research: Conceptual, strategic, and statistical considerations. *Journal of Personality and Social Psychology, 51*(6), 1173–1182.

Brewin, C. R. (1986). Internal attribution and self-esteem in depression: A theoretical note. *Cognitive Research and Therapy, 10,* 469–475.

Brewin, C. R. (1990). Attributions of blame for marital violence: A study of antecedent and consequences. *Journal of Marriage and the Family, 52,* 757–767.

Brown, J. D., & Siegel, J. M. (1988). Attributions for negative life events and depression: The role of perceived control. *Journal of Personality and Social Psychology, 54*(2), 316–322.

Cascardi, M., & O'Leary, K. D. (1992). Depressive symptomatology, self-esteem, and self-blame in battered women. *Journal of Family Violence, 7*(4), 249–259.

Cohen, S., & Edwards, J. R. (1989). Personality characteristics as moderators of the relationship between stress and disorder. In W. I. Neufeld (ed.), *Advances in the investigation of psychological stress* (pp. 235–283). New York: Wiley.

Compas, B. E., Banez, G. A., Malcarne, V., & Worsham, N. (1991). Perceived control and coping with stress: A developmental perspective. *Journal of Social Issues, 47*(4), 23–34.

Derogatis, L. R., Lipman, R. S., Rickels, K., Uhlenhuth, E. H., & Covi, L. (1974). The Hopkins Symptom Checklist (HSCL): A self-report symptom inventory. *Behavioral Science, 19,* 1–14.

Folkman, S. (1984). Personal control and stress and coping processes: A theoretical analysis. *Journal of Personality and Social Psychology, 46,* 839–852.

Follingstad, D. R., Brennan, A. F., Hause, E. S., Polek, D. S., & Rutledge, L. L. (1991). Factors moderating physical and psychological symptoms of battered women. *Journal of Family Violence, 6,* 81–95.

Follingstad, D. R., Neckerman, A. P., & Vormbrock, J. (1988). Reactions to victimization and coping strategies of battered women: The ties that bind. *Clinical Psychological Review, 8,* 373–390.

Frazier, P, A. (1990). Victim attributions and post-rape trauma. *Journal of Personality and Social Psychology, 59*(2), 298–304.

Frazier, P. A., & Schauben, L. (1994). Causal attributions and recovery from rape and other stressful life events. *Journal of Social and Clinical Psychology, 13*(1), 1–14.

Green, D. E., Walkey, F. H., McCormick, I. A., & Taylor, A. J. W. (1988). Hopkins Symptom Checklist with New Zealand and United States respondents. *Australian Journal of Psychology, 40*(1), 61–70.

Janoff-Bulman, R. (1979). Characterological versus behavioral self-blame: Inquiries into depression and rape. *Journal of Personality and Social Psychology, 37*(10), 1798–1809.

Janoff-Bulman, R. (1992). *Shattered assumptions: Towards a new psychology of trauma.* New York: Free Press.

Katz, B., & Mazur, M. (1979). *Understanding the rape victim.* New York: Wiley.

Lazarus, R. S., & Folkman, S. (1984). *Stress, appraisal, and coping.* New York: Springer-Verlag.

Moss, V. A. (1991). Battered women and the myth of masochism. *Journal of Psychosocial Nursing, 29*(7), 9–23.

Pearlin, L. L., & Schooler, C. (1978). The structure of coping. *Journal of Health and Social Behavior, 19,* 2–21.

Porter, C. A. (1983). Blame, depression and coping in battered women. Unpublished doctoral dissertation, University of British Columbia, British Columbia, Canada.

Skinner, E. A. (1992). Perceived control: Motivation, coping, and development. In R. Schwarzer (ed.). *Self-efficacy: Thought control of action* (pp. 91–106). Washington, DC: Hemisphere.

Straus, M. A. (1979). Measuring intrafamily conflict and violence: The Conflict Tactics Scale. *Journal of Marriage and the Family, 41,* 75–88.

Taylor, S. E. (1983). Adjustment to threatening events: A theory of cognitive adaptation. *American Psychologist, 38,* 1161–1173.

Taylor, S. R, Lichtman, R. R., & Wood, J. V. (1984). Attributions, beliefs about control, and adjustment to breast cancer. *Journal of Personality and Social Psychology, 46*(3), 489–502.

Tennen, H., & Affleck, G. (1990). Blaming others for threatening events. *Psychological Bulletin, 108,* 209–232.

Turnquist, D., Harvey, J., & Andersen, B. (1988). Attributions and adjustment to life-threatening illness. *British Journal of Clinical Psychology, 27,* 55–65.

Weaver, T. L., & Clum, G. A. (1995). Psychological distress associated with interpersonal violence: A meta-analysis. *Clinical Psychology Review, 15*(2), 115–140.

Chapter Nine

Labeling Partner Violence
When Do Victims Differentiate among Acts?

Sherry L. Hamby
Bernadette Gray-Little

When is a woman a battered woman? If her partner has physically assaulted her, is she battered as of the first time? The second? Must the assault be of a minimum level of severity? Relatively little empirical attention has been paid to these questions, although it is clear that the answers are a source of controversy. On the one hand, some domestic violence professionals advocate using labels such as "battering" for all physical violence (e.g., Hamberger & Arnold, 1989), what might be called an "inclusive" perspective. Advocates of this perspective assert that if the definition of battering needs to be changed at all, then it should be made broader to incorporate all acts of coercive control (Stark, 1995). They argue that applying a "calculus of harms" (Stark, 1995, p. 980) that discriminates among victims of violence can lead to minimizing some forms of violence. Such a strategy may limit the scope of public policy and intervention and, in the long run, reduce protection for assault victims. Most prevention and intervention programs in Western countries adopt an inclusive strategy; that is, the definitions of "abuse" and "violence" tend to be broad and the cessation of all violence, including controlling and abusive behavior, is the treatment goal (e.g., Gondolf, 1995; McMahon & Pence, 1996; Pence & Paymar, 1993; also see Feldman & Ridley, 1995, for a review). Recent policy initiatives tend to adopt an inclusive perspective as well (e.g., Domestic Violence: Probation Act of California, 1995; Department of Public Health, Commonwealth of Massachusetts, 1995).

From *Violence and Victims*, 15(2): 173–186, copyright © 2000 by Springer Publishing Company, Inc., New York 10012. Used by permission.

Other professionals argue that there are equal dangers in labeling all violence the same (e.g., Rouse, 1989). From this "differentiating" perspective, using the same terms for all physical force trivializes the experiences of women who have suffered the most horrific extremes of violence. Those advocating distinctions among levels and forms of violence suggest that their approach will be most helpful in terms of shaping theory, policy, and intervention because of the potential increases in specificity in each of these domains (Jacobson, Gottman, & Shortt, 1995; Johnson, 1995; O'Leary, 1996; Rouse, Breen & Howell, 1988; Sedlak, 1988). Recent theoretical and empirical work suggests a marked trend in the direction of differentiating among levels of violence. Studies that differentiate among levels of violence are becoming increasingly common (e.g., Gottman et al., 1995). For example, many authors separate violence into minor forms, such as grabbing, versus more severe forms, such as beating up (Hamby, Poindexter, & Gray-Little, 1996; Sugarman, Aldarondo, & Boney-McCoy, 1996). Johnson (1995) has suggested that partner violence be divided into "patriarchal terrorism" and "common couple violence." These authors believe such a shift would have significant implications for the field.

Although the distinction between the inclusive and differentiating perspectives has been fairly well articulated among domestic violence professionals, little is known about the labeling strategies of women who have sustained physical assault by their partners. Much of what is known focuses on perceived deficits in the strategies that women use to label their experience of relationship violence. Apparently, battered women do not adopt the same inclusive labeling strategy as most domestic violence activists. Usually, victims' unwillingness to apply abuse-related labels is seen as pathological and evidence of denial about the seriousness of their situation (e.g., Ferraro, 1983; Graham, Rawlings, & Rigsby, 1994; Henton, Cate, Koval, Lloyd, & Christopher, 1983; Herbert, Silver, & Ellard, 1991; Walker, 1984, 1993). For example, the symptom of denial is a primary focus of research on the Battered Woman Syndrome (Walker, 1984) and the Stockholm Syndrome (Graham et al., 1994). That research, however, is driven by an inclusive perspective and has not specifically examined the link between victimization experiences and labels. A more accurate, less deficit-focused understanding of victims' perspectives on violence is needed. Although denial may lead some victims to reject abuse labels, it is also possible that rejection of abuse labels by some assaulted women reflects a differentiating perspective on violence more than it reflects denial. Some domestic violence researchers reserve abuse-related labels for a subset of physical assaults, and it is possible that this is also the labeling strategy adopted by the broader community.

This article focuses on the labeling strategies—the link between act and name—used by women who have sustained physical assault. Specifically, we examined their application of labels such as "abuse," "victim" and "battered" to physical force experienced in intimate relationships. We investigated women's use of labels for their own experiences and for violence experienced by others. Because not all assaulted women see themselves as abused (e.g., Graham et al.,

1994; Walker, 1984), the first hypothesis was that labeling would not be universal; that is, that some women would decline to endorse abuse-related labels for physical violence. Second, we hypothesized that attributes of the violence would influence the use of labels; we expected that more frequent and more severe force would be associated with greater use of labels, consistent with a differentiating strategy. Third, we hypothesized that attributes of the women and of their relationships would influence their use of labels. Past research conducted with women seeking assistance for abuse (Babcock, Waltz, Jacobson, & Gottman, 1993; Strube, 1988) has documented that level of commitment, resources, and relationship power influence whether women leave relationships, but these factors have not previously been explored in nonhelpseeking samples. We hypothesized that the same relationship factors will also influence the use of abuse labels in our community sample. Other differences associated with demographic and relationship characteristics were explored.

Method

RESPONDENTS

The respondents were 78 women from a random sample of all nonfaculty female employees at a large southeastern state university. The 78 respondents for this study are the women who indicated that "physical force" had been used against them at least once in their current or most recent relationship (39% of all 200 respondents). The study included questions on responses to violence in addition to those presented here (cf. Hamby & Gray-Little, 1997). The women averaged 38.7 years of age (*SD* 9.62). They were generally White (79%), had at least some college, and had average to above-average incomes (median income $20,000 to $24,000). Most were married (80%) and 75% had been with the current partner for several years. Most (69%) had at least one child. The respondents' partners had virtually identical demographic characteristics, except that their partners had a higher median income ($25,000 to $29,999 per year). Thus household income for the majority of respondents was more than $45,000. All partners were males.

PROCEDURE

Respondents for the study were randomly selected from the campus directory and contacted at work. An initial letter of inquiry (with response card) was followed by telephone contact for those who did not respond. The overall response rate was 51%. Respondents were contacted at work to give them the opportunity to complete the questionnaires without their partner's knowledge. Questionnaires, presented in a booklet, were sent to those who agreed to participate. It took approximately 30–40 minutes to complete the questionnaires. Follow-up letters were mailed 1 week after the questionnaires. In order to reduce the imposition on those who did not wish to participate, the reason for nonparticipation was not solicited, but most who volunteered a reason said that they were not in a relationship. For the analyses below, respondents who had not experienced any partner violence were excluded, as the focus of the study is on the labeling patterns among victims of physical force.

LABELING MEASURES

All measures were pretested with a group of 96 females prior to use in the present study.

Self-Labeling (Labeling of Personally Experienced Violence)

Three items assessed whether women applied to themselves some of the labels commonly adopted by violence researchers. The items were chosen to tap into the emotionally laden language that often surrounds discourse in this area. Each item was presented as a Likert-type scale that ranged from 1 ("Definitely Not") to 7 ("Definitely"). The abuse label referred to their description of the "worst" forceful incident in their relationship: "Do you believe this event is an instance of physical abuse?" The victim label asked whether they applied the term "victim" to themselves ("Do you think of yourself as a victim of violence?"), and the battered label was similarly phrased ("Do you think of yourself as a battered woman?").

The distributions of all three labels were markedly nonnormal and generally bimodal with peak clusters at Score 1 and Score 7 on the Likert-type scale (see table 1). Because of nonnormal distributions, these variables were dichotomized for further analyses, which is the only transformation possible for bimodal distributions (Tabachnik & Fidell, 1989). Median splits would have entailed placing individuals with scores of only 2 or 3 into the "high" category, even though substantively they were largely rejecting the label. Thus, variables were dichotomized so that individuals using scores of 3 and below were placed in the "low" group and those with scores of 4 and above into the "high" group.

Table 1
Distributions of Three Labeling Variables among a Sample of Women Reporting Having Sustained Physical Force in Their Relationships

Likert-scale Score	Abuse episode (%)	Violence victim (%)	Battered woman (%)
1	26	40	65
2	12	15	8
3	4	8	5
4	18	10	6
5	6	4	1
6	12	4	1
7	23	19	13

Note: The anchor points of the Likert scale were labeled as 1 ="Definitely Not" and 7 = "Definitely." Thus, higher scores indicate greater endorsement of labels.
$n = 78$.

Finally, these labels were combined into a single self-labeling variable in order to explore factors associated with self-labeling patterns. The self-labeling variable had 3 levels or groups. Women who endorsed no labels (i.e., had "low" scores for all 3 labels) were placed into the No Labels Group. Women who endorsed 1 or 2 but not all 3 labels became the Some Labels Group, while women who endorsed all 3 labels became the All Labels Group.

Violent Acts Scale (VAS, Walker, 1984)—Labeling Violent Acts

A modified version of this scale was used to obtain ratings of respondents' attitudes toward various forms of physical violence for which no information about context was provided. Two modifications were made to the original scale, which asks respondents to make severity ratings of the force. First, we added a separate rating of whether they considered each act to be spouse abuse. Second, 6 of the original 16 items were dropped because a pretest sample showed no variability in rating these 6 acts. The remaining 10 acts were the following: push, claw, verbal abuse, hit with an object, knife, throw an object, slap, kick, wrestle, and punch. For this study, ratings for each act from 0 ("Definitely is not spouse abuse") to 10 ("Definitely is spouse abuse") were examined.

Vignettes—Labeling Violence Experienced by Others

The items from the VAS described above are used to obtain ratings of violent acts without reference to context or to the consequences of the acts. In order to assess reactions to violence occurring in the context of an ongoing relationship, we also asked respondents to rate three brief vignettes. The vignettes depicted a grab, a slap, and a punch during the course of an argument. They were intended to provide minimal context and to represent increasing levels of severity. Respondents rated each vignette on the same 0 to 10 scale of abusiveness that was used for the VAS. The text of each of the vignettes follows:

"Kim and Steve were arguing heatedly. Steve grabbed Kim's arm to keep her from leaving. Kim could not get out of his grasp."

"Linda and Michael were arguing heatedly when Michael reached out and slapped Linda in the face. Linda's face stung sharply afterwards."

"David and Laura were arguing heatedly when David pulled back and punched Laura in the face. Laura's nose was broken and required medical attention."

FORCE MEASURES

Frequency

Respondents were asked to indicate how many times physical force was used during the course of their relationship, using the following seven categories: 0, 1, 2, 3–5, 6–10, 11–20, and more than 20 (however, individuals with scores of 0 were dropped in this sample as outlined in the Respondents section). This measure of aggregate frequency was shown in another sample to be a very reliable measure of having sustained violence (Hamby, Poindexter,

& Gray-Little, 1996). It has the added benefit that, unlike many measures of partner violence, the respondent must herself classify the act as physical force to be judged to have sustained violence.

Severity

Judges rated the severity of the incidents related in participants' narrative descriptions. Judges' severity ratings have been shown to adequately assess the construct of partner violence (Hamby et al., 1996). The directions to the participants were as follows: "We are trying to learn about the ways people act in different relationships, especially if and when partners use force. Please think about the most forceful or physically threatening episode in your relationship, even if you would not normally consider it violent. All respondents should answer these questions. Some examples of forceful acts that sometimes happen are pushing, hitting, shouting, slapping, slamming the door, biting, cursing, threatening with a weapon, and so forth." Examples were included because pretesting indicated that some respondents omitted descriptions of verbal aggression or only described the emotional consequences of the actions and not the acts. The first question following these instructions read, "Describe what you and your partner did (or said), including what kind of force was used."

Two female undergraduate psychology majors were trained to rate the severity of the incident described on a 7-point scale; the judges were blind to other information about the respondents and to the hypotheses of the study. Both judges rated all descriptions and they achieved an effective reliability of .95. This coefficient indicates the aggregate consistency of the two judges' scores and is appropriate for noncategorical ratings (Rosenthal & Rosnow, 1991).

Judges rated about half of the incidences in the lowest two violence categories: grabbing (10%), and pushing or shaking that did not knock the victim off balance (40%). The rest of the acts were judged as moderate-to-severe levels of violence such as slapping (18%), hitting or knocking down (19%), or punching, hitting repeatedly, and more injurious acts (13%).

DEMOGRAPHIC CHARACTERISTICS

Respondents were asked to provide their age, educational level, race, and individual yearly income. The same questions were asked about their partners in order to determine if their partner's social resources affected labeling. Relationship length, marital status, relationship status (current or terminated), and number of children were obtained in the demographics section of the questionnaire.

RELATIONSHIP CHARACTERISTICS

Relationship Commitment Scale (Rusbult, 1980)

A 5-item questionnaire developed by Rusbult was included to assess respondents' degree of commitment to their relationship. Questions asked how likely it was that the respondent would end the relationship, for what length of time she thought it would last for what length of time she wanted it to last, how attached she was to the relationship, and how committed she was to the relationship. Each question was scaled on a 9-point Likert-type scale, with higher scores indicating more commitment. The mean was used in analyses. For this group of women, internal consistency was .93 as measured by coefficient alpha.

Decision Making in Intimate Relationships (DMIR) Scale

The DMIR is an 11-item scale of relationship power (Hamby, 1996). The DMIR was patterned after the scale used by Blood and Wolfe (1960) to study decision-making power, but the original scale was modified so that the items are appropriate for use with both cohabiting and noncohabiting couples. For each of 11 specific content areas (e.g., what to do on weekends, when to have sex), participants indicated on a 5-point scale who usually had the final say (partner always, partner usually, equal, myself usually, myself always). Higher scores indicate that more decision-making power resides with the respondent. Internal consistency (alpha) was .79.

Results

SELF-LABELING: DESCRIPTIVE DATA

The patterns of endorsement across the three dichotomized labels ("abuse," "victim of violence," and "battered woman") were examined. Figure 1 shows that a substantial portion (38%) of the respondents did not endorse any labels for their own experiences of force. The next largest group, about a

Figure 1.
Self-labeling: Application of "abuse," "victim," and "battered" labels to personally experienced physical assaults by partners in a sample of women (*n* = 78).

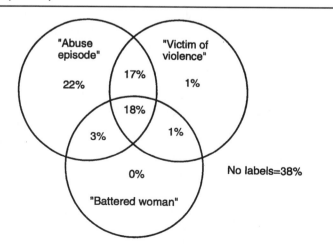

fifth (22%) of respondents, endorsed the abuse label, but not the other two labels. Interestingly, the next largest group consisted of women who endorsed all three labels (18%), while an almost equal number endorsed the abuse and victim labels but not the battered label (17%). If one examines only those women who reported multiple (2 or more) physical assaults (47 of 78 women in the sample, or 60% of the sample), 26% of multiply victimized women still declined all labels and only 26% endorsed all three. Thus not all women who have sustained violence consider themselves to be victims, abused, or battered.

OTHER-LABELING:
DISTRIBUTIONS AND ASSOCIATION WITH SELF-LABELING

Violence Acts Scale (VAS)

Every item on the VAS was rated as abuse (M 8.04 to 9.89). In order to examine the relationship of self-labeling (No, Some, or All labels) to labeling of VAS items, we conducted a multivariate analysis of variance (MANOVA), with self-labeling as the independent variable and the 10 VAS items as dependent variables. This analysis indicated that ratings of the VAS items were not significantly associated with self-labeling (all $p > .15$).

Vignettes

A repeated measures analysis in which ratings of the vignettes was the dependent measure revealed that respondents differentiated among levels of abuse depicted in the vignettes; $F(2, 74) = 29.21, p < .0001$. Mean abusiveness ratings increased from the grab (7.19, $SD = 2.86$) to the slap (9.40, $SD = 1.35$), to the punch (9.96, $SD = 0.25$) vignette. This pattern of increasing abusiveness ratings across the three vignettes was not associated with self-labeling, however ($p > .50$); nor was there any effect for self-labeling on labeling of any of the individual vignettes, (all $ps > .55$).

A similar pattern of differentiation among the vignettes is observed if the distribution of vignette ratings is dichotomized in a manner similar to the self-labeling variables. If the responses are dichotomized so that scores at or above the midpoint are considered to be endorsing the label, then 82% labeled a grab as spouse abuse, 99% labeled a slap as abuse, and 100% labeled a punch as abuse (see figure 2).

INFERENTIAL ANALYSES: SELF-LABELING

Self-labeling (No labels, Some labels, and All labels) was used as the independent variable in a series of multivariate analyses of variance (MANOVA). In the sections below we present a series of analyses examining the relationship of self-labeling to (a) frequency and severity of force experienced by the respondent; (b) demographic characteristics; and (c) relationship characteristics. Significant univariate results were further examined with two orthogonal planned comparisons, one comparing the No Labels Group to both of the other two groups, and one comparing the Some Labels Group to the All Labels. Further, frequency and severity of force were tested as

Figure 2. Other labeling: Application of "abuse" label to hypothetical partner violence vignettes in a sample of women who have sustained physical assault by their partner (*n* = 78).

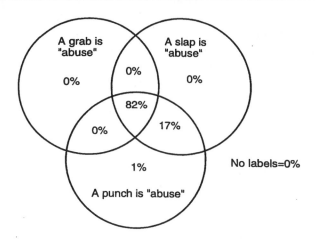

covariates to see if the association between labeling and demographic and relationship attributes was mediated by differences in degree of force.

Frequency and Severity of Force

See table 2 for the means and standard deviations of the force variables. The overall MANOVA for the force variables was significant; $F (4, 146) = 9.34$, $p < .0001$. As expected, both increasing frequency [$F (2, 74) = 7.79, p < .001$] and severity [$F (2, 74) = 12.09, p < .0001$] of physical force were associated with a greater endorsement of labels. Planned contrasts indicated that women using no labels reported less frequent [$F (1, 74) = 15.38, p < .001$] and less severe [$F (1, 74) = 24. 10, p < .0001$] violence than women using any labels. Contrasts comparing the women in the Some Labels Group to those in the All Labels Group revealed no significant differences in their experience of force; for frequency, $F (1, 74) = 2.26, p > .10$, and for severity, $F (1, 74) = 1.11, p > .25$.

Demographic Characteristics

We found that severity of force (but not frequency) was associated with demographic characteristics [$F (8, 59) = 2.58, p < .051$]. In order to examine the unique association of demographic characteristics to self-labeling, severity was used as a covariate in the analyses. Overall, there was a significant association between self-labeling and demographic characteristics, $F (16, 118) = 3.33, p < .0001$. Inspection of univariate effects revealed that labeling differed as a function of respondents' race, $F (2, 66) = 11.59, p < .0001$, and partner's race, $F (2, 66) = 9.60, p < .001$. Planned comparisons indicated that being Black was associated with a greater endorsement of labels. The force covariate was significant, too, because White respondents reported more forceful acts than did Black respondents. A virtually identical pattern was found for partners' race, because the two race variables are highly inter-correlated with each other ($r = .96$).

Partners' income also differed across self-labeling groups, $F(2, 66) = 9.43$, $p < .001$. Contrasts indicated that women in the No Labels Group reported significantly more income than those in the other two groups, $F(1, 66) = 18.64$, $p < .0001$, but women in the Some Labels and All Labels groups did not differ in income from each other, $F(1, 66) = 0.94$, $p > .30$. Increased partners' income was also associated with greater severity of force. Other demographic characteristics did not distinguish the groups. The means and standard deviations for these analyses ran also be found in table 2.

Table 2
Means and Standard Deviations of Force, Sociodemographic, and Relationship Variables as a Function of Labeling

Variable	No Labels		Some Labels		All Labels	
	M	*SD*	*M*	*SD*	*M*	*SD*
Force Measures						
Frequency****	2.69	1.04	3.74	1.60	4.43	1.79
Severity****	2.90	1.84	4.65	1.43	5.21	1.97
Sociodemographic Characteristics						
Respondent's characteristics						
Age	38.00	8.93	39.06	11.88	41.27	8.67
Education	14.38	1.70	14.80	2.07	14.18	1.40
Income	25,394.62	8,417.02	23,333.33	10,346.02	24,318.18	8,950.62
Race****	0.23	0.43	0.07	0.25	0.64	0.50
Partner's characteristics						
Age	39.38	8.60	41.43	12.76	42.18	9.71
Education	13.77	2.07	14.13	2.10	13.09	2.26
Income***	31,826.92	9,396.68	24,833.33	11,743.18	22,045.45	13,730.36
Race****	0.23	0.43	0.10	0.31	0.64	0.50
Relationship Attributes						
Status (%/ended)**	0.04	0.19	0.10	0.31	0.45	0.52
Commitment*	7.79	2.18	6.73	2.81	5.16	3.17
Decision making[1]	3.07	0.40	2.90	0.45	2.72	0.55
Length	12.61	8.45	11.70	8.23	8.55	8.02
Marital status	1.32	0.67	1.33	0.71	1.27	0.65
No. of children	1.61	1.42	0.93	1.08	1.36	2.01

Notes. For force measures, higher scores indicate greater force. Age and education are in years; income is in dollars. Race is dichotomized (0 = White; 1 = Black); higher scores indicate a higher percentage of Black respondents. For commitment, higher scores indicate greater commitment. For decision making, lower scores indicate more male-dominant decision making. For overall univariate effects, **** $p < .0001$; *** $p < .001$; ** $p < .01$; * $p < .05$; and [1]$p < .08$. Means with different superscripts are significantly different as determined by planned contrasts, $p < .05$.

Relationship Characteristics

There were significant overall differences among the labeling, groups on relationship variables, $F(12, 126) = 2.24, p < .05$. Neither force covariate was significant, $p > .40$, and hence neither was included in the final analyses. Relationship status was related to self-labeling. Having terminated the relationship was associated with increased self-labeling, $F(2, 66) = 7.41, p < .01$; both planned contrasts were significant, $F(1, 66) = 9.02, p < .01$; and $F(1, 66) = 10.45, p < .01$. Relationship commitment was lowest among those who used labels, $F(2, 66) = 4.03, p < .05$, although only the contrast comparing the No Labels Group to the other two was significant $[F(1, 66) = 7.27, p < .01]$. The contrast between the Some Labels and All Labels group approached but did not achieve significance $[F(1, 66) = 2.85, p < .10]$. The overall effect for decision-making power only approached significance $[F(2, 66) = 2.64, p < .08]$, but the planned contrast between women in the No Labels Group versus other women was significant, $F(1, 66) = 5.10, p < .05$. The No Labels group described their relationships as less male dominated than those of the other groups. The contrast between the Some and All Labels Groups was not significant for decision-making power, $p > .25$. Relationship length, marital status, and number of children were not associated with self-labeling, all $p > .15$. In summary, increasing endorsement of abuse labels was associated with having terminated the relationship, lower relationship commitment, greater likelihood of view[ing] the relationship as male dominated.

INFERENTIAL ANALYSES: LABELING OTHERS

A parallel set of MANOVAs was conducted to examine the association of other-labeling to the frequency and severity of force as well as to demographic and relationship characteristics. However, neither the labeling of acts on the VAS, nor the vignettes, was associated with frequency nor severity of one's own sustained violence (all $p > .05$). Furthermore, there were no associations among any of the demographic and relationship characteristics and labeling of the VAS items or for the vignettes, all $p > .05$.

Discussion

USE OF BOTH INCLUSIVE AND DIFFERENTIATING STRATEGIES

This study indicates that women who reported that they have experienced assault by their partners generally adopt a differentiating labeling strategy with respect to their own abuse and an inclusive one with respect to abuse that does not personally involve them. Moreover, in this sample, women's labeling of hypothetical acts was not associated with their self-labels, suggesting that two rather different processes may be at work. Women's use of a differentiating labeling strategy for their own experiences is similar to the strategy of researchers who argue that terms like battering should be reserved for more frequent and more severe violence (e.g., Johnson, 1995; Rouse, 1989). Their use of an inclusive strategy for other's experience parallels the practice of other domestic violence professionals who believe that all relationship force should be labeled as violent (e.g., Family Violence Prevention Fund, 1995; Hamberger &Arnold, 1989; Stark, 1995).

Several factors appear to be associated with women's use of labels for their own experiences. Besides the effects of violence frequency and severity, self-labeling is also influenced by the context created by qualities of the relationship. Most of our findings are consistent with the proposition that violence occurring in the context of more valued relationships is less likely to lead to labeling. Thus, women who were more committed to their partners were less likely to adopt labels. Rusbult's commitment measure, used in this study, emphasizes wanting to continue in the relationship and probably reflects a personal valuing of the relationship more than commitment due to moral obligations or structural constraints (Johnson, Caughlin, & Huston, 1999). Similarly, women who were still in a relationship with their partners were less likely to adopt labels. Less male dominant, more egalitarian relationships, which may, in today's society, be associated with the perceived value of the relationship (Risman & Johnson-Sumerford, 1998), were also characterized by less labeling. Similarly, partners' resources influenced labeling; women who declined labels had partners who made considerably more money, on average, than did women who used labels. Finally, the observed racial differences suggest that the broader sociocultural context may also affect labeling, but interpretations should take into account the limited number of Black respondents. These racial differences would need to be replicated before firm conclusions can be drawn.

Do These Findings Indicate Denial?

Context might partially explain why women adopt inclusive strategies for violence not directed at them and differentiating strategies for their own experiences. Researchers have long noted similar actor-observer differences in perceptions of events (e.g., Jones & Nisbett, 1971). The kind of force experienced by the women in this study was similar to that depicted in the vignettes and VAS. All of them had experienced something at least as forceful as a grab, yet more than twice as many of the respondents rated the grab vignette as abusive as rated their own experience of "being grabbed" as abusive. It seems likely that disparity in the amount of available information is the important difference between actors and observers. This type of actor-observer difference is often assigned to the fundamental attribution error, the tendency to explain events involving the self in situation-specific terms, but to attribute the behavior of others to transsituational factors (Ross & Sicoly, 1979). This study indicates that relationship-specific circumstances might include strong commitment and often present messages without a context. For example, slogans like "There's NO excuse for domestic violence" and "Some men break more than their girlfriends' hearts" (FVPF, 1995) may do an excellent job of communicating general societal attitudes about domestic assault. The lack of context in these ads, however, may be one reason that they are not very effective in changing women's behavior. By contrast, the contextualized formats seen in movies such as *The Burning Bed* or *What's Love Got to Do with It*, and well-publicized incidents such as the murder of Nicole Brown Simpson (Jones, 1995) have led to large increases in help-seeking by victims of domestic violence. These personalized formats are uniquely well suited for conveying the relational and sociocultural contexts that often surround violence.

Intervention programs for victims may benefit from a greater incorporation of a differentiating perspective. Clients of shelters and other services may find it difficult to integrate their own beliefs with the ideology of shelters, which tend to be based on ideas that developed from Western forms of feminism (Timmins, 1995), and which may be seen as antimale or antimarriage. It is possible that a differentiating approach, with a more explicit recognition of context including positive relationship features, could help alleviate some of these problems. For example, providers could encourage women to explore ways of identifying all of the factors that affect their responses to the violence and discuss how adopting abuse, victim, or battered labels affects their ideas about themselves, their relationships, and the violence they have experienced.

To understand fully how victims make sense of violence, researchers should include individuals who have sustained all levels of violence. A limitation of the present study, for example, is that the most extreme forms of violence were not well represented. The levels of violence included in this sample, however, are typical of most forms of relationship violence. National data suggest that minor violence is approximately 4 times more common than severe violence (Straus & Gelles, 1990), and other avenues of research (e.g., Aldarondo & Sugarman, 1996; Feld & Straus, 1989) suggest that a significant number of relationships do not remain violent over time. Sample selection strategies focusing on only the most extreme forms of violence will tend to promote portrayals of dysfunction that may be erroneously generalized to represent all couples who experience violence. Those failing to include the severe abuse may miss the opportunity to examine qualitative differences occurring in women's response to severe violence. Thus a framework that accounts for all levels of violence is needed, and it seems likely that such a framework will incorporate both the inclusive and differentiating perspectives.

REFERENCES

Aldarondo, E., & Sugarman, D. B. (1996). Risk marker analysis of the cessation and persistence of wife assault. *Journal of Consulting and Clinical Psychology, 64,* 1010–1019.

Babcock, J. C., Waltz, J., Jacobson, N. S., & Gottman, J. M. (1993). Power and violence: The relation between communication patterns, power discrepancies, and domestic violence. *Journal of Consulting and Clinical Psychology, 61,* 40–50.

Blood, R. O., & Wolfe, D. M. (1960). *Husbands and wives: The dynamics of married living.* Glencoe, IL: Free Press.

Crosby, F. J., Pufall, A., Snyder, R. C., O'Connell, M., & Whalen, P. (1989). The denial of personal disadvantage among you, me and all the other ostriches. In A. Crawford & M. Gentry (Eds.), *Gender and thought* (pp. 79–99). New York: Springer-Verlag.

Department of Public Health, Commonwealth of Massachusetts. (1995). Massachusetts Guidelines and Standards for the Certification of Batterers Intervention Programs. Boston, MA: Author.

Domestic Violence: Probation Act of California, Statutes of California and Digests of Measures, Chapter 641. (1995).

Feld, S. L., & Straus, M. A. (1989). Escalation and desistance of wife assault in marriage. *Criminology, 27,* 141–161.

Feldman, C. M., & Ridley, C. A. (1995). The etiology and treatment of domestic violence between partners. *Clinical Psychology: Science and Practice, 2,* 317–348.

Ferraro, K. J. (1983). Rationalizing violence: How battered women stay. *Victimology, 3–4,* 203–212.

Gondolf, E. W. (1995, July). Discharge criteria for batterer programs. Presented at the 4th International Family Violence Research Conference.

Gottman, J. M., Jacobson, N. S., Rushe, R. H., Shorn, J. W., Babcock, J., La Thillade, J. J., & Waltz, J. (1995). The relationship between heart rate reactivity, emotionally aggressive behavior, and general violence in batterers. *Journal of Family Psychology, 9,* 227–248.

Graham, D. L. R., Rawlings, E. I., & Rigsby, R. K. (1994). *Loving to survive: Sexual terror, men's violence, and women's lives.* New York: New York University Press.

Hamberger, L. K., & Arnold, J. (1989). Dangerous distinctions among "abuse," "courtship violence," and "battering": A response to Rouse, Breen, and Howell. *Journal of Interpersonal Violence, 4,* 520–522.

Hamby, S. L. (1996). The Dominance Scale: Preliminary psychometric properties. *Violence and Victims, 11,* 199–212.

Hamby, S. L., & Gray-Little, B. (1997). Responses to partner violence: Moving away from deficit models. *Journal of Family Psychology,* 339–350.

Hamby, S. L., Poindexter, V. C., & Gray-Little, B. (1996). Four measures of partner violence: Construct similarity and classification differences. *Journal of Marriage and the Family, 58,* 127–139.

Harvey, J. H., Town, J. P., & Yarkin, K. L. (198 1). How fundamental is the "fundamental attribution error"? *Journal of Personality & Social Psychology, 40,* 346–349.

Henton, J., Cate, R., Koval, J., Lloyd, S., & Christopher, S. (1983). Romance and violence in dating relationships. *Journal of Family Issues, 4,* 467–482.

Herbert, T. B., Silver, R. C., & Ellard, J. H. (1991). Coping with an abusive relationship: I. How and why do women stay? *Journal of Marriage and the Family, 53,* 311–325.

Jacobson, N. S., Gottman, J. M., & Shortt, J. W. (1995). The distinction between Type 1 and Type 2 batterers—further considerations: Reply to Ornduff et al. (1995), Margolin et al. (1995), and Walker (1995). *Journal of Family Psychology, 9,* 272–279.

Johnson, M. P. (1995). Patriarchal terrorism and common couple violence: Two forms of violence against women. *Journal of Marriage and the Family, 57,* 283–294.

Johnson, M. P., Caughlin, J. P., & Huston, T. L. (1999). The tripartite nature of marital commitment: Personal, moral, and structural reasons to stay married. *Journal of Marriage and the Family, 61,* 160–177.

Jones, C. (1995, October 15). Nicole Simpson, in death, lifting domestic violence to the forefront as national issue. *The New York Times,* p. A28.

Jones, E. E., & Nisbett, R. E. (1971). *The actor and the observer: Divergent perceptions of the causes of behavior.* Morristown, NJ: General Learning Press.

McMahon, M., & Pence, E. (1996). Replying to Dan O'Leary. *Journal of Interpersonal Violence, 11,* 452–455.

Norris, J., Nurius, R. S., & Dimeff, L. A. (1996). Through her eyes: Factors affecting women's perception of and resistance to acquaintance sexual aggression threat. *Psychology of Women Quarterly, 20,* 123–145.

O'Leary, K. D. (1996). Physical aggression in intimate relationships can be treated within a marital context under certain circumstance. *Journal of Interpersonal Violence, 11,* 450–452.

Pence, E., & Paymar, M. (1993). *Education groups for men who batter: The Duluth model.* New York: Springer Publishing.

Risman, B. J., & Johnson-Sumerford, D. (1998). Doing it fairly: A study of postgender marriages. *Journal of Marriage and the Family, 60,* 23–40.

Rosenthal, R., & Rosnow, R. L. (1991). *Essentials of behavioral research: Methods and data analysis* (2nd ed.). New York: McGraw-Hill.

Ross, M., & Sicoly, F. (1979). Egocentric biases in availability and attribution. *Journal of Personality & Social Psychology, 37,* 322–336.

Rouse, L. P. 0 989). Reply to Hamberger and Arnold. *Journal of Interpersonal Violence, 4,* 523–527.

Rouse, L. P., Breen, R., & Howell, M. (1988). Abuse in intimate relationships: A comparison of married and dating college students. *Journal of Interpersonal Violence, 3,* 414–429.

Rusbult, C. E. (1980). Commitment and satisfaction in romantic associations: A test of the investment model. *Journal of Experimental Social Psychology, 16,* 172–186.

Sedlak, A. J. (1988). Prevention of wife abuse. In V B. Van Hasselt, R. Morrison, A. Bellack, & M. Hersen (Eds.), *Handbook of family violence* (pp. 319–358). New York: Plenum Press.

Stark, E. (1995). Re-presenting woman battering: From battered woman syndrome to coercive control. *Albany Law Review, 58,* 973–1026.

Straus, M. A., & Gelles, R. J. (1990). How violent are American families? Estimates from the National Family Violence Resurvey and other studies. In M. A. Straus & R. J. Gelles (Eds.), *Physical violence in American families: Risk factors and adaptations to violence in 8,145 families* (pp. 95–112). New Brunswick, NJ: Transaction Publishers.

Strube, M. J. (1988). The decision to leave an abusive relationship: Empirical evidence and theoretical issues. *Psychological Bulletin, 104,* 236–250.

Sugarman, D. B., Aldarondo, E., & Boney-McCoy, S. (1996). Risk marker analysis of husband-to-wife violence: A continuum of aggression. *Journal of Applied Social Psychology, 26,* 313–337.

Tabachnik, B. G., & Fidell, L. S. (1989). *Using multivariate statistics* (2nd ed.). New York: Harper & Row.

Timmins, L. (Ed.). (1995). *Listening to the thunder. Advocates talk about the battered women's movement.* Vancouver, Canada: Women's Research Centre.

Walker, L. E. (1984). *The battered woman syndrome.* New York: Springer Publishing.

Walker, L. E. (1993). The battered woman syndrome is a psychological consequence of abuse. In R. Gelles; & D. Loseke (Eds.), *Current controversies on family violence* (pp. 133–153). Newbury Park, CA: Sage Publications.

Chapter Ten

Deviant Homicide
A New Look at the Role of Motives and Victim-Offender Relationships

Scott H. Decker

All crime has a certain normative character. The set of normative expectations that develop about crime are a reflection of the social organization of those crimes. Burglaries tend to be committed when residents are away from home, assaults more often occur between people who know each other, and robberies are typically committed against strangers. The organizational characteristics of offenses create a set of routine expectations about "normal" crimes, that is, crimes that correspond to the modal category. The perception of crime by the public, and the response of the criminal justice system, is in large part structured by the characteristics of the typical or routine crimes. Events that fall beyond the bounds of normal crimes are problematic, because they confront people with circumstances for which they lack a conceptual framework for understanding such events. In this sense, these are deviant or nonnormative crimes.

Part of the way society orders itself is through norms about violence—when it can be used and against whom. The intersection of those two guidelines (motives and targets) provides us with our conception of the tolerable limits of violence. Even the most serious of violent crimes, homicide, has a normative character. Indeed, homicide is a crime generally regarded as having less diversity than many other offenses. Homicide has a strong social organization, particularly in the relationship between victims and offenders and motives. Previous research has characterized the victim-offender relationship as a dichotomy, either as strangers and nonstrangers or primary and

From *Journal of Research in Crime & Delinquency*, 33(4): 426–449, copyright © 1996 by Sage Publications, Inc. Reprinted by permission of Sage Publications, Inc.

secondary relationships. Motives have been conceptualized as instrumental (in pursuit of gain) or expressive (an expression of outrage or emotion). Homicides within primary relationships usually have an expressive nature, whereas homicides within secondary relationships typically have an instrumental motive. As long as the great majority of homicide events fall into these normative categories of victim, offender, and motive classifications, society possesses mechanisms to cope with homicide. However, when a substantial fraction of homicide events exceed the normative boundaries for that event, it creates a public dilemma about the nature of crime and calls into question traditional explanations of homicide. This article examines deviant homicides, events that do not correspond to normative expectations about the intersection of motives and victim-offender relationships.

Victim-Offender Relationships and Motives in Homicide

Much prior research has characterized the victim-offender relationship in homicide as a dichotomy. Some of this research has defined this relationship as being between strangers or nonstrangers (Messner and Tardiff 1985; Sampson 1987), whereas others (Parker and Smith 1979; Smith and Parker 1980) have defined them either as primary or secondary. In this classification scheme, primary relationships occur between intimates (relatives, lovers, and friends), whereas secondary relationships include those with little or no prior relationship (such as strangers or acquaintances). Despite several recent exceptions (R. Block and C. Block 1992; Polk 1994), motives generally also have been operationalized as dichotomies. Instrumental homicides are events in which offenders seek to improve their position through some rational calculation or planning that involves minimizing risk, increasing gain, or both. Robbery is the textbook example of an instrumental crime involving an offender who seeks to maximize gain or advantage while minimizing the risk of apprehension. Expressive homicides are less likely to be motivated by such "rational" considerations. Instead, expressive or impulsive killings stem from "character contests" (Luckenbill 1977–78), desires to retaliate or seek revenge (Felson 1978), or as expressions of "righteous slaughter" (Katz 1988).

In general, primary or nonstranger homicides have been thought to have expressive motives (Loftin 1986; Maxfield 1989; Rojek and Williams 1993).[1] From this perspective, more intimate or primary relationships (those among family, the romantically linked, or friends) produce homicides that, as the expression of strongly held emotions or rage, are the product of more intense relationships and interactions. Homicides that occur within secondary relationships (between acquaintances or strangers) are presumed to have instrumental motives; that is, these homicides occur in the context of violence committed for gain (Block 1981; Riedel 1981, 1987; Rojek and Williams 1993). The instrumental motive in homicide (and criminal events in general) has been identified in events in which participants are less intimately related, and stranger homicides have traditionally been regarded as instrumental events (R. Block 1977, p. 9). Recent research has emerged that questions this association. Riedel and Zahn (1985) found that between one third and one half of all stranger homicides did not involve concurrent felonies. In a careful analysis of a rich data set of Australian homicides, Polk and Ranson (1991) demonstrated the complex relationship between motive and victim-offender relationship. They focused on three broad inclusive categories of homicide: (a) discord in intimate relationships, (b) confrontations between males, and (c) the commission of a concurrent felony. Within these categories of events, they identified variations in motive and relationship. According to Polk and Ranson, such categories more accurately capture the motivation and interaction in homicides and enable researchers to better measure the impact of relationships on events.

If instrumental homicides are generally concentrated in nonprimary relationships and expressive homicides occur within primary relationships, we can conclude that the victim-offender relationship has important consequences for (a) offering protection from some kinds of fatal interactions, such as instrumental violence among intimates or expressive violence among strangers; and (b) increasing the likelihood that fatal interactions will occur among others, such as primary violence among intimates and expressive violence among strangers. From this perspective, the stranger relationship offers no protection from instrumental violence of the sort provided by the intimate relationships and the shared role definitions of nonstranger categories. In the case of instrumental violence, nonstrangers are presumed to be protected from homicides with the intent of tangible gain or advantage on the part of the offender. Instrumental violence represents the felony-murder category identified by R. Block and Zimring (1973), Zimring and Zuehl (1986), and R. Block and Skogan (1984). And as Cook (1987) has observed, expressive homicides involve people more intimately related than in instrumental homicides, especially those that occur in the context of robbery. These relational ties and shared expectations about behavior and values usually play a role in insulating nonstrangers from instrumental violence by each other. The set of common experiences that distinguishes strangers from others provides moral bonds of the sort that serve to inhibit violence, especially instrumental violence. Breaking these bonds is more difficult for intimates than would be the case for strangers. As such, nonstranger relationships provide a protective stake in the well-being of others such as family members, friends, or acquaintances. This stake varies with the nature of the relationship, being strongest for children, next for spouses, weaker for friends, weaker yet for acquaintances, and generally nonexistent for strangers (Wilson and Daly 1985; Wilson, Daly, and Weghorst 1980).

The absence of prior relationships, however, should be linked to low levels of expressive violence, as expressive violence is a product of frequent interaction and more intense relationships. The frequency and intensity of interactions with persons one is intimately involved with creates circumstances that lead to disputes and potentially fatal violence of an expressive nature. In this case, the intensity of the stake in another's well-being can be turned "upside down" and facilitate violence rather than insulate nonstrangers from it. This process involves the inversion or rejection of strongly internalized norms against within-group violence (e.g., the killing of a spouse, blood relative, or close friend).

A long line of previous research (Cook 1987; Daly and Wilson 1982; Maxfield 1989; Riedel and Przybylski 1993; Rojek and Williams 1993) found that expressive violence is concentrated in more intense (primary) relationships and instrumental violence is found most often in secondary relationships (such as friends, acquaintances, and strangers). Prohibitions against violence are strongest in primary relationships. Such strictures traditionally have been broken only when levels of rage exceeded the bonds of control, usually resulting in expressive violence. Strong as those bonds are, controls on instrumental violence among intimates are even stronger and thus should be violated only rarely. Lacking the moral commitments against violence for gain, most instrumental homicides should occur between those who do not know one another. Moreover, interactions among strangers lack the history or intensity of interaction necessary to generate expressive violence. However, C. Block (1985) presented evidence that this issue may not be so straightforward. Two propositions result from these considerations and are examined in the present analysis: (a) Expressive violence is concentrated in primary relationships and (b) instrumental violence is concentrated in secondary relationships.

Data Sources

Data for this analysis were drawn from the Records Division of the St. Louis Metropolitan Police Department. St. Louis is a particularly appropriate city to use for this analysis for a number of reasons. It has high rates of homicide, typically ranking among the top five cities in the United States. In addition, the pattern of change in St. Louis rates shows a strong correspondence with national data (Rosenfeld and Decker 1993). Equally important, the St. Louis police department clears a high percentage of cases and, as a consequence, has more complete records than in cities with lower clearance rates. All 792 homicides for the years 1985 through 1989 for the city of St. Louis are included in this study. We use the homicide event as the unit of analysis; thus characteristics of victims and offenders can be linked to those of the homicide event. We did not routinely accept police descriptions of these events; instead, each case file and every supplemental report was read to determine the appropriate category for coding such variables as victim-offender relationships, drug or alcohol use, and number of witnesses, among others. Coding was done by two research assistants and reviewed by a third. Discrepancies in classification decisions were resolved by a conference between the parties. Qualitative descriptions of each homicide event, "homicide narratives," were written after coding was completed. These narratives provide what Polk

(1994) has called "the missing voice" in homicide events (p. 173). Such reconstructions provide the "voices" of a variety of witnesses and participants, broadening the view of events beyond that of the police. In addition, these narratives provide a more reliable basis for determining motives.

Motives for each event were classified as either instrumental or expressive, applying classification schemes used by Berkowitz (1986), R. Block and Zimring (1973), Riedel (1987), and R. Block and C. Block (1992).[2] Following Berkowitz (1986, p. 89), instrumental motives include a mechanism designed to gain an advantage for the offender over the victim. Much of the violence (but not all) with an instrumental (or "incentive") motive is grounded in the desire for fiscal or financial gain. Other instrumental motives include gaining control over the victim, such as in cases of self-protection. Expressive motives are found in violent events where "hostile" or "angry" aggression is the primary goal. That is, the primary goal of expressive violence is to inflict injury or create "dread" (Katz 1988) independent of instrumental gain. It is the expression of a strongly held emotion that most often characterizes expressive motives. In order for a motive to be successfully classified, two independent reviewers had to agree that the motive was clearly instrumental or expressive. Five hundred seventy-one (72%) of the 792 cases were successfully classified as either instrumental or expressive. For another 98 cases no suspect had been identified, and a motive could not be determined. In a final group of 108 cases, it was not possible to determine a single motive because the events included elements of both instrumental and expressive violence. For example, the drug dealer who was a robbery victim, and retaliated by killing the robber, often acted from both instrumental and expressive motivations. Only cases in which a single motive could be identified were included in this analysis.

In our initial analysis, we classify victim-offender relationships as dichotomies; primary relationships (including relatives, those romantically linked, and friends) and secondary relationships (acquaintances and strangers). Similar to Polk's (1994) approach, these relationships are reclassified in later analyses so that the primary (or intimate) category consists of relatives, persons romantically linked, and friends; the second category consists of acquaintances; and the third category is composed of strangers. Friends were those who had a mutually reinforcing relationship of a positive nature that had endured for an extended period of time. Acquaintances, on the other hand, lacked the positive, reinforcing aspects and enduring nature of the friend relationship, although this category often included those who had known each other only casually or by sight for an extended period of time. Friends were often distinguished from acquaintances by the frequency of their interaction and also by the extent to which they engaged in supportive acts, such as providing transportation, loaning small amounts of money, and doing things (crime, attending social events, meals) together. These three categories represent a rank ordering of the intensity of relationships and as such allow for a test of the proposition that motive and the intensity of relationships are linked. The coding of individual attributes (race, sex, age) was straightforward. The "premises" variable was the actual location of the homicide event. We were liberal in our approach to coding drug or alcohol involvement. Any mention of drugs or alcohol in the files led us to classify the event as related to that substance.

Analysis Plan

This article focuses on the measurement and interpretation of homicide data. We examine two categories of homicide: (a) homicides where the bonds or insularity provided by primary relationships are broken to commit instrumental offenses and (b) expressive homicides within secondary relationships. These categories represent deviations from our general understanding of homicide, where instrumental violence is most often directed against strangers (e.g., in the case of robbery) and expressive violence is targeted against intimates (as in the killing of a spouse). The common conception of homicide and much prior research (see Polk's [1994] review) support the contention that homicides occur primarily within the intimate/expressive and secondary/instrumental categories. This creates a set of expectations regarding the intersection of motives and victim-offender relationships in homicide. These expectations assume a normative character, defining "normal" homicides. It is important to study the "off-diagonal" or deviant cases to determine both their frequency and characteristics.

The analysis proceeds along two directions. First, I explore the bivariate relationship between victim-offender relationships and motive. Motive is defined as either instrumental or expressive, and victim-offender relationship is coded as intimate, acquaintance, or stranger. I then examine the ratio of instrumental to expressive homicide within each victim-offender relationship. I construct a series of ratios so that a number less than 1.0 indicates a greater proportion of nondeviant homicides and a number greater than 1.0 indicates that the majority of homicides in that category were classified as deviant homicides, and a ratio of 1.0 indicates an equal number of expressive and instrumental homicides. In the case of homicides between intimates, instrumental homicides are the numerator and expressive homicides are the denominator. For both the acquaintance and stranger categories, expressive homicides are the numerator and instrumental homicides are expressed in the denominator. These ratios were constructed in this way to conform to the theoretical expectations developed above so that any ratio greater than 1.0 reflects a proportion of "deviant" homicides greater than "typical" homicides. These ratios are cross-classified with four individual attributes important to understanding homicide: (a) race (both inter- and intraracial homicides), (b) sex (inter- and intrasexual homicides), (c) age (age of suspect), and (d) marital status (married, not married). Six event variables are also examined: the presence of weapons (firearm or personal contact), the location of the event (inside, outside, or in an auto), the number of suspects (one or more than one), number of "witnesses" at the scene (none, one, two or more), drug involvement (yes, no), and alcohol involvement (yes, no).

The second line of analysis examines the "homicide narratives" (qualitative descriptions of homicide events) to explore in greater detail the characteristics of "deviant homicides." In the case of intimate instrumental homicides, there is a *prohibition against the violence*. Thus we ask the question, "What are the factors that produce motivations strong enough to overcome these prohibitions?" In the case of stranger expressive homicides there is a lack of motivation (i.e., the rage that can be created or intensity of emotions generated by intense or intimate relationships) so a motive must be generated.

Prior research leads us to several expectations for the outcomes of our analysis. The results of earlier research suggest that more intimate relationships should have a much higher proportion of expressive homicides, and that secondary (acquaintances and strangers) relationships should have a higher proportion of instrumental homicides. Kapardis (1990), however, suggested that there is greater variation among stranger homicides than past research has uncovered. I expect those excluded from the mainstream of urban life (Blacks, males, single people, and younger persons) to be found in greater numbers in the categories of deviant homicide (i.e., primary instrumental and secondary expressive homicides). These expectations are built from the knowledge that such individuals are isolated from institutions that produce conformity in American society, such as the family, school, and job market (Hacker 1992; Nightingale 1994; Wilson 1987). Because of this isolation, they are more likely to engage in homicides generally defined as deviant, often involving what Bernard (1990) has called "angry aggression." I also expect these categories to contain higher proportions of drug-related homicides, as well as events in which a third party—the audience—links victims and offenders not previously known to each other.

‎■■■■■‎

Findings

The results of the cross-tabulation of victim-offender relationship and motive are presented in table 1. The findings in this table stand in contrast to the expectations about the intersection of victim-offender relationship and motive. Twenty-eight percent of homicides between intimates had an instrumental motive, homicides that could be classified as "deviant." These include events such as bad drug deals, debts, and disputes over property that occur among those who knew each other well. For example, a fight between brothers over debts or drugs may result in homicide. Thus, even among intimates, the desire to gain material advantage leads to fatal disputes. For secondary relationships, 46% of homicides had expressive motives, a far greater proportion than expected. This category consists of killings of nonprimary associates over matters that do not lead to material gain, and they conform roughly to what Katz (1988) identified as "righteous slaughter," as many of them contain ele-

Table 1
The Intersection of Victim-Offender Relationship and Motive (*N* = 533)

| | Motive | | |
Victim-Offender Relationship	Expressive	Instrumental	Total
Primary			
n	124	47	171
Row percentage	72	28	
Total percentage	23	9	32
Secondary			
n	166	196	362
Row percentage	46	54	
Total percentage	31	37	68
Total			
N	290	243	533
Percentage	54	46	

ments of retaliation. In total, 40% of the homicides over a 5-year period differed from normative expectations, as 9% of all homicides were primary instrumentals and 31% were secondary expressive events. These proportions are far higher than suggested by the literature and indicate the need for an analysis of the factors associated with such "deviant" homicides. My classification scheme suggests that the intersection of the two variables produces results that differ from a priori expectations. I describe these as "deviant homicides" because they represent the "off-diagonals" of the cross-classification of motive and relationship, and because they violate our traditional understanding of the way these variables have been related. This group represents a far larger share of events than would be expected. The analysis to follow focuses specifically on these cases, examining the ratio of deviant to nondeviant cases.

In table 2, I consider the effect of several individual-level attributes on the homicide types. Here, I expand the dichotomy of victim-offender relationships to three categories—intimates, acquaintances, and strangers. Interestingly, interracial crimes contain smaller ratios of deviant to normative homicides than do the intraracial homicides. For Black on Black homicides, both the intimate and acquaintance categories reflect fewer deviant than "typical" homicides. For White on White homicides, however, there are 5 times as many acquaintance expressive homicides as acquaintance instrumental homicides. This indicates a greater willingness of Whites whose ties are looser to each other to engage in expressive violence. The ratios for White on White and Black on Black stranger homicides were much closer; for each category more expressive than instrumental homicides were observed. This evidence clearly shows that race alone cannot account for the emergence of nonnormative homicides and that interracial homicides more closely conform to the findings of prior research.

The results for comparing the ratio of deviant to normative homicides for categories of sex more closely correspond with the findings of prior research. Similar to the pattern observed for race, the acquaintance relationship provides the category in which the greatest number of deviant homicides is found. In particular, when women kill men who are acquaintances, there are 3 times as many expressive as instrumental homicides. Most striking in this panel, however, is the ratio of male on male stranger homicides. More of these offenses are deviant; that is, they have an expressive motive. Because stranger homicides have long been incorrectly viewed as almost exclusively instrumental in character, a revision in our understanding of these events is called for. This category of events may include a disproportionate number of gang killings or street culture identity disputes, likely to draw combatants who do not know each other but struggle over expressive concerns such as revenge or reputation.

A similar pattern is found for the acquaintance category when considering the role of age. I created a dichotomy for age; the first category includes suspects between 19 and 34 years old, the peak years of homicide involvement in St. Louis. The second category includes all others. Because of the

Table 2
Deviant Homicides and Victim-Offender Relationships by Demographic Group[a]

	Intimate Instrumental/ Expressive	Acquaintance Expressive/ Instrumental	Stranger Expressive/ Instrumental
Race			
Black on Black (423)	0.49 (137)	0.68 (212)	1.05 (74)
White on White (60)	0.07 (30)	5.33 (19)	1.75 (11)
Interracial (33)	0.00 (3)	0.60 (8)	0.83 (22)
Sex			
Male-male (372)	0.50 (78)	0.68 (202)	1.36 b (92)
Female-female (15)	0.25 (10)	1.50 (5)	—b
Female-male (52)	0.27 (38)	3.33 (13)	0.00 (1)
Male-female (83)	0.33 (44)	1.09 (23)	0.33 (16)
Age			
Suspect 19–34 (369)	0.39 (111)	1.44 (186)	1.00 (72)
Suspect < 19, > 34 (151)	0.38 (58)	0.81 (56)	1.31 (37)
Marital status (of offender)			
Married (55)	0.03 (34)	2.40 (17)	3.00 (4)
Single (108)	0.33 (53)	0.80 (18)	1.31 (37)

a. In each case, the victim is listed first, the offender second. The ratio is presented first and the number of cases used to construct the ratio is in parentheses.
b. Denotes no cases in this category.

relevance for epidemiology and policy, it is important to examine the high-rate ages as a separate category. For the 19- to 34-year-olds, more expressive than instrumental homicides were recorded for acquaintance relationships. For strangers, both age categories recorded high proportions of deviant homicides, in this case, events with expressive motives. Finally, offenders who were married were more likely to engage in expressive homicides against intimates than were single offenders, a result not surprising, because single offenders were less likely to have intimate relations than were married individuals. However, the acquaintance and stranger categories displayed unexpected findings. Married suspects were more likely to have an expressive motive when they killed an acquaintance, and single suspects were more likely to have an expressive motive when they killed a stranger.

The results of table 2 provide several interesting findings. For stranger homicides, expressive motives were more likely to be recorded than were instrumental motives. For acquaintances, the ratio of deviant to normative homicides greatly exceeded expectations based on prior research. These two categories of victim-offender relationships account for roughly two thirds of all homicides in St. Louis during the study period, 1985–1989. Only homicides involving intimates conformed to the findings of prior research.

In table 3, I examine the intersection between the typology and event characteristics. The first of five event characteristics considered was the location of the homicide event. In general, this panel of results conformed to expectations about the ratio of deviant to normative homicides. A somewhat different result is found for the panel containing information about the weapon used to commit the homicide. When physical contact was the method of inflicting death, more instrumental motives were present for intimates and more expressive motives for acquaintances, both counterintuitive findings. Intimate homicides with a gun were more likely to be instrumental, suggesting that motive has clear implications for the choice of means by which death is inflicted, a finding also reflected for acquaintances. Acquaintance homicides that involved the use of physical force were more likely to be expressive. Stranger killings with a firearm were more likely to have an expressive than instrumental motive.

An important characteristic of homicide events is the number of persons who participate in the event as suspects, as well as the number of witnesses present at the scene.[3] In only one of six outcomes—when stranger homicides were committed by one suspect—did the ratio of deviant to normative homicides exceed 1.0. When two or more witnesses were present, an unexpected combination of motive and victim-offender relationship was found for both the acquaintance and stranger categories. In each case, more expressive than instrumental motives were observed. The role of multiple witnesses in creating a backdrop for homicides between those who have weak or nonexistent relationships is well documented (Campbell 1986; Felson 1981; Oliver 1994), and the present results confirm the salience of an audience for homicide. Finally, alcohol seems to affect the intersection of motives and relationships differently than do drugs. Drug-related homicides among intimates more often have

Table 3
Deviant Homicides and Victim-Offender Relationships
by Situational Characteristics

	Intimate Instrumental/ Expressive	Acquaintance Expressive/ Instrumental	Stranger Expressive/ Instrumental
Premises			
Inside (242)	0.31 (108)	1.11 (97)	0.85 (37)
Outside (244)	0.47 (53)	0.65 (127)	0.94 (64)
Auto (28)	0.50 (3)	0.23 (16)	1.25 (9)
Weapon			
Gun (363)	0.48 (89)	0.59 (187)	1.18 (87)
Physical contact(142)	3.47 (76)	2.36 (47)	0.72 (19)
Number of suspects			
1 (412)	0.37 (156)	0.86 (179)	1.26 (77)
2 or more (105)	0.56 (14)	0.58 (60)	0.72 (31)
Number of witnesses			
None (231)	0.38 (91)	0.59 (102)	0.43 (28)
One (114)	0.48 (31)	0.68 (59)	0.85 (24)
Two or more (188)	0.32 (49)	1.26 (86)	1.94 (53)
Drug or alcohol related			
Drug related (143)	1.82 (31)	0.09 (83)	0.52 (29)
Alcohol related (134)	0.29 (45)	1.39 (62)	2.38 (27)

instrumental motives than expressive motives (Goldstein, 1985). Alcohol, on the other hand, is more likely to be present when acquaintance and stranger homicides have expressive motives. This suggests, especially in the case of intimates, that drugs exacerbate the already weak nature of "strong" or intimate ties. Alcohol, long linked to expressive behavior (Parker, 1995), is likely to be present when expressive motives dominate acquaintance or stranger killings.

Homicide Narratives

I now examine the dynamics of "deviant homicides" in greater detail. This analysis was facilitated by the construction of "homicide narratives." Primary instrumental homicides are the first category of events that are examined. These events are characterized by close relationships between victims and offenders and attempts on the part of one of the actors to achieve material gain or tangible outcome. Bad deals and bad debts comprise the basis for a substantial portion of these events. In many cases, disputes over drugs form the basis for many such disagreements, as shown in table 3. A number of primary instrumental homicides include felony homicides over issues not related to drugs.

Kin relationships have long been assumed to "protect" or insulate individuals against instrumental crimes. Three homicide narratives illustrate the nature of deviant homicides within this category. The first occurred between two brothers who fought over a debt owed by one to the other.

> Argument over money suspect owed victim. Victim kept asking suspect what he was going to do about the debt. Suspect wanted victim to stop hassling him and let him "chill out." Victim said he wanted his half, suspect said he did not have half coming to him. Victim went into suspect's closet to get his half. Suspect tried to stop victim. They struggled and suspect shot victim. (HN 8800162757)[4]

The characteristics of this event closely resemble a dispute over money that may occur between those whose relationships are less strong than that of brothers. A second narrative presents another dispute between brothers, this one over drugs.

> Suspect was a known drug user, released from halfway house just before murder. Suspect was killed before an arrest could be made. Since getting out of prison, suspect had been selling drugs for a dealer he met in prison. Victim did not like people coming in and out of the house to buy drugs. Suspect also brought prostitutes to the house, which further angered the victim. When victim found suspect's drugs, he flushed them down the toilet. Suspect then shot and killed victim. (HN 8800042748)

Such disputes are not confined to male siblings, as the following example of a homicide between sisters illustrates:

> Argument over money for drugs. During argument and fight with stick, victim threatened to kill suspect. Victim wanted suspect to lend her money. Suspect claimed she refused because victim only wanted money for drugs. Victim called suspect names. Argument started in tavern. The two left the tavern, the fight continued and the victim was stabbed. (HN 8800110185)

Other primary relationships have instrumental motives, as the following examples of homicides between a girlfriend and boyfriend demonstrate:

> After the victim's death, her family discovered that jewelry, a handgun, insurance policy, and checkbook were missing from the house. (HN 8800143993)

> Victim and suspect dated. Suspect robbed victim for money to get crack. Suspect's cousin was aware that suspect was thinking of robbing the victim. While she was sitting outside of victim's apartment waiting for suspect, two guys came by and they all went and smoked primos. Suspect stole victim's handgun and bought some rocks and smoked them. Then she stole victim's wallet, bought five more rocks, and smoked them with her cousin. When she stole the wallet, she killed the victim. She then stole her mother's dishes in an attempt to bring more crack. (HN 8900179216)

These narratives demonstrate that drugs, especially crack cocaine, have created instrumental motives within primary relationships, diminishing the insularity that such relationships previously provided. It is also possible that changes in family structure (Hacker 1992; Wilson et al. 1980) among the urban underclass have altered the insularity previously found in such relationships. Daly and Wilson (1982) reported that "blood ties" provide this insularity. My results suggest that among some population subgroups, these "strong" ties have begun to become undone.

Friends also represent a primary relationship in which instrumental homicides occur. Daly and Wilson (1982) reported that relational distance is inversely related to the probability of homicide. Our results for primary instrumental homicides are consistent with this finding, as friends are more likely to be represented in this category than relatives. And like those related by blood, primary instrumental homicides involving friends often occur over disputes involving bad debts or bad deals, often about drugs. Despite the heavy involvement of drugs in homicides within this category, most of the drug involvement is associated with drug roles (seller, buyer, supplier) and drug transactions rather than "high" homicides (Rosenfeld, 1989).

> This argument occurred outside a dope crib. Victim threatened suspect's wife in an argument over a PCP bottle. A short time later, suspect (accompanied by wife and another friend) encountered the victim who came running up to their car. Victim was reportedly armed and, according to the suspect's wife, was "quicker on the draw." (HN 8700069379)

In the case above, a dispute over drugs provided a motive for the homicide. In the cases below, the homicides occurred in the context of a drug role, illustrating that a long-standing friendship and the protection it typically offers from instrumental homicides can be set aside in the face of the need to make money.

> Sellers killed the victim because he bothered their customers. The victim had been drinking that evening and had been bothering the suspects' dope customers. The victim knew the suspects from the neighborhood. He had been begging from the suspects' customers. Suspects had intended to scare the victim away. The first suspect had been given cocaine to try to detain the victim until the other two suspects could catch up to him and kill him. (HN 8700039742)

> Suspect and victim had known each other well for approximately 8 or 9 years. Victim was known to be an alcoholic and had been in many fights. Suspect gave money to the victim to buy beer, and the victim tried to take the money without buying the beer. A fight resulted and the suspect punched the victim in the face, causing the victim to fall and hit the back of his head on the pavement. The suspect claimed that he was simply trying to retrieve his money. (HN 8500056761)

A final narrative illustrates a key ingredient found in many of the primary instrumental homicides, prior involvement in criminal activities.[5] As Loftin (1986) has observed, "[V]iolent victimization is the best predictor of the prevalence of a serious assaultive offense in the careers of cohort members" (p. 552). The insularity against instrumental homicides provided by primary relationships is neutralized most easily, not surprisingly, by those with prior involvement in criminality.

> Around 12:30 a.m. the suspect confronted the victim concerning a bur-
> glary. The suspect believed the victim had burglarized his house. There
> was an argument followed by a fight. Friends of the suspect also became
> involved in the fight. The suspect went to one of his friends' house and had
> a few beers. The victim followed and taunted one of the friends. At this
> point the suspect and victim fought again. The victim left the area. The sus-
> pect decided to confront the victim again and killed him. (HN 8700056693)

Primary instrumental homicides comprise a relatively small (9%) yet distinct category of events. A much larger group, 31%, was classified as secondary expressive homicides. In secondary relationships, the "protection"
against instrumental violence provided in primary relationships does not
exist. However, secondary relationships (here defined as strangers or
acquaintances) have seldom been thought to produce expressive forms of
violence. Lacking the intensity of primary relationships, these associations
have typically led to instrumental, not expressive violence. The finding that
31% of homicides fall into the secondary expressive category suggests a
redefinition of the intersection of motives and relationships. Several characteristics distinguish these homicides: (a) revenge or retaliation, (b) "identity"
killings, or (c) killings between strangers who are linked by a third party in a
primary relationship with either the victim, offender, or both.

I first examine secondary expressive homicides that have a strong element of retaliation or revenge. In many of these cases, the ultimate outcome
can be linked to a prior dispute of noninstrumental origin that often centers
on some form of harassment, and thus contains some element of "reciproc-
ity" (Loftin 1986). Another feature common to many of these homicides is
the role of the victim in precipitating the event that led to his or her death.
The first narrative illustrative of this category involved a dispute common to
most neighborhoods, "fast driving."

> Victim had been "laying rubber" in the street with his auto, then parked
> auto in front of suspect's home. Banged on suspect's door and screamed,
> "have I got your attention now mother fucker," and dared suspect to call
> the police. The suspect got a golf club, and when victim saw it, he got a
> baseball bat from his car, beat his own car with the bat, and threatened to
> beat and kill the suspect. The suspect went back in the house for a rifle,
> returned, and shot the victim. The suspect claimed that the victim had
> scared him, and he feared for his life. The victim's girlfriend said that the
> victim was drunk and acting like a "total asshole." (HN 8700143167)

Another feature of retaliation homicides is an underlying feud that may
have simmered for some time. These events are most often thought to occur
exclusively within primary relationships; however, as the following narrative
shows, they occur within secondary relationships as well.

> The suspect was dressed as a "ninja" (face was masked except for the
> eyes). A crowd of people was outside when the suspect approached the
> victim, pushing several people out of the way. The suspect shot the vic-

tim once. The victim fell, telling kids near him to run, which most of them did. As the victim lay on the ground, the suspect stood over him and shot him 4 or 5 more times, then fled. One onlooker said there had been "bad blood" between the two since the victim shot a relative of the suspect the year before. (HN 8800086491)

The following narrative documents how the process of contagion may work to generate an increase in homicide.

Suspect and victim had been drinking earlier in the evening. They got into an argument. The victim had once stabbed the brother of the suspect, though not fatally. An argument ensued over the prior stabbing of the suspect's brother and a gun was pulled. During the struggle over the gun, the suspect shot the victim. (HN 8800041192)

I classify a second category of secondary expressive homicides as "identity" killings, or events in which a threat to the identity of the suspect (or victim) initiates the conflict. In these cases violence often occurs in response to "status-inappropriate" (Wilson and Daly 1985) behavior. These killings most closely resemble the "righteous slaughter" described by Katz (1988) in which victims are killed not for instrumental gain but rather as a demonstration of identity or toughness by criminals Katz referred to as "badasses." The acts of such persons reflect their immersion in street-life culture.

Suspect claimed that earlier in the evening he argued with the victim because suspect had been sitting on steps of a vacant house. The victim didn't want the suspect to sit there because it may draw the attention of the police. The suspect told the victim he could sit wherever he liked, that the victim didn't pay the rent there, etc. Suspect went to a party and shot the victim after the party. (HN 8700093200)

Clearly, the suspect had no intention of being directed by the victim to appropriate places to sit. His response was to engage in "righteous slaughter" over the victim's temerity to suggest where the suspect could or could not "hang out." The following narratives further illustrate the "dangers" in challenging the identity or territory (however loosely defined) of "badasses."

Suspect was a drug dealer and was killed before he could be arrested for this incident. The victim had been drinking and in his rush to catch up with his girlfriend, he tripped up the porch where the suspect was sitting. The suspect said, "You don't know me. Are you too good for me?" The victim and suspect argued and the suspect pulled a gun and shot the victim in the neck from about 2 feet away. (HN 8900083223)

The following narrative describes another identity killing that occurred when the victim told the suspect how to behave. After the killing, the suspect returned to the scene of the crime for a "victory lap," as if to demonstrate to those in the neighborhood that he was no one to "mess with."

Victim and suspect had first contact earlier the day of the shooting. The victim apparently thought the suspect was a nuisance or annoying people and told the suspect so. The suspect became angry and left the area to get a gun and returned to shoot the victim. Suspect was arrested because he returned to the scene shortly after the shooting and was pointed out to the police by the victim (who was still conscious) and other witnesses. (HN 8800150533)

These narratives point to the dangers of intervening in the lives of the "badass." There are times, though, when such individuals are confronted by situations that they do not control, and the perceived challenges to their identity that provokes their rage is turned against them. In such an instance, living out the street-defined identity of the badass leads them into trouble.

The victim kept driving up and down the street fast, making U-turns at each end of the street. Once he drove up on the sidewalk while U-turning, nearly hitting the suspect who was walking his dog. The suspect said, "Man, you almost hit me." Victim got out of car and cursed the suspect. Suspect then took out a gun and fired a shot, missing the victim, then ran. Victim got in car and chased suspect, stating to friends that he was going to get the old man and hit him with the car (which was one of four victim had stolen that evening). Suspect shot and killed victim. (HN 8900130418)

The following narrative demonstrates the brashness with which "street elites" (Katz 1988) operate on their territory, taking liberties with whomever they please in whatever way they please.

The victim walked the witness home after the tavern had closed. The suspect followed them, not approaching them until the pair had reached their destination. Suspect approached victim and victim's companion on the street. The suspect fondled the witness's breasts, which angered the victim. The victim told the suspect, "I'll see you hang." Then the suspect shot the victim. (HN 8700166044)

Other challenges to identity can be couched in racial or sexual terms. Racial bias crimes often can be classified as secondary expressive events, especially when they involve perceived threats to identity. Such "threats" often require little force behind them.

Victim and witness were stopped in their car. Suspects pulled up in a truck next to them. Victim glanced over and suspect said, "What the hell are you looking at?" Victim said. "We don't want no trouble, we're going our way." Suspect said, "Go about your business you f—— niggers." Suspect then shot victim. (HN 8900099278)

Sometimes strangers are brought together in homicide by third parties who know the victim, the suspect, or both. This can be particularly true for homicides that involve conflicts over women; as Daly and Wilson (1982) have noted, male sexual jealousy plays an especially large role in violent assaults. Although these homicides do occur between strangers, they often have many of the characteristics of primary homicides. It is a third party who links the victim and suspect and creates the conditions that make these "stranger" homicides resemble primary homicides in motive. In the following narratives, one stranger was killed by another stranger who had met only because of a romantic relationship with the third party.

> Suspect and victim had same girlfriend. Suspect walked in on victim and suspect's girlfriend in bed together. An argument ensued. Suspect entered the witness's home because he had the key. When suspect found the victim in bed with her, suspect and victim fought, then ran in different directions. Victim collapsed outside and was found by a passing acquaintance. (HN 8500138575)

And the following narrative shows how third parties can bring strangers into contact for homicides. In this instance, the victim and suspect were strangers, but the suspect's girlfriend knew the victim, thus "facilitating" the homicide.

> Victim was dating suspect's ex-girlfriend. The girlfriend did not want to talk to suspect, but he called several times and was insistent. She finally agreed and tried to keep him on the front porch. Suspect wanted girlfriend back and she did not want to resume the relationship. When ex-girlfriend went into house for a beer, suspect followed her. While still on the porch, suspect asked the ex-girlfriend, "Where is that punk-ass?" When the suspect followed her into the house and was introduced to the victim, he shot him immediately. There was no argument between suspect and victim. Girlfriend did not think the suspect knew anything about the victim or her relationship with the victim. (HN 8600072187)

Similarly, mistaken identity about a girlfriend led to the following expressive homicide between strangers.

> The suspects were in the neighborhood because they had gone to the home next door (the victim's residence) to collect a debt. One of the suspects had been seeing a young girl in the neighborhood. Six weeks prior she had been sitting in an auto with the suspect when the victim had returned from work. When she saw the victim she ran into her house. The victim thought it was his girlfriend who had been with the suspect and wanted to fight. The suspect refused to fight at that time, but said, "I'll remember this. I'll be back." (HN 8700166354)

These homicide narratives demonstrate the diversity of events that can be found within primary instrumental and secondary expressive homicides.

Conclusion

The data reviewed here demonstrate that the motive in homicide interacts with the victim-offender relationship in important and unexpected ways. Instrumental homicides do not occur exclusively among strangers; the level of instrumental violence—especially among those well known to each other—was higher than expected, and the narratives ascribe a rational character to such events. In addition, expressive homicides are not confined to those who are well known to each other. Expressive violence often occurs among strangers; indeed, it is almost as likely to be found among strangers as intimates and it takes an aggressive form. These results suggest that the intensity of relationships is not as strong a predictor of motive as has been previously suggested. In addition, those intimately related may not be immune from homicides that arise from disputes of an instrumental nature.

One of the characteristics of homicide that is difficult to explain using only quantitative data is sudden increases in homicide. Most cities experience what is commonly referred to as a "rash" or "epidemic" of homicides. During these periods of time, homicides increase rapidly. By examining qualitative data, we can begin to suggest explanations for these sudden changes in the distribution of homicides over time. Loftin (1986) recommended the concept of "contagion" as useful in explaining such sudden upturns in homicide rates. It is apparent that structural characteristics alone could not explain these rapid changes, because their fluctuation is much slower and is generally measured at annual intervals. Our narratives, especially in the secondary expressive category, suggest that many homicides are linked through what we call "homicide networks." These networks link victims, suspects, and witnesses to assaultive violence and can explain how a witness to one event can become the victim or suspect in another event. It is often the case that a prior act of instrumental motivation generated an expressive homicide, as in the case of retaliation for wrongs, both actual and perceived. The narratives described above illustrate how many of these networks facilitate the contagious spread of violence, especially those with an expressive motivation among strangers. Many of these events comprise what Black (1983) referred to as "capital punishment administered on a private basis" (p. 35). Those individuals most isolated from social institutions have the least confidence that the criminal justice system takes the victimization of their friends and family seriously. This creates the motivation to mete out justice on the street, independent of the criminal justice system. In addition, these networks can explain how motives for one killing are generated out of a prior assault or murder. Because of the "collective liability" (Black 1983, p. 33) that exists within secondary relationships, the victim need not be the perpetrator of an earlier offense and need only be a suitable representative for the perpetrator.

A most important question arises with the presentation of these findings: "Why do they differ so from earlier research?" Several explanations are possible. First, homicide may be changing dramatically. Like all social behavior, crime is dynamic. Without question, the urban contexts in which a large proportion of homicides occur have changed drastically in the last two decades (Anderson 1990; Hacker 1992; Wilson 1987). As these and other commentators have noted, the family has all but ceased to exist in large numbers of urban neighborhoods. The strength of family ties may have eroded in the process, removing constraints on instrumental homicides among intimates. The emergence of crack cocaine has also fundamentally altered the relationship between motives and victim-offender relationships. Also, the presence of gangs in American cities has contributed to a growth in expressive homicides committed between people who do not know each other. These insights suggest policy interventions that are linked to disrupting easy access to such criminogenic commodities as firearms and illegal drugs, as well as the markets that provide them. The data presented here, however, are inadequate to determine whether these observations depict a trend, as 5 years of annual data are inadequate for such purposes. Second, although change in the nature of urban life (and correspondingly urban homicide) may be at the heart of these findings, a measurement issue may also be of significance. In much prior research, victim-offender relationships and motives were viewed as alternative measurements of the same concept. For example, all homicides involving strangers were recorded as having instrumental motivation. For my data, however, determinations of motive were based on a reading of the data and construction of narratives describing the homicide process. Thus motives were determined independently of relationships, and with reference to extensive police reports, including the statements of suspects and witnesses. These findings caused me to question the fundamental premise about the relationship between motives and victim-offender relationships in homicide. Nearly half of all homicides did not conform to my expectations based on prior research, suggesting that there is considerable variation in homicide events.

These findings call into question our understanding of the effect of relationships on motives, particularly when such concepts cannot be measured independently. Polk (1994) and Daly and Wilson (1988) have each suggested that measuring these variables is complex, and often not well-done. The current research underscores the conclusion that our understanding of homicide events depends on access to the most detailed descriptions possible. Absent such descriptions, serious measurement error is likely to accompany analyses.

NOTES

[1] Block and Block's . . . work (1992) stands as a notable exception to the cross classification of these dichotomies. They have developed "syndromes," multiple categories that reflect greater diversity in motive, circumstance, and victim-offender relationship.

[2] Some classification schemes depend on situational characteristics of the offense such as whether it originated from an argument. From our perspective, arguments are the product of relationships and interactions, and can occur in either category.

[3] Here "witnesses" refers to people present at the scene, regardless of their future participation in the legal processing of the case.

[4] HN refers to "Homicide Number," the case number of a homicide event in the records.

[5] As this classification was determined from homicides files and not offender histories, it underestimates prior criminal involvement.

REFERENCES

Anderson, Elijah. 1990. *A Place on the Corner*. Chicago: University of Chicago Press.

Berkowitz, Leonard. 1986. "Some Varieties of Human Aggression: Criminal Violence as Coercion, Rule-Following, Impression Management and Impulsive Behavior." Pp. 87–103 in *Violent Transactions*, edited by A. Campbell and J. Gibbs. New York: Basil Blackwell.

Bernard, Thomas. 1990. "Angry Aggression among the 'Truly Disadvantaged.'" *Criminology* 28: 73–96.

Black, Donald. 1983. "Crime as Social Control." *American Sociological Review* 48: 34–45.

Block, Carolyn R. 1985. *Lethal Violence in Chicago over Seventeen Years: Homicides Known to the Police, 1965–1981.* Chicago: Illinois Criminal Justice Information Authority.

Block, Richard. 1977. *Violent Crime: Environment, Interaction and Death.* Lexington, MA: D. C. Heath.

Block, Richard. 1981. "Victim Offender Dynamics in Violent Crime." *Journal of Criminal Law and Criminology* 72 (2): 743–61.

Block, Richard, and Carolyn Block. 1992. "Homicide Syndromes and Vulnerability: Violence in Chicago's Community Areas over 25 Years." Pp. 61–87 in *Studies on Crime and Crime Prevention, 1,* by D. Chappell. Oslo, Norway, and Stockholm, Sweden: Scandinavian University Press.

Block, Richard, and Wesley Skogan. 1984. *The Dynamics of Violence between Strangers: Victim Resistance and Outcomes in Rape, Assault and Robbery.* Evanston, IL: Center for Urban Affairs and Policy Research.

Block, Richard, and Franklin Zimring. 1973. "Homicide in Chicago, 1965–1970." *Journal of Research in Crime and Delinquency* 10: 1–12.

Campbell, Anne. 1986. "The Streets and Violence." Pp. 115–32 in *Violent Transactions: The Limits of Personality,* edited by Anne Campbell and John J. Gibbs. New York: Basil Blackwell.

Cook, Philip J. 1987. "Robbery Violence." *Journal of Criminal Law and Criminology* 78: 357–76.

Daly, Martin, and Margo Wilson. 1982. "Homicide and Kinship." *American Anthropologist* 84: 372–8.

Daly, Martin, and Margo Wilson. 1988. *Homicide.* New York: Aldine.

Felson, Richard B. 1978. "Aggression as Impression Management." *Social Psychology* 41: 205–13.

Felson, Richard B. 1981. "An Interactionist Approach to Aggression." Pp. 181–99 in *Impression Management Theory and Social Psychological Research,* edited by James T. Tedeschi. New York: Academic Press.

Goldstein, Paul. 1985. "The Drugs/Violence Nexus: A Tripartite Conceptual Framework." *Journal of Drug Issues* 14: 493–506.

Hacker, Andrew. 1992. *Two Nations.* New York: Basic Books.

Kapardis, Andros. 1990. "Stranger Homicides in Victoria, January, 1984–December 1989." *Australian and New Zealand Journal of Criminology* 23: 241–58.

Katz, Jack. 1988. *Seductions of Crime.* New York: Basic Books.

Loftin, Colin. 1986. "Assaultive Violence as a Contagious Social Process." *Bulletin of the New York Academy of Medicine* 62: 550–5.

Luckenbill, David, 1977–78. "Criminal Homicide as Situated Transaction." *Social Problems* 25: 176–86.

Maxfield, Michael. 1989. "Circumstances in Supplementary Homicide Reports: Variety and Validity." *Criminology* 27: 671–95.

Messner, Steven F., and Kenneth Tardiff. 1985. "The Social Ecology of Urban Homicide: An Application of the 'Routine Activities' Approach." *Criminology* 23: 241–67.

Nightengale, Carl H. 1993. *On the Edge: A History of Poor Black Children and Their American Dreams.* New York: Basic Books.

Oliver, William. 1994. *The Violent Social World of Black Men.* Boston: Lexington Books.

Parker, Robert Nash. 1995. *Alcohol and Homicide: A Deadly Combination of Two American Traditions.* Albany: State University of New York Press.

Parker, Robert Nash, and M. Dwayne Smith. 1979. "Deterrence, Poverty and Type of Homicide." *American Journal of Sociology* 85: 614–24.

Polk, Kenneth. 1994. *Why Men Kill*. New York: Cambridge University Press.

Polk, Kenneth, and David Ranson. 1991. "Patterns of Homicide in Victoria." Pp. 53–119 in *Australian Violence: Contemporary Perspectives*, edited by D. Chappell and H. Strang. Canberra: Australian Institute of Criminology.

Riedel, Mark. 1981. "Stranger Homicides in an American City." Paper presented at the American Society of Criminology, November, Washington, DC.

Riedel, Mark. 1987. "Symposium: Stranger Violence: Perspectives, Issues and Problems." *Journal of Criminal Law and Criminology* 78 (2): 223–58.

Riedel, Mark, and Roger Przybylski. 1993. "Stranger Murders and Assault: A Study of a Neglected Form of Stranger Violence." Pp. 359–82 in *Homicide: The Victim/Offender Connection*, edited by Anna Victoria Wilson. Cincinnati, OH: Anderson.

Riedel, Mark, and Margaret Zahn. 1985. *The Nature and Patterns of American Homicide*. Washington, DC: U.S. Department of Justice.

Rojek, Dean, and James Williams. 1993. "Interracial vs. Interracial Offenses in Terms of the Victim/Offender Relationship." Pp. 249–66 in Homicide: *The Victim/Offender Connection*, edited by Anna Victoria Wilson. Cincinnati, OH: Anderson.

Rosenfeld, Richard. 1989. "Anatomy of the Drug-Related Homicide." St. Louis Homicide Project, University of Missouri—St. Louis.

Rosenfeld, Richard, and Scott H. Decker. 1993. "Responding to Youth Violence: Where Public Health and Law Enforcement Meet." *American Journal of Police* 12 (3): 11–57.

Sampson, Robert J. 1987. "Personal Violence by Strangers: An Extension and Test of the Opportunity Model of Predatory Victimization." *Journal of Criminal Law and Criminology* 78 (2): 327–56.

Smith, M. Dwayne and Robert Nash Parker. 1980. "Type of Homicide and Variation in Regional Rates." *Social Forces* 59: 136–47.

Wilson, Margo, and Martin Daly. 1985. "Competitiveness, Risk Taking and Violence: The Young Male Syndrome." *Ethology and Sociobiology* 6: 59–73.

Wilson, Margo, Martin Daly, and Suzanne Weghorst. 1980. "Household Composition and the Risk of Child Abuse and Neglect." *Journal of Biosocial Science* 12: 333–40.

Wilson, William Julius. 1987. *The Truly Disadvantaged*. Chicago: University of Chicago Press.

Zimring, Franklin E., and James Zuehl. 1986. "Victim Injury and Death in Urban Robbery: A Chicago Study." *Journal of Legal Studies* 15: 1–40.

Chapter Eleven

Victimology and
the Victims of White-Collar Crime

David Shichor

There has been a growing professional interest in the study of victims and victimization since the early 1970s. This interest was reflected in the publication of a large volume of victimological books and articles in academic journals; in the establishment of national and international organizations including the World Society of Victimology; and in victimological conferences and professional workshops. The number of researchers and helping professionals dealing with crime victims and victimization also has grown rapidly.

At the same time, victimology, having aspirations of becoming a respected academic discipline, has come under serious criticism by several social scientists. For example, the well-respected criminologist Cressey (1992 p. 57) declared that victimology is neither a scientific nor an academic principle "to which scholars and scientists trained in various disciplines make theoretical and research contributions." This situation was attributed to the differences between the scientific and humanistic approaches to victimology, between those who try to establish victimology as a scientific enterprise and those who focus on helping, in various ways, the plight of crime victims.

Generally, with the growing interest in the victims of crimes, there are efforts to find ways to reduce their sufferings, because they are "natural targets for human sympathy" (Fattah 1992 p. 4). However, this positive public attitude has focused predominantly on victims of street crimes, particularly violent crimes, and such "newly discovered" crimes as domestic violence, child abuse and sexual molestation. Relatively little attention has been paid to the victims of white-collar crimes. Fattah (1986 p. 5) relates to this issue by

From Section III, Verbrechensopfer und Verbrechensfurcht, of *Festschrift für Hans Joachim Schneiderzum 70. Geburtstag am 14.* November 1998, Hans-Dieter Schwind, Edwin Kube, Hans-Heiner Kühne, editors, pp. 332–351. Berlin: Walter de Gruyter GmbH & Co. Copyright © 1998 by Walter de Gruyter GmbH & Co., D-10785 Berlin. Used with permission.

pointing out that: "despite the scope of white-collar crime and despite the fact that its depredations far exceed those of conventional crime it is totally left out from victim campaigns." Even general victimology textbooks, that supposedly should provide an overview of the discipline and cover the entire scope of the subject matter, do not deal with the victims of white-collar crimes. For example, Karmen (1996) in the introduction of his widely used textbook makes clear that he focuses only on the victims of street crimes.

The above concentration on the victims of street crimes is not completely unique to American scholars, it is true to a large degree for European traditional victimology as well (see Joutsen 1994). The neglect of a major area of study such as white-collar victimization and its victims hurts the development of victimology as a bona-fide scientific discipline. Lately, however, there are some modest changes in this regard. For example, feminist scholars studied several aspects of victimization of women by corporations (Szockyj and Fox 1996; Gerber and Weeks 1992), a handful of other works that dealt with various forms of white-collar crime dedicated some attention to the victims of these crimes as well (Clinard and Yeager 1980; Friedrichs 1996; Levi 1992), and a few small-scale studies focused on the victims of white-collar fraud (Mason and Benson 1996; Shichor et al. 1996; Shover et al. 1994). Also, in a few countries, there were some studies and surveys on commercial fraud victimization (see Maguire and Shapland 1997). In spite of promising developments, the overwhelming majority of victimological research (empirical and theoretical) remains to be occupied by the study of street crime victims and their victimization.

Before trying to analyze the reasons for the victimological neglect of the topic of white-collar victimization, there is a need to define white-collar crime for the purposes of this chapter. It is well known, that currently there are several definitions of "white-collar crime," and there is no full consensus regarding the acceptance of any one of them by criminologists and social scientists.

In this chapter, a recent definition of white-collar crime, that was forwarded by the participants of the Academic Workshop on White-Collar convened by the National White-Collar Crime Center, was adopted:

> Planned illegal or unethical acts of deception, committed by an individual or organization, usually during the course of legitimate occupational activity by persons of high or respectable social status, for personal or organizational gain that violates public trust. (Helmkamp et al. 1996 p. III)

This definition was adopted because it includes both occupational and corporate offenses, maintains the original idea of depicting violations by persons having relatively high status during their legitimate occupational activity, and includes "deception" and "violation of trust" which are two important characteristics present in most white-collar crimes.

This chapter attempts to review some of the major reasons for the neglect of victims of white-collar crime and their victimization, and the theoretical as well as the pragmatic ramifications of this neglect. The analysis, because of the limitations of a short chapter, is general and focuses mainly on the American scene. It is recognized that some of the conclusions drawn may be more relevant for one type of white-collar crime than for another, and the relevance of the analysis may vary by the type of offense, offenders and victims (individuals, public organizations, private corporations, etc.).

Political Issues

During the 1980s, several major legislations were passed and various victim aid programs were established throughout the United States. Many of these measures were implemented without too much scrutiny of the underlying issues and legal considerations. For example, the California Victim's Bill of Rights, voted in by the electorate in 1982, has raised some constitutional questions concerning the exclusionary rule, pretrial detention, restrictions on bail, and on several other legal matters. This and similar other bills contributed to the increased use of long-term incarceration, to the problems of overcrowding in correctional facilities, and to the continuously rising criminal justice expenditures.

There was a strong support for these measures by politicians from all levels (local, state, national) and from all sides of the political spectrum. It was easily recognized that conventional victimization is a "valance issue" which means that it "elicits a single, strong, fairly emotional response and does not have any adversial quality" (Fattah 1992 p. 3). Thus, clearly, it could muster broad-scale public support. However, while the overt concern with the plight of the victims of street crimes was impressive, the motives behind the support of various groups and individuals promoting victim causes often were not revealed.

There is a growing volume of evidence that victim causes that were presented as humanitarian concerns have been "hijacked" by conservative "law and order" groups and even by certain business interests that could benefit from their implementation (e.g. the gun lobby). These groups and politicians used this issue to further their political agenda and to press for more repressive crime control policies. This trend culminated in the notorious "three-strikes" laws legislated in the 1990s (Shichor and Sechrest 1996).[1]

Traditional grassroots victim advocacy and support groups, trying to influence legislation dealing with issues of victimization, seem to be successful mainly in increasing the punishment for offenders rather than mustering support for long-term victimization prevention programs that often are seen as too liberal. For example, women victim advocacy organizations supported the Community Protection Act of 1989 of the State of Washington which included the control of sexual violence and stiff sentences for violators, but failed to gain significant financial support from the legislature for programs of detection and treatment of juvenile delinquency (Scheingold, et al., 1994).

Conservative efforts to use victim causes for punitive purposes are enhanced by the media's distorted presentation of crime, offenders, and victims. The focus is on violent crimes because of their "newsworthyness" and their visibility (see Karmen 1996). This is especially true for television and movies. Television reporting is the main source of news for a large portion of the population, because short one- to two-minute reports can present gory crime scenes and grab the attention of the audience. This way of reporting provides a distorted picture of crime since it emphasizes the sensational and violent aspects, increases the public's fear and anxiety (Matthews and Young 1992), and diverts attention from and interest in white-collar crimes and their victims. The lack of reporting of white-collar crimes is explained by Chermak (1995 p. 120):

> White-collar crimes rarely satisfy the visual format needs of television because there is rarely a specific crime scene or a victim on which to focus. In addition, white-collar crime is generally not a threat to the immediate safety of the audience. When a serial rapist strikes, the news report serves as an easily visualized warning. In television, it is difficult to warn people about white-collar victimization because too much explanation is needed.

Movies and television shows focusing on crime, with relatively few exceptions, concentrate on street, mainly violent, crimes and on their perpetrators and victims. These topics are more action oriented, more understood by the public, and can be presented more easily on the screen than white-collar crimes.

The exploitation of victims and victim issues reached its peak during the 1980s in the U.S. The President's Task Force on Victims of Crime, appointed by President Reagan in 1982, interviewed a large number of victims and persons dealing with victims throughout the country, and made a set of recommendations to criminal justice agencies and private institutions regarding the handling of victims of violent crimes, with a special emphasis on sex crimes. This elaborate document did not make any mention of victims of white-collar crimes.

The conservative socio-political trend which put a major emphasis on "family values" and on efforts to stop the "moral decay" afflicting modern industrialized society, emphasized the "war on drugs" and showed a major concern with domestic violence, child abuse, and sex crimes. Since most of the reported and officially processed domestic violence, child abuse, sexual attack, and drug violation cases involve lower class, often minority families and individuals, to focus on these issues became even more attractive for conservative politicians and interest groups. At the same time, victims of domestic violence became also a major concern for feminist groups who otherwise tend to pursue a more liberal social agenda (particularly pro-choice on abortion, support for single parent families, and financial support for day care centers). Thus, on various victimization issues unusual social and political alliances emerged. However, these concerns with the victims of violent crimes seldom were followed with substantial financial support. During the early part of the 1990s many victim aid services were downsized or even closed down because of lack of funding. Similarly, in the United States and in Britain, conservative legislators often rejected comprehensive criminal injuries compensation claiming budgetary problems (Mawby 1992).

Also victimologists, regardless whether they follow the conservative, liberal or left-oriented approaches to victimology, and various helping professionals, tend to focus on the victims of street crimes and street crime victimization. Walklate (1992), in making a comparison between mainline and left-oriented victimology, observed that empirical research, following either one of these directions, relies heavily on victimization surveys using them as the major data source. Among others she stated that "both focus on crimes as it is commonly understood; that is neither tackles the question of victimization by corporations. . . ." (p. 112).

It is an important for victimology to analyze the reasons for the neglect of victims of white-collar crimes and their victimization by the conservative approach[2] on the one hand and by the liberal, left-realist, and critical approaches to victimology on the other.

Victims of White-Collar Crimes and Victimology

In many cases, white-collar crime is perpetrated by upper- and middle-class offenders, often in the name of or in the behalf of corporations. Focusing on this kind of victimization would reveal wide-scale law breaking among supporters of the conservative socio-political agenda. Gottfredson and Hirschi (1990 p. 17) observe, that based on empirical research "victims and offenders tend to share nearly all social and personal characteristics." By concentrating on the victims of street crimes and by focusing their demands for harsh punishments of street crime offenders, middle- and upper-class advocates of the conservative agenda tend to neglect the cause of the victims of white-collar crimes. In turn, this may further the commission of more white-collar crimes and more victimization of middle- and upper-class people, because only meager efforts are dedicated to curb these crimes, their perpetrators are punished relatively lightly and are exposed to only minor public denunciation.

Similarly, the mainstream liberal and the left-oriented approaches of victimology also show little interest in the victims of and victimization by white-collar crimes. There are several possible reasons for this neglect. The liberal approach is similar to the conservative one in the sense that it does not ask "fundamental questions about the viability or desirability of mainstream American life" (Scheingold 1984 p. 4). Both the liberal and the left-oriented approaches are focusing on the plight of lower class, politically powerless victims of street crime and domestic victimization (see Young and Rush 1994). The various left-orientations usually adopt a Marxist view and look at violent victimization as a result of the social conditions created by the capitalist system which emphasizes competition and the "survival of the fittest" rather than a more equal distribution of resources and wealth. This line of reasoning follows to a large extent the premises of Bonger (1916) who argued that capitalism furthers selfishness which produces egoistic and violent acts by lower class people. According to him, because of their "false class consciousness" the exploited poor victimize other poor people who live close to them and who are the least able to protect themselves.

It was already recognized by Sutherland (1940) over fifty years ago that white-collar crimes are economically far more costly than street crimes are. Also, in terms of social cost, they may be more harmful than street crimes because they tend to undermine the social fabric of society (Meier and Short 1983), they question the validity of the capitalist value system, they violate trust which is a fundamental basis of social relations (Shapiro 1990), and they involve the abuse of power by important and influential members of society (Geis 1992).

In spite of this situation, white-collar crimes and the ways they victimize people do not seem to command a serious public concern. One of the reasons is that certain types of these crimes, while they victimize a large number of people and yield large sums of money to their perpetrators, they are highly diffusive and the individual losses are relatively small. For example, in the case of commercial victimizations "the injuries caused by most corporate violations are highly diffused, falling almost imperceptively upon each of a great number of widely scattered victims" (Geis 1973 p. 248). In many cases, the victims are even unaware of the fact that they were victimized. Furthermore, even when victims are aware of their victimization, relatively few of them report the crime to the authorities, oftentimes because they feel that they were duped and are embarrassed of their gullibility.

Another contributing factor, to the limited public exposure of and interest in white-collar victimization, is that in some instances there are no clearly recognized direct victims of the scheme, but only potential victims can be depicted. This is the case in most ponzi and pyramid schemes, or in certain commercial frauds such as escrow fraud when various individual accounts are commingled and the handlers of these funds cover their embezzlement with new incoming deposits (Doocy and Shichor 1994).

In other cases of corporate violations in which the direct victims are government agencies or the public at large, such as tax evasion or air/water pollution, individuals, even if they become aware of the violations, in most cases do not feel the immediate effects of victimization (Shichor 1989). When tax evasion is concerned, many may side more with the perpetrator of the offense than with the direct victim (the government entity). Only in relatively few major cases, when serious physical injuries or deaths are the result of white-collar violations and victimization, like in the Pinto automobile case, will the public furor and indignation be demonstrated and a demand for government action be heard (Cullen, et al. 1987).

Another factor that contributes to the limited attention being paid to the victims of white-collar crime is that many white-collar violations are processed and handled through administrative and civil courts, thus the crimogenic nature of these violations is deflected and not easily seen. However, it can be argued that this feature of white-collar crimes should compel left-oriented victimologists to focus even more on their victims rather than to forget about them. Also, many victimologists do not have the skills and/or the interest to devote the time needed to study the civil and administrative procedures in order to understand how white-collar victimization is handled and how the interests of victims of white-collar crimes could be better protected. Mann

(1992 p. 347) emphasizes the above point in the following: " . . . more attention should be given to civil processes that bring into the open offenses that we want to study as part of the larger phenomenon of white-collar crime."

Images of Victims of White-Collar Crime

The ways in which the victims of white-collar crimes are seen and perceived by the public, by the authorities, and by the professionals, also contribute to the neglect of white-collar crime victimization.

There is a tendency by left-oriented victimologists and helping professionals to view most victims of white-collar crimes as middle- or upper-class people whose plight is not a major concern for them. This perspective is demonstrated by Matthews and Young (1992 p. 2):

> Victimization studies have shown that the impact of crime is uneven. It falls disproportionately on the poorer and more vulnerable section of the population and serves to compound the growing economic and social inequalities which have risen dramatically over the past decade.

According to this orientation, for example, victims of financial crimes such as investment fraud, are seen as rich speculators who cannot be considered as "deserving" or "ideal" victims. Christie (1986 pp. 18–19) defines an "ideal victim" as "a person or a category of individuals who—when hit by crime—most readily are given the complete and legitimate status of being a victim." He adds to this description that the "ideal victim is weak compared to the unrelated offender" and has put a reasonable amount of effort into self-protection. In the case of financial victimization, it is often hard to claim that the victims are weak and have made sufficient efforts to protect themselves. In many instances they were defrauded because they were not very careful in trying to protect themselves, they were not aware of the risks involved with the investment, and even more so, often they were driven by greed rather than by their concern for fiscal safety (Schlegel and Weisburd 1992).

The public concern with victimization and the readiness to do something about it depends to a large degree on the extent to which large numbers of people can identify, empathize, and sympathize with the victims. Since most of the above victims do not fit the "ideal victim" image, they receive little sympathy. Furthermore, victims of white-collar crimes often are private or government organizations (e.g., in many cases of embezzlement, antitrust violations, and tax evasion). In these cases, individuals have a difficult time empathizing with the victims. Often, as in embezzlement or tax evasion cases, for many citizens it is easier to identify with the perpetrators of the offense than with their direct victims (e. g. banks, government, etc.). Therefore, it is not surprising that there is a relatively small volume of research available concerning the victimization of organizations and corporations which hardly can be characterized as powerless, helpless, and "innocent" victims who deserve a great deal of sympathy and public concern. Dugan's comment (1994 p. 372) regarding the victimization of organizations is timely and poignant by stating that the "'person-centered' perspective has distorted understanding of both the extent and nature of victimization."

Paradoxically, most of the theoretical and empirical work of left-oriented victimology, by neglecting the study of white-collar crime victims, white-collar victimization, and the victimization of organizations by white-collar crime, unintentionally contributes to the deemphasis of the importance and impact of white-collar and corporate crime. This neglect helps to maintain the focus on violent and street crimes which are committed mainly by lower class offenders against lower class victims. In other words, left-oriented victimology contributes to the very same focus and direction of mainstream criminology and victimology which is often criticized by left-oriented victimologists as reactionary and politically conservative.

As noted, one notable exception in this regard is related to the victimization of women by corporations that has received attention lately by feminist writers (see Szockyj and Fox 1996), although there is much more emphasis by feminist victimologists on the victims of sex crimes and domestic violence. The feminist analysis of corporate victimization focuses on the structural arrangements of capitalist industrial societies that put women in especially vulnerable positions for becoming victims of corporate crimes. Gerber and Weeks (1992 p. 343) present this view in the following:

> We postulate that ignoring female victimization of corporate crime is to accept the dominant world view and its values. . . . we argue that feminist theories provide a unique approach that will lead to a clearer picture of corporate victimization in all its forms.

This development demonstrates a welcome change in victimology in general and the study of white-collar crime victimization in particular. However, by definition, it covers only a relatively limited aspect of victimization by white-collar crimes and relates to a relatively limited group of victims.

Visibility

The well known fact that white-collar offenses tend to be much less visible than violent, predatory and street crimes has been dealt with earlier. As noted, often the public and even the direct victims are not aware that a white-collar offense was committed, and in many consumer fraud cases, the victims do not have any suspicion that they were cheated or shortchanged. This is the case in many white-collar offenses perpetrated against the elderly. Braithwaite and Geis (1982 p. 190) have pointed out that one of the major characteristics of corporate crimes, which is relevant to other types of white-collar crimes as well, is that: "with most traditional crimes, the fact that an offense has occurred is readily apparent; with most corporate crimes the effect is not readily apparent."

Obviously, the visibility or the lack of visibility of a crime influences the ways in which the public, the media, the politicians, the criminal justice system, policy makers, and social scientists approach and handle certain crimes and their victims. Visibility plays a major role in defining whether these violations and the plight of their victims will be considered as an important social problem, and what if any efforts and resources will be committed to deal with them. In respect to white-collar crimes, even in those cases in which the victims are aware of the fact that they have been victimized, they often fail to report the crime to the authorities. Generally, in all victimization situations, the main reasons for not reporting crimes to the police are a result of the victims' beliefs that the offense was "not important enough" or that "nothing could be done/lack of proof" (Laub 1990 p. 42). This is probably even more so in the case of white-collar crimes and their victims.

In a recent small-scale study Mason and Benson (1996) tried to learn about the factors that influence the reporting behavior of personal fraud victims. This study found strong similarities between the reporting of victims of personal fraud and the reporting of victims of street crimes. The similarities were the following: (a) those who were encouraged by people close to them were more likely than others to report, (b) those who blamed themselves for becoming a victim, rather than the offenders, were less likely to report the crime, and (c) the amount of monetary loss was positively correlated with the likelihood of reporting. These researchers, however, acknowledged that their findings may be less relevant for victims of other kinds of white-collar crimes than fraud.

The relatively low rate of victim reporting and low visibility of white-collar crime and white-collar crime victimization contribute to the complexity of studying this issue and to the paucity of available research reports pertaining to this subject. Researchers who want to focus on this subject often need, besides the usual criminological and victimological research competence, professional expertise in such areas as accounting, marketing, and management. These skills are not readily found among criminologists and victimologists.

Methodological Issues

The first victimization survey was conducted in the United States during the 1960s. Since 1972, victimization surveys, NCS (National Crime Survey), currently called NCVS (National Crime Victimization Survey), have become the most systematic procedure to collect information on victims and victimization in the United States. Annual reports on victims and victimization and topical reports on certain types of victimizations are published routinely and the data are readily available for researchers. Similarly, many other industrial countries conduct victimization surveys on a more or less regular basis.

The NCVS cover the personal offenses of rape, robbery, aggravated assault, simple assault, and personal larceny with and without contact, and household offenses of burglary, household larceny, and motor vehicle theft.

There is no attempt to collect any information about the victims of various white-collar crimes and their victimization.

As noted, the NCVS became the main database for large-scale aggregate research not only for victimological studies, but for many criminological projects as well. An increasing volume of research focuses on the analysis of these surveys because of the large number of respondents, sophisticated sampling procedures, applicability for computer analysis, and the easy availability of the data for researchers who can conduct their studies in their offices without getting bogged down in the time-consuming, complex, costly, and often problematic phase of field work and data collection. In fact, the National Institute of justice (NIJ) encourages the use of victimization surveys for further research by providing special grants for projects using the accumulated data for secondary analysis. The available information is used not only for academic purposes but also for policy applications. The growing volume of published criminological and victimological research based on the secondary analysis of this data source is substantial.

It was pointed out that the NCVS does not collect information about the victims of and victimization by white-collar crime. Thus, this influential database, which provides a wealth of information on the victims of street crimes, while it increases the opportunities for research on street crime victimization and facilitates the dissemination of information on violent and predatory crimes, does not further any research on white-collar victims and their victimization.

The prospects for future victimological research forecast the continuation of this trend of data driven computerized analyses, because of the shrinking resources available for independent research projects and the pressure of "publish or perish" for academic researchers. As mentioned, the readily available data relieve researchers from the arduous tasks of collecting good quality (reliable and valid) information by themselves, and allow for faster publication of results of projects based on secondary data analysis using sophisticated and trendy statistical methods. This situation does not offer a great promise for the future study of white-collar victims and their victimization.

It should be mentioned as a positive development for the study of white-collar victims and white-collar victimization that, as noted, recently in several countries surveys were conducted on commercial victimization (Maguire and Shapland 1997).[3] Hopefully, these kinds of surveys and others dealing with various types of white-collar crime victimization will be conducted on a more regular basis.

The Effects of White-Collar Victimization

In spite of the relative neglect of this subject during the last two decades, there has been an increase in the number of publications dealing with the various aspects of white-collar, corporate, organizational, and occupational crimes. However, as stated above, only a few of these works deal with white-collar crime victims and with the details of their victimization. Even when they do mention these topics, in most cases they are considered only as side issues and handled accordingly. One would assume that there would be more concern with these issues in the United States at the aftermath of the Wall Street scandals of the 1980s, the savings and loan debacle during the Reagan administration, and with the collapse of the Bank of Credit and Commerce International. These cases were widely publicized and seriously affected the securities, finance, and banking industries. In these scandals many business organizations suffered losses, and many well-to-do and middle-class individuals lost large sums of money, and some even their life savings. The lack of attention to and the lack of concern with these victims has a symbolic importance, because it reinforces the "caveat emptor" mentality that is pervasive among many in the business world. Furthermore, this approach conveys to the general public and to the potential offenders the message that white-collar offenses are not considered to be serious violations or real crimes in modern industrial societies and their victims do not need any special concern. The lax attitude toward white-collar crimes and the victimization accrued by them seems to prevail, in spite of the fact that their consequences may be serious, not only for their direct victims, but for society as a whole. In addition to their tremendous financial cost (the savings and loan scandal alone cost U.S. taxpayers an estimated $500 billion), white-collar crimes, which almost always involve the breach of trust (Shapiro 1990), seriously weaken public confidence in the social arrangements and the value system of society (see Meier and Short 1983).

It was mentioned earlier that in certain types of white-collar crimes, such as consumer fraud or violations against the public-at-large (e. g. air and water pollution), many victims are unaware of the fact that they are being victimized. In other violations the individual harm may be minor for each individual, but the aggregate amount of gain may be substantial for the violators as it occurs in a large number of corporate and white-collar crimes.

In other cases, such as investment frauds, victims may be seriously harmed by the crime. Individual victims, in spite of the fact that they are seen as well-to-do, greedy, and sophisticated investors who are taking calculated risks and who are familiar with the intricacies of the business world, are not necessarily such. For example, Shapiro (1984) in her research on securities violations found that among the victims were relatively few who could be considered as a wealthy and sophisticated investor. In fact many of them were quite naive and gullible in their investing behavior. They were investing in phony gold mines, dry oil wells, fantastic cancer remedies, wingless airplanes, expeditions to retrieve sunken treasures, and even in machines that were supposed to turn sand into gold.

In another study that focused on the collapse of a small loan company because of the criminal activity of its management, the authors found that the majority of victims were people seeking safe investments and were of modest means (Shover, et al. 1994). This kind of victimization may have dire consequences for many victims, especially for the elderly living off their retirement money. The authors of this study mention the case of an 82-year-old victim who had "difficulty sleeping for months for fear that she would lose her home" (Shover, et al. 1994 p. 88). Very similar fears were expressed by several victims of a large-scale investment fraud perpetrated during the 1980s (Shichor et al. 1996). In the widely publicized Lincoln Savings and Loan case, a large number of retirees were duped into buying junk bonds without being informed that their investment is not insured by the federal insurance agencies, and they lost their life savings (Calavita and Pontell 1990). The savings and loan debacle caused major financial losses also for pension funds that invested with firms involved in fraudulent practices, leaving many workers without adequate pension benefits (Zey 1993).

In addition to neglecting the financial aspects of white-collar crime victimization, cases that result in physical injuries and deaths are also neglected. For example, several studies have shown that over one-third of job-related accidents are the result of crimes and violations of safety regulations by employers (Messner and Rosenfeld 1994). The physical injuries are often attributed by the businesses to the negligence of the workers, rather than to the wrongdoing of the employers. While safety regulations are often breached, the regulatory agencies are often limited in their enforcement abilities (see Friedrichs 1996). Even when these agencies could act upon these violations they refrain from doing so, because of the threats of large corporations that they will take their business somewhere else, probably to third-world countries, where the safety regulations are minimal or nonexistent. . . . [There are] victims of physical injuries caused by faulty products manufactured by companies that knew about the dangerousness and harmfulness of their products. . . . For example, it became clear that some Ford executives knew about the problems of the Pinto model, but they decided not to correct them for financial reasons; this decision cost several lives and serious injuries. Furthermore, there is a growing volume of evidence that cigarette manufacturers, who were aware of the harmfulness of their product a long time ago, have purposively increased nicotine levels in cigarettes in order to achieve higher levels of addiction and consequently more sales. Also, there are known cases of production of unsafe drugs by pharmaceutical companies to increase their profits (Braithwaite 1984).

There are indications that victims of white-collar crimes often go through many of the same or similar psychological experiences as victims of traditional street crimes do. In some respects, these negative effects may be even more severe than those of violent crimes. It is known, that many victims of all crimes ask questions, such as "why me?" and "what did I do wrong?", after being victimized. These questions reflect a tendency of self-blaming, because the victims seek the cause of their victimization (or at least some portion of it) in their own behavior. This pattern is even more prevalent among the victims of certain white-collar crimes, especially among victims of fraud. Most of these crimes involve various degrees of deceit, and victims often are manipulated into participating in their own deception. Edelhertz (1970 p. 16) elaborates on this point:

> White-collar crimes are unique. They generally require the victim to acquiesce in being victimized. In the great majority of cases, we are confronted with crimes which require affirmative acts of cooperation by victims before the fraud can be completed. Put another way, victims must help to "dig their own graves."

Victims of fraud often confront themselves with the embarrassing question of "how could I be so stupid?" Thus, in addition to the financial effects of the actual victimization, these crimes may have serious psychological impacts on the victims' self-concept and self-esteem. Also, there is evidence that victims of fraud-related crimes often are seen as easy marks and stupid and are widely ridiculed by their victimizers (e.g. Granelli 1997). All these indicate that there are not only financial but psychological consequences (which are mostly immeasurable) related to this kind of victimization (Levi 1992). This problem was demonstrated vividly by a victim of a large-scale investment fraud in the following:

> I did not know there was a scheme or scam until it went into "bankruptcy" or whatever. I almost had a nervous breakdown. I have practically no income. I'm almost 71 years old and I borrowed from equity on my house. I owe almost $75,000. The first mortgage was paid off after 30 years. It has totally caused a major loss of self-esteem and realization of victimization. I considered suicide. I am losing my home. (quoted in Shichor et al. 1996 p. 105)

In the same study, a husband reported that he lost his wife's respect because he invested in this fraudulent operation against her advise and lost a large sum of money. Victim embarrassment, coupled in most cases with the lack of available venues to recover the losses, contributes to a great extent to the gross underreporting of these kinds of offenses (Tomlin, 1982). Furthermore, victim compensation programs administered by government agencies do not cover financial victimization, and even if the principal offenders have tangible assets, restitution often is not forthcoming (Granelli 1992) and the legal process is so slow that many victims find themselves in a situation of financial hardship. The lack of arrangements for official compensation, by itself, is a symbolic statement of neglect and lack of public interest in most white-collar victimizations. While civil procedures are available for victims, often they are not practical because they may cost too much in legal fees, may take years to complete, the offenders either do not have enough assets or know how to hide them, and in the case of corporate violators they usually have access to the best legal services to fight the claims (see Mann 1985).

Also, many white-collar victimizations are not reported because there are victims who do not know where and to whom to report them. Many others do not report because they have doubt that the criminal justice system or other public agencies would do anything about their complaint (Jesilow et al.

1992). When victimization is reported, victims often experience a "second injury" from the justice system itself. Victim dissatisfaction and frustration with the criminal justice process are well known (Shichor 1987). This situation prevails in the case of white-collar victimization as well. One of the main reasons for this phenomenon is, as noted before, the constant questioning of the role of the victim in the commission of the crime. In the case of white-collar victimization the doubts about the victims' role may be even amplified, and the victims are often treated similarly to rape victims:

> . . . the victim might be presumed to have cooperated in order for the crime to occur, the statutory proofs required to sustain the charge will hinge on a showing of the blamelessness of the victim's conduct. The victim cannot logically suggest that cooperation was not forthcoming, since the fact of cooperation is already presumed. (Walsh and Schram 1980 pp. 42–43)

Accordingly, as noted earlier, many victims of white-collar crime are not considered to be bona-fide victims, neither by the public nor by the criminal justice system. In addition, there is seldom strong public pressure to be harsh on white-collar crimes and on their perpetrators. Therefore, there is no major emphasis on trying to use the victims of white-collar crimes in clamping down on these offenses, as is the case with street crimes. Thus, victim/witness and various victims' aid programs, which are designed to provide help and support to street crime victims in order to ensure their readiness to cooperate with the criminal justice process, seldom come to the support of white-collar crime victims. The fact that the criminal justice system fails to make an effort to prosecute effectively offenders of white-collar crimes contributes to the neglect of the victims of these crimes as well (Moore and Mills 1990).

In one of the rare empirical studies touching upon this subject, the role of the victims of white-collar crime in sentencing was dealt with by Wheeler et al. (1988). This research found that judges were particularly concerned with the loss incurred to the victim. They focused on this item because "in most ordinary crimes, both the victim and the loss are clear, but in white-collar cases often neither is clear" (p. 70). Some judges viewed white-collar crimes as "victimless" crimes and obviously this perception has influenced their sentencing. The authors observed that usually judges relate to white-collar crime as a more serious violation when "there are visible and particular victims and where the relationship between offense and loss to the victims is direct" (p. 71). In the same research a distinction was made between individual victims on the one hand, and public and private organizations on the other. For example, price-fixing and tax fraud were not seen as serious crimes, because it was hard to pinpoint an individual victim who is suffering a loss. Judges did show a special concern for victims who appeared defenseless and had fewer resources to handle their losses, in other words, the judges were looking for individuals who would resemble "ideal victims" and who are much harder to find among the victims of white-collar crimes than those of street crimes.

Some Suggestions for the Further Study of White-Collar Victims

The theoretical and practical importance to bring the victims of white-collar crime and their victimization into the spectrum of systematic victimological study has been the underlying theme of this chapter. Here, a few suggestions to expedite this development are suggested:

(a) There should be an increased effort by government agencies to collect systematic data on various types of "white-collar" offenses and to eliminate general categories such as "fraud" in their statistics, which often include many types of different offenses. These kinds of "waste basket" categories should be divided into separate, unidimensional charges.

(b) Victimologists, and other social scientists, should lobby for the inclusion of detailed questions concerning white-collar crime victimization into the victimization survey (NCVS) schedule on a permanent basis.

(c) Victimology courses and victimology textbooks should cover the topic of white-collar crime victims, their victimization, and the victim experiences in society in general, and in the criminal justice system in particular.

(d) Public agencies, that deal with victim-related issues, should recognize that the harm caused to white-collar crime victims may have serious consequences, and should devote their efforts to help the victims of white-collar crimes as well.

Conclusion

Victimology, as a relatively new area of study, came under criticism on several accounts. One of the most important and serious claimed that it hardly can be considered as an academic or scientific discipline because it lacks a clear distinction between the theoretical and empirical approach followed by researchers and the advocate/therapeutic approach of the practitioners. Another problematic issue that was highlighted is the omission and neglect of certain kinds of victims and their victimization by both approaches mentioned above. In the preceding discussion several reasons were suggested for the theoretical and practical neglect of the victims of white-collar crimes; these included:

(a) Political reasons play an important part in this issue. The conservative sociopolitical atmosphere that is dominant in American society since the presidency of Ronald Reagan was conducive to the "getting tough" policies on street crimes and street criminals. Politicians used street crime victims as a potent vehicle to legislate stricter laws carrying longer prison sentences and to receive more political support from the public. Also, intentionally or unintentionally, some academics and victim advocates allied themselves with these efforts. On the other side of the political spectrum, mainstream liberals, left-oriented victimologists, and victim advocates continued to focus on the victims of street crimes, at least in some part, because of ideological reasons. Most victims of street crimes are from the poorer segments of society, and focusing on their plight fits into the liberal and left-oriented sociopolitical agenda.

The paradox is that on the one hand, the conservatives' focus on the victims of street crimes neglects large numbers of well-to-do and high status people, many of them conservatives themselves. On the other hand, liberal and left-oriented victimologists in their neglect of white-collar crime victimization help to reduce the public interest to scrutinize middle- and upper-class white-collar offenders and corporate crimes. In this way, they contribute to the perception that criminal behavior is rampant among lower class people and is rare among the higher classes.

(b) The perception that many victims of white-collar crimes are "unworthy" and are not bona-fide victims and they are victimized because of their own greediness opens the door for victim blaming. This, combined with the fact that many victims are government or private organizations, reduces the sympathy for white-collar crime victims and limits the readiness to help them. Furthermore, these views lead to the lack of understanding of the plight of the individual victims of these offenses, in spite of the fact that the impacts of white-collar crimes on individual victims are often similar, or in some cases are even more severe, than the effects of street crime victimization.

(c) White-collar crimes and white-collar crime victimization are low-visibility occurrences. They are not as readily seen, reported, and known in the public as street crimes are. Consequently, they raise much less public furor, condemnation, and demands for official reactions than street crimes and street crime victimization do.

(d) Methodological and research developments favor the study of street crime victims and the neglect of white-collar victims. The extended and officially encouraged use of victimization surveys for secondary data analysis provides a clear direction for the study of street and traditional household crimes while simultaneously discouraging the study of white-collar crime victims and their victimization by not having information on these subjects in their database.

If victimology seeks to become a respectable academic discipline, whether related to or independent from criminology, it will have to put more emphasis on the study of white-collar crime victimization and victims of white-collar crime. Similarly, helping agencies and helping professionals who deal with crime victims will have to open themselves to the victims of white-collar crime, recognize that they are being harmed, legitimize their victim status, and help them in their efforts to cope with their plight.

NOTES

[1] For example, in the 1994 elections in California there was a ballot measure to reinforce the "Three Strikes and You are Out" law, that stipulates 25 years to life prison

terms for a felony conviction for offenders who had two previous convictions for "serious" crimes. This law was enacted earlier that year by the California legislature. The initiator of the ballot measure was the father of a murder victim whose mailers were issued by the Republican politician who was the candidate for the U.S. Senate in that election. The proposition was strongly supported by the state governor and the attorney general, both running for reelection on a conservative platform.

[2] Miers (1989) referred to the professional approach based on conservative concepts as "positivist victimology" while Walklate (1992) called it "conventional victimology."

[3] Levi (1987 p. XIX) provides a distinction among the various forms of "commercial fraud" on the basis of the nature of violations and offenders/victims involved: " . . . there are frauds by business people against each other; by business people against investors—who, by volume of securities traded, are predominately institutions or professionals—as well as against small investors, consumers and tax authorities (who may be regarded as 'corporate crime' rather than 'white-collar crime' victims); and by directors and employees against their companies."

REFERENCES

Bonger, W., 1969. *Criminality and Economic Conditions.* Bloomington: Indiana University Press. (Abridged edition).

Braithwaite, J., 1984. *Corporate Crime in the Pharmaceutical Industry.* London: Routledge & Kegan Paul .

Braithwaite, J. and G. Geis, 1982. "On theory and action for corporate crime control." In: Geis, G., *On White-Collar Crime.* Lexington, MA: D. C. Heath.

Calavita, K. and H. N. Pontell, 1990. "Heads I win, tails you lose: Deregulation, crime and crisis in the Savings and Loans industry." *Crime and Delinquency,* 36 (3) pp. 309–341.

Chermak, S. M., 1995. *Victims in the News: Crime and the American News Media.* Boulder, CO: Westview.

Christie, N., 1986. "The ideal victim." In: Fattah, E. A. (editor), *From Crime Policy to Victim Policy.* New York: St. Martin's Press.

Clinard, M. B. and P. C Yeager, 1980. *Corporate Crime.* New York: Free Press.

Cressey, D. R., 1992. "Research implications of conflicting conceptions of victimology." In: Fattah, E. A. (editor), *Towards a Critical Victimology.* New York: St. Martin's Press.

Cullen, F., W. Maakestad, and G. Cavender, 1987. *Corporate Crime Under Attack: The Ford Pinto Case and Beyond.* Cincinnati, OH: Anderson.

Doocy, J. and D. Shichor, 1994. "Escrow fraud: An exploratory study of a neglected crime." *Journal of Security Administration,* 17 (1) pp. 18–36.

Dugan, M., 1994. "Organizations as victims of crime." In: Kirchoff, G. F., E. Kosovski and H. J. Schneider (editors), *International Debates on Victimology.* Mönchengladbach, Germany: WSV Publishing.

Edelbertz, H., 1970. *The Nature, Impact and Prosecution of White-Collar Crime.* Washington, DC: U.S. Department of Justice, Law Enforcement Assistance Administration.

Fattah, E. A., 1986. *From Crime Policy to Victim Policy: Reorienting the Justice System.* London: Macmillan.

Fattah, E. A., 1992. "The need for critical victimology." In: Fattah, E. A. (editor), *Towards a Critical Victimology.* New York: St. Martin's Press.

Friedrichs, D. O., 1996. *Trusted Criminals: White-Collar Crime in Contemporary Society.* Belmont, CA: Wadsworth.

Geis, G., 1973. "Deterring corporate crime." In: Nader, R. and M. J. Green (editors), *Corporate Power in America.* New York: The Viking Press.

Geis, G., 1992. "White-collar crime what is it?" In: Schlegel, K. and D. Weisburd (editors), *White-Collar Crime Reconsidered.* Boston: Northeastern University Press.

Gerber, J. and S. L. Weeks, 1992. "Women as victims of white-collar crime: A call for research on a neglected topic." *Deviant Behavior,* 13, pp. 325–347.

Gottfredson, M. R. and T. Hirschi, 1990. *A General Theory of Crime.* Stanford, CA: Stanford University Press.

Granelli, J. S., 1992. "Getting their day in court." *Los Angeles Times,* March 1, p. D1.

Granelli, J. S., 1997. "Telemarketers convicted of fraud charges." *Los Angeles Times,* April 11, pp. D 1, 7.

Helmkamp, J., R. Ball, and K. Townsend (editors), 1996. *White-Collar Crime.* Morgantown, WV: National White-Collar Center.

Jesilow, P., E. Klempner, and V. Chiao, 1992. "Reporting consumer and major fraud: A survey of complaints." In: Schlegel, K. and D. Weisburd (editors), *White-Collar Crime Reconsidered.* Boston, MA: Northeastern University Press.

Joutsen, M, 1994. "Victimology and victim policy in Europe." *The Criminologist,* 19 (3) p. 1.

Karmen A., 1996. *Crime Victims: An Introduction to Victimology.* Belmont, CA: Wadsworth.

Laub, J. H., 1990. "Patterns of criminal victimization in the United States." In: Lurigio, A. J., W. G. Skogan, and R. Davis (editors), *Victims of Crime: Problems, Policies and Programs.* Newbury Park, CA: Sage.

Levi, M., 1987. *Regulating Fraud: White-Collar Crime and the Criminal Process.* London: Tavistock.

Levi, M., 1992. "White-collar crime victimization." In: Schlegel, K. and D. Weisburd (editors), *White-Collar Crime Reconsidered.* Boston, MA: Northeastern University Press.

Maguire, M. and J. Shapland, 1997. "Provision for victims in an international context." In: Davis, R. C., A. J. Lurigio, and W. G. Skogan (editors), *Victims of Crime.* Thousand Oaks, CA: Sage.

Mann, K., 1985. *Defending White-Collar Crime: A Portrait of Attorneys at Work.* New Haven: Yale University Press.

Mann, K., 1992. "Procedure, rules and informal control: Gaining leverage over white-collar crime." In: Schlegel, K. and D. Weisburd (editors), *White-Collar Crime Reconsidered.* Boston, MA: Northeastern University Press.

Mason, K. A. and M. L. Benson, 1996. "The effect of social support on fraud victims' reporting behavior." *Justice Quarterly,* 13 pp. 511–523.

Matthews R. and J. Young, 1992. "Reflections on realism." In: Young, J. and R. Matthews (editors), *Rethinking Criminology: The Realist Debate.* London: Sage.

Mawby, R. L., 1992. "Trends in research on crime victims in the United Kingdom." In: Ben-David, S. and G. F. Kirchoff (editors), *International Faces of Victimology.* Mönchengladbach, Germany: WSV Publishing.

Meier, R. F. and J. F. Short, Jr., 1983. "The consequences of white-collar crime." In: Edelhertz, H. (editor), *White-Collar Crime an Agenda for Research.* Lexington, MA: D. C. Heath.

Messner, S. F. and R. Rosenfeld, 1994. *Crime and the American Dream.* Belmont, CA: Wadsworth.

Meirs, D., 1989. "Positivist victimology." *International Review of Victimology,* 1 pp. 3–22.

Moore, M. H. and M. Mills, 1990. "The neglected victims and unexamined costs of white-collar crime." *Crime and Delinquency,* 36 pp. 408–418.

Scheingold, S. A., 1984. *The Politics of Law and Order: Street Crime and Public Policy.* New York: Longman.

Scheingold, S. A., T. Olson, and J. Pershing, 1994. "Sexual violence, victim advocacy, and republican criminology: Washington state's Community Protection Act." *Law and Society Review,* 28 pp. 729–763.

Schlegel, K. and D. Weisburd, 1992. "White-collar: The parallax view." In: Schlegel, K. and D. Weisburd (editors), *White-Collar Crime Reconsidered.* Boston, MA: Northeastern University Press.

Shapiro, S. P., 1984. *Wayward Capitalists.* New Haven, CT: Yale University Press.

Shapiro, S. P., 1990. "Collaring the crime, not the criminal: Reconsidering the concept of white-collar crime." *American Sociological Review,* 55 pp. 346–365.

Shichor, D., 1987. "The ramifications of victim dissatisfaction with the criminal justice system." *Prosecutor's Brief,* X (4) pp. 24–27.

Shichor, D., 1989. "Corporate deviance and corporate victimization." *International Review of Victimology,* 1 pp. 64–78.

Shichor, D., J. H. Doocy, and G. Geis, 1996. "Anger, disappointment and disgust: Reactions of victims of a telephone investment scam." In: Sumner, C., M. Israel, M. O'Connell, and R. Sarre (editors), *International Victimology: Selected Papers from the 8th International Symposium.* Canberra, Australia: Australian Institute of Criminology.

Shichor, D., and D. K. Sechrest (editors), 1996. *Three Strikes and You're Out: Vengeance as Public Policy.* Thousand Oaks, CA: Sage.

Shover, N., G. Lipton Fox, and M. Mills, 1994. "Long-term consequences of victimization by white-collar crime." *Justice Quarterly,* 11 pp. 75–98.

Sutherland, E. H., 1940. "White-collar criminality." *American Sociological Review,* 5 (February) pp. 1–12.

Szockyj, E. and J. G. Fox (editors), 1996. *Corporate Victimization of Women.* Boston, MA: Northeastern University Press.

Tomlin, J. W., 1982. "Victims of white-collar crimes." In: Schneider, H. J. (editor), *The Victim in International Perspective.* Berlin: Walter de Gruyter.

Walklate, S., 1992. "Appreciating the victim: Conventional, realist or critical victimology?" In: Matthews, R. and J. Young (editors*), Issues in Realist Criminology.* London: Sage.

Walsh, M. E. and D. D. Schram, 1980. "The victim of white-collar crime: Accuser or accused?" In: Geis, G. and E. Stotland (editors), *White-Collar Crime: Theory and Research.* Beverly Hills, CA: Sage.

Wheeler, S., K. Mann, and A. Sarat, 1988. *Sitting in Judgement: The Sentencing of White-collar Criminals.* New Haven, CT: Yale University Press.

Young, A. and P. Rush, 1994. "The law of victimage in urban realism: Thinking through inscriptions of violence." In Nelken, D. (editor), *The Futures of Criminology.* London: Sage.

Zey, M., 1993. Banking on Fraud: Drexel, Junk Bonds, and Buyouts. New York: Aldine De Gruyter.

Chapter Twelve

Victims of Investment Fraud

David Shichor
Dale K. Sechrest
Jeffrey Doocy

There is a growing volume of literature that focuses on various kinds of white-collar crimes, including corporate crime. There are some who refer to most white-collar crimes as business crimes, because they are committed in the course of otherwise legitimate business activities, usually for material gain. Often, the business organization involved in illegal activities is in a financially pressed situation. On the other hand, professional literature dealing with organizations established for illegal business practices is sparse. Illegal activities conducted through these entities cannot always be characterized as white-collar crimes or business crimes, according to the traditional definitions, because in these cases illegal behavior is not incidental to legitimate, everyday business activities. Due to the similarities, the distinction between white-collar crime and fraud victimizations are often blurred; thus, for this article the terms are used interchangeably. Many boiler-room type of telemarketing operations are involved in fraudulent activities, although not all of them necessarily promote scams (Stevenson, 1998). A notable exception to the paucity of empirical research on fraud victimization is the study conducted by Titus, Heinzelmann, and Boyle (1995), on the victims of personal fraud, which they define as "involving the deliberate intent to deceive with promises of goods, services, or other financial benefits that in fact do not exist or that were never intended to be provided" (p. 54).

The growth of telemarketing as a tool of modern marketing strategy for legitimate, as well as for illegitimate, businesses may make the operation of fraudulent schemes and scams harder to recognize. It is easier for smooth-talking boiler-room salespersons to find prospective victims off-guard and victimize them through the phone when they do not have to establish a face-to-face relationship with them.

The telemarketing scheme that this article focuses on was devised to get potential investors involved in bogus investments. It belongs to the category of offenses that Moore (1980, 32) calls "sting and swindles," which are described as "stealing by deception by individuals (or 'rings') who have no continuing institutional position and whose major purpose from the onset is to bilk people of their money." Edelhertz (1983) calls these schemes "white-collar crime as business." In offenses that fit into this category "the provision of goods, services, or property is only an excuse to grasp monies that bear no recognizable relationship to what is provided" (p. 116). He specifically mentions the "sale of worthless desert land or investment securities . . . based on fraudulent descriptions" (p. 117). Investments and "fiduciary" frauds typically target individual victims.

Edelhertz pointed to several problem areas in the control of white-collar crimes. One of them has a special relevance for our research, namely, the problem of "reconciling the need to protect the public with deregulation policies" (p. 120). The sociopolitical atmosphere of the 1980s, with the business-friendly Reagan administration promoting a free-market system and deregulation, have facilitated the reinvigoration of the caveat emptor approach to business, resulting in an increase in various kinds of white-collar crime and fraud. This trend reached its crescendo in the national savings and loan debacle (Pontell and Calavita, 1993).

Since our interest is in learning about the victims of fraud and their victimization, Edelhertz's analysis of the elements of fraudulent operations is useful. He finds five elements present in a fraud:

(a) Intent to commit a wrongful act . . .
(b) Disguise of purpose or intent.
(c) Reliance by perpetrator on ignorance or carelessness of the victim.
(d) Acquiescence by victim in what he believes to be the true nature and content of the transaction.
(e) Concealment of crime by
  1. Preventing the victim from realizing that he has been victimized, or
  2. Relying on the fact that only a small percentage of victims will react to what has happened, and making provisions for restitution to or other handling of the disgruntled victim, or
  3. Creation of a deceptive paper, organizational, or transactional facade to disguise the true nature of what has occurred (Edelhertz, 1970, 12).

The last point is emphasized by Wheeler and Rothman (1982), who note the importance of organizations in white-collar crimes, because organizations are viewed by the public as more substantial than individuals and, therefore, prospective victims are more likely to trust them. This was seen in the fraudulent operations on which our research focuses. In this study the two major perpetrators of the fraud created between 150 and 200 partnerships to conduct their investment scheme (Goldman, 1995).

The Effects of Fraud on Victims

The above elements of fraud victimization may have profound effects on the victims. They often reinforce the victims' perception that they acted "foolishly" and may cause them to be deeply embarrassed. Also, victims of fraud easily can be blamed for their own victimization. Often they are not seen as bona fide victims by the public, by the officials, and even by the various victim services. An "ideal victim," according to Christie (1986, 18–19), is "a person or a category of individuals who—when hit by crime—are most readily given the complete and legitimate status of being a victim." He further indicates that the ideal victim has put a reasonable effort into self-protection. In the case of investment fraud, on which this study focuses, it is hard to claim that the victims have made sufficient efforts for self-protection. Many of them were defrauded because they were not vigilant enough to find out about the risks involved in investing with telemarketers unknown to them, and even more so, often they were driven by greed rather than by prudence and concern for financial safety (Schlegel and Weisburd, 1992). Walsh and Schram (1980, 42–43) draw an interesting parallel between victims of fraud and the victims of rape regarding their "innocence":

> The victim might be presumed to have cooperated in order for the crime to occur, the statutory proofs required to sustain the charge will hinge on a showing of the blamelessness of the victim's conduct. The victim cannot logically suggest that cooperation was not forthcoming, since the fact of cooperation is already presumed.

Some people may become "chronic victims"; in other words, they may be victimized repeatedly by fraud. Blum (1972, 238) found three characteristics that describe this kind of victim: one, that they were "always looking for a deal"; second, some of them could not resist the aggressive sales techniques; and third, they had an unrealistic belief in other people. The plight of these victims can be neutralized by claiming that the first type of victims were "greedy," and in the case of the other two types of victims that they had not learned from their experiences while they should have done so.

There are some additional reasons that victims of white-collar crimes in general, and victims of investment fraud in particular, are viewed and related to differently than victims of "street crimes." The limited concern shown fraud victims is undoubtedly a reflection of the more lenient official and public attitude toward white-collar and fraud-related crimes and their perpetrators than toward street crimes and street criminals. Generally, investment fraud victims are seen as economically well-to-do people; therefore they do not seem to need as much sympathy because they can take their losses with relative ease. The professional interest in these victims is limited also among victimologists (Shichor, 1998), a fact that can be seen in the contents of victimology textbooks. For example, Karmen, in his introduction (1996, p. 10) states that his widely used textbook "focuses almost entirely on victims of street crimes." Similarly, other recently published victimology textbooks either do not deal with fraud victims or deal with them very briefly in just a few pages (see Doerner and Lab, 1995; Kennedy and Sacco, 1998; Meadows, 1998; Wallace, 1998). This neglect stems, at least partially, from the "paternalistic" approach of many social scientists who try to be helpful and supportive of weak, poor, and vulnerable victims. This is true for "liberal" and various shades of "left-oriented" victimologists, who look at victimization as the outcome of the culture of violence rooted in the core of the capitalist social structure. Consequently, they consider victims as pawns in the hands of conservatives, who use them to initiate strict laws and policies against street crimes and street criminals (Elias, 1993; Phipps, 1986).

According to this view, the most vulnerable individuals for victimization by street crimes are the poor and disenfranchised elements of society. This approach toward victims and victimization is not unique to the American scene but can be found in other industrial societies as well (see Mawby and Walklate, 1994). On the policy level, victim compensation and victim assistance programs that are usually operated or supported by government agencies and by nonprofit organizations concentrate on street crime victims (Roberts, 1990). This policy is based on the observation that:

> Victimization studies have shown that the impact of crime is uneven. It falls disproportionately on the poorer and more vulnerable section of the population and serves to compound the growing economic and social inequalities which have risen dramatically over the past decade. (Matthews and Young, 1992, p. 2)

Conservatives also jumped on the bandwagon of violent victimization. In the 1980s, President Reagan appointed a task force to address the problems of victims of violent crime. Similarly, a Victims' Bill of Rights was enacted by several states. These measures, which focused on the problems of victims of violent crimes, not only were prompted by the genuine concern for the plight of these victims but were also often disguised attempts to increase the severity of punishment for street criminals and the limitations of their legal rights. These policies were further supported by business interest groups that could cash in on the fear of crime generated by the media and by politicians who kept the crime issue on the front burner for their own political advantage. As for business, whole industries thrived on crime-related products and services and the profits derived from them. These included personal and home security products (alarms, detection systems, guns, etc.), private security services, insurance, counseling services, and various industries connected with different forms of crime control and corrections (see Lilly and Knepper, 1993). Women and other social activist groups who usually fought for liberal causes also joined this trend in their efforts to bring attention to violent crimes that are primarily directed against females, such as sex crimes, domestic violence, and child abuse.

Victim Experiences

All these developments diverted interest from white-collar and fraud-related crimes and consequently from the victims of such crimes. Since the 1970s the main source of information on victims and victimization became the National Crime Survey (NCS), which is now called the National Crime Victimization Survey (NCVS). These surveys collect a large amount of data but do not contain information on white-collar and fraud victimization and victims. The collected aggregate data serve as the basis of most victimological analysis and literature, and further add to the neglect of white-collar and fraud victimization.

In most cases, when white-collar and/or financial fraud victims are mentioned this topic is considered only as a side issue. One would expect more interest in and concern with these victims in the aftermath of the Wall Street securities scandals and the savings and loan debacle of the 1980s, in which many middle-class people lost their life savings. This lack of concern has a symbolic importance because it reinforces the caveat emptor mentality that is pervasive in the business world and conveys to the public, and especially to potential offenders, the message that fraud victims are not "real" victims. However, individual victims of these offenses, in spite of the fact that they are seen as well-to-do, greedy, and sophisticated investors who are taking calculated risks and who know about the business world, are not necessarily such. Shapiro (1984, 34), in her research on securities violations, found that among the victims there were only a few who could be considered wealthy and/or sophisticated investors. She came to the conclusion that the majority of them demonstrated "considerable naiveté and gullibility-investing."

In another study focusing on the collapse of a small Southern loan company because of fraud by its management, Shover, et al. (1994) found that the majority of victims were of modest means and seeking safe investments. This kind of victimization may have long-term effects on elderly victims. The authors cite the case of an 82-year-old widow who could not sleep for months because of the fear that she would lose her home. These kinds of fears were expressed by several victims of the large-scale investment fraud perpetrated during the 1980s (Shichor, et al., 1996) on which this chapter is focusing. Similarly, in the widely publicized Lincoln Savings and Loan case, many retirees were duped into unsafe investments and lost their life savings (see Calavita and Pontell, 1990).

Victims of fraud, in certain aspects, may have more negative experiences than victims of street crimes. It is common for the victims of all crimes to ask the penetrating question: "why me?" or "what did I do wrong?" That is, what was the reason for being "targeted" to become the victim? This question reflects a degree of self-blaming. Fraud and most white-collar crimes involve deceit. Victims are often tricked into participating in their own deception. Generally, these crimes involve breach of the victim's trust (Shapiro, 1990).

Victims tend to ask themselves the disturbing question: "how could I be so stupid to fall for this scheme?" Thus, apart from the financial effects, this type of victimization impacts their self-concept and self-esteem, which in many cases may be even more devastating for the victim than their material loss. Therefore, victimization by fraud tends to cause not only financial harm but psychological damage as well (Levi, 1992). It can even affect husband-and-wife relationships (Sechrest, et al. 1998). The cumulative effect of material and psychological problems on the victims is expressed vividly by a victim of the investment fraud that is the focus of the current study:

> I did not know there was a scheme or a scam until I went into "bankruptcy" or whatever. I almost had a nervous breakdown. I have practically no income. I'm almost 71 years old and I borrowed from equity on my house. I owe almost $75,000. The first mortgage was just paid off after 30 years. It has totally caused a major loss of self-esteem and realization of victimization. I considered suicide. I am losing my home. (Quoted in Shichor, et al., 1996, 105)

Victim embarrassment, coupled with the lack of compensation, results in a gross underreporting of these kinds of offenses (Tomlin, 1982). Victim compensation programs by state agencies do not cover financial victimization, and restitution from the offenders is usually not forthcoming (Granelli, 1992). Recovery of some losses must be pursued through civil procedures that are often too lengthy and may become expensive. If corporations are involved in questionable practices, individual victims may have a hard time being compensated because of the superior legal services that big companies can afford. There is also a neglect and differential handling of these crimes by the media which, in turn, contribute to the neglect of fraud victims (Chermak, 1995).

Justice System Response

Victims of fraud have problems also with the justice system. As mentioned earlier, in many respects they are treated much like rape victims in that it is often presumed that they have cooperated with the alleged offenders. In this sense they have to prove that they are blameless (Walsh and Schram, 1980). Victims often feel that the system is not there to protect them and to punish the offender, and this appears to be more likely in the case of fraud. A victim of a consumer fraud expressed this opinion: "the court should be there to protect the innocent. I have come to the conclusion that our system is set up specifically to protect the criminal" (Jesilow, et al. 1992, 166). Similarly, Shover, et al. (1994) found that many victims of bank fraud that they interviewed were more upset with the ways the authorities handled their case than with the perpetrators of the fraud. It is sometimes hard to accept, but victims should be aware that they deal with the "criminal justice system" and not with a "victim justice system."

Victims often feel defenseless, and many believe that the authorities should better control and regulate the telemarketing business; however, legal and constitutional issues (e.g., the First Amendment) are involved in the regulation of this industry. These legal complexities are exploited by slick and skillful operators. While the victims are still licking their wounds, impostors such as the "two Daves," the main operators of the investment scam that we are dealing with, not only remained unpunished more than seven years after their operation was closed by state investigators, but there are reports that at least one of them is still involved in fraudulent schemes.

Victims of the "Two Daves" Fraud

The current study focuses, as noted, on the victims of a large-scale investment fraud that was perpetrated by the "two Daves," David Bryant and David Knight, during the 1980s until 1991, when their operation was closed down by the investigators of the California Department of Corporations. The two perpetrators set up companies that were selling phony investment schemes, mostly gas and oil leases through telemarketing. They basically ran large-scale boiler-room operations. While the headquarters of the 150 to 200 partnerships operated by the "two Daves" were in southern California, they were selling their "investments" nationwide. The number of victims of these operations is estimated to be between 7,000 and 8,000, although some estimates put the number around 12,000. The amount of money involved exceeded $160 million and may have been well over $200 million (Goldman, 1995).

The data for this study were based on two sources. One, the demographic and personal information available on 8,516 identifiable victims of these investment schemes in the files of the California Department of Corporations. This database deals with the victims of twenty-four of the above mentioned "companies" for the period of 1984 to 1992. These companies were operating under names that projected a certain level of credibility, such as "Remington Securities, Inc." (25 percent of the victims), "Broker's Investment Corporation" (14 percent), "Ellman & Howe Securities" (11 percent), and "Brighton Industries, Inc." (8 percent). The second source of information is based on the data that were collected through a questionnaire mailed to a random sample of the victims. From the 281 questionnaires sent, 152 (54.1 percent) completed questionnaires were returned, a figure considered to be a relatively high return rate.

DATA ANALYSIS

The analysis of 8,489 cases in which information was available indicated that among the victims-investors, 4,106 (48.4 percent) were males only, 1,194 (14.1) percent were females only, and in 2,837 (33.4 percent) of the cases couples were listed as investors. As mentioned, the scope of the investment fraud was nationwide, but the majority of the victims (55.8 percent) were from California, which is not surprising considering that the "two Daves" headquarters was in southern California; thus the scam operations were run from this state, possibly because of the size of the population and the relative affluence of the region: 10.1 percent of the victims were from Illinois, 8.1 percent from Minnesota, 6.9 percent from Ohio, and 5.0 percent from Colorado. The reasons for this distribution are not clear. It may be that the Daves had professional and personal connections in the above states, or there were other factors that made these states attractive for their scam operations or in other ways facilitated them, such as the favorable legal environment.

The amount of investment by the victims varied a great deal. The smallest amount was $500 by two investors (apparently that was the minimum sum that could be invested in a partnership); the largest amount was $550,000 by one investor. About one-third, 2,803 (32.9 percent) invested less than $10,000; 40.6 percent invested between 10 and 20,000; 21.4 percent between 20 and 40,000, and the remaining 5.1 percent invested more than $40,000. The most frequently invested amount (the mode) was $10,000 by 2,905 victims, a bit over one-third of the total (34.1 percent). The median amount of investment was $9,687. Only about one-quarter, 2,257 (26.5 percent) put $20,000 or more into these partnerships. The amount invested varied by gender. Males tended to invest higher amounts, 5.9 percent of them more than $40,000; 4.7 percent of the females invested more than $40,000; and 3.9 percent of the couples invested more than $40,000.

As mentioned, a questionnaire was sent to 281 randomly selected victims in January 1994. This figure was roughly 3 percent of the known victims. Out of these, 152 questionnaires that could be used for analysis were returned. This 53.9 percent return was considered adequate for analysis.

The responses to this survey reveal additional information about the identity of the victims, the ways they were recruited to participate in these schemes, their attitudes and perceptions toward their victimizers and their victimization, and the ways the authorities handled their case.

The perception of investors as an affluent group seemed erroneous. In dollars based on 1990 values, over half the investors (59.1 percent) had a yearly family income of less than $60,000; 15 percent had less than $30,000. Only 17.3 percent had more than $90,000 annual income. About one-third, 34.4 percent, lived in metropolitan areas, 37.1 percent in cities having more than 50,000 population, 19.9 percent in small towns, and 6.6 percent in rural areas. Thus the large majority, more than 70 percent, came from urban environments where usually people are exposed to various investment opportunities and supposedly more informed about them.

The overwhelming majority of the respondents (97.3 percent) listed "promises of gain" as the most often mentioned promise made by telemarketers at the first call. Another often mentioned selling point was tax breaks; 86.8 percent reported this factor, which was probably more important among respondents in the higher income brackets. The mentioning of possible risk factors by the agents was reported by 88.2 percent of the respondents, and this high figure shows that the agents were aware of the legal responsibilities of investment marketing and wanted to be sure that they fulfilled them, at least formally. It was not mentioned how they talked about these risks, although it is likely that they mostly played down the possibility of losing money in their sales pitch.

After receiving three to four initial calls, almost all the victims reported that there were later calls to them from the agents; in fact, more than two-thirds (66.7 percent) of the victims reported that they received six or more calls. About half the investors reported receiving additional material concerning their "investment" after the receipt of the prospectus, which is legally required to be sent by all companies that seek investments from the general public.

The majority of the victims (59.6 percent) reported that they discussed the investment with someone else before making their final decision. However, there was a major difference between males and females in this regard. While among the males only 56.2 percent reported doing so, 80 percent of females discussed their investment decision. Most of the participants (64.4 percent) discussed the issue with only one person. The most-often mentioned person with whom they discussed the investment was their spouse (32.8 percent) followed closely by discussion with an expert (30.3 percent). In spite of the relatively high percent of discussion with "experts" (the qualification of the experts was not detailed, i.e., whether they were gas and oil, financial, or other experts) the victims got involved in this fraudulent investment.

Interestingly, the great majority of respondents (82.3 percent) reported that initially they had reservations about investing in the above partnerships. There was a clear difference in this respect between males and females—86.6 percent of the male victims reported such reservations, compared with only 55.5 percent of the females. The obvious question is: what convinced these individuals to invest in spite of the high level of reservations reported? The first and most important reason by far was the "agent's persuasiveness"; 72.4 percent indicated this factor. Two other factors mentioned as second and third in importance were the attractiveness of the "prospectus," and the "advice of others." These answers highlight the importance of the verbal skills and the manipulative ability of individual agents, which was probably enhanced by the instructions and "pep talks" of the boiler-room operators themselves. Stevenson (1998, 92) emphasizes the importance of middle-class verbal skills among boiler-room pitchmen and the repetitious learning of the pitches. The salesmen have to learn "how to open a pitch, mastering the close and comeback techniques, practicing voice control, and taking charge of a telephone conversation." Also, the presentation of the scheme as a legitimate, "dignified," and successful operation illustrated by a well-written and nicely illustrated prospectus was important. Almost all the victims expressed their suspicion that many details were falsely represented to them. According to the respondents, the most-often mentioned (38.3 percent) misrepresentation was the claim of a "high return" on the investment; "low risk" as another misrepresentation was mentioned by 14.3 percent, and being a "reliable and legitimate company" was mentioned by 13.5 percent of the respondents.

The distribution of amounts invested by the sample of survey participants was somewhat different from the distribution for the total population of victims discussed earlier. There was a slightly higher percent of small investments ($10,000 or less); 37.1 percent in the sample vs. 32.9 percent in the total population, but there was a greater difference in the major investments ($100,000 or more); 9.8 percent among the sample vs. 1.0 percent in the total victim population. Many investors in the survey invested more than once with the "Daves." About 60 percent invested more than three times, and about 30 percent six times or more. This pattern may have been influenced by the fact that the perpetrators tried to manipulate the victims through the familiar way of providing some returns at the beginning in order to gain their victims' confidence and encourage them to continue to pour money into their schemes. An indication of this practice is the fact that more than half of the respondents (55.4 percent) reported that they received some return on their investment, most of them up to $1,000, although thirteen of them received more than $5,000. Regarding the relationship between the sum invested and the extent of the return, the greater the amount invested, the more likely the subject was to report some return. However, of 69 subjects who reported the amount of cash returned, 82 percent got back less than $5,000, and most (45%) got less than $1,000 on investments of up to $50,000. Larger investments yielded slightly greater returns.

A further review of the pattern of reinvestment indicated that females were more likely to reinvest (60 percent), than males (50.9 percent). The participants also were asked whether they had any previous experience with similar investments. About one-third of them (34.7 percent) answered in the affirmative. The next question to those who were previously involved in similar investments asked about the outcome of their experiences. Seventeen percent reported that the previous experience turned out "very well," 43.4 percent thought that it was "OK," and 39.6 percent reported that it turned out "poorly." Interestingly, the relatively high percent of respondents who had a negative experience with their previous investments were ready to try it again. It would be instructive to know how many of these respondents were finally deterred from investing again in similar investments.

When the victims' reactions to their loss in these fraudulent investments were solicited in the survey, the largest group (39.2 percent) expressed anger and dismay; 23.1 percent reported similar sentiments, but presented their feelings more mildly, stating that they were disappointed, shocked, and could not believe that this would happen to them. A smaller proportion, 10.9 percent, were philosophical about their loss, showing an acceptance of the fact. One respondent even looked at this outcome with a stoic view as a part of the risk one takes when he/she invests; another 5.9 percent expressed helplessness and sadness rather than anger; and, finally, a small number (five, 2.9 percent) showed some "active" response by stating that they will never again be involved in such a scheme. One respondent even demanded legal action against the perpetrators; sadly, it was reported that one victim apparently died because of effects of his loss in this fraud.

A few questions were asked concerning the actual actions taken as a reaction to the fraud. It turned out that most of the victims did not do much about the current situation concerning the case. There was an attempt to take some action in this case through an organization that had been established for purposes of recovering the losses; 37.8 percent of the victims belonged to this organization, while 62.2 percent did not join. Among the fifty-seven individual victims who did join, the majority forty-five (78.9 percent) reported that they are active or very active in this organization. When the respondents were asked to evaluate the activities of this organization, more than 40 percent did not answer. Among those who did rate the activities of this organization, about half had a positive view and the other half expressed various degrees of dissatisfaction. Obviously, this evaluation was dependent on the expectations that individuals had concerning the possibility of certain actions that would lead to the recovery of at least some of their investments.

Similar considerations were taken into account when questions were asked regarding the actions of the authorities in this case. The first question posed focused on the respondents' satisfaction or dissatisfaction with the authorities' handling of the case. The overwhelming majority of respondents, 69.5 percent, as expected, were not satisfied, versus only 16 percent who reported that they were satisfied with the authorities' actions in this case; 13.7 percent reported that they didn't know anything about the authorities' response to this apparently fraudulent scheme. This may indicate that the respondents in this last group were uninformed about what was happening with this case and/or it may be a further indication of the authorities' failure to keep the victims informed about the status of their investigation. It is worthwhile to mention that there were some differences in the answers of males and females. While among males 17.4 percent were satisfied with the authorities' handling of the case, only one (6.3 percent) female expressed the same view. While we do not have any direct answer for this discrepancy, we may speculate about some reasons, e.g., males may have more investing experience and are more familiar with the "relaxed" attitudes of the authorities in protecting the public from victimization by fraud.

Following this line of questioning, the respondents were asked their opinion about what actions should be taken in this case. Roughly one-third of the victims surveyed did not answer this question, either because they did not know what to suggest or because they considered this as a "lost case." Among those who did relate to this question, 32.7 percent claimed that they don' know what action should be taken. These two groups ("no answer" and "don't know") accounted for 53.6 percent of the total number of respondents. The fact that the majority of victims didn't know or didn't suggest any actions regarding this large-scale fraud may indicate the prevalence of an anomic state of mind among the victims. It was a situation which they did not expect, were not familiar with, and didn't know how to relate to. Among those who suggested some actions, the majority wanted a more aggressive stand to be taken against the perpetrators, so that they will be punished, and some suggested that the case should be settled (it was not completely clear what was meant by this suggestion).

Finally, the respondents' recommendations for future preventive actions to avoid similar kinds of victimization by fraud of other potential investors were solicited. This was an open-ended question, therefore, a wide variety of suggestions were offered, which were not easily summarized. The suggestions can be divided into two major categories: (1) actions by government agencies; (2) actions by potential individual investors.

The suggested actions by government may be subdivided into legislative actions and actions by control agencies. Legislative actions include stricter laws and regulations for the investment industry (licensing, bonding); outlawing solicitation; prohibiting dealings that are unregulated by the SEC; establishing a government office that can advise on these investments; dissemination of more public information, and printing warnings on advertising literature. These suggestions were given by 45.9 percent of the respondents. Actions by the control agencies include punishing fraudsters to deter them from defrauding victims; reporting to the police (with the assumption that some action will be taken); and to monitor boiler-room operations. These control agencies' activities were recommended by 13.9 percent of the survey participants.

The various recommendations for individual investors implied that there is a personal responsibility either not to get involved in these investment schemes at all ("hang up the phone," "invest only with known companies," "avoid limited partnerships," etc.), or to be careful and to conduct personal investigations making sure that the investments are legitimate, to "be skeptical" of investment offers, and/or to make sure that the investor can afford the investment and the potential loss of money ("don't invest if can't afford it"). These recommendations for the potential investors were made by 40.2 percent of the respondents.

Discussion and Conclusions

One of the recurring themes in the analysis of white-collar and fraud-related crimes is that the victims of these crimes tend to be neglected in comparison to the victims of the so-called "street crimes," in spite of an increase in studies dealing with these victims. It is not an isolated occurrence that the "two Daves" were not seriously punished for their large-scale fraud, which victimized thousands of would-be investors, and that their victims were not able to recover even a fragment of their losses.

Our research is not unique with respect to this outcome. The case of one of the better-known investment frauds, the Home-Stake oil scam (McClintick, 1977), which started in the 1950s and continued into the early 1970s, showed many similarities to the current case, but there were some differences as well. Probably the major difference was that among the Home-Stake investors there were a number of celebrities, well-known lawyers, politicians, businessmen, and business executives. Quite a few of them invested six-figure sums in the project. The main purpose of the investment was to create tax shelters. This case also demonstrated that the regulatory and the criminal justice systems did not pay enough attention to early warnings about fraudulent activities by the perpetrators, and that they were not seriously punished when the case was handled by the criminal justice system. The main figures were placed on probation and had to pay relatively modest fines, and the victims lost their investments. It was interesting to learn that even rich, seasoned, and influential investors can be duped and are not immune to becoming victims of fraud.

In many cases, even if the Federal Trade Commission (FTC) is successful in putting the fraudulent operations out of business through the courts, the regulators and the criminal investigators fail to collect what they win in court and to distribute it to the victims (Leeds, 1999, p. A6). An article in the *Los Angeles Times* reported that "con artists who have made Southern California the nation's fraud capital operate in a world where crime pays—so long as they make the cash disappear." Often the scam operators transfer the money that they made to offshore financial havens, find legal loopholes to use the bankruptcy laws for protection, or simply spend it. The end result is the same, and the victims do not get restitution. The authorities are not successful, and often are not very interested in following these cases. They do not seem to be a high priority for the criminal justice system, while many victims are forced into serious financial hardships because of the scams.

This situation obviously raises hostile feelings and negative attitudes among the victims toward the regulators and against the entire criminal justice system. These feelings and attitudes are sometimes as strong or even stronger than the animosity against the perpetrators themselves, because of the recognition that the very same system that should enforce the laws does not provide protection for victims who abide by the same laws. These feelings are exacerbated by the fact that many street criminals go to prison for relatively minor crimes (such as some of the three-strikes sentences in California), and these offenders often get away with large sums of money and then return to "business as usual" before too long. A fact that clearly adds insult to injury.

REFERENCES

Blum, R. H. 1972. *Deceivers and Deceived*. Springfield, IL: Charles C. Thomas.

Calavita, K., and H. N. Pontell. 1990. "Heads I win, tails you lose: Deregulation, crime and crisis in the Savings and Loan industry. *Crime and Delinquency* 36 (3): 309–341.

Chermak, S. M. 1985. *Victims in the News: Crime in the American News Media*. Boulder, CO: Westview.

Christie, N. 1986. "The ideal victim." In Fattah, E. A., ed. *From Crime Policy to Victims Policy*. New York: St. Martin's Press.

Doerner, W. G., and S. P. Lab. 1995. *Victimology*. Cincinnati, OH: Anderson.

Edelhertz, H. 1983. "White-collar and professional crime: The Challenge for the 1980s." *American Behavioral Scientist* 27 (1): 109–128.

Edelhertz, H. 1970. *The Nature, Impact and Prosecution of White-Collar Crime*. Washington, DC: U.S. Department of Justice, Law Enforcement Assistance Administration.

Elias, R. 1993. *Victims Still: The Political Manipulation of Crime Victims*. Newbury Park, CA: Sage.

Goldman, S. 1995. "The Two Daves." *California Lawyer*, February, 44–49.

Granelli, J. S. 1992. "Getting their Day in Court." *Los Angeles Times*, A1 (March 1).

Jesilow, P., E. Klempner, and V. Chiao. 1992. "Reporting consumer and major fraud: A survey of complaints." In Schlegel, K., and D. Weisburd, eds. *White-Collar Crime Reconsidered*. Boston, MA: Northeastern University Press.

Karmen, A. 1996. *Crime Victims: An Introduction to Victimology*, 3rd ed. Belmont, CA: Wadsworth.

Kennedy, L. W., and V. F. Sacco. 1998. *Crime Victims in Context*. Los Angeles: Roxbury.

Leeds, J. 1999. "For Nation's Scam Artists Crime Does Pay." *Los Angeles Times*, pp. A1, A6 (April 20).

Levi, M. 1992. "White-Collar Crime Victimization." In Schlegel, K., and D. Weisburd, eds. *White-Collar Crime Reconsidered*. Boston, MA: Northeastern University Press,

Lilly, J. R., and P. Knepper. 1993. "The Corrections-Commercial Complex." *Crime and Delinquency* 39(2): 150–166.

Matthews, R., and J. Young. 1992. "Reflections on Realism." In Young, J., and R. Matthews, eds. *Rethinking Criminology: The Realist Debate*. London: Sage.

Mawby, R. I., and S. Walklate. 1994. *Critical Victimology*. London: Sage.

McClintick, D. 1977. *Stealing from the Rich: The Home-Stake Oil Swindle*. New York: M. Evans and Company.

Meadows, R. J. 1998. *Understanding Violence and Victimization*. Upper Saddle River, NJ: Prentice Hall.

Moore, M. H. 1980. "Notes Toward a National Strategy to Deal with White-collar Crime." In Edelhertz, H., and C. Rogovin, eds. *A National Strategy for Containing White-Collar Crime*. Lexington, MA: D.C. Heath.

Phipps, A. 1986. "Radical Criminology and Criminal Victimization: Proposals for the Development of Theory and Intervention." In Matthews, R., and J. Young, eds. *Confronting Crime*. London: Sage.

Pontell, H. N., and K. Calavita. 1993. "White-collar Crime in the Savings and Loan Scandal." *Annals of the Academy of Political and Social Science* 525:31–45.

Roberts, A. R. 1990. *Helping Crime Victims*. Newbury Park, CA: Sage.

Schlegel, K., and D. Weisburd, eds. (1992). *White-Collar Crime Reconsidered*. Boston: Northeastern University Press.

Sechrest, D. K., D. Shichor, J. H. Doocy, and G. Geis. 1998. "A Research Note: Women's Response to a Telemarketing Scam." *Women & Criminal Justice* 10 (1): 75–89.

Shapiro, S. P. 1990. "Collaring the Crime, not the Criminal: Reconsidering the Concept of White-Collar Crime." *American Sociological Review*, 5:346–365.

Shapiro, S. P. 1994. *Wayward Capitalists*. New Haven, CT: Yale University Press.

Shichor, D. 1998. "Victimology and the Victims of White-collar Crime." In Schwindt, H. D., E. Kube, and H. H. Kuhne, eds. *Festschrift fur Hans Joachim Schneider*. Berlin: Walter de Gruyter.

Shichor, D., J. H. Doocy, and G. Geis. 1996. "Anger, Disappointment and Disgust: Reactions of Victims of a Telephone Investment Scam." In Sumner, C., M. Israel, M. O'Connell, and R. Sarre, eds. *International Victimology: Selected Papers from the 8th International Symposium*. Canberra, Australia: Australian Institute of Criminology.

Shover, N., G. L. Fox, and M. Mills. 1994. "Long-term Consequences of Victimization by White-Collar Crime." *Justice Quarterly* 11:75–98.

Stevenson, R. J. 1998. *The Boiler Room and Other Telephone Sales Scams*. Urbana, IL: University of Illinois.

Titus, R. M., F. Heinzelmann, and J. M. Boyle. 1995. "Victimization of Persons by Fraud." *Crime and Delinquency* 41(1): 54–72.

Tomlin, J. W. 1982. "Victims of White-collar Crimes." In Schneider, H. J., ed. *The Victim in International Perspective*. Berlin: Walter de Gruyter.

Wallace, H. 1998. *Victimology: Legal, Psychological, and Social Perspectives*. Boston: Allyn and Bacon.

Walsh, M. E., and D. D. Schram. 1980. "The Victim of White-collar Crime: Accuser or Accused?" In Geis, G., and E. Stotlend, eds. *White-Collar Crime: Theory and Research*. Beverly Hills, CA: Sage.

Wheeler, S., and M. L. Rothman. 1982. "The Organization as Weapon in White-Collar Crime." *Michigan Law Review* 80 (7): 1403–1426.

Chapter Thirteen

The Characteristics of Hate-Crime Victimizations in the United States

Brian Levin

Unlike most of the other 14,086 murders in the United States in 1998, the slayings of James Byrd in Jasper, Texas, and Matthew Shepard in Laramie, Wyoming, garnered extraordinary national attention (FBI, 1999). Byrd, an African American, was decapitated and dismembered on the night of June 7 after being tied by the ankles with a metal chain to the back of a pickup truck and dragged along a desolate street by three white supremacists who had offered him a ride. Shepard, a 5 foot 2 college student with braces on his teeth weighing barely 100 pounds, was severely beaten by two local toughs and left in the near freezing cold, tied to a wooden fence on a flat plain on the edge of town (Southern Poverty Law Center, 2000)

If the significance of hate-crime were measured only by the prevalence of reported cases, it would hardly warrant a chapter in a book on criminal victimization. Of the 11,605,751 index crimes reported to the FBI in 2000, only 8,063 were hate crimes—less than .0007%. In New York City, for instance, more robberies are reported every five days than hate crimes reported in an entire year (FBI, *Crimes*, 2001; FBI, *Hate Crimes*, 2001). Hate crimes are relatively infrequent events, especially when compared to other dangerous situations faced by Americans. An African American is far more likely to be victimized by a fellow African American than he or she is to be victimized at the hands of a hate-crime offender. Similarly, a Jewish person is more likely to be killed in a traffic accident than to be the direct target of a hate crime (Levin, 1992–93). While the relative number of reported hate crimes is small—and definitions the subject of some debate—the category has nonetheless achieved broad public recognition in the United States (Jacobs and Potter, 1998).

Prepared especially for *Victims and Victimization*.

An Incomplete Composite of a Serious Type of Victimization

Available data, which are admittedly incomplete, nevertheless paint a picture of a crime that is more serious than previously thought. Hate crimes are much more likely to be directed against persons than is overall crime. Religious hate crime, however, had the lowest proportion of person-directed attacks. Generally, hate-crime offenses appear to be primarily clustered around simple and aggravated assault, vandalism, and threats. Person-directed hate crimes appear twice as likely to result in injury than overall person-directed crime. Aggravated assaults also appear to occur with greater frequency in hate crime than they do in overall crime. Weapon use in hate-crime attacks appears to involve primarily imprecise weapons of opportunity that can be accessed spontaneously, such as fists, blunt objects, and knives. Hate-crime victims are more likely to face unknown assailants, who are most often strangers. Most, but not all, research indicates that multiple offenders are more likely in hate-crime cases. Hate crimes are most likely to occur at residences, and it appears that there is a relationship between changing racial and ethnic housing patterns and hate crime. Hate-crime frequency also appears to be related at various times to the existence of a trigger event that ignites a cycle of retaliatory violence between or against certain communities, as was the case with anti-Muslim hate crimes after the September 11, 2001, terrorist attacks.

At least 60% of hate-crime victims are male. Racial bias accounts for about 55% of reported hate crime, with 66% of those victims being African-American (FBI, *Hate Crimes*, 2001). Research indicates that the vast majority of assailants are not confirmed to be members of bigoted hate groups. Hate crimes also appear to be less likely to be reported to authorities than crime overall. Hate-crime victims often face serial victimizations, and they face greater psychological and behavioral consequences as a result of their attacks. These negative indicators last longer for hate-crime victims than they do for similarly situated victims of non-hate crime.

The enforcement of hate-crime laws varies greatly among different jurisdictions. Even in jurisdictions where hate-crime enforcement is aggressive, few offenders are caught and the number of convictions is low. There is a paucity of scholarly research relating to how hate crime affects secondary victims such as coworkers and community members, but it would stand to reason that the effect would be significant because of the perceived interchangeability of victims within a targeted group. Presumably, the terror generated by hate crime would extend beyond direct victims to those who feel that they share the characteristics and attendant vulnerability of someone targeted for a crime—particularly since assailants are most frequently unknown or strangers.

Legal Definition and Coverage

Hate crimes are those offenses where a person or property is targeted for a crime because of his or her actual or perceived group affiliation or association. In 2002, 45 states and the District of Columbia had criminal statutes punishing bias-based victimizations, but there was significant variation relating to coverage, data collection, and enforcement. Race, religion, and ethnicity or national origin are covered in all states that explicitly list categories. Over 20 states cover gender and sexual orientation, while a smaller number cover disability. Some states have created a distinct, separate offense for hate crimes that do not require the charging of an additional offense (Anti-Defamation League, 2001). California Penal Code 422.6, for example, makes it a crime to interfere through force or threat with a person's civil rights on the basis of characteristics such as race, religion, national origin, sexual orientation, disability, and gender. In contrast, New York State's hate-crime law is in the form of a penalty enhancement, which requires the charging of an underlying offense. New York's hate enhancer adds an additional period of incarceration onto the sentence for an underlying criminal conviction when a jury finds beyond a reasonable doubt that the offender discriminated on the basis of a protected status in the selection of a crime victim. In many states, victims have used civil law tools such as mediation, injunctions and stay-away orders, and monetary judgments to enforce their rights on their own (Hate Crimes Act of 2000).

The federal hate-crime penalty enhancement law protects on the basis of race, religion, national origin, sexual orientation, and disability. The law is rarely used because it requires the charging of an underlying federal crime, which limits its applicability (Hate Crime Sentencing Enhancement Act of 1994). Another federal law punishes conspiracies that deprive victims of civil rights, while others punish the interference with certain specified rights on the basis of race or other group status (18 U.S.C. 241, 245; 42 U.S.C. 363).

Hate-Crime Cases and the Supreme Court

The Supreme Court has held that hate-motivated crime may be punished more severely, but it has also established guidelines for the application of such punishments. In *Barclay v. Florida* (1983) the United States Supreme Court held that a defendant's anti-white racial animus and motivation to ignite a race war were relevant in determining punishment in a race murder case. While the government may not penalize abstract bigoted beliefs, it may introduce evidence of a defendant's constitutionally protected beliefs to show motive or to establish intentionality.

In *R.A.V. v. St. Paul* (1992), the Supreme Court invalidated a municipal "hate speech" ordinance used to prosecute a teenage skinhead for burning a

Hate-Crime Criminal Law Overview

Federal

18 USC 241
Punishes conspiracies that interfere with civil rights; no racial motivation needed.

18 USC 242
Punishes government officials who use their authority to interfere with civil rights.

18 USC 245
Punishes interference with particular enumerated rights on the basis of race, color, religion or national origin.

42 USC 3631
Punishes interference with housing rights on the basis of race, color, religion, sex or national origin.

Hate Crime Sentencing Enhancement Act (HCSEA)
Increases the penalties by approx. 1/3 for underlying federal offenses committed on the basis of race, color, religion, national origin, ethnicity, gender, disability or sexual orientation.

18 USC 247
Increases the coverage and penalties under federal law for attacks against houses of worship.

State

Hate Crime Penalty Enhancement Laws
Increases the sentences for underlying crimes when a fact finder establishes beyond a reasonable doubt that a victim or property is selected on the basis of group characteristics.

Hate Crime Stand Alone Laws
Punishes violence, threats and or property destruction on the basis of group characteristics without the necessity of charging another offense.

Cross Burning Statutes
Punishes the hostile use of a burning cross on the property of another without the owner's permission

cross in the yard of an African-American family with several young children. While the justices unanimously rejected the statute, they were sharply divided as to their rationales. The statute read in relevant part:

> Whoever places on public or private property a symbol, object, appellation, characterization, or graffiti, including but not limited to a burning cross or Nazi swastika, which one knows or has reasonable grounds to know arouses anger, alarm or resentment in others on the basis of race, color, creed, religion or gender, commits disorderly conduct and shall be guilty of a misdemeanor. (St. Paul, Minn., Legis. Code § 292.02)

All the justices found the law impermissibly overbroad by punishing constitutionally protected speech that merely evoked anger or resentment. The First Amendment has consistently been held to protect extremely offensive speech and political discourse that fails to rise to the level of a threat, immediate incitement to criminality, or solicitation of a crime. The mere offensiveness of a belief is an impermissible basis for the government to punish its expression.

Four of the justices supported the contention that it was constitutional to punish expression whose severity went beyond merely offending someone. Since threats and so-called fighting words were traditionally held to be unprotected by the First Amendment, these justices maintained that it was constitutional for the government to punish bigoted speech selectively within these narrow categories on the basis of content. In his opinion Associate Justice John Paul Stevens argued:

> Conduct that creates special risks or harms may be prohibited by special rules. Lighting a fire near an ammunition dump or a gasoline storage tank is especially dangerous, such behavior may be punished more severely than burning trash in a vacant lot. Threatening someone because of her race or religious beliefs may cause particularly severe trauma or touch off a riot . . . such conduct may be punished more severely than threats against someone based on, say, his support of a particular athletic team. (*R.A.V.* at p. 416)

The controlling opinion, authored by Associate Justice Antonin Scalia, disagreed. These justices believed that even traditionally unprotected areas of speech cannot be punished based on the content of the idea expressed. They held that punishing certain types of threatening cross burnings such as those based on racial supremacy, but not others, such as those degrading the mentally ill, violated that principle. The *R.A.V.* decision invalidated those hate-crime laws where the criminality hinged solely on the idea expressed.

The issue of the overall constitutionality of hate-crime laws as a category was settled in *Wisconsin v. Mitchell* (1993). There, the Court unanimously upheld the constitutionality of another type of hate-crime statute—a penalty enhancement law. Specifically, the enhancement law at issue punished an offender's intentional selection of a victim or property based on the status characteristics of another person. The characteristics covered by Wisconsin's law included race, religion, color, national origin, and ancestry. Todd Mitchell was a nineteen-year-old African-American resident of Kenosha, Wisconsin, angered over a scene in the movie *Mississippi Burning*, where an African-American child was beaten by white supremacists as he knelt to pray. Mitchell used incendiary rhetoric to incite a crowd to beat Gregory Riddick, a fourteen-year-old white passerby, viciously. Mitchell was convicted of aggravated battery and sentenced to two years for the underlying assault. He was assessed another two-year term for intentionally selecting his victim on the basis of race. He was sentenced to a total of four years incarceration out of a possible seven-year term (*Wisconsin v. Mitchell*, 1993).

In reversing the Wisconsin Supreme Court, Chief Justice William Rehnquist cited three basic reasons for affirming the statute. First, while the government may not punish abstract beliefs, it can punish a vast array of depraved motives. The Court further found that penalty-enhancement laws, unlike the statute at issue in *R.A.V.* did not prevent people from expressing their views or punish them for doing so. Lastly, the Court pointed to the severity of hate crimes, stating that they are "thought to be more likely to provoke retaliatory crimes, inflict distinct emotional harm on their victims and incite community unrest" (*Wisconsin v. Mitchell*, 1993, p. 487–88).

In June 2000, the United States Supreme Court struck down a New Jersey hate-crime law in *Apprendi v. New Jersey*. The hate-crime law at issue allowed a judge, rather than a jury, to increase the sentence of a convicted defendant beyond the maximum enumerated in the criminal code for the underlying offense on a showing of racial bias by a preponderance of the evidence. The Court held 5–4 that when a factor impacts a sentence as substantially as racial bias did in *Apprendi*, it must be established to a jury by a higher standard—beyond a reasonable doubt. The impact of the decision in the area of hate-crime law was limited because the overwhelming majority of hate-crime statutes already meet the Court's standards (*Apprendi v. New Jersey*, 2000).

Data Collection Issues and Limitations

Before analyzing existing official hate-crime data it is important to stress that much of it is incomplete because of faulty or nonexistent law enforcement data collection in many states. Because of negligible hate-crime reporting from southern states other than Virginia, Texas, and Florida there is probably an undercount of African-American hate-crime victims because they represent a greater proportion of the population of those states than they do nationally (FBI, *Hate Crimes*, 2001). In addition, there is also probably an undercount of crimes linked to traditional organized hate groups like the Ku Klux Klan. Traditional, organized hate groups like the Klan have a greater representation in rural areas in Georgia, Alabama, Mississippi,

Arkansas, Louisiana, and the Carolinas than they do in the major metropolitan areas of California and the Northeast (Southern Poverty Law Center, 2000). The aforementioned seven southern states reported less than 150 hate crimes combined while the metropolitan areas of the Northeast and California account for over 25% of all reported hate crime (FBI, *Hate Crimes,* 2001). Furthermore, there is an undercount of Asian and Pacific Islander hate-crime victims and perpetrators owing to Hawaii's failure to supply hate-crime data to the federal government. In addition various individuals with cultural distrust of police, unlawful immigration status, or language difficulties appear less likely to report cases. Lastly, while many states list gender as a protected class under hate-crime statutes, gender has not been meaningfully included in recent hate-crime data collection and enforcement efforts and is thus excluded from this analysis (Levin & Weisburd, 1994).

Boston was the first police department in the United States to develop a hate-crime police unit and data collection in 1978 (Wexler & Marx, 1986). New York began collecting "bias crime" data in December 1980, followed by Los Angeles County, San Francisco, and Chicago. Maryland was the first state to collect hate-crime data in 1981, followed by Pennsylvania in 1986 (Levin, 1992–93). Eleven states mostly in the Mid-Atlantic and Northeast had begun compiling data by the end of the decade (Bibel et al., 1992). The Anti-Defamation League (ADL), a Jewish civil rights organization began compiling private data on anti-Semitic incidents in 1979 and issues annual reports (Anti-Defamation League, 2001). By the late 1980s and early 1990s additional compilation or analysis of hate-crime victimizations was conducted by the University of California, Davis; Northeastern University; University of Maryland, Baltimore-National Institute Against Prejudice & Violence; University of Pennsylvania; Atlanta's Center for Democratic Renewal; The National Gay & Lesbian Task Force; and the Southern Poverty Law Center.

Initially introduced in 1985, the federal Hate Crime Statistics Act was signed into law by President George H. Bush on April 23, 1990. The act authorized the attorney general to direct the Uniform Crime Reporting Section (UCR) of the Federal Bureau of Investigation (FBI) to collect data voluntarily submitted to it from law enforcement agencies on hate crime committed on the basis of race, religion, ethnicity, sexual orientation, and disability. Wide variation exists between jurisdictions, with many states submitting thousands of cases, while others submit none. New Jersey, widely regarded as a leader in enforcement, counted 710 in 2000, while Alabama and Hawaii failed to report any (FBI, *Hate Crimes,* 2001).

Over the last ten years there has been a steady increase in the number of agencies officially participating in the data-collection program. However, many of these newly participating agencies merely submit forms stating that there were zero reported hate crimes, leading some to believe that many jurisdictions are inaccurately reporting zero incidents. The Bureau of Justice Statistics funded an analysis of 2,657 of the nation's 16,000 police agencies.

An estimated 37% of departments that failed to submit reports had at least one hate crime committed within their jurisdiction. The study further found that 31% of jurisdictions reporting zero hate crimes actually failed to account for hate crime in their jurisdiction. The study extrapolated that nearly 6,000 departments had hate-crime victimizations, but failed to report them. An investigation by the Southern Poverty Law Center (SPLC) indicated that at least seven states routinely report zero hate crimes when departments fail to submit reports, despite FBI prohibition of the practice. The SPLC also reported instances where obvious hate-crime cases were intentionally or accidentally not reported to the FBI. Alabama, which routinely submitted "zero" hate-crime cases for several years, failed to record the murder of Billy Jack Gaither. Gaither was killed with an ax handle and his body set on fire in rural Sylacauga, Alabama, because he was gay. State authorities acknowledged that the murder was homophobic, but still declined to follow FBI reporting procedures because Alabama's penalty enhancement law (which has no bearing on reporting requirements) excludes gays and lesbians. In 1999 in Elkhart, Indiana, 19-year-old Sasezley Richardson was murdered by white supremacists, including an Aryan Brotherhood member. A clerical error prevented the case from being reported to the FBI despite the police and prosecutor's designation of the homicide as a hate crime. In addition, Washington State authorities revealed that the FBI did not include three agencies that recorded hate crimes in 1999 in its national tally (Southern Poverty Law Center, 2001). The BJS study further found that an unidentified capital city in the southern United States forwarded 20 hate-crime incidents to state authorities, but those numbers inexplicably never were reported to the FBI (McDevitt & Weiss, 2000).

Data about hate-crime victimizations is hampered not only by instances of police misclassification but also by the refusal or inability of many victims themselves to report incidents. Many victims do not even make an initial notification to police. Analysts estimate that the actual number of hate-crime victimizations is between 36,000 to 50,000 nationally (Southern Poverty Law Center, 2001; Weisburd & Levin, 1994). The data on hate-crime victimizations come from three basic sources: government reports, scholarly research, and private monitoring groups.

Government Data Collection

There are three sources of federal empirical data on hate-crime victimizations. As mentioned earlier the UCR has prepared uniform, but partial, annual national summaries of hate-crime data since 1991 (FBI, *Hate Crimes*, 1992–2001). An analysis of 1990 data from 11 states was also compiled for the FBI under contract and released in December 1992 (Bibel et al., 1992). The FBI has recently developed a more comprehensive subset of the UCR program that collects additional information on an expanded number of offenses. This new, more detailed data-collection system, the National Incident-Based Reporting System (NIBRS), will eventually be implemented nationally. (In 1997, 1,878 agencies from 10 states, about 6% of the U.S. population, submitted data to the FBI. In 1999, the number of agencies increased to 3,396 from 17 states, 13% of the total population.) NIBRS data on hate crime from the 2-year period 1997–1999 was published in September 2001. The third federal crime data initiative is the National Crime Victimization Survey (NCVS). The survey, which involves a comprehensive national sampling of residents who are questioned about victimizations, commenced operation in 1973 and was redesigned and renamed in 1992. The NCVS complements crime data reported to police by including both reported and unreported crimes. Hate-crime questions were recently added to the NCVS, but results are not yet available (Strom, 2001).

While national data is admittedly incomplete, it does offer interesting insights into the characteristics of hate crimes. Reported hate crimes appear to be more violent than non-bias motivated offenses. Hate motivated offenses are almost six times more likely to involve crimes against persons than are crimes generally. Nearly all of the NIBRS person-based hate crimes were clustered around three offenses: intimidation (verbal or related threats of bodily harm) (23.1%), simple assault (21.9%), and aggravated assault (12.9%). The next most common NIBRS person-based hate-crime offense was robbery (1.3%). The last four person offenses accounted for less than 1% combined (Strom, 2001).

The 2000 UCR hate-offense data is similar to that of the smaller but more detailed NIBRS sampling. As in previous years, intimidation was the most commonly reported UCR hate-crime offense at 34.9%. Vandalism and property destruction had ranked first among the NIBRS hate-crime data but was second in the UCR data set at 29.3%, followed by simple assault at 17.1%, and aggravated assault at 12.6% (FBI, *Hate Crimes*, 2001).

National data for overall crime indicates that hate crime is more likely to be violent and directed against persons than is crime overall. Part I of the UCR index for overall crime consists of eight representative offenses reported to police and is evenly divided between property offenses and person-based offenses. Person-directed or "violent" crime accounts for 12.2% of crime reported to police (FBI, *Crime*, 2001). For both hate crime and crime in general, homicide offenses are very infrequent events. The 15,517 murders and non-negligent homicides nationally recorded by the UCR in 2000 represented just .13% of the 11.6 million index crime offenses, while the 19 UCR hate-crime homicide offenses constituted .2% of the 9,430 hate-crime offenses reported in 2000 (FBI, *Hate Crimes*, 2001; *Crime*, 2001).

Aggravated assault was the most represented violent crime accounting for 7.8% of all reported Part I crimes. By contrast the FBI found that aggravated assault accounted for 12.6% of reported UCR hate-crime offenses and 12.9% of NIBRS hate-crime offenses. Since Part I of the UCR index of reported crime does not count simple assaults, it is not possible to compare

Hate-Crime Incidents by Offense		
	%	#
Person Offenses	60.0	1785
Assault, intimidation	23.1	687
Assault, simple	21.9	651
Assault, aggravated	12.9	385
Robbery	1.3	38
Other property offenses	.8	24
Property Offenses	38.3	1139
Vandalism	28.0	832
Larceny/Theft	5.1	153
Burglary	3.0	88
Other property offenses	2.2	66
Other Offenses	1.7	52
(Strom, 2001) NIBRS data 1997–99 10–17 States		

Hate-Crime Statistics by Offense in 2000		
	%	#
Person Offenses	65	6130
Intimidation	34.9	3292
Simple Assault	17.1	1615
Aggravated Assault	12.6	1184
Property Offenses	34.4	3241
Damage/Destruction/Vandalism	29.3	2765
Other	5.1	476
Other	.6	59
(FBI, Hate Crimes, 2001) UCR data 2000 48 states and DC		

the proportion of reported simple assaults to aggravated assaults for crime reported to police. However, Part II of the UCR, which tracks arrests from 6,400 agencies, includes a greater number of offenses, including assault and aggravated assault. In Part II there are 2.45 arrests for simple assault for every aggravated assault arrest. By contrast UCR 2000 hate-crime data indicate that there are 1.36 reported simple assaults for every aggravated assault, while the NIBRS hate-crime report shows the ratio of simple assault to aggravated assault to be 1.69. Not all serious crime had a higher representation in hate-crime data sets than in the data sets for overall crime. Rape and robbery represented a much greater proportion of overall crime than of hate crime (FBI, *Hate Crimes*, 2001; FBI, *Crime* 2001; Strom, 2001).

WEAPON USE AND INJURY

The only federally compiled composite information on weapon use during hate-crime offenses is in the NIBRS data. The data on weapon use during aggravated hate-crime assaults appear to be the most reliable. Weapon use was reported in 96% of the hate-crime aggravated assaults. The most common type of weapon was a personal weapon such as hands, fists, and feet, which were used 27% of the time. Blunt objects were used 19% of the time, and firearms and knives were tied at 17% each. The use of weapons for aggravated hate assaults is almost identical to that of aggravated assaults overall as the chart on the following page illustrates (Strom, 2001).

Victims of person-based hate crimes appear twice as likely to sustain an injury as victims of person-based crimes in general.

Aggravated Assault by Weapon Type*

	NIBRS Hate Crime	UCR Overall Assaults
Firearms	17%	18%
Knives/Cutting Devices	17%	18%
Personal Weapons	27%	28%
Other (Blunt object, etc.)	35%	36%

*Totals do not add up to 100% because of rounding. Cases in which no weapon was used (4%) were not included in NIBRS data.
(Strom, 2001; FBI, *Crime* 2001).

	All Person-Directed Crime	Person-Directed Hate Crime
No Injury	74.7%	47%
Injury	25.3%	53%
Minor Injury	20.8%	45%
Severe Injury	3.4%	8%
Other/ Unspecified Injury	1.1%	-----

(Strom, 2001; Mercy, Perkins, & Simon, 2001).

OFFENSE DISTRIBUTION VARIES BY GROUP TARGETED

The distribution of offenses is not even across targeted groups. Victimization appears to vary by victim type in both the UCR and NIBRS hate-crime data.

With the exception of hate crime motivated by religious bias, all other target groups were involved in incidents primarily directed against persons. Religious targets were much more likely to involve property, accounting for 69% of the incidents in the NIBRS data. The Jewish faith was the most targeted, accounting for 41% of religious-based hate crime in the NIBRS sample and 75% in the 2000 UCR data. This differential can partly be explained by the fact that the NIBRS data do not include several states with the largest concentration of Jews, such as New York, New Jersey, Pennsylvania, and California (American Jewish Committee, 1999). The UCR data reported that about 61.5% of both religiously motivated hate crime and hate crime directed at Jewish targets involved property damage or destruction (FBI, *Hate Crimes*, 2001; Strom, 2001). Two factors may account for differential representation of property offenses in this type of hate crime. First, property is sometimes more obviously connected to a religious faith; an individual's faith may not be as readily apparent. A house of worship, surname on a mailbox, or sign at a community center are examples where property characteristics yield immediate clues about the owners. Many Jewish peo-

Type of Bias Motivation 1997–1999 (NIBRS)

	Race	Religion	Ethnicity	Sexual Orient.	Disability
Person Directed	66.1%	29.9%	69.3%	56.2%	70.6%
Aggrav. Assault	14.3%	3.9%	18.5%	11.9%	11.8%
Simple Assault	24.1%	8.4%	22.8%	24.8%	41.2%
Intimidation	25.9%	16.5%	24.6%	16.4%	11.8%
Property Offenses	31.8%	68.9%	30.1%	42.2%	23.5%
Vandalism	23.1%	52.7%	20.7%	30.3%	11.8%

(Strom, 2001)

ple live in suburban areas where property crime is more prevalent than violent crime. According to the 2000 UCR data, houses of worship are the second most targeted location for religious hate crime (23%), while residences are the most common (37%). The NIBRS hate-crime data found that 29% of religiously motivated hate crime targeted residences, while commercial establishments, houses of worship, educational institutions, and open spaces all comprised about 16% each (FBI, *Hate Crimes*, 2001; Strom, 2001).

For overall hate crime in the 2000 UCR data, residences were the most frequent location, accounting for 36% of known locations, followed by streets at 20%, and schools and colleges at 12.6%. In descending order, residences, streets, and schools and colleges were the three most represented locations for hate crime motivated by race, sexual orientation and ethnicity. The NIBRS hate-crime data showed residences were the location of hate crimes 32% of the time, followed by open space at 28%, and commercial establishments at 19% (FBI, *Hate Crimes*, 2001; Strom, 2001).

The UCR 2000 hate-crime data showed this distribution of motivation: racial bias 54.5%, religious bias 17.2%, sexual-orientation bias 15.7%, ethnicity bias 12.35%, and disability bias less than 1/2 of 1%. Anti-Black incidents accounted for 66% of the cases motivated by racial bias, "anti-male homosexual" bias accounted for 68% of sexual orientation cases, anti-Hispanic cases accounted for 63% of ethnicity cases, while physical disability accounted for 56% of disability-related hate crime (FBI, *Hate Crimes*, 2001). The NIBRS data was similar: 61% of cases were racially motivated, 14.4% were religiously motivated, 11.1% ethnicity motivated, 12.7% were sexual-orientation motivated, and .6% physical disability related (Strom, 2001).

Victim-Offender Information

Person-directed hate crimes are more likely to involve offenders who are unknown or who are strangers to the victims, accounting for 56% of NIBRS

Hate Crime Incidents by Bias Motivation

	1992	1993	1994	1995	1996	1997	1998	1999	2000
Total Incidents†	6623	7587	5932	7947	8759	8049	7755	7876	8063
Agencies Participating†	6181	6551	7356	9584	11354	11221	10730	12122	11690
Bias Motivation									
Race:	4025	4732	3545	4831	5396	4710	4321	4295	4337
Anti-White	1342	1471	1010	1226	1106	993	792	781	875
Anti-Black	2296	2815	2174	2988	3674	3120	2901	2958	2884
Anti-Asian/ Pac. Islander	217	258	211	355	355	347	293	298	281
Eth./Nat. Origin:	669	697	638	814	940	836	754	829	911
Anti-Hispanic	369	472	337	516	564	491	482	466	557
Religion:	1162	1298	1062	1277	1401	1385	1390	1411	1472
Anti-Jewish	1017	1143	915	1058	1109	1087	1081	1109	1109
Anti-Christian	46	62	46	67	110	84	120	84	115
Anti-Islamic	15	13	17	29	27	28	21	32	28
Sexual Orient.:	767	860	685	1019	1016	1102	1260	1317	1299
Anti-Gay/Lesbian	760	830	664	984	991	1081	1231	1280	1257

†Year by year comparisons are discouraged because the number of agencies participating in the hate-crime data-collection program varies from year to year.
(FBI, *Hate Crimes*, 1993–2001)

hate-crime cases, compared to 47% for crime overall. The victim-offender relationship was unknown in 30% of all NIBRS hate-crime cases, a much higher percentage than that found with overall crime. For overall person-directed violent crime, the NCVS found that 45% were strangers, and 2% were unknown (Strom, 2001; Rennison, 2001).

The NIBRS person-directed hate-crime data showed that strangers represented 36% of offenders where the victim-offender relationship was known, with acquaintances accounting for 53.5%, and another 10% consisting of friends, intimates, and

NIBRS
Hate-Crime Victims by Age

Age	All Hate-Crime Offenses	Person-Directed Hate Offenses
0–12	6%	8%
13–17	17%	21%
18–24	21%	23%
25–34	21%	21%
35–44	19%	17%
45 & Up	16%	10%

(Strom, 2001)

relatives combined. Acquaintance offenders committing person-directed hate-crime attacks, however, varied significantly by the age of the victim, while stranger offenders remained relatively stable. Victims of person-directed hate-crime attacks who were 12 years old or younger were targeted by acquaintances 67% of the time, for those 13–17 the frequency drops to 46%. For victims 21 and older only 21% of attacks were committed by acquaintances. For hate-crime aggravated assaults 47% of known offenders were strangers. NIBRS data further indicate that young hate-crime victims were more likely to suffer from a person-directed attack than crime victims in general. Over half of person-directed hate-crime victims were under 25 years old, while almost one-third were below 18. In contrast NIBRS data for overall crime during the same period found that only about 20% of person-directed offenses involved victims under 18, while over 40% involved victims below age 25. The NIBRS data further revealed that 62% of hate-crime victims and 65% of person-directed hate-crime victims were males (Strom, 2001).

OTHER GOVERNMENT DATA

Various states with highly regarded reporting programs collect detailed supplemental hate-crime data that have not been included in federal data-collection programs. California, the nation's most populous state recently surpassed New Jersey for the most recorded hate-crime cases. While California hate-crime data were included in the 2000 UCR hate-crime report, not all information collected in California was included in federal reports. California supplemental information on hate-crime locations was similar to that collected by the NIBRS.

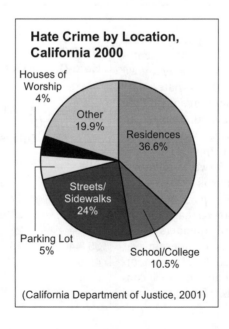

Hate Crime by Location, California 2000

- Houses of Worship 4%
- Other 19.9%
- Residences 36.6%
- Streets/Sidewalks 24%
- Parking Lot 5%
- School/College 10.5%

(California Department of Justice, 2001)

New Jersey was one of the first states to institute data collection in the late 1980s and has consistently ranked in the top three for most reported hate-crime cases. After collecting over one thousand cases annually in previous years, New Jersey recorded 710 hate crimes in 2000.

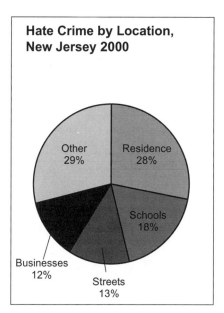

Hate Crime by Location, New Jersey 2000

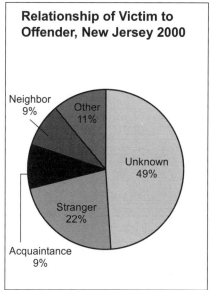

Relationship of Victim to Offender, New Jersey 2000

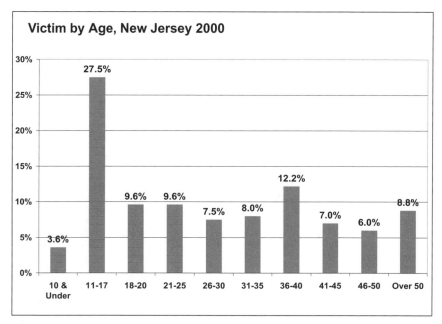

Victim by Age, New Jersey 2000

(New Jersey Department of Law & Public Safety, 2001)

While Pennsylvania collects a smaller number of incidents per capita than neighboring New Jersey, it recently compiled a five-year data collection retrospective that contained supplemental victim data (Pennsylvania Office of Attorney General, 1999).

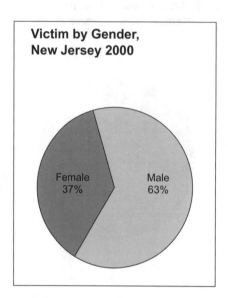

Victim by Gender, New Jersey 2000

Female 37%

Male 63%

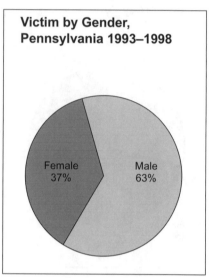

Victim by Gender, Pennsylvania 1993–1998

Female 37%

Male 63%

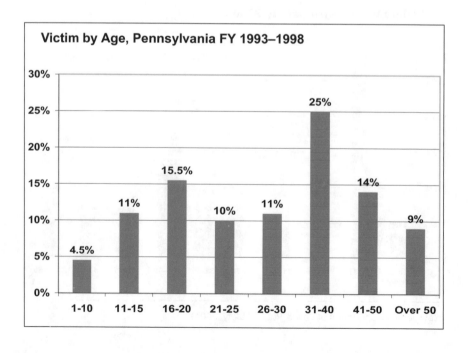

Victim by Age, Pennsylvania FY 1993–1998

Age	Percent
1-10	4.5%
11-15	11%
16-20	15.5%
21-25	10%
26-30	11%
31-40	25%
41-50	14%
Over 50	9%

Hate Group Involvement

Maryland's data-collection effort was one of the only official state data sets to track the involvement of hate groups in "hate incidents," which may or may not be crimes. The state published known hate-group involvement in "hate incidents" into the mid-1990s. In 1995 the data indicated that out of 546 hate incidents, only 37 involved hate groups: 22 involved the Ku Klux Klan, while most of the others involved various associations of young people (Maryland State Police, 1992, 1996). Confirmed hate-group involvement in hate-crime cases in other states was similar to that of Maryland. In 1990 only 7.5% of Minnesota hate-crime cases involved suspected hate groups. Massachusetts 1990 data showed confirmed hate-group involvement in hate crime only 2.3% of the time while another 11.8% of the cases were inconclusive (Bibel et al., 1992).

Scholarly Research

In 1986 the National Institute Against Prejudice and Violence found that victims of "ethnoviolence" exhibited 21% more negative "pyschophysiological symptoms" and a greater number of social and behavioral changes than those subjected to "violence" generally. The study included criminal and non-criminal acts under their definition of violence: verbal abuse, assaults, threats, burglaries, sexual assault and harassment. The study found that 6.5% of those surveyed had experienced criminal or non-criminal "violence" in the previous year. Victims of "ethnoviolence" reported their victimization to police 24% of the time, while those subjected to other violence reported incidents to police 39% of the time. The study also found that the majority of victims faced serial attacks (National Institute Against Prejudice & Violence, 1989).

A 1989 study by Jack McDevitt of Northeastern University analyzed Boston Police hate-crime data from 1983–87. That study concluded that some hate-crime cases reported to police, particularly property offenses, were preceded by other attacks that went unreported to police; while serious assaults usually had no preceding history of discord. McDevitt also found that hate-crime assaults result in injury 74% of the time and that 30% required hospitalization, a rate higher than that for overall crime. The study also found that 85% of Boston hate-crime cases involved unknown offenders or offenders who were strangers to the victim—a somewhat higher percentage than the NIBRS hate-crime data (McDevitt, 1989).

McDevitt further found that hate-crime offenders were more likely to attack in groups, doing so in 75% of the Boston cases, compared to 25% for crime overall in the United States (McDevitt, 1989). Using data from New York City, James Garafalo (1990) reached a similar finding: a significant majority of hate-crime cases involved multiple offenders. However, while

1991 Maryland data showed 71% of hate-crime "incidents" involved multiple offenders, its 1995 data indicated that only 49% did (Maryland State Police, 1992, 1996). NIBRS data diverged even more, indicating that multiple offenders were involved in only 25% of person-directed hate crimes and in about one-third of the assaults (Strom, 2001). Other results of McDevitt's (1989) study are presented below.

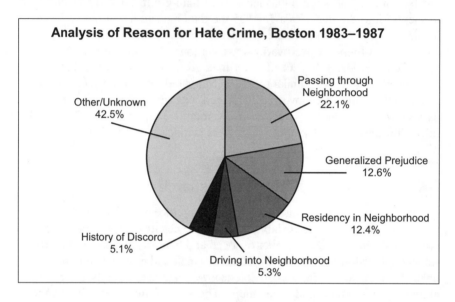

Analysis of Reason for Hate Crime, Boston 1983–1987

Other/Unknown 42.5%

Passing through Neighborhood 22.1%

Generalized Prejudice 12.6%

Residency in Neighborhood 12.4%

Driving into Neighborhood 5.3%

History of Discord 5.1%

Researcher Kevin Berrill (1992) released findings of composite victimization surveys of gays and lesbians. Of those surveyed, 19% reported being beaten or battered at least once in their lives because of their sexual orientation, and 44% had been threatened because of it. Of those who were threatened with violence, over 60% were subject to serial victimizations, as were 47% of those who had been physically assaulted. Between 48 and 78% of victims of anti-gay hate crime faced multiple attacks.

This author (Levin, 1992–93) found in 1992 that hate crimes were more likely to involve attacks against persons and a higher proportion of multiple offenders. The study also found that these crimes had a significant risk of retaliatory violence that could spread throughout a metropolitan area. The study also presented Boston police data that analyzed hate crime over a thirteen-year period by type of victimization (see chart opposite page).

A 1999 victimization study by Gregory Herek, J. Roy Gillis, and Jeanine Cogan (1999) included 2,300 gays, lesbians, and bisexuals in the Sacramento, California, metropolitan area and concluded that this population faced high risk of homophobic victimization. Almost one-fifth of female respondents and over 25% of males had been subject to a homophobic hate crime or attempted hate crime during their lives. One-eighth of the females and one-sixth of the males were victimized in a hate crime in the previous

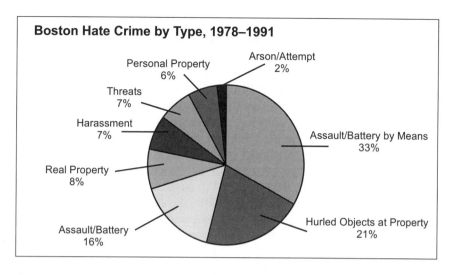

Boston Hate Crime by Type, 1978–1991

Personal Property 6%

Arson/Attempt 2%

Threats 7%

Harassment 7%

Real Property 8%

Assault/Battery by Means 33%

Assault/Battery 16%

Hurled Objects at Property 21%

five years. Hate-crime victims were also less likely to report their victimization to police. Another disturbing finding of the study was that those who were victimized by hate crimes experienced more severe psychological distress than did lesbian and gay victims of non-hate crime. Moreover, the study concluded that crime-related psychological problems for hate-crime victims remained for up to five years—over twice as long as for other crime. Ed Dunbar concluded that those most severely victimized in hate-crime attacks were the least likely to contact police because of fear of further abuse (Dunbar, 1997).

A 1998 study of Los Angeles hate-crime cases over a 3-year period led by Karen Umemoto revealed some disturbing findings. First, 47% of reported racial hate crimes were inter-minority crimes, particularly between African Americans and Latinos. The study also found that neighborhoods experiencing racial demographic changes were locations of clusters of hate crimes. The study further found that minority gangs and skinheads were oftentimes related to these geographically clustered hate crimes (Umemoto & Mikami, 2000). Donald Green, using a New York City data set, concluded that changing neighborhood demographics had an impact on the frequency of hate-crime incidents, as opposed to the overall state of the economy, as had been previously thought (Green, 1997; Green, Glaser & Andrew, 1998). For gays and lesbians, however, attacks appeared to be clustered in neighborhoods known to have a high gay population (Los Angeles County, 2001).

This author found that hate crimes appeared to cluster chronologically soon after the occurrence of a triggering event. For instance, New York City had a significant spike in hate crime after a black man was killed after being forced onto a highway by a white mob. Similarly, after the acquittal of four police officers in the Rodney King incident in 1992, every American jurisdiction with meaningful data collection experienced an increase in hate crime, with some experiencing rioting (Levin, 1992–93; Levin, 1993). Lastly, people and institutions perceived to be Muslim or South Asian became a more frequent target of hate crime after the September 11, 2001, terrorist attacks. For instance Los Angeles County, California, had 92 hate crimes, including 2 homicides, committed on the basis of anti-Muslim or anti-Middle Eastern bias in the three months following September 11, 2001—compared to 12 cases for the whole of the previous calendar year (Winton, 2001).

A 2001 study by Jack McDevitt and other Boston researchers compared various characteristics of bias and non-bias victimizations in 146 cases of aggravated assault from Boston. The researchers found that bias crime attacks involve multiple offenders in 49% of the cases compared to 35% for the non-bias victim sample. The study also found that bias crime victims had no prior relationship in 83.5% of the cases compared to 68.2% for the non-bias crime sample. Bias crime victims categorized incidents as unprovoked 76% of the time compared to 53% for non-bias crime victims. Victims from both groups reported nearly identical percentages relating to hospital stays. More non-bias victims reported emergency room treatment, but the response sample to this question set was too low for the researchers to draw any conclusions (McDevitt et al., 2001). The study also found that almost identical proportions of bias and non-bias crime victims modified their behavior in response to their victimization. However, bias crime victims reported more intense and severe psychological trauma after their victimization than their non-bias counterparts. Bias crime victims were about one-third more likely to report feeling less safe after their attack and almost three times as likely to categorize overcoming their victimization as very difficult (McDevitt et al, 2001).

Prosecution Information

The Los Angeles County Human Relations Commission reported 933 hate crimes in 2000. The district attorney reviewed 214 cases, while city attorneys reviewed 65. The district attorney filed 158 hate-crime charges, with 91 against adults, and 67 against juveniles. The city attorney filed another 17 charges. The United States attorney pursued three federal hate-crime cases in 2000, all of which resulted in convictions or guilty pleas (Los Angeles County, 2001).

California has various jurisdictions where there are prosecutors specifically assigned to hate-crime cases. In 1999 there were 1,962 hate-crime events, 2,001 offenses, and 2,021 known suspects. In 1999, 1,039 cases (not all of which took place in 1999) were referred to California prosecutors. Of those referrals, 372 complaints were filed; of the cases filed, 229 resulted in convictions or guilty pleas. Hate-crime charges were involved in 174 of those convicted or offering guilty pleas (California Department of Justice, 2000).

McDevitt's 1989 study of hate crime in Massachusetts tracked the disposition of 452 hate-crime cases. Of the 452 cases, 369 had known dispositions. The victim declined to pursue the case in 127 (34.4%) of those cases. Of the 242 cases that remained, no suspect was apprehended in 130 of them. An arrest was made in 15% of the cases. Only 40 cases went to criminal court, and 81% of those resulted in a conviction or guilty plea. Out of the 452 cases initially reported to police, only five actually resulted in incarceration of the defendant (McDevitt, 1989).

Monitoring Organizations

Private organizations also collect data on hate crimes and hate incidents. A coalition of gay, lesbian, and bisexual organizations counted 2,362 hate-motivated criminal events from 15 metropolitan areas, including 33 homicides in 1998. The data indicated that there were 907 assaults and attempted assaults, with 248 of them resulting in serious injuries, and 110 resulting in hospitalization. FBI UCR hate-crime data from the same year recorded 1,248 anti-gay incidents including four homicides (National Coalition, 1999; FBI, *Hate Crimes*, 1999).

A consortium of Asian organizations has produced an annual audit of anti-Asian violence over the last decade. The audit has counted between 450 and 550 incidents annually since 1994, with 486 in 1999.

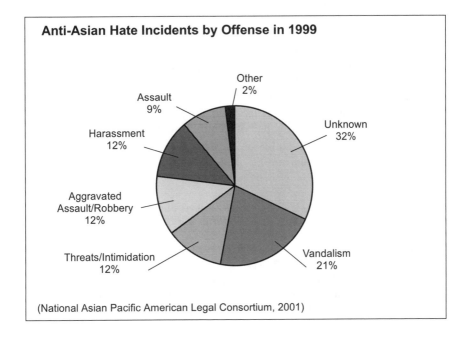

Anti-Asian Hate Incidents by Offense in 1999

- Other 2%
- Assault 9%
- Harassment 12%
- Aggravated Assault/Robbery 12%
- Threats/Intimidation 12%
- Unknown 32%
- Vandalism 21%

(National Asian Pacific American Legal Consortium, 2001)

The Anti-Defamation League has monitored anti-Semitic "incidents" for over two decades. In 2000 the ADL counted 1,606 incidents with 877 harassment, threat, and assault incidents and 729 incidents directed against property. Person-directed incidents first outpaced property incidents in 1991 and have remained in the majority every year since then. The most incidents occurred in 1994 when 2,066 were recorded (Anti-Defamation League, 2001).

Conclusion

Critics of hate-crime legislation argue that bias motivation does not create additional injuries for victims. Continuing research disputes that conclusion. "Hate crimes are inherently more harmful to the social fabric of society than comparable crimes without bias motive" (McDevitt et al., 2001, p. 698). Four aspects of hate crime contribute to differential impact on victims: (1) victim interchangeability—victims are usually hard pressed to alter the perceived status that precipitated the hate crime; an African American cannot prevent future victimizations by changing his or her ethnicity; (2) secondary victimization—the impact of bias crime extends beyond the primary victim to all members of the community who share the targeted characteristics; (3) the first two elements can interact to create violent disruption in the community; courts have noted the potential for bias crime to incite mass disturbances; (4) victims of hate-motivated batteries face a greater risk of injury than do victims of batteries overall.

Hate crimes are serious criminal events with significant consequences for victims, communities, and our pluralistic democracy. While many states have hate-crime laws, enforcement—as evidenced by data collection—varies widely by jurisdiction. Despite legislation directing that uniform national data be collected on hate crime, complete data are currently not available. Existing data and research from a variety of sources, however, create a composite that strongly suggests that hate-crime victimizations are a criminologically distinct and severe form of criminal conduct. The United States Supreme Court has upheld the constitutionality of statutes that enhance the punishment for crimes where a person is intentionally selected for victimization on the basis of group status, in part because of research showing the severe effects of hate crime.

BIBLIOGRAPHY

American Jewish Committee (1999). *American Jewish yearbook, 1998.* New York: Author.
Anti-Defamation League (2001). *2000: Audit of anti-Semitic incidents.* New York: Author.
Apprendi v. New Jersey, 530 U.S. 466 (2000).
Barclay v. Florida, 463 U.S. 939 (1983).
Berrill, K. (1992). Anti-gay violence and victimization in the United States: An overview. In G. T. Herek & K. T. Berrill (Eds.), *Hate crimes: Confronting violence against lesbians and gay men.* Newbury Park, CA: Sage.

Bibel, D., McDevitt, J., Miliano, R., Ross, D., & Stone, W. (December 1992). *Hate crime statistics, 1990: A resource book*. Washington, DC: U.S. Department of Justice/Federal Bureau of Investigation.

California Department of Justice (2001). *Hate crime in California: 2000*. Sacramento: Author.

California Department of Justice (2000). *Hate crime in California: 1999*. Sacramento: Author.

California Penal Code, 422.6 (West 2001).

Dawson v. Delaware, 503 U.S. 159 (1992).

Dunbar, E. (1997, November). *Hate crime patterns in Los Angeles County: Demographic and behavioral factors of victim impact and reporting of crime*. Paper presented at a congressional briefing cosponsored by the American Psychological Association and the Society for the Psychological Study of Social Issues, Washington, DC.

Garafalo, J. (1990, November). *Bias and non-bias crimes in New York City: Preliminary findings*. Unpublished paper presented at the meeting of American Society of Criminology, Baltimore, MD.

Federal Bureau of Investigation (1999). *Crime in the United States: 1998*. Washington, DC: U.S. Department of Justice.

Federal Bureau of Investigation (2001). *Crime in the United States: 2000*. Washington, DC: U.S. Department of Justice.

Federal Bureau of Investigation (1992–2001). *Hate crimes in the United States: 1991–2000*. Washington, DC: U.S. Department of Justice (multiple annual reports).

Green, D. (1997, November). *Cause of hate: Economics versus Demographics*. Paper presented at a congressional briefing sponsored by the American Psychological Association et al., Washington, DC.

Green, D., Glaser, J., & Rich, A. (1998). From lynching to gay bashing: The elusive connection between economic conditions and hate crime. *Journal of Personality and Social Psychology, 75*(1), 82–92.

Hate Crimes Act of 2000, NY Crim. Proc. Law, § 485.10 (2000).

Hate Crime Sentencing Enhancement Act of 1994. Violent Crime Control and Law Enforcement Act of 1994, Pub. L. No. 103–322, § 280003, 108 Stat. 1796, 2096.

Hate Crimes Statistics Act of 1990, Pub. L. No. 101–275, 104 Stat. 140, *codified as amended at* 28 U.S.C.A. § 534 (West 2001).

Herek, G. M., Gillis, J. R., & Cogan, J. C. (1999). Psychological sequelae of hate crime victimization among lesbian, gay, and bisexual adults. *Journal of Consulting and Clinical Psychology, 67*(6), 945–951.

Jacobs, J., & Potter, K. (1998) *Hate crimes: Criminal law & identity politics*. New York: Oxford University Press.

Levin, B. (1992–93). Bias crimes: A theoretical & practical overview. *Stanford Law & Policy Review, 4,* 165.

Levin, B. (Fall 1993). A dream deferred, *Journal of Intergroup Relations, 20,* 3.

Levin, B., & Weisburd, S. (1994) On the basis of sex: Recognizing gender based bias crimes. *Stanford Law & Policy Review, 5,* 21.

Los Angeles County Commission on Human Relations (2001). *Hate crime report: 2000*. Los Angeles: Author.

McDevitt, J. (1989, July). *The study of the character of civil rights violations in Massachusetts (1983–1987)*. Paper presented at the meeting of American Society of Criminology, Reno, NV.

McDevitt, J., Balboni, J., Garcia, L., & Gu, J. (2001). Consequences for victims: A comparison of bias and non-bias-motivated assaults. *American Behavioral Scientist*, 45 (4), 697–713.

McDevitt, J., & Weiss, J. (2000). *Improving the quality and accuracy of bias crime statistics nationally: An assessment of the first ten years of bias crime data collection.* Washington, DC: U.S. Department of Justice.

Maryland State Police (1992). *Hate bias incident assessment 1991.* Pikesville, MD: Author.

Maryland State Police (1996). *Hate bias incident assessment 1995.* Pikesville, MD: Author.

Mercy, J., Perkins, C., & Simon, T. (June 2001). *Injuries from violent crime, 1992–98.* Washington, DC: U.S. Department of Justice/Bureau of Justice Statistics.

National Asian Pacific American Legal Consortium (2001). *1999: Audit of violence against Asian Pacific Americans, seventh annual report: Challenging the invisibility of hate.* Washington, DC: Author.

National Coalition of Anti-Violence Programs (1999). *Anti-lesbian, gay, bisexual, and transgender violence in 1998.* New York: Author.

National Institute Against Prejudice & Violence (1989). *National Victimization Survey.* Baltimore, MD: The Prejudice Institute.

New Jersey Department of Law & Public Safety (2001). *Bias incident offense report: 2000.* Trenton, NJ: Author.

New York Hate Crimes Act of 2000, 2000 N.Y. ALS 107, 2000 N.Y. Laws 107, 2000 N.Y. S.N. 4691.

Pennsylvania Office of Attorney General and Pennsylvania Human Relations Commission (1999). *Hate crimes report: 1993–1998.* Harrisburg, PA: Author.

R.A.V. v. St. Paul, 505 U.S. 377 (1992).

Rennison, M. (June 2001). *Criminal victimization 2000: Changes 1999–2000 with trends 1993–2000.* Washington, DC: U.S. Department of Justice/Bureau of Justice Statistics.

Southern Poverty Law Center (2001, Winter). *Discounting hate (Intelligence report No. 104).* Montgomery, AL: Author.

Southern Poverty Law Center (2000, Winter). *The decade in review (Intelligence report No. 97).* Montgomery, AL: Author.

St. Paul, MN. Legis. Code § 292.02 (Invalidated).

Strom, K. J. (2001, September). *Special report: Hate crimes reported in NIBRS, 1997–99.* Washington, DC: U.S. Department of Justice/Bureau of Justice Statistics.

Umemoto, K., & Mikami, C. (2000). A profile of race-bias hate crime in Los Angeles County. *Western Criminology Review,* 2(2). Retrieved June 8, 2000, from *http://wcr.sonoma.edu/ v2n2/umemoto.html*

18 U.S.C. 241.

18 U.S.C. 242.

18 U.S.C. 245.

42 U.S.C. 363.

Wexler, C., & Marx, G. (1986). When law & order works. *Journal of Crime & Criminology, 32,* 205.

Winton, R. (2001, December 21). Hate crimes soar following attacks; Violence: The number of incidents targeting middle easterners is seven times the total for all of last year, a county report says. *Los Angeles Times,* p. B1.

Wisconsin v. Mitchell, 508 U.S. 476 (1993).

Chapter Fourteen

First Response to Victims of Crime

Office for Victims of Crime

Basic Guidelines on Approaching Victims of Crime

BACKGROUND

The way people cope as victims of crime depends largely on their experiences immediately following the crime. As a law enforcement officer, you are usually the first official to approach victims. For this reason, you are in a unique position to help victims cope with the immediate trauma of the crime and to help restore their sense of security and control over their lives. Circumstances of the crime and the crime scene determine when and how the first responding officers are able to address victims and their needs. This publication recognizes that each crime and crime scene is different and requires officers to prioritize their performance of tasks in each situation. Generally, officers must attend to many tasks, including assessing medical needs, determining facts and circumstances, advising other personnel, and gathering and distributing suspect information. It is helpful to keep in mind that apprehension of the suspect is the primary duty of law enforcement and that accomplishing this task helps not only the suspect's current victims but potential victims as well. Sometimes the first responders must delay their attendance to the victims if the situation requires. For example, if the crime is ongoing, or if the collection of evidence or investigation of the crime is extremely time-sensitive, first responders may not be able to direct their immediate attention to the victims. However, as soon as the most urgent and pressing tasks have been addressed, officers will focus their attention on the victims and their needs. At this point, how the officers respond to the victims,

Source: Office for Victims of Crime, *First Response to Victims of Crime* (NCJ 176971), pp. 8–24, May 2000.

explain the competing law enforcement duties, and work with the victims is very important.

By approaching victims appropriately, officers will gain their trust and cooperation. Victims may then be more willing to provide detailed information about the crime to officers and later to investigators and prosecutors, which, in turn, will lead to the conviction of more criminals. Remember that you are there for the victim, the victim is not there for you. You can help victims by understanding the three major needs they have after a crime has been committed: the need to feel safe; the need to express their emotions; and the need to know "what comes next" after their victimization. . . .

TIPS FOR RESPONDING TO VICTIMS' THREE MAJOR NEEDS

Victims' Need to Feel Safe

People often feel helpless, vulnerable, and frightened by the trauma of their victimization. As the first response officer, you can respond to victims' need to feel safe by following these guidelines:

- Introduce yourself to victims by name and title. Briefly explain your role and purpose.
- Reassure victims of their safety and your concern by paying close attention to your own words, posture, mannerisms, and tone of voice. Say to victims, "You're safe now" or "I'm here now." Use body language to show concern, such as nodding your head, using natural eye contact, placing yourself at the victims' level rather than standing over seated victims, keeping an open stance rather than crossing your arms, and speaking in a calm, sympathetic voice.
- Ask victims to tell you in just a sentence or two what happened. Ask if they have any physical injuries. Take care of their medical needs first.
- Offer to contact a family member, friend, or crisis counselor for victims.
- Ensure privacy during your interview. Conduct it in a place where victims feel secure.
- Ask simple questions that allow victims to make decisions, assert themselves, and regain control over their lives. Examples: "Would you like anything to drink?"; "May I come inside and talk with you?"; and "How would you like me to address you, Ms. Jones?"
- Assure victims of the confidentiality of their comments whenever possible.
- Ask victims about any special concerns or needs they may have.
- Provide a "safety net" for victims before leaving them. Make telephone calls and pull together personal or professional support for the victims. Give victims a pamphlet listing resources available for help or information. This pamphlet should include contact information for local crisis intervention centers and support groups; the prosecutor's office and the victim-witness assistance office; the state victim compensation/assistance office; and other nationwide services, including toll-free hotlines.

- Give victims—in writing—your name and information on how to reach you. Encourage them to contact you if they have any questions or if you can be of further help.

Victims' Need to Express Their Emotions

Victims need to air their emotions and tell their story after the trauma of the crime. They need to have their feelings accepted and have their story heard by a nonjudgmental listener. In addition to fear, they may have feelings of self-blame, anger, shame, sadness, or denial. Their most common response is: "I don't believe this happened to me." Emotional distress may surface in seemingly peculiar ways, such as laughter. Sometimes victims feel rage at the sudden, unpredictable, and uncontrollable threat to their safety or lives. This rage can even be directed at the people who are trying to help them, perhaps even at law enforcement officers for not arriving at the scene of the crime sooner. You can respond to victims' need to express their emotions by following these guidelines:

- Avoid cutting off victims' expression of their emotions.
- Notice victims' body language, such as their posture, facial expression, tone of voice, gestures, eye contact, and general appearance. This can help you understand and respond to what they are feeling as well as what they are saying.
- Assure victims that their emotional reactions to the crime are not uncommon. Sympathize with the victims by saying things such as: "You've been through something very frightening. I'm sorry"; "What you're feeling is completely normal"; and "This was a terrible crime. I'm sorry it happened to you."
- Counter any self-blame by victims by saying things such as, "You didn't do anything wrong. This was not your fault."
- Speak with victims as individuals. Do not just "take a report." Sit down, take off your hat, and place your notepad aside momentarily. Ask victims how they are feeling now and listen.
- Say to victims, "I want to hear the whole story, everything you can remember, even if you don't think it's important."
- Ask open-ended questions. Avoid questions that can be answered by "yes" or "no." Ask questions such as "Can you tell me what happened?" or "Is there anything else you can tell me?"
- Show that you are actively listening to victims through your facial expressions, body language, and comments such as "Take your time; I'm listening" and "We can take a break if you like. I'm in no hurry."
- Avoid interrupting victims while they are telling their story.
- Repeat or rephrase what you think you heard the victims say. For example, "Let's see if I understood you correctly. Did you say . . . ?"; "So, as I understand it, . . . "; or "Are you saying . . . ?"

Victims' Need to Know "What Comes Next" after Their Victimization

Victims often have concerns about their role in the investigation of the crime and in the legal proceedings. They may also be concerned about issues such as media attention or payment for health care or property damage. You can help relieve some of their anxiety by telling victims what to expect in the after-math of the crime. This will also help prepare them for upcoming stressful events and changes in their lives. You can respond to victims' need to know about what comes next after their victimization by following these guidelines:

- Briefly explain law enforcement procedures for tasks such as the filing of your report, the investigation of the crime, and the arrest and arraignment of a suspect.
- Tell victims about subsequent law enforcement interviews or other kinds of interviews they can expect.
- Discuss the general nature of medical forensic examinations the victim will be asked to undergo and the importance of these examinations for law enforcement.
- Explain what specific information from the crime report will be available to news organizations. Discuss the likelihood of the media releasing any of this information.
- Counsel victims that lapses of concentration, memory losses, depression, and physical ailments are normal reactions for crime victims. Encourage them to reestablish their normal routines as quickly as possible to help speed their recovery.
- Give victims a pamphlet listing resources available for help and information. This pamphlet should include contact information for local crisis intervention centers and support groups; the prosecutor's office and the victim-witness assistance office; the State victim compensation/assistance office; and other nationwide services, including toll-free hotlines.
- Ask victims whether they have any questions. Encourage victims to contact you if you can be of further assistance.

Elderly Victims

BACKGROUND

When elderly people are victimized, they usually suffer greater physical, mental, and financial injuries than other age groups. Elderly victims are twice as likely to suffer serious physical injury and to require hospitalization than any other age group. Furthermore, the physiological process of aging brings with it a decreasing ability to heal after injury—both physically and mentally. Thus, elderly victims may never fully recover from the trauma of their victimization. Also, the trauma that elderly victims suffer is worsened by their financial difficulties. Because many elderly people live on a low or fixed income, they often cannot afford the professional services and products that could help them in the aftermath of a crime.

It is understandable why the elderly are the most fearful of crime. Elderly people, in fact, face a number of additional worries and fears when victimized. First, they may doubt their ability to meet the expectations of law enforcement and worry that officers will think they are incompetent. They may worry that a family member, upon learning of their victimization, will also think they are incompetent. Further, they may fear retaliation by the offender for reporting the crime. Finally, elderly people may experience feelings of guilt for "allowing" themselves to be victimized. Depending on your approach as a first responder, you can do much to restore confidence in and maintain the dignity of the elderly victims you work with.

TIPS FOR RESPONDING TO ELDERLY VICTIMS

- Be attentive to whether victims are tired or not feeling well.
- Allow victims to collect their thoughts before your interview.
- Ask victims if they are having any difficulty understanding you. Be sensitive to the possibility that they may have difficulty hearing or seeing, but do not assume such impairments. Ask victims if they have any special needs, such as eyeglasses or hearing aids.
- Ask victims whether they would like you to contact a family member or friend.
- Be alert for signs of domestic violence or neglect, since studies indicate that 10 percent of the elderly are abused by their relatives.
- Give victims time to hear and understand your words during the interview.
- Ask questions one at a time, waiting for a response before proceeding to the next question. Avoid interrupting victims.
- Repeat key words and phrases. Ask open-ended questions to ensure you are being understood.
- Avoid unnecessary pressure. Be patient. Give victims frequent breaks during your interview.
- Protect the dignity of victims by including them in all decision-making conversations taking place in their presence.
- For hearing-impaired victims, choose a location free of distractions, interference, and background noise, and:
  - Face the victim so your eyes and mouth are clearly visible.
  - Stand or sit at a distance of no more than 6 feet and no fewer than 3 feet from the victim.
  - Begin speaking only after you have the victim's attention and have established eye contact.
  - Never speak directly into the victim's ear.
  - Speak clearly, distinctly, and slightly slower than usual. Keep your questions and instructions short and simple. Do not overarticulate your words.
  - If necessary, talk slightly louder than usual but do not shout. Extremely loud tones are not transmitted as well as normal tones by hearing aids.
  - Be prepared to repeat your questions and instructions frequently. Use different words to restate your questions and instructions.

- Provide enhanced lighting if victims are required to read. Ensure that all print in written materials is both large enough and dark enough for victims to read.
- Provide victims written information that summarizes the important points you communicated verbally so they can refer to this information later.
- Remember that elderly victims' recollections may surface slowly. Do not pressure them to recollect events or details; rather, ask them to contact you if they remember anything later.
- In all your comments and interactions with elderly victims, their families, and other professionals involved in the case, focus on the goals of restoring confidence to and maintaining the dignity of the elderly victims you work with.

Victims of Sexual Assault

BACKGROUND

Sexual assault is one of the most traumatic types of criminal victimization. Whereas most crime victims find it difficult to discuss their victimization, sexual assault victims find it especially painful. One obvious reason for this is the difficulty that many people have in talking about sex. A more important reason, however, is that many victims of sexual assault are intensely traumatized not only by the humiliation of their physical violation but by the fear of being severely injured or killed.

The three primary responsibilities of law enforcement in sexual assault cases are to (1) protect, interview, and support the victim; (2) investigate the crime and apprehend the perpetrator; and (3) collect and preserve evidence of the assault that will assist in the prosecution of the assailant.

In the investigation and prosecution of most sexual assault cases, the role of the victim is much more important than in other crimes since the victim is usually the sole witness to the crime. Unfortunately, sexual assault victims are sometimes reluctant to cooperate with law enforcement because they fear the perpetrator will return to retaliate.

Only men and women who have suffered the trauma of sexual assault themselves can begin to understand the depth and complexity of the feelings experienced by sexual assault victims. Even so, your approach as a first responder to sexual assault victims can significantly affect whether the victims begin the road to recovery or suffer years of trauma and anguish.

TIPS FOR RESPONDING TO VICTIMS OF SEXUAL ASSAULT

- Be prepared for virtually any type of emotional reaction by victims. Be unconditionally supportive and permit victims to express their emotions, which may include crying, angry outbursts, and screaming.

- Avoid interpreting the victim's calmness or composure as evidence that a sexual assault did or did not occur. The victim could be in shock. (Note: False accusations of sexual assault are estimated to occur at the low rate of 2 percent—similar to the rate of false accusations for other violent crimes.)
- Approach victims calmly. Showing your outrage at the crime may cause victims even more trauma.
- Ask victims whether they would like you to contact a family member or friend.
- Offer to contact a sexual assault crisis counselor. Ask victims whether they would prefer a male or female counselor. In addition, ask the victims whether they would prefer talking with you or a law enforcement officer of the opposite sex.
- Be careful not to appear overprotective or patronizing.
- Remember that it is normal for victims to want to forget, or to actually forget, details of the crime that are difficult for them to accept.
- Encourage victims to get medical attention, especially to check for possible internal injuries. In addition, a medical examination can provide evidence for the apprehension and prosecution of the victim's assailant. Keep in mind, however, that victims may feel humiliated and embarrassed that their bodies were exposed during the sexual assault and must be exposed again during a medical examination. Explain what will take place forensically during the examination and why these procedures are important.
- Notify the hospital of the incoming victim/patient and request a private waiting room. Escort victims to the hospital. If no crisis intervention counselor is available, wait at the hospital until victims are released and escort them to their destination.
- Be mindful of the personal, interpersonal, and privacy concerns of victims. They may have a number of concerns, including the possibility of having been impregnated or contracting sexually transmitted diseases such as the AIDS virus; the reactions of their spouse, mate, or parents; media publicity that may reveal their experience to the public; and the reactions and criticism of neighbors and coworkers if they learn about the sexual assault.
- Interview victims with extreme sensitivity. Minimize the number of times victims must recount details of the crime to strangers. If possible, only one law enforcement officer should be assigned to the initial interview and subsequent investigation.
- Offer to answer any further questions victims may have and provide any further assistance they may need.
- Encourage victims to get counseling. Explain that your recommendation for counseling is based on having seen other victims benefit from it in the past. Explain that they may experience posttraumatic stress symptoms in the next few months. Identify and refer them to support services for assistance.

Child Victims

BACKGROUND

The victimization rate for children 12 through 19 is higher than that for any other age group. (Note: Criminal victimization data are not collected for children under 12 years of age.) In addition, according to the American Medical Association, approximately 1,100 children die each year from abuse and neglect while 140,000 are injured. Uniform Crime Report data indicate that almost 2,000 children under the age of 18 were murdered in 1996. Finally, murder and nonnegligent manslaughter are the causes of death for approximately 17 percent of children under the age of 19.

When children are victimized, their normal physiological and psychological adjustment to life is disrupted. Furthermore, they must cope with the trauma of their victimization again and again in each succeeding developmental stage of life after the crime.

Child victims suffer not only physical and emotional traumas from their victimization. When their victimization is reported, children are forced to enter the stressful "adult" world of the criminal justice system. Adults—perhaps the same adults who were unable to provide protection in the first place—are responsible for restoring the children's sense that there are safe places where they can go and safe people whom they can turn to. As a law enforcement officer, you can play a key role in this process and lessen the likelihood of long-term trauma for child victims.

TIPS FOR RESPONDING TO CHILD VICTIMS

- Choose a secure, comfortable setting for interviewing child victims, such as a child advocacy center. If such an interview setting is not available, choose a location that is as comfortable as possible. Take the time to establish trust and rapport.
  - Preschool children (ages 2 through 6) are most comfortable at home—assuming no child abuse took place there—or in a very familiar environment. A parent or some other adult the child trusts should be nearby.
  - For elementary school-age children (ages 6 through 10), the presence of a parent is not usually recommended since children at this age are sometimes reluctant to reveal information if they believe they or their parents could "get into trouble." However, a parent or some other adult the child trusts should be close by, such as in the next room.
  - Preadolescents (ages 10 through 12 for girls and 12 through 14 for boys) are peer-oriented and often avoid parental scrutiny. For this reason, they may be more comfortable if a friend or perhaps the friend's parent(s) is nearby.

- – Since adolescents (generally, ages 13 through 17) may be fearful of betraying their peers, it may be necessary to interview them in a secure setting with no peers nearby.
- Realize that children tend to regress emotionally during times of stress, acting younger than their age. For example, 8-year-olds may suck their thumb.
- Use language appropriate to the victim's age. Remember your own childhood and try to think like the victim. Avoid "baby talk."
- Since young children often feel they may be blamed for problems, assure preschool and elementary school-age children that they have not done anything wrong and they are not "in trouble."
- Be consistent with the terms you use and repeat important information often.
- Ask open-ended questions to make sure victims understand you.
- Use care in discussing sexual matters with preadolescent and adolescent children, as their embarrassment and limited vocabulary can make conversation difficult for them. At the same time, do not assume that victims, including elementary school-age children, are as knowledgeable about sexual matters as their language or apparent sophistication might indicate.
- Maintain a nonjudgmental attitude and empathize with victims. Because elementary school-age children are especially affected by praise, compliment them frequently on their behavior and thank them for their help.
- Remember the limited attention span of children. Be alert to signs that victims are feeling tired, restless, or cranky. When interviewing preschool children, consider conducting a series of short interviews rather than a single, lengthy one. Also, consider postponing the interview until the victim has had a night's sleep. However, in this case, be sure not to wait too long before interviewing preschool children because victims at this age may have difficulty separating the events of the victimization from later experiences.
- Encourage preschool children to play, as it is a common mode of communication for them. You may find that as children play, they become more relaxed and thus more talkative.
- Limit the number of times victims must be interviewed. Bring together for interviews as many persons from appropriate public agencies as possible, including representatives from the prosecutor's office, child protective services, and the medical/health care community.
- Include victims, whenever possible, in decision-making and problem-solving discussions. Identify and patiently answer all of their questions. You can reduce victims' insecurity and anxiety by explaining the purpose of your interview and by preparing them, especially elementary school-age children, for what will happen next.
- Show compassion to victims. Children's natural abilities to cope are aided immensely by caring adults.

- Although the immediate victim is the child, do not forget to comfort the nonoffending parents. Referrals regarding how they can cope, what they can expect, as well as how to talk to and with their child should be provided.

Victims of Domestic Violence

BACKGROUND

Domestic violence is a crime, not a family matter, and should be approached as such by law enforcement. U.S. Department of Justice statistics indicate that approximately 20 percent of homicides are committed within families or within intimate relationships, and one out of three female homicide victims is killed by an intimate. Furthermore, approximately 28 percent of violent crimes against females are committed by husbands or boyfriends. Finally, approximately 50 percent of domestic violence occurs between married partners and 25 percent between nonmarried partners living together, both involving mainly male assailants and female victims.

The three primary responsibilities of law enforcement in domestic violence cases are to (1) provide physical safety and security for victims, (2) assist victims by coordinating their referral to support services, and (3) make arrests of domestic violence perpetrators as required by law.

Unlike most other victims of crime, victims of domestic violence do not usually suffer a "sudden and unpredictable" threat to their safety or lives. More often, domestic violence involves years of personal stress and trauma, as well as physical injury. Thus, in domestic violence cases—unlike in other crimes—your ability to help victims cope with and recover from their victimization may be limited.

TIPS FOR RESPONDING TO VICTIMS OF DOMESTIC VIOLENCE

- Because domestic violence cases present potential dangers, responding officers should arrive in pairs at the scene if possible. Introduce yourself and explain that you were called because of a possible injury. Ask permission to enter the residence to make sure everything is okay.
- Separate the parties involved in domestic violence before interviewing them, even if they are not violent or arguing when you arrive.
- Ask victims whether they would like you to contact a family member or friend.
- Avoid judging victims or personally commenting on the situation. Abusive relationships continue for many reasons. Offering advice to the victim at the scene will not solve this complex problem.
- Even if no children are present at the scene, ask whether there are children in the family, and, if so, find out their whereabouts. Keep in mind that children sometimes hide or are hidden in these circumstances.

- Approach children with care and kindness. Look for signs of emotional trauma or distress. Be attentive to physical indications of child abuse since domestic violence is sometimes linked with child abuse.
- Even when no domestic violence charges can be filed, encourage the parties to separate for a short period—at least overnight. If victims' safety at home can be assured, consider asking assailants to leave. Although law enforcement officers have traditionally asked victims to leave the home, this serves to disrupt their lives even further, especially when children are involved.
- Assure victims that the purpose of your intervention is to help address the problem, not to make the situation worse.
- Provide victims referral information on domestic violence shelters and battered women's programs. This should be done away from the offender.
- Remember that domestic violence can occur in same-sex relationships.
- Be sure to complete a thorough report.

Survivors of Homicide Victims

BACKGROUND

Homicide is a crime with more than one victim. Nothing can ever prepare survivors for the day they are suddenly told their loved one has been murdered. Survivors suffer the shock of the sudden loss of their loved one and anger that the loved one did not have to die. Murder crushes survivors' trust in the world and their belief in social order and justice.

Many survivors of homicide victims say that the most traumatic event of their lives was when they were notified of the death. One of the most difficult duties a law enforcement officer must perform is providing notification to the family of murdered victims. An inappropriate notification can prolong survivors' grieving process and delay their recovery from the crime for years. Proper notification by you can restore some of the survivors' trust and beliefs and help them to begin a new life.

TIPS FOR RESPONDING TO SURVIVORS OF HOMICIDE VICTIMS

- Know the details surrounding the homicide victim's death before notification. Survivors often want to know the exact circumstances of their loved one's death.
- Have confirming evidence of the homicide victim's identity in the event of denial by the survivors. Be sensitive to the possibility that the victim may have been leading a life unknown to the survivors, such as involvement in drugs, extramarital affairs, or homosexuality.
- Know as much as possible about the homicide victim's survivors before notification. Notify the appropriate closest survivor first.
- Make notifications in person.

- Conduct notifications in pairs. You can contact local volunteers who are specially trained in death notification through your local clergy or crisis intervention agency. Also, the National Organization for Victim Assistance (800–879–6682) may be able to refer you to volunteers in your area.
- Do not bring personal articles of the homicide victim with you to the notification.
- Conduct the notification in a private place after you and the survivors are seated.
- Avoid engaging in small talk upon your arrival. Do not build up slowly to the reason for your visit or to the actual announcement of the death of the survivor's loved one. Finally, do not use any euphemisms for the death of the loved one, such as "She passed away," "We lost her," "She expired," or "She left us." Be compassionately direct and unambiguous in giving notification to survivors. For example: "We've come to tell you something very terrible. Your daughter has been killed in a carjacking. I'm so sorry."
- Ask survivors whether they would like you to contact a family member or friend.
- Have one person take the lead in conducting the notification. The other person should monitor survivors for reactions dangerous to themselves or others.
- Accept survivors' reactions—no matter how intense or stoic—in a non-judgmental, empathetic manner. Survivors may cry hysterically, scream, collapse, sit quietly, or go into shock.
- Be prepared for survivors' possible hostility toward you as a representative of law enforcement and avoid responding impolitely or defensively.
- Show empathy for survivors' pain and suffering, but do not say "I understand" when clearly no one can.
- Refer to the homicide victim by name out of respect to the victim and survivors. Do not use terms like "the deceased" or "the victim."
- Listen to survivors and answer all of their questions.
- Make telephone calls to other survivors of the homicide victim at the request of the immediate survivors. If possible, make arrangements for someone to be with these survivors before they receive your telephone notification. If this is not possible, ask the survivors to sit down once you've contacted them before you make the notification. Ask for permission to call a neighbor, a friend, or a crisis intervention counselor to be with the survivors after the notification. Tell each person you contacted the names of others who have been notified.
- Show respect for survivors' personal and religious or nonreligious understandings of death. Do not impose your personal beliefs about death on survivors by saying of the victim, for example, "She's in a better place now."
- Explain to survivors that everyone grieves differently. Encourage them to be understanding and supportive of one another.
- Before leaving survivors, make sure that someone can stay with them and that they have contacts for support services.

Part III

Society and the Victim

One of the more notable developments in recent years has been the growing interest by the public, legislatures, and researchers in the active influence of victims in the processing and/or release of offenders. Since the earliest societies, victims have always desired vengeance and justice against those who wronged them. As civilization and common law evolved, the state (i.e., governments) replaced the victim as the primary element in the justice process. The greater good and the promotion of the concept of justice in society replaced the individual interests of the direct victims involved.

Despite the logic of extrapolating individual retribution to the aggregate/societal level, something valuable was lost in this evolution. In the last few decades, victims in the United States have begun to demand more rights—from being treated with respect by authorities to requesting notification of the progress of the case against the offender to receiving restitution. In the last two decades, numerous victims' rights bills have been proposed and many have become law. For example, by 1987 virtually all states had authorized some form of victim participation in sentencing offenders (McLeod, 1988). The widespread support that these measures have received, from the public and politicians alike, is largely due to a significant rise in the public's fear of crime and actions to try to address the problem.

The desire for justice is the topic of the first selection in this section. Lucy Friedman, Susan Tucker, and Peter Neville provide brief anecdotes of pain and loss due to crime and to the failure to be acknowledged or heard by authorities. The authors review the range of problems victims suffer and the benefits of programs that intervene to provide services and protection. The article gives examples of how community involvement can help victims deal with their feelings of being harmed. The authors claim that participation in programs such as Mothers Against Drunk Driving (MADD) and Parents Of Murdered Children (POMC) facilitates recovery from the psychological damage incurred by the crimes. The authors survey a variety of victims' rights groups that have influenced public views and legislation. They also discuss

261

the problems involved with becoming a "victim activist" and the potentially negative effects of activism. We hope that readers will weigh the benefits and drawbacks carefully, while increasing their awareness of the needs of victims of particularly tragic crimes. Decisions about rights and services for victims require an informed public.

To provide an overview of the range and effectiveness of victims' rights laws, we have selected as article 16 a 1998 Department of Justice report written by Dean Kilpatrick, David Beatty, and Susan Smith Howley. This report summarizes findings from a survey of over 1,300 crime victims in states with both strong and weak victim protection laws/services. More specifically, the authors collected data on such issues as: the percentage of victims who were notified of events in their cases, who were informed of their rights as victims and the services available to them, and who exercised their rights. The evaluation by Kilpatrick et al. reveals how legislative and justice system support can (and sometimes cannot) affect the victims' role in processing their cases in the justice system.

In quite another light, for selection 17 we have included a manuscript by Gregory Orvis that discusses the evolution of the victims' rights movement and its potential conflict with due process rights of offenders. Many readers will find the author's argument quite controversial. Namely, Orvis claims that the rights of defendants have been historically and rationally crafted over the past 225 years, whereas the rights of victims have been the result of public fervor over the last 25 years and are likely to undermine the rights of defendants. In light of the extremely rapid growth of laws in the area of victims' rights, this perspective urges careful and cautious consideration. If we want to protect our constitutional rights, it may be advantageous to reflect critically before developing new victims' rights provisions.

One of the more controversial areas of reform is victim impact statements, in which victims testify in court (usually during the sentencing phase) about the impact of the crime on their lives and/or their loved ones. In article 18, Robert Davis and Barbara Smith examine the effects of victims' statements on actual sentences of offenders in Bronx County, New York. The findings and conclusions of this study are not congruent with previous studies, exposing the necessity for further studies to determine the effects of victim impact statements and the nature of these effects.

In the next selection, Emilio Viano explores the extent to which stereotypical roles, images, and verbal cues impact the responses of society and the justice system to victims of crime. He discusses the possible obstacles presented by the stereotyping of and discrimination against victims and the additional burden of this "secondary victimization." Viano pays particular attention to the added burden these issues place on minorities and the elderly.

Recently, the issue of restorative and/or peace-making justice has been a focus of many scholars. Such approaches often support an active role for the victim in the reentry of the offender into the community. Although the extent of victim involvement is still unclear, we believe this relatively new aspect of the criminal justice process will become much more prevalent in the future. Therefore, it is important to examine the advantages and disadvantages of such an approach before finalizing any programs. Susan Herman and Cressida Wasserman examine the various issues involved in victim input to the offender's reentry into the community. The authors note the variety of victims and the varied relationship to offenders. They then discuss the role of victims in the recovery of offenders. While some victims of crime will not want to be involved with the offenders, others may find that the involvement alleviates the pain experienced as a result of the crime committed.

In the final selection, Mike Niemeyer and David Shichor report on a victim-offender reconciliation program (VORP). The authors discuss a sentencing alternative whereby offenders and their victims, with the help of a mediator, negotiate an appropriate restitution for the severity of harm caused by the offense. This study addresses the issue of whether victims who choose more community involvement were more satisfied with the justice system than those who did not.

We chose the articles in this section because they provide good coverage of the important issues involved in victims' rights and the role of victims in the disposition of the people who offended against them. As all of these studies discuss, an active role for the victim in various stages of the criminal justice process is a means of reaching a sense of closure and efficacy.

It is our hope that all the selections in this collection will be beneficial to students, researchers, policymakers, and—most importantly—victims themselves.

Chapter Fifteen

From Pain to Power
Crime Victims Take Action

Lucy N. Friedman
Susan B. Tucker
Peter Neville

Introduction: Two Stories

In 1985, Ralph Hubbard's 23-year-old son was shot and killed in New York City. After years of feeling angry, frustrated, and powerless, Hubbard resolved to help other families work through their suffering. In a Victim Services support group for families of homicide victims in New York, he began to speak out, telling his family's story to the police, criminal justice officials, social service providers, and the public. He found that telling others what his family had gone through helped him cope with his pain and anger and inspired other victims to address their feelings. He started a self-help group for men who had lost family members to violence. He also became an adviser to New York's Crime Victims' Board, vice president of Justice For All, a victims' rights advocacy group, and a board member of the National Organization for Victim Assistance. A leading spokesperson for victims' rights in New York State, Hubbard feels no less compelled to be an advocate for victims ten years after his son's murder: "It's something I need to do. This is therapeutic for me."

Survivors from the 1993 Long Island Railroad massacre were determined to prevent similar atrocities from happening to others. Colin Ferguson's shooting spree transformed a number of those who were either on the train or lost family members into outspoken advocates for gun control and

Source: Office for Victims of Crime, September 1998.

victims' rights. Today, they speak at vigils, rallies, on television talk shows, and with legislators about the personal impact of the event, and they lobby for a ban on assault weapons, including the model used in the shooting. Tom McDermott, who was on the train that evening, believes he was spared in order to join the fight against gun violence. "I'm a radical now," he often says. "I'm a radical for the safety of us all."[1]

The Trauma of Violence Leaves Its Mark

Long after the physical wounds have healed, many crime victims continue to feel overwhelmed by the psychic pain of loss, powerlessness, low self-esteem, isolation, fear, rage—feelings that often are shared by their family and friends, as well as by the extended community.

From the ashes of criminal violence, victims and their families are struggling to rebuild their communities, as well as their own lives. Through community activism, individuals like Ralph Hubbard and Tom McDermott are transforming their pain into power, helping change society, and healing themselves in the process. Moving from the personal to the political, they work to correct causes of crime that are systemic, such as poverty, racism, sexism, the culture of violence and easy access to guns; to hold those who commit crimes accountable; and to enact victim-sensitive reforms and programs. As the crime victims' movement enters its third decade, advocates should look for ways to nurture victims' desires to help others by providing educational and organizational opportunities for community action.

Without intervention, victims can become chronically dysfunctional afraid to venture out at night, unable to work productively, alienated from neighbors and friends, distrustful of police and courts, and overly dependent on social services. Their withdrawal from life hurts their families and weakens the fabric of the community.

Individual counseling and practical assistance help people deal with the psychological aftermath of crime and reconstruct a sense of equilibrium. When crime victims move from their personal experiences to a broader social analysis and to activism, they can also aid their own recovery from the trauma of victimization. Recognizing or addressing the social conditions that lead to violence and victimization is important. Helping other victims, working to change laws, or mobilizing violence prevention initiatives can help victims and survivors regain a sense of control and channel their fear and rage into efforts for reform.

The history of grassroots efforts in other movements shows that community activism can be a powerful catalyst for social change. Individual stakeholders—those whose lives were directly affected by the movement's cause—have brought about landmark reforms. The movements for civil rights, elder rights, welfare, environmental protection, and AIDS research and treatment have been spearheaded by those directly affected by the issues. Like crime victim activism, each of these movements arose from victimizing conditions of neglect, persecution, or marginalization; and the involvement of "victimized" individuals legitimized the cause.

A crucial step toward activism may be the individual's self-identification as a member of a group victimized by particular social conditions. Yet within the crime victims' and battered women's movements, the "victim" label remains controversial. Some believe it is a stigmatizing label that hinders recovery and reinforces society's perception of victims as helpless, hopeless, and dependent. Others see it as an empowering identification that promotes connection with others and spurs community involvement.

As Crenshaw points out, "[I]dentity-based politics has been a source of strength, community and intellectual development [for many individuals and groups], African-Americans, other people of color, and gays and lesbians, among others."[2] The individual's self-identification as a victim—as a temporary and active condition, as opposed to an inherent or static one—may be both a step toward recovery and a source of empowerment. Mahoney's framing of the controversy with respect to battered women may be equally applicable to other crime victims: "[F]irst, the abuse of women and its consequences must be explained without defining the woman herself by the experience of abuse; second, the woman's perceptions and the context of her life must be explained—defending the reality of this woman's experience—in a way that locates her experience within patterns of systemic power and oppression."[3] By acknowledging themselves as victims and survivors, some people achieve a more realistic understanding of blame, realize a connection with other victims, and mobilize to address the social conditions that contribute to victimization.

The impetus for community involvement and political empowerment often comes from victims themselves or from their families and friends. Victim Services' Families of Homicide Victims program initially offered individual counseling. By talking with each other, participants found they were not alone in their suffering and could give each other valuable affirmation and support. They formed a self-help group, which provided the first real sense of community since their tragedies. When members wanted to become more politically active, the group spun-off as an independent organization. Those who wanted to help other survivors were trained to work with Victim Services staff as group co-facilitators. More recently, members have become involved in crime prevention. One participant who lost three sons to violence started an afterschool program for at-risk youth.

Community Involvement
Since the 1982 Task Force Report

The journey from victim to advocate taken by Hubbard, the Long Island Railroad victims, and participants in the Families of Homicide Victims program followed a line of recovery that was largely unrecognized when the 1982 Final Report of the President's Task Force on Victims of Crime was written. The report only indirectly touched on victim involvement in communities, addressing "involvement" primarily in terms of permitting victims to participate in their own court cases. Many of the 1982 recommendations for judicial reform have been enacted, including provisions for victim impact statements and victim allocution. In addition, 29 states have enacted some kind of constitutional amendment to guarantee victims the right to be involved in the prosecution of their cases. Many of these successes were attributable to the efforts of crime victims. For example, Mothers Against Drunk Driving and Parents of Murdered Children played a key role in moving the 1988 amendments to the 1984 Victims of Crime Act (VOCA) that expanded the kinds of victims eligible for services supported by the legislation.

Victim leadership and activism can be credited with many of the substantive public policy and legislative achievements that have been won over the past 20 years. Aside from its trauma healing benefits, victim involvement is important because it helps maintain the direction and integrity of the movement.

This article expands the original focus of the 1982 Final Report of the President's Task Force on Victims of Crime by considering how victim activism can help speed the individual's recovery from trauma, reform the criminal justice system, and promote crime prevention through addressing some of the underlying conditions of violence. Recognizing that community activism is not for all crime victims, it also explores the potential risks of activism and outlines considerations to guide activist efforts.

The Impact of Crime

Crime victims often suffer a broad range of psychological and social injuries that persist long after their physical wounds have healed. Intense feelings of anger, fear, isolation, low self-esteem, helplessness, and depression are common reactions.[4] Like combat veterans, crime victims may suffer from post-traumatic stress disorder, including recurrent memories of the incident, sleep disturbances, feelings of alienation, emotional numbing, and other anxiety-related symptoms. Janoff-Bulman suggests that victimization can shatter basic assumptions about the self and the world which individuals need in order to function normally in their daily lives—that they are safe from harm, that the world is meaningful and just, and that they are good, decent people.[5] This happens not only to victims of violent assaults but also to victims of robbery and burglary[6] and to their friends and family.[7] Herman has suggested that "survivors of prolonged, repeated trauma," such as battered women and abused children, often suffer what she calls "complex post-traumatic stress disorder," which can manifest as severe "personality changes, including deformations of relatedness and identity [which make them] particularly vulnerable to repeated harm, both self-inflicted and at the hands of others."[8]

The emotional damage and social isolation caused by victimization also may be compounded by a lack of support, and even stigmatization, from friends, family and social institutions, that can become a "second wound" for the victim. Those closest to the victim may be traumatized by the crime in ways that make them unsupportive of the victim's needs. Davis, Taylor and Bench found that close friends and family members, particularly of a victim of sexual assault, sometimes withdraw from and blame the victim.[9] Crime victims must also contend with society's tendency to blame them for the crime, which compounds the trauma of the event. To protect their belief in a just world where people get what they deserve, and to distance themselves from the possibility of random or uncontrollable injury, many prefer to see victims as somehow responsible for their fate.[10] The lack of support for victims trying to recover from a crime can exacerbate the psychological harm caused by victimization and make recovery even more difficult.

When victims do seek help, they may be treated with insensitivity. They may feel ignored or even revictimized by the criminal justice process, which has traditionally been more concerned with the rights of the accused than with the rights and needs of the victim. Family members of homicide victims in particular may feel left out of the justice process. When one woman whose child had been murdered asked to be informed as the case progressed, she was asked, "Why do you want to know? You're not involved in the case."

Benefits of Community Involvement

Community involvement can help victims overcome feelings of low self-esteem, isolation, powerlessness, fear, and anger. The process of connecting with others, confronting and overcoming real-life challenges, striving for justice and giving something back to the community can provide recovery benefits not achieved solely by traditional counseling or therapy.

REBUILDING LOW SELF-ESTEEM

Participating in peer self-help groups can improve victims' self-images by demonstrating they are neither abnormal nor guilty for the victimization. Before joining groups such as Families of Homicide Victims, survivors often blame themselves for their children's deaths, seeing themselves as inadequate parents because they could not protect their children from harm. By talking with other parents who seem nurturing and loving, they are able to look at themselves and the question of blame more realistically. When those who once lamented, "If only we had moved to a safer neighborhood," meet residents of safer neighborhoods who have also lost family members, they begin to recognize that it was not their fault. Self-help groups can create an "adaptive spiral"; acceptance by other group members boosts the individual's self-esteem, in turn increasing his or her empathy and support for others.[11]

Community involvement generally involves some degree of risk; there is no guarantee that victims' efforts will pay off. Efforts to pass legislation, increase services for victims, or establish prevention programs will often be disappointing. By standing up to these challenges and failures, victims prove to themselves and others that they are neither weak nor helpless, and that they are able to fight their own battles.

Self-esteem also can be enhanced by joining a particular cause "from which one derives reflected power and glory."[12] Creating psychological strength through numbers—banding together to advance the cause of victims or to reduce violence—can provide a dividend of empowerment that may be considerably greater than victims might receive through individual action. When victims share their personal experiences with others, they are no longer alone in their struggle.

REDUCING ISOLATION

Victims of crime often feel alienated from family, friends and community. They may consider themselves stigmatized or tainted by the crime, a feeling reinforced by insensitive treatment from those who "shun victims, sensing their 'spoiled identities.'"[13] Battered women are especially at risk of feeling isolated because they are often separated from society by their abusers. According to Stark, "the hallmark of the battering experience [is] 'entrapment'. . . a pattern of control that extends . . . to virtually every aspect of a woman's life, including money, food, sexuality, friendships, transportation, personal appearance, and access to supports, including children, extended family members, and helping resources."[14]

Lebowitz, Harvey and Herman describe the process of overcoming this isolation and reestablishing ties with others as one of the key stages of trauma recovery.[15] Social action can serve as one effective means of achieving this reconnection. When victims work with those who have had similar experiences, they begin to realize they are not alone.

Peer support groups or victim-initiated advocacy groups may help to create a new community for victims that can be strengthened by grappling with the larger social problems that affect it,[16] and may serve as a bridge to relationships outside the group.[17] Publicly embracing the victimization experience through advocacy or other public actions can reduce feelings of deviance and stigmatization that perpetuate isolation from others.

REGAINING A SENSE OF POWER

A common reaction to crime is to ask, "Why me?" Unable to find a reason for their victimization, crime victims may feel a loss of control over their surroundings. By joining with others to prevent violence or improve the treatment of crime victims, victims can have an impact on the community and recapture a sense of power. They "transform the meaning of their personal tragedy by making it the basis for social action."[18] Victims who are able to answer "Why?" perhaps by taking on a survivor mission, may be less likely to be psychologically incapacitated;[19] they create something positive out of a negative experience by carving out an area of their lives where they are in control. Sarah Buel, a battered woman who became a district attorney specializing in domestic violence cases, said, "I feel very much like that's part of my mission, part of why God didn't allow me to die in that marriage, so that I could talk openly and publicly . . . about having been battered."[20]

DEALING WITH FEAR AND ANGER

Fear of revictimization, which is related to feelings of powerlessness and isolation, is a powerful, sometimes paralyzing result of crime. Fear of crime can be "divisive . . . creat[ing] suspicion and distrust,"[21] but it also can "motivate citizens to interact with each other and engage in anticrime efforts."[22] Crime victims can master their fear by working on community crime prevention projects. In a study not limited to crime victims, Cohn, Kidder and Harvey[23] found that those involved in community anticrime projects felt more in control of their surroundings and had less fear of crime. Other studies linking isolation from the community with fear of crime suggest that, as victims become more involved with others, they become less afraid.[24] After witnessing the murder of his father, a student in a school-based victim assistance program overcame his fear of being victimized again by launching an antiviolence campaign in his school. By finding a more positive way to increase the safety of his environment, he no longer felt the need to be overly defensive or to resort to violence to protect himself.

The anger that follows victimization—at the offender, at the criminal justice system and at society for letting it happen—can productively be redirected through activism. By speaking out at conferences, schools, churches and public hearings, Tom McDermott found that he "transferred [his] hatred, bitterness and white-hot anger into something positive." Some victims may focus on the pursuit of justice, not only for their own suffering but also because they recognize the detrimental impact of crime on society. Herman notes that in the later stages of recovery, victims often embrace abstract principles that "transcend [their] personal grievance against the perpetrator [and] . . . connect the fate of others to their own."[25]

Thus, in addition to wanting the individual offender brought to justice, they might work to ensure that victims are given the support they need or to fight the social conditions that may have contributed to the crime. In these ways, feelings of rage and anger are transformed into constructive social action.

Some victims find release by sharing their experiences with others, who also are helped in the process. After telling the story of his son's murder at conferences, Ralph Hubbard found that his words helped other men talk about the loss of their own child after years of silence and denial. Hubbard describes this experience as "one of the most rewarding things ever." Similar benefits from sharing have been described by victims of AIDS and other serious illnesses who, as Susan Sontag describes in *Illness as Metaphor*, have historically been ostracized and silenced.[26]

Others feel compelled to testify publicly about their victimization—in court, in church, to community groups, or in print. Like the physician narrator of Albert M. Camus' *The Plague*, whom Felman and Laub describe as feeling "historically appointed 'to bear witness in favor of those plague-stricken people, so that some memorial of the injustice done them might endure,'"[27] victims sometimes need to testify to feel that some degree of justice is achieved. Describing the survivors of the Holocaust, Felman and Laub note that, "The witness's readiness to become himself a medium of the testimony—and a medium of the accident—in his unshakable conviction that the accident [or the crime] . . . carries historical significance . . . goes beyond the individual and is thus, in effect, in spite of its idiosyncrasy, not trivial."[28]

By continuously reminding the populace of the injustice, victims prevent society from acquiescing to what they may prefer to deny or forget. Lorna Hawkins was frustrated that no one else seemed outraged by the death of her two sons by gang violence; random shootings were so common in Los Angeles that her story was not considered "news" by the media. To raise awareness about the pain, suffering, and injustice of urban violence, Hawkins began "Drive-By Agony," a weekly cable show.[29] Countless other victims have spoken out against violence and advocated for reforms. Since 1990, 72 noteworthy activists have been recognized by the president's annual National Crime Victim Service Award.

Examples of Community Involvement

Over the past two decades, the viability of community activism by crime victims has been demonstrated at the local, state, and national levels. In general, victim activism has focused on three objectives: victim assistance, victims' rights advocacy, and violence prevention. (See appendix for more detailed descriptions of programs.)

VICTIM ASSISTANCE

If crime victims have sufficiently recovered from their own traumatic experiences and have received appropriate training, they often are well-suited to help other crime victims because of their capacity to empathize. Facilitating victim support groups (such as the Families of Homicide Victims or the nationwide Parents of Murdered Children (POMC)), accompanying victims through the criminal justice process, or becoming in-court advocates are practical, valuable services. The Youth Empowerment Association in New York City trained teenagers recovering from sexual assault to work as peer counselors with youth victims who were at earlier stages of recovery. Victims also have played large roles in establishing and staffing rape crisis centers.[30]

VICTIMS' RIGHTS ADVOCACY

Having experienced poor treatment from the criminal justice and social service systems, some victims choose to advocate for social change. By speaking to government officials, legislators, or the press and by campaigning for reform, victims often find that they are accorded greater respect than service professionals and that their words carry weight with decision makers. When Victim Services staff travel to Albany, New York, accompanied by crime victims, to talk with state legislators, they usually are met by the legislator; when they go alone, they are more likely to be met by staff. Victim Services offers public speaking training to crime victims, as well as to agency staff, and maintains a Crime Victim Speakers Bureau. Another good example of the effectiveness of this kind of victim advocacy is the Stephanie Roper Committee, which has contributed significantly to the passage of three dozen victims' rights bills in Maryland since 1983.

Some victims may work to ensure that the criminal justice system functions as it should and that offenders are brought to justice. The Roper Foundation, the direct service component to the Roper Committee, operates a Courtwatch program that places volunteers, many of them victims, in courtrooms to monitor whether victims' rights are being respected. Mothers Against Drunk Driving (MADD) and Remove Intoxicated Drivers (RID) developed Victim Impact Panels, through which victims speak directly to offenders about the devastating impact of drunk driving. POMC's Truth-In-Sentencing program mobilizes its national membership to make sure that those convicted of murdering their children serve at least the minimum sentences; when an offender comes up for early parole, the network launches a letter-writing campaign to oppose the offender's release. Taking another approach, Murder Victims Families for Reconciliation, a national group based in Virginia, campaigns against capital punishment.[31]

VIOLENCE PREVENTION

Victims often say that what they want most is for the crime never to have happened. Accordingly, some focus their efforts on crime prevention through public awareness and education campaigns or by creating programs for at-risk youth and self-defense training.

In its public education work, MADD launched the national Designated Driver program. The California-based Teens on Target (TNT) trains at-risk youth and young victims to be antiviolence advocates. Based on their firsthand experiences, these advocates talk to their peers about the causes of violence and suggest alternative approaches for resolving conflicts. In a new TNT project, "Caught in the Crossfire," advocates visit young gunshot victims who are still hospitalized to dissuade them from seeking revenge. In New York City, P.O.W.E.R. (People Opening the World's Eyes to Reality), a group of victims of gun violence who use wheelchairs, visit young people to show what can result from a life of drugs and violence. The group also has advocated for stricter state legislation against assault guns, and has testified in Washington, D.C. at a hearing on gun control before the House Judiciary Subcommittee on Crime and Criminal Justice.

Caveats Regarding Victim Activism

Though beneficial for many, becoming a victim activist is not a requisite step in trauma recovery and may be problematic for some. Because people recover in different ways and have different needs, community action is not necessarily appropriate for all crime victims. The individual's personality and history of victimization may play a role in determining whether community involvement will be helpful to recovery, while the availability of emotional and financial supports may be a factor in determining whether the victim has the time and energy to spend on community issues. Some victims of crime, though able to lead normal lives, may never feel prepared to deal with the pain of others or the frustrations of advocacy efforts. Being a victim may not be enough by itself to lead to activism; there is some evidence that victims who become active in community efforts are likely to have been activists before the crime.[32] In the absence of clear criteria for when activism is likely to benefit a traumatized individual, a victim's own interest and desire to participate should be the determining factor. Rather than prescribing activism as a necessary part of the recovery process, professionals can provide people with opportunities for action, and support those who choose to get involved.

Timing is also an important consideration in community involvement. Advocating for legislative reform or helping others before coming to terms with their own trauma may impede some victims' recovery. Lebowitz, Harvey and Herman note that what they call the third stage of trauma recovery—reconnecting with others—should not be attempted until the earlier steps of achieving a sense of safety and exploring and integrating the traumatic event have been achieved.[33] Unless they have reached this stage, victims may be unable to cope with other people's trauma on top of their own. Listening to others' crime stories may exacerbate fears and bring back disturbing, even overwhelming, memories of their own experiences, thereby retraumatizing them.[34] Research on MADD's Victim Impact Panels has shown that the act of speaking out was beneficial for the overwhelming majority (87 percent) of participants; the few participants (3 percent) who felt they were harmed by it had become involved too close to the incident—they were still using coping strategies, such as denial, that conflicted with telling their stories publicly.[35] This suggests that victims who invest themselves in advocacy efforts too soon may be taking on more than they are ready to handle. If individual change is difficult, societal change is even more so, especially in the face of political opposition. To avoid these pitfalls, activism generally should be encouraged later rather than earlier in the recovery process.

Certain types of activism may cause victims to feel exploited, potentially revictimizing them and setting back their recovery. For example, some victims who have spoken out through television and other news media feel that they have been taken advantage of—that their messages were misrepresented or their words cut or edited to alter their meaning. In an attempt to make a story more compelling, some journalists recast victim activists' identities, portraying them as powerless and pitiable rather than empowered and brave. As a result, victims may feel embarrassed or betrayed, and may be less likely to speak out in the future. To avoid revictimization and to appropriately access the power of the media, victim activists need to understand how the media works—for example, that their page-one story may fade completely from the news a day later. Victim services organizations can provide training for crime victim activists as to what they might expect from working with the media. And the news media need to become sensitive to the risk of revictimization as well as the value of victim activism. Finally, some victims interested in activism may not feel comfortable getting involved through organizations that are labeled as "victim" activist or "victim" assistance, which is one reason why other community groups—religious institutions, community organizations, neighborhood and parent groups and other formal and informal organizations—should support crime prevention and activist efforts. Some individuals who already have ties with these groups may feel more comfortable taking action in familiar settings within their support networks than venturing into new organizations. Thus, institutions outside the victim field need to be supportive of victims, and recognize that victim involvement can benefit both their own individual members' well-being and their efforts for community improvement.

Barriers to Involvement

Given the successful programs described above and their benefits for both victims and communities, why is victim activism not more widespread? One reason cited by Skogan and Maxfield is that those crime victims who see conditions in their communities improving are more likely to try to do something about crime, whereas people living in more traumatized neighborhoods may feel relatively more "incapacitated" by fear for their safety.[36] Research has suggested that, although victimization may lead to community involvement, the very social conditions that contribute to victimization can also discourage activism. A disproportionate number of crime victims already feel disempowered by racism, poverty, sexism, and a lack of political power. Victimization makes them feel even more helpless and estranged from society. For many, the combined effects of living on the margins of society, being victimized, and living in constant fear of crime can make social activism seem irrelevant and futile.

Society's tendency to blame victims further inhibits their ability to become effective public players. The common misperception that victims are responsible for their victimization (especially victims of domestic violence or sexual assault) can inhibit them from becoming advocates, damage their credibility as victim activists, and cause them to pull back. In this way, some crime victims miss out on the recovery benefits of involvement, and society loses their potential contributions for social reform. This tendency to blame victims suggests that the friends or relatives of crime victims who fight on their behalf may be less subject to personal criticism and social backlash than those victims who act on behalf of themselves.

Moreover, people who are subjected to ongoing violence or abuse—victims of sexual assault, domestic violence,[37] stalking or gang violence and those who live in neighborhoods characterized by chronic violence—face multiple barriers to activism. For example, the feelings of low self-esteem and degradation resulting from the "coercive control" that characterizes partner violence, as well as the symptoms of what Judith Herman calls "complex post-traumatic stress disorder,"[38] can inhibit the capacity of women (and no doubt others suffering persistent victimization) for living, much less taking public action.[39] In some cases, individuals may not even imagine the possibility of activism because they do not identify or label themselves as victims, or they may be silenced out of shame and embarrassment. This is often the case where community violence is the norm, when society explicitly or tacitly condones men's power and control over women,[40] or if the violence occurring within families (against women, children or the elderly) is denied. Of course, real fear of being found or of violent retribution keeps other victims (women who have fled violent relationships, gang members) from going public who might otherwise want to.

In view of such substantial barriers, the effective activism of some victims is especially noteworthy. For example, Barbara Hart in Pennsylvania, Vickii Coffey in Chicago, and Sarah Buel in Quincy, Massachusetts, are formerly battered women whose names are synonymous with the leadership to end violence against women. Many others across the country—perhaps less publicly and without necessarily identifying themselves as battered women—work in shelters and provide peer counseling for other battered women. In recent years, adult victims of child sexual assault have become a vocal and effective force in raising awareness about the prevalence and trauma of incest. In many communities beset by violence, poverty and racism, committed residents—many of whom have lost friends and family to violence—have stayed to fight for education, job training, and opportunities, especially for young people.

Building primarily on their own initiative, commitment, and resources, crime victims have demonstrated the viability of activism and its value for themselves and society. The role of "victim as activist," however, has not yet become a recognized role in society, its benefits for victims' recovery have not been sufficiently examined, and most victims lack the opportunity or support they need to become involved. By creating structures for community involvement, forging links with existing victim programs and conducting further research, the public sector and victim assistance organizations could mobilize many more crime victims to help others and to participate in grassroots initiatives for victims' rights and crime prevention, thereby enhancing their recovery and helping to improve society.

The self-determination that contributes to victims' healing needs to be supported but not co-opted. By placing a higher priority on victim activism, government and assistance organizations can ensure that community involvement efforts remain community-based, rooted in the soil of individual victims' dedication and experience.

Victim Activism Recommendations

RECOMMENDATIONS FOR VICTIM SERVICE PROGRAMS

Working directly with crime victims, victim service programs are in an excellent position to educate them about the larger political and social context of crime and violence and to create opportunities for activism. Victim service programs should:

1. Train staff to understand the benefits of community activism for victims and to be aware of opportunities for victims both within and outside victim assistance organizations.
2. Engage crime victims in the leadership and guidance of the organization through serving on boards and developing new services and programs.
3. Create speakers' bureaus which recruit and prepare victims to speak at conferences and with legislators, criminal justice officials, police, medical personnel, and others about the needs and rights of victims and the causes of violence.
4. Include battered women as presenters in domestic violence training programs for police, service providers, and others.
5. Actively engage victims in paid and volunteer positions throughout the organization, from facilitating self-help groups to managing programs.
6. Prepare victim activists to work with the media.
7. Promote and disseminate information about the value of victim activism through local and national associations of victim assistance programs. For example, the National Organization for Victim Assistance and the National Victim Center have provided training and technical assistance to foster victim involvement.

RECOMMENDATIONS FOR GOVERNMENT

As new legislation and criminal justice reforms have increased the involvement of victims in their own cases, the public sector has gained the ability to expand victims' involvement in their communities, even with current financial constraints. Many of the following recommendations require little or no new resources; instead, they focus on shifting priorities for decision making or program funding. Public-sector agencies and organizations should:

1. Actively engage crime victims in the policy decisions that affect them. Public hearings on legislation and public policies that affect victim services, victims' rights, and violence prevention should always include testimony from victims themselves.

2. Require victim involvement as part of professional curricula in all disciplines that work with victims (e.g., criminal justice, social work, medicine, and law enforcement).
3. Incorporate community involvement as a funding guideline. This will encourage the creation of programs that engage crime victims in service, advocacy and violence prevention roles. Requests for proposals should require victim participation on advisory boards, as designers of services and projects, and as paid or voluntary staff.
4. Launch demonstration programs to develop the most effective program models for victim involvement. One possible route might be AmeriCorps, where youth could work in their communities to engage crime victims in social action.
5. Create opportunities for battered women to become more openly and actively involved in their communities. Services to empower battered women and increase their sense of self-determination—including education, job training, and placement—would provide them with the skills and confidence they need to reach out to others. Public education programs that debunk the myth of battered women as helpless would increase society's acceptance of women who do speak out.
6. Engage crime victims through community policing programs. Designed to create partnerships between police and the communities they serve, these efforts are ideal situations for victims to work with police to reduce crime and help others in need.
7. Encourage the involvement of all citizens, along with crime victims, on issues of victim assistance and violence prevention, through public education (public service announcements, news and entertainment media). When victims initiate or join community-based efforts, they often do so with the understanding that the injustice they experienced affects all of society. A more widespread recognition that crime affects everyone would create a more supportive atmosphere for victim involvement, and could reduce some of the social barriers to community activism, such as the common tendency to blame the victim.
8. Support research to document more clearly the benefits of community involvement for victims' recovery. This would provide the rationale and motivation necessary for victim assistance programs to create opportunities for victim activism and establish links with victims' organizations.

Conclusion

Victim assistance organizations, professionals and policymakers have much to gain by looking more closely at victim activism. A better understanding of the healing benefits of community involvement would encourage partnerships between victim assistance programs and community initiatives. Expanded opportunities for involvement would create new avenues for reintegrating crime victims into society while mobilizing a dedicated force for social change. Through better communication between groups, victim activists might stimulate victim assistance professionals to look beyond individual needs to the broader social conditions that lead to violent crime.

Appendix: Victim Involvement in Action

The following examples of victim activist efforts demonstrate the viability of victim activism and its benefits for both victims and their communities. They are both local and national in scope, and they include programs created to encourage victims to get involved, as well as entire organizations initiated and operated by victims.

MOTHERS AGAINST DRUNK DRIVING (MADD)

Mothers Against Drunk Driving (MADD) was founded in 1980 by Candy Lightner and Cindy Lamb, whose daughters were, respectively, killed and maimed by drunk drivers. In the case of Cari Lightner, the driver, who was out on bail from another drunk-driving crash only two days before, had three prior drunk-driving arrests; sentenced to only two years, he was allowed to serve his time in a work camp and a halfway house. Laura Lamb became the country's youngest quadriplegic after being hit by a driver without a license who had a record of 37 traffic violations, three for drunk driving. MADD is one of the most successful victim activist organizations in the nation. With three million members and more than 600 chapters, MADD provides a wide range of victim assistance, advocacy, and prevention activities. The Victim Advocate Training Program is a 40-hour course that teaches volunteers to counsel victims, accompany them through court proceedings, and speak to the media. The Court Monitoring Program trains volunteers to serve as watchdogs for victims' rights in courts. Court-mandated Victim Impact Panels compel offenders to hear from victims about the devastating impact of drunk driving on their lives. Studies have found these panels to have benefits for both offenders and victims—offenders' attitudes are changed and rates of recidivism are reduced, and victims' traumatic symptoms often are diminished.[41] In the words of one victim impact panelist, "I do not want my daughter, Amy, and what happened to her to be forgotten. I can't have her back, but I do believe that by telling her story, I am making a difference for my three beautiful grandchildren."[42]

MADD also has played a key role in the passage of state and federal bills, including the Age 21 Law (setting the minimum age for drinking at 21). Other efforts, like the Project Red Ribbon "Tie One On for Safety" campaign and Designated Driver programs, have helped raise awareness of the problem and prevent drunk driving injuries through simple, straightforward messages. Victim involvement is at the heart of all of MADD's activities. The majority of local volunteers, two-thirds of board members, and a considerable portion of the employed staff are victims of drunk drivers or family members of those killed or injured.

PARENTS OF MURDERED CHILDREN (POMC)

Parents of Murdered Children (POMC) is a nationwide network of self-help groups and advocacy and assistance programs which help families deal with the aftermath of homicide. The organization was founded in 1978 by Charlotte and Bob Hullinger in Cincinnati, Ohio, after their daughter, Lisa, was murdered. The loss of a child to violence is often an intensely isolating experience; survivors often find that others are unable to understand how it feels and are reluctant to talk about it. POMC's goal is to allow family members to share their grief with others who have been through similar experiences, thereby breaking down the isolation that many families face.

POMC has grown from its first self-help group in Cincinnati to a network of more than 100 local chapters serving 38,000 survivors each year. It also has become active in more extensive community involvement projects. Praised by survivors for helping them "see justice," the Truth-in-Sentencing program mobilizes the POMC membership to ensure that the convicted murderers of members' children serve at least their minimum sentences. When an offender comes up for early parole, the network helps victims respond. POMC's annual national conference offers survivors the chance to meet one another, network, and participate in workshops and seminars. National and local newsletters serve as a forum for members to communicate and express themselves. Survivors also help provide a range of other services on behalf of POMC, including court accompaniment, writing anniversary letters of consolation to other survivors, and serving on a speakers' bureau.

P.O.W.E.R. (PEOPLE OPENING THE WORLD'S EYES TO REALITY)

Following the shooting deaths of two New York City high school students in 1992, mobility-impaired victims of gun violence at Goldwater Memorial Hospital created P.O.W.E.R., a group that visits at-risk youth in schools, community organizations, and detention centers to show what can result from a life of drugs and violence. Ranging in age from 19 to 44, most of the group's members are former drug dealers, addicts, or gang members. Their personal stories and physical conditions present a compelling argument for youth to reassess the direction of their lives. P.O.W.E.R. also has testified at the state and federal level for passage of stricter gun control laws and has participated in demonstrations against street violence. Many of the P.O.W.E.R. members feel that they have been given a second chance at life and that their victimization will have meaning if it can benefit others. Staff at the hospital have found that participation in the group has helped to increase members' self-esteem and has enabled them to come to terms with their disabilities.

REMOVE INTOXICATED DRIVERS (RID)

In 1977, Karen and Timothy Morris, ages 17 and 19, were killed by a 22-year-old drunk driver. A newspaper article about this tragedy struck a nerve with Doris Aiken, the mother of two children the same ages as the victims. She was particularly concerned that the offender was not only not jailed, but allowed to continue driving. Together with friends, she began investigating how drunk driving cases were handled by the criminal justice system. They were stunned to learn that drunk driving was rampant—killing 25,000 people each year—yet arrests, convictions, and suspended licenses were rare.

In 1978, in Schenectady, New York, Aiken formed Remove Intoxicated Drivers (RID). RID currently consists of 151 chapters in 41 states. Its activities include counseling and guidance for victims and family members, legislative advocacy, court monitoring, speakers' bureaus, and public education. Based on the work of victims and other volunteers, a string of successful legislative efforts in New York State have reduced plea bargaining by drunk drivers, ensured that drivers lose their license temporarily if they refuse to take an alcohol test, and instituted other strategies to strengthen the state's response. One study by the New York State Police Superintendent estimated that, over a ten-year period, these measures saved over 6,000 lives. RID helped to pioneer the use of Victim Impact Panels, in which drunk drivers hear directly from victims about how their lives have been affected. Stressing the accountability of government officials to the will of the people, RID provides materials and information for victims and others in the community to help them find their voices and demand stronger action against drunk driving.

Almost entirely a volunteer effort, RID has enjoyed strong participation by victims and their families. In many instances, one victim's story has served as the spark to create new chapters. In 1981, RID-Missouri was founded by Marge Charleville, whose letter to a local newspaper about her daughter's death in 1980 received 128 letters in response and led to funding to establish the chapter.

Victims are empowered and trained to work actively to monitor courts, review pending legislation and appear as spokespersons on national radio and television programs, with RID acting as sponsor and agent. These public activities help to heal the wounds inflicted by drunk drivers. In one survivor's words, "Since the most tragic loss . . . that anyone can endure [one's child], I have been clinging to everyday survival by my work helping other DWI victims, and by giving talks to high school assemblies, . . . state troopers, and in victim witness panels to defendant drunk drivers. It is my reason for living."

THE STEPHANIE ROPER COMMITTEE AND FOUNDATION

Based in Maryland, the Stephanie Roper Committee and Foundation were created in 1982 to improve the criminal justice system's treatment of victims and their families. After the brutal murder of their daughter Stephanie, Roberta and Vince Roper were astounded both by the way they were left out of the court proceedings and with the outcome of the trial. Stephanie's convicted murderers were eligible for parole in just 12 years. Roberta began speaking out before local groups about the insensitivity of the justice system to victims. Friends and neighbors joined her efforts, sparking a movement that quickly spread throughout the state. Members collect petitions, hold rallies, and support other activities in the fight for victims' rights.

Both the Committee and Foundation are staffed by trained volunteers, half of whom are themselves crime victims. The Committee focuses on legislative reforms to protect victims' rights and increase services in Maryland, and it has been a major force in passing three dozen victims' rights bills since 1983 (e.g., laws ensuring mandatory victim impact statements, restitution and court attendance rights, and a state constitutional amendment for victims' rights). The Committee issues a regular newsletter to inform members of pending legislation and to encourage them to support the bills.

The Foundation provides direct services to crime victims, including support groups, a Court Companion program to help victims and their families during the trial, and a Courtwatch program to monitor the enforcement of victims' rights. Through its newsletter and other channels, the Foundation actively recruits new volunteers to be trained in providing these services.

TEENS ON TARGET (TNT)

Following an increase in the number of on-campus shootings, the Oakland Unified School District in California started Teens on Target in 1989 to involve young victims of violence and at-risk youth in violence prevention. An additional chapter was later opened in Los Angeles. Pointing out that "those who are most at risk have not been invited to be part of the solution," the program's founders have trained 100 students to be violence prevention advocates. They make presentations that explore the causes of youth violence and suggest solutions, based on their firsthand experiences, for schools and school boards, city and state legislators, national conferences, and the media. With a specific aim to get victims involved, the Los Angeles chapter operates in partnership with a local spinal cord injury program and trains youth with firearm-related spinal injuries to become TNT advocates. In addition to providing a voice that other youth will listen to, these advocates find that their actions help their recovery. One advocate who was paralyzed by a gunshot wound said, "Talking to other kids in the program and in classes has helped me get through it." By speaking out, he has received support and encouragement from others that has helped him rebuild his own life.

TNT recently began "Caught in the Crossfire," a peer visitation program for victims of gun violence. TNT advocates visit young victims at Highland Hospital in Oakland. By sharing their own personal experiences and statistical information on gun violence, they attempt to dissuade victims and their friends from seeking revenge. These advocates can give a uniquely convincing argument against continuing the violence because they often speak from the same perspective as the victim.

YOUTH EMPOWERMENT ASSOCIATION

Created by a young adult survivor of sexual assault, the Youth Empowerment Association (YEA) was initiated to improve the treatment of teen survivors of sexual assault by the mental health system and to enhance their recovery through peer counseling and personal empowerment. Based in

New York City, YEA operated from 1992 to 1995, when it closed due to the loss of funding and key staff members. YEA trained teens who had spent time in the inpatient ward recovering from sexual assault and related symptoms (substance abuse, depression) to serve as peer counselors to other recovering youth and to speak about their experiences at conferences and policymaking forums. In addition to creating an opportunity for youth to learn new skills and improve their self-esteem, YEA created a comforting support system for victims in the mental health system, which is sometimes criticized for failing to diagnose sexual abuse among its patients.

To participate in the training, young people had to express an interest in serving as counselors and to have been out of the inpatient ward for at least six months to demonstrate sufficient progress in their own recovery. If substance abuse had been a problem, they also had to have been clean and sober for six months. To prepare participants to counsel other youth in the hospital's inpatient ward, the training program gave basic information on sexual assault, substance abuse, and other mental health consequences of victimization, as well as communication and peer counseling skills. YEA also prepared young people to speak publicly about their treatment and other experiences before professional conferences, policymaking task forces, and legislative hearings. YEA participants found that, by becoming peer counselors and youth advocates, they advanced their own recovery, increased their feelings of control over their lives, and realized they had something of value to contribute. Many first entered the inpatient ward feeling they had somehow failed in life and were incapable of helping themselves or others. By taking on these new responsibilities, participants were able to increase their feelings of self-worth and set higher goals for their own recovery. Working with others who had shared similar experiences also allowed both counselors and patients to talk about their problems without fear of stigmatization.

NOTES

[1] D. Katz, "A Journey We Did Not Want To Take," *Worth*, (April 1995), pp. 87–96, 118–125.

[2] K. W. Crenshaw, "Race, Reform and Retrenchment: Transformation and Legitimization in Antidiscrimination Law," *Harvard Law Review*, 101 (1988), p. 1331.

[3] M. R. Mahoney, "Victimization or Oppression? Women's Lives, Violence, and Agency," in *The Public Nature of Private Violence: The Discovery of Domestic Abuse*, ed. M. A. Fineman and R. Mykitiuk (New York: Routledge, 1994), pp. 59–92.

[4] R. C. Davis and L. N. Friedman, "The Emotional Aftermath of Crime and Violence," in *Trauma and Its Wake*, ed. C. R. Figley (New York: Brunner/Mazel, 1985), pp. 90–112; A. J. Lurigio and P. A. Resick, "Healing the Psychological Wounds of Criminal Victimization: Predicting Postcrime Distress and Recovery," in *Victims of Crime: Problems, Policies, and Programs*, eds. A. J. Lurigio, W. G. Skogan, and R. C. Davis (Newbury Park, CA: Sage, 1990), pp. 50–67.

[5] R. Janoff-Bulman, "The Aftermath of Victimization: Rebuilding Shattered Assumptions," in *Trauma and Its Wake*, ed. C. R. Figley (New York: Brunner/Mazel, 1985), pp. 15–33.

[6] Lurigio and Resick, "Healing the Psychological Wounds of Criminal Victimization: Predicting Postcrime Distress and Recovery," pp. 50–67; D. S. Riggs and D. G. Kilpatrick, "Families and Friends: Indirect Victimization by Crime," in *Victims of Crime: Problems, Policies, and Programs*, eds. A. J. Lurigio, W. G. Skogan, and R. C. Davis (Newbury Park, CA: Sage, 1990), pp. 120–138.

[7] R. Davis, B. Taylor and S. Bench, *The Impact of Sexual and Non-Sexual Assault on Secondary Victims* (New York: Victim Services, 1994).

[8] J. L. Herman, *Trauma and Recovery* (New York: Basic Books, 1992), p. 119.

[9] R. Davis, B. Taylor and S. Bench, *The Impact of Sexual and Non-Sexual Assault on Secondary Victims*.

[10] M. J. Lerner, D. T. Miller, and J. G. Holmes, "Deserving and the Emergence of Forms of Justice," in *Advances in Experimental Social Psychology*, Vol. 9, ed. L. Berkowitz and E. Walster (New York: Academic Press, 1976).

[11] Herman, *Trauma and Recovery*.

[12] B. Simos, *A Time to Grieve: Loss as a Universal Human Experience* (New York: Family Service Association of America, 1979), p. 228.

[13] W. G. Skogan and M. G. Maxfield, *Coping with Crime: Individual and Neighborhood Reactions*, (Beverly Hills: Sage, 1981), p. 230.

[14] E. Stark, "Framing and Reframing Battered Women," in *Domestic Violence: The Criminal Justice Response*, ed. E. Buzawa (New York: Auburn House, 1992), p. 282.

[15] L. Lebowitz, M. R. Harvey, and J. L. Herman, "A Stage-By-Dimension Model of Recovery from Sexual Trauma," *Journal of Interpersonal Violence*, 9 (3) (1993), pp. 378–391.

[16] A. A. Stein, "Conflict and Cohesion: A Review of the Literature," *Journal of Conflict Resolution*, 20 (1976), pp. 143–172.

[17] Herman, *Trauma and Recovery*.

[18] Ibid.

[19] R. L. Silver, C. Boon and M. L. Stones, "Searching for Meaning in Misfortune: Making Sense of Incest," *Journal of Social Issues*, 39 (1983), pp. 83–103.

[20] Herman, *Trauma and Recovery*, p. 209.

[21] Skogan and Maxfield, *Coping with Crime: Individual and Neighborhood Reactions*, p. 230.

[22] Law Enforcement Assistance Administration, 1977, cited in Skogan and Maxfield, *Coping with Crime: Individual and Neighborhood Reactions*, p. 230.

[23] E. S. Cohn, L. Kidder and J. Harvey, "Crime Prevention vs. Victimization: The Psychology of Two Different Reactions," *Victimology*, 3 (3–4) (1978), pp. 285–296.

[24] Skogan and Maxfield, *Coping with Crime: Individual and Neighborhood Reactions*.

[25] Herman, *Trauma and Recovery*, p. 209.

[26] Susan Sontag, *Illness as Metaphor* (New York: Ferrar, Straus and Giroux, 1978).

[27] S. Felman and D. Laub, *Testimony: Crisis of Witnessing in Literature, Psychoanalysis, and History* (New York: Routledge, 1992), p. 24.

[28] Ibid.

[29] "Mother of Two Murder Victims Provides Solace for Others on Her Talk Show," *New York Times*, 17 April 1995.

[30] S. Schechter, *Women and Male Violence* (Boston: South End, 1982).

[31] D. Terry, "Victims' Families Fight for Mercy," *The New York Times*, 1 February 1996, p. A–10.

[32] F. J. Weed, "The Victim-Activist Role in the Anti-Drunk Driving Movement," *The Sociological Quarterly*, 31 (3) (1990), pp. 459–473.

[33] Lebowitz, Harvey, and Herman, "A Stage-By-Dimension Model of Recovery from Sexual Trauma."

[34] Skogan and Maxfield, *Coping with Crime: Individual and Neighborhood Reactions.*

[35] J. H. Lord, Personal Communication, 1995.

[36] Skogan and Maxfield, *Coping with Crime: Individual and Neighborhood Reactions.*

[37] E. Stark, "Mandatory Arrest of Batterers: A Reply To Its Critics," *American Behavioral Scientist*, 36 (5), (Jones & Schechter, 1993).

[38] Herman, *Trauma and Recovery.*

[39] A number of writers have pointed out how society's common misperception of battered women as "victims without agency" fails to recognize their capacity to act even within a system of oppression. M. R. Mahoney, "Victimization or Oppression? Women's Lives, Violence and Agency"; K. W. Crenshaw, "Race, Reform and Retrenchment: Transformation and Legitimization in Antidiscrimination Law"; E. M. Schneider, "Particularity and Generality: Challenges of Feminist Theory and Practice in Work on Woman Abuse," *New York University Law Review*, 67 (3) (1992), pp. 520–568.

[40] Stark, "Mandatory Arrest of Batterers: A Reply To Its Critics," *American Behavioral Scientist*, pp. 651–680.

[41] J. H. Lord, *Victim Impact Panels: A Creative Sentencing Opportunity* (Dallas: Mothers Against Drunk Driving, 1990); D. Mercer, R. Lorden, and J. Lord, "Victim and Situational Characteristics Facilitation of Impending Post-Victimization Functioning." Presentation at the International Society for Traumatic Stress Studies, San Antonio, 27 October 1993.

[42] Lord, *Victim Impact Panels: A Creative Sentencing Opportunity.*

REFERENCES

Cohn, E. S., L. Kidder, and J. Harvey. "Crime Prevention vs. Victimization: The Psychology of Two Different Reactions." *Victimology*, 3 (3–4) (1978), pp. 285–296.

Crenshaw, K. W. "Race, Reform and Retrenchment: Transformation and Legitimization in Antidiscrimination Law." *Harvard Law Review*, 101 (1331) (1988).

Davis, R. C., and L. N. Friedman. "The Emotional Aftermath of Crime and Violence." *Trauma and Its Wake*. Ed. C. R. Figley. New York: Brunner/Mazel, 1985, pp. 90–112.

Davis, R., B. Taylor, and S. Bench. *The Impact of Sexual and Non-Sexual Assault on Secondary Victims*. New York: Victim Services, 1994.

Felman, S., and D. Laub. *Testimony: Crises of Witnessing in Literature, Psychoanalysis, and History*. New York: Routledge, 1992.

Herman, J. L. *Trauma and Recovery*. New York: Basic Books, 1992.

Janoff-Bulman, R. "The Aftermath of Victimization: Rebuilding Shattered Assumptions." *Trauma and Its Wake*. Ed. C. R. Figley. New York: Brunner/Mazel, 1985, pp. 15–33.

Katz, D. "A Journey We Did Not Want to Take." *Worth*, (April 1995), pp. 87–96, 118–125.

Lebowitz, L., M. R. Harvey, and J .L. Herman. "A Stage-by-Dimension Model of Recovery from Sexual Trauma." *Journal of Interpersonal Violence*, 8 (3) (1993), pp. 378–391.

Lerner, M. J., D. T. Miller, and J. G. Holmes. "Deserving and the Emergence of Forms of Justice." *Advances in Experimental Social Psychology*, Vol. 9. Ed. L. Berkowitz and E. Walster. New York: Academic Press, 1976.

Lurigio, A. J., and P. A. Resick. "Healing the Psychological Wounds of Criminal Victimization: Predicting Postcrime Distress and Recovery." *Victims of Crime: Problems, Policies, and Programs*. Ed. A. J. Lurigio, W. G. Skogan, and R. C. Davis. Newbury Park, CA: Sage, 1990, pp. 50–67.

Lord, J. H. *Victim Impact Panels: A Creative Sentencing Opportunity*. Dallas: Mothers Against Drunk Driving, 1990.

Lord, J. H. Personal communication, 1995.

Mahoney, M. R. "Victimization or Oppression? Women's Lives, Violence, and Agency." *The Public Nature of Private Violence: The Discovery of Domestic Abuse*. Ed. M. A. Fineman and R. Mykitiuk. New York: Routledge, 1994, pp. 59–92.

Mercer, D., R. Lorden, and J. Lord. "Victim and Situational Characteristics Facilitation of Impeding Post-Victimization Functioning." Presentation at the International Society for Traumatic Stress Studies. San Antonio, 27 October 1993.

"Mother of Two Murder Victims Provides Solace for Others on Her Talk Show." *New York Times*, 17 April 1995.

Riggs, D. S., and D. G. Kilpatrick. "Families and Friends: Indirect Victimization by Crime." *Victims of Crime: Problems, Policies, and Programs*. Eds. A. J. Lurigio, W. G. Skogan, and R. C. Davis. Newbury Park, CA: Sage, 1990, pp. 120–138.

Schechter, S. Women and Male Violence. Boston: South End, 1982.

Schneider, E. M. "Particularity and Generality: Challenges of Feminist Theory and Practice in Work on Woman-Abuse." *New York University Law Review*, 67 (3) (1992), pp. 520–568.

Silver, R. L., C. Boon, and M. L. Stones. "Searching for Meaning in Misfortune: Making Sense of Incest." *Journal of Social Issues*, 39 (1983), pp. 83–103.

Simos, B. *A Time to Grieve: Loss as a Universal Human Experience*. New York: Family Service Association of America, 1979.

Skogan, W. G., and M. G. Maxfield. *Coping with Crime: Individual and Neighborhood Reactions*. Beverly Hills: Sage, 1981.

Sontag, S. *Illness as Metaphor*. New York: Farrar, Straus and Giroux, 1978.

Stark, E. "Framing and Reframing Battered Women." *Domestic Violence: The Criminal Justice Response*. Ed. E. Buzawa. New York: Auburn House, 1992, pp. 271–289.

Stark, E. "Mandatory Arrest of Batterers: A Reply to Its Critics." *American Behavioral Scientist*, 36 (5) (1993), pp. 651–680.

Stein, A. A. "Conflict and Cohesion: A Review of the Literature." *Journal of Conflict Resolution*, 20 (1976), pp. 143–172.

Stein, J. Interview, 18 April 1995.

Terry, D. "Victims' Families Fight for Mercy." *The New York Times*, 1 February 1996, p. A-10.

Weed, F. J. "The Victim-Activist Role in the Anti-Drunk Driving Movement." *The Sociological Quarterly*, 31 (3) (1990), pp. 459–473.

Chapter Sixteen

The Rights of Crime Victims
Does Legal Protection Make a Difference?

Dean G. Kilpatrick
David Beatty
Susan Smith Howley

The President's Task Force on Victims of Crime concluded in its 1982 Final Report that there was a serious imbalance between the rights of criminal defendants and the rights of crime victims. This imbalance was viewed as so great that the task force proposed an amendment to the U.S. Constitution to provide crime victims with "the right to be present and to be heard at all critical stages of judicial proceedings."[1] The recommended amendment has not been enacted by Congress, but the report led to a proliferation of victims' rights legislation at the state level.

By the early 1990s, every state had enacted statutory rights for crime victims, and many had adopted constitutional amendments protecting victims' rights. Today, all 50 states have passed some form of a statutory crime victims' bill of rights, and 29 have amended their constitutions to include rights for crime victims.[2] At the federal level, the Victim's Rights and Protection Act of 1990, and several subsequent statutes, gave victims of federal crime many of the rights accorded at the state level.

Despite the widespread adoption of legal protection, the implementation of such protection and its impact on victims have not been widely studied, nor has much research been directed at how this legislation has influenced victims' views of the criminal justice system.[3] One reason the latter issue is important is that victims who view the criminal justice system unfavorably are likely to share that opinion with others, thereby undermining confidence in the system. The current debate in the U.S. Congress over a

Source: *National Institute of Justice: Research in Brief*, December 1998, pp. 1–11. http://www.ojp.usdoj.gov/nij

proposed crime victims' rights constitutional amendment highlights the relevance of victims' rights legislation and the need for research in this area.

This research project, conducted by the National Center for Victims of Crime,[4] was designed to test the hypothesis that the strength of legal protection for crime victims' rights has a measurable impact on how victims are treated by the criminal justice system and on their perceptions of the system. A related hypothesis was that victims from states with strong legal protection would have more favorable experiences and greater satisfaction with the system than those from states where legal protection is weak.

Overall, the research revealed that strong legal protection makes a difference, but it also revealed that even in states where legal protection is strong, some victims are not afforded their rights. In other words, enactment of state laws and state constitutional amendments alone appears to be insufficient to guarantee the full provision of victims' rights in practice. The likely reason is that a host of other factors mediates the laws' effects. Thus, although the disparities between strong and weak victims' rights laws indicate the need to strengthen legal protection, additional steps may be necessary to address the other, intervening factors, to better ensure that the laws have their intended effects.

Measuring the Effectiveness of Victims' Rights Laws: The Study Design

The first step in the study was identifying states that were weak in protecting victims' rights and those that were strong. Next, crime victims from two "weak" states and two "strong" states were asked about their experiences in the criminal justice process. Their experiences were compared and contrasted to find out whether there is a measurable difference in the two groups of states in victim protection. State and local level criminal justice professionals, policymakers, and victim assistance professionals in both groups of states were asked their opinions of victim protection, and their responses were also compared and contrasted.[5]

Selecting strong and weak states. To identify strong and weak states, a legal analysis of victims' rights laws in all 50 states was conducted. Criteria were developed to rate statutory and state constitutional protection of victims' rights on the basis of comprehensiveness, strength, and specificity. The criteria were then used to rate each state in four areas: (1) the right to notification, (2) the right to be present, (3) the right to be heard, and (4) the right to restitution. Applying these ratings, each state was ranked according to the strength of its legal protection of victims' rights. Groups of strong- and weak-protection states were identified, and two states from each group were selected as sites for study. (Both strong states hadconstitutional amendments covering victims' rights, whereas neither weak state did.)

Crime victims' views. From the four states, adult (age 18 and older) crime victims' names and locational information were obtained from department of corrections and victims' compensation agencies. Of the 2,245 victims who could be located, 665 (29.6 percent of the contacted sample) denied that they or a family member had been a recent Victim of Crime.[6] Of the remaining 1,580 respondents, interviews were completed with 1,308 crime victims (83 percent of the victims who could be located and disclosed their victimization).

The sample consisted of victims of physical assault (25 percent), robbery (24 percent), sexual assault (11 percent), other crimes (10 percent), and relatives of homicide victims (30 percent).[7]

Interviews were conducted by phone, and information was obtained about the crime, experiences with the criminal justice system, satisfaction with treatment by the system, and crime-related injuries and losses.[8] Interviews averaged 40.2 minutes and were conducted between April and October 1995.

Views of government and victim assistance professionals. Criminal justice officials, other government officials, and professionals in victim assistance organizations were asked their opinions, perceptions, and suggestions about the rights of crime victims and crime victim services. These individuals, 145 at the local level and 53 at the state level, fell into the following categories.

Local	State
Judges*	Agency directors
Prosecutors	Legislators
Parole and probation officials	Victim coalition directors
Victim assistance coordinators	Other government officials
Victim-witness staff	
Defense attorneys	
Police and sheriffs	

*Judges constituted almost half the people interviewed at the local level.

Can the findings be generalized? By their very nature, the findings of social science studies that are not true experiments can establish relationships among various factors; more difficult is establishing definitive, cause-and-effect relationships. In this study, strong- and weak-protection states were not identical in certain factors that might determine case outcomes or how victims are treated; the differences may have affected the findings. Another limitation to generalizing the findings is that the victims selected for this study were not a representative sample of all crime victims. That is because most crimes are not reported to the police and, if they are, do not progress beyond the report stage. Because the cases in this study progressed further, the victims surveyed were likely to be more satisfied than the average crime victim. In addition, the legal analysis of state laws and state constitutional amendments reflected the situation at a single point in time (January 1, 1992), and many changes in applicable statutes and constitutional provisions have been made since then.

Assessing the Implementation of Victims' Rights

The experiences of crime victims in the two states studied where legal protection of victims' rights is strong were compared with those in the two states studied where protection is weak. In each group, the victims were asked whether they were afforded their rights in several areas. Were they kept informed of case proceedings and their rights as victims? Did they exercise those rights? Did they receive adequate notification of available victim services?[9] Did they receive restitution for the crime committed against them? They also were asked what losses they suffered as a result of the crime, and they rated their satisfaction with the criminal justice process and its various representatives.

Representatives of the criminal justice system are the implementors of laws that provide victims access to information and facilitate victims' participation in the criminal justice process. For this reason, officials from various components of the system, as well as victim assistance professionals, were asked how much they were aware of victims' rights and how well they believed these rights are implemented in their jurisdiction.

NOTIFICATION OF CASE EVENTS AND PROCEEDINGS

Perhaps the most fundamental right of a crime victim is the right to be kept informed by the criminal justice system. Notification plays a key role in a victim's ability to participate in the system because victims cannot participate unless they are informed of their rights and of the time and place of the relevant criminal justice proceedings in which they may exercise those rights. Victims clearly attested to the importance of their rights to attend and be heard at proceedings, but unless they receive notice of proceedings and of their rights, cannot exercise those rights.

At most points in the criminal justice process, from arrest through the parole hearing, victims in strong-protection states were much more likely to receive advance notification than those in weak-protection states. (See exhibit 1.) At certain other points in the process, however, the difference between the two groups was not significant. For example, the proportions of victims who were not informed of plea negotiations were nearly the same in strong- as in weak-protection states, despite the fact that both strong-protection states—but neither weak-protection state—had a law requiring that victims be informed of such negotiations. In other words, the relative strength, and even the existence, of laws providing this right made no difference to the provision of the notice.

In other cases, while the strength of the legal protection for a victim's right did appear to affect the rate at which the right was provided, it was not sufficient to ensure that most victims in fact received the right. For example, far more victims in strong-protection than weak-protection states were notified of the defendant's pretrial release, but more than 60 percent of victims in those strong-protection states did not receive such notice. (See exhibit 1.) Similarly, nearly twice as many victims in strong-protection states as in weak-protection states were notified in advance of the sentencing hearing, but more than 40 percent of such victims were not notified. (See exhibit 1.) Lack of such advance notice would directly affect the ability of victims to exercise their rights to attend and/or be heard at such proceedings.

NOTIFICATION OF THEIR RIGHTS AS VICTIMS

Crime victims not only need to be notified about events and proceedings in the criminal justice process, they also need to be informed of their legal rights. They need to know, for example, not only that the trial has been scheduled, but also that they have a right to discuss the case with the prosecutor. As expected, there were significant differences on this score between strong- and

Exhibit 1
Notification of events in the case—percentage notified

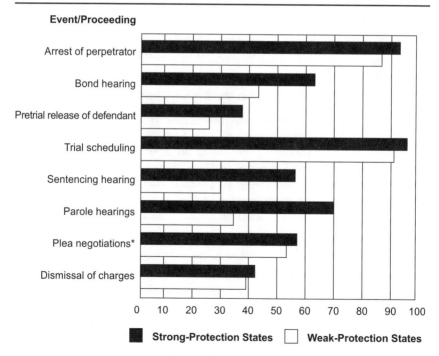

*Difference between groups is not statistically significant.

The Importance of Victims' Rights to Victims Themselves

The right to participate in the process of justice, including the right to attend criminal proceedings and to be heard at various points in the criminal justice process, is important to crime victims. The researchers reached this conclusion by presenting victims with the following list of rights and asking them to rate the importance of each one.[10]

- Being informed about whether anyone was arrested
- Being involved in the decision to drop the case
- Being informed about the defendant's release on bond
- Being informed about the date of the earliest possible release from incarceration
- Being heard in decisions about the defendant's release on bond
- Discussing the case with the prosecutor's office
- Discussing whether the defendant's plea to a lesser charge should be accepted
- Making a victim's impact statement during the defendant's parole hearing
- Being present during the grand jury hearing
- Being present during release hearings
- Being informed about postponement of grand jury hearings
- Making a victim's impact statement before sentencing
- Being involved in the decision about what sentence should be given

On each item, more than three-fourths of the victims rated the particular right as "very important." Topping the list was the right to be informed about whether there was an arrest, rated "very important" by more than 97 percent of the victims. The sole item rated "very important" by less than 80 percent was involvement in the decision about the sentence.

weak-protection states. It was much more common in the strong-protection states for crime victims to be notified of their various rights and of the availability of services. (See exhibit 2.) For example, almost three-fourths of victims in strong-protection states were informed of the availability of victim services, while less than half in weak-protection states received such information.

There were similar differences when it came to being informed of the right to discuss the case with the prosecutor, make a victim's impact statement, and make a statement at the parole hearing. Victims in the strong-protection states fared better. But again, as with notification of case-processing

Exhibit 2
Notification of services and rights—percentage notified

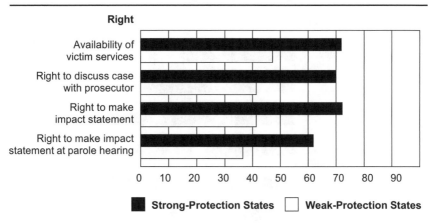

Note: All figures are statistically significant at the 0.05 level or less.

events, even in the strong-protection states large proportions of crime victims were not notified of their rights and of available services. Thus, almost 40 percent of victims in the strong-protection states were not informed they could make an impact statement at the parole hearing.

EXERCISING THEIR RIGHTS

Notifying crime victims in advance of events and proceedings in the criminal justice process, and informing them of their rights to participate in that process, are prerequisites to the exercise of the rights to participate. Researchers asked crime victims who indicated they had received such information whether they had in fact exercised their rights to attend, make statements at, or otherwise participate in the criminal justice process. The responses of victims in strong-protection and weak-protection states were then compared.

At some points in the criminal justice process, among victims who had received the prerequisite notice, victims in the strong-protection states were more likely to exercise their rights than those in weak-protection states. They were more likely to make recommendations at bond hearings, to make recommendations about sentences, and to make an impact statement at the parole hearing. (See exhibit 3.) At other stages, such as making an impact statement at sentencing, or attending the parole hearings, similar percentages of victims from both groups of states, who knew of the proceeding and of their legal rights, exercised those rights.

While the strength of the legal protections of victims' rights to participate did appear to influence the numbers of victims who exercised some rights to participate, victims in both groups of states were more likely to exercise some rights than others. For instance, most victims in both strong- and

Exhibit 3
Exercising their rights as victims—percentage exercising their right[a]

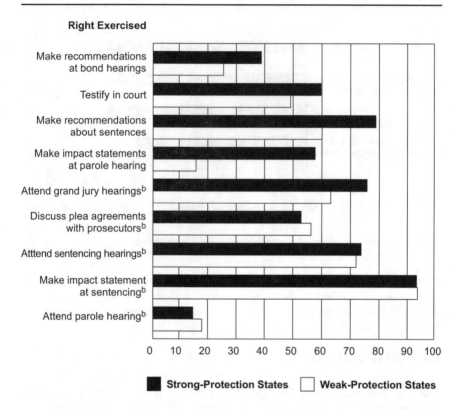

Right Exercised

Make recommendations at bond hearings	
Testify in court	
Make recommendations about sentences	
Make impact statements at parole hearing	
Attend grand jury hearings[b]	
Discuss plea agreements with prosecutors[b]	
Atttend sentencing hearings[b]	
Make impact statement at sentencing[b]	
Attend parole hearing[b]	

■ Strong-Protection States   □ Weak-Protection States

[a] In each case, percentages are based on number of relevant cases. For example, the percentages that attended the grand jury hearing were based on the number of victims who knew of the hearing; the percentages who testified in court were based on the number of cases that went to trial.
[b] Difference between groups is not statistically significant.

weak-protection states who were notified of the sentencing hearing and their rights to participate attended sentencing hearings (72 percent) and made an impact statement at sentencing (93 percent). Relatively few victims in either group, even when they were aware of their rights and of the proceeding, exercised their rights to make recommendations at bond hearings or to attend parole hearings. (See exhibit 3.)

OBTAINING RESTITUTION

Another important area of victims' rights examined in this study was the right of victims to restitution—the court orders a convicted defendant to repay the victim for crime-related economic losses. Contrary to the hypothesis that judges in strong-protection states would be more likely to order restitution whenever a victim had sustained economic losses, they were significantly *less* likely to do so (22 percent, in contrast to 42 percent in the weak-protection states).[11] In the cases in which restitution was ordered, there was no significant difference in the percentages of victims from strong- and weak-protection states who actually received restitution (37 percent versus 43 percent). Overall, victims in strong-protection states who were eligible for restitution were significantly less likely than their counterparts in weak-protection states ever to receive *any* restitution (8 percent, in contrast to 18 percent).

Because these results were contrary to the hypothesis, exploratory analyses were conducted to determine if other factors might explain them. The analyses revealed that defendants in restitution-eligible cases in strong-protection states were more likely than those in weak-protection states to have been incarcerated (89 percent, in contrast to 72 percent). Restitution in both groups of states was less likely to have been ordered in cases involving a sentence of incarceration. However, the analyses also revealed that weak-protection states were significantly more likely to order restitution than strong-protection states, regardless of whether the sentence included incarceration (44 percent, in contrast to 23 percent), or did not include incarceration (61 percent in contrast to 36 percent). Thus the analyses were unsuccessful in identifying the incarceration of convicted defendants as a reason for the superiority of the weak-protection states in ordering restitution.

The most striking finding was the relatively small percentage of eligible victims overall (less than 20 percent) who received *any* restitution (whether ordered or not). The low percentage suggests that factors other than legislative mandates are driving whether restitution is paid. When criminal justice officials were surveyed (See "How the criminal justice system views crime victims' rights," page 298, they indicated that the factors influencing the ordering of restitution might include lack of knowledge about victims' economic losses or the amount of defendants' assets, lack of knowledge about the victims' right to restitution, and opinions about the appropriateness of ordering restitution.

RATING THE CRIMINAL JUSTICE PROCESS AND ITS AGENTS

Crime victims need to have confidence in the criminal justice process. To measure their level of confidence, the researchers asked them to assess the adequacy of criminal justice system performance at several points in the criminal justice process. Again, the findings were consistent with the hypothesis: victims who came from states where legal protection is strong were more likely to rate the system favorably. (See exhibit 4.) Still, the comparative figures cannot conceal the fact that many victims, even in states where legal protection is strong, gave the system very negative ratings.

Rating the outcome of the case. As predicted by the hypothesis, victims in weak-protection states were more likely to believe the fairness of the sentence was completely inadequate" (the lowest rating). However, a sizeable minority of victims in the strong-protection states also believed the sentence

Exhibit 4

Victims rate criminal justice processing—percentage who rate it more than adequate or completely inadequate*

Aspect of Processing	Strong-Protection States		Weak-Protection States	
	More Than Adequate	Completely Inadequate	More Than Adequate	Completely Inadequate
Efforts to apprehend the perpetrator	44	6	27	11
Efforts to inform the family about progress on the case	29	9	13	19
Their ability to have input in the case	21	15	9	25
Thoroughness of case preparation	28	10	14	20
Fairness of the trial	20	11	10	20
Fairness of the verdict or plea	17	21	6	28
Fairness of sentence	14	25	5	34
Speed of the process	17	15	6	27
Support services	16	15	8	22

*The ratings continuum was "more than adequate," "adequate," "somewhat less than adequate," and "completely inadequate."
Note: All figures are statistically significant at the 0.05 level or less.

imposed was "completely inadequate" (34 percent in weak-protection versus 25 percent in strong-protection states).

Similarly, more than one in four victims from weak-protection states and one in five from strong-protection states believed the fairness of the verdict or plea was completely inadequate. More than 25 percent of victims from weak-protection states and 15 percent from strong-protection states felt the speed of the process was completely inadequate. Finally, 22 percent of victims from weak-protection states and 15 percent from strong-protection states said support services for victims were completely inadequate.

These negative ratings are particularly noteworthy in view of the fact that, from the victims' perspective, the outcomes of these cases were much more favorable than most; that is, a higher than usual proportion resulted in a plea or verdict of guilty that led to incarceration of the defendant. Clearly, to many crime victims, even in cases resulting in a conviction and imprisonment of the defendant, the criminal justice process did not meet their expectations.

Rating the system and its agents. Victims gave high marks to the various agents of the criminal justice system, such as the police. Again, victims in the strong-protection states tended to be more satisfied than those in the weak-protection states. But the proportions who said they were very satisfied or somewhat satisfied with the performance of police, prosecutors, victim/witness agency staff, and judges were high across the board, irrespective of the strength of legal protection. Thus, in the strong-protection states, 83 percent of the victims were very or somewhat satisfied with the police and, at 77 percent, the proportion in the weak-protection states was similarly high. (See exhibit 5.)

The criminal justice system overall was rated somewhat lower than each of its component representatives: Only 55 percent of victims in strong-protection states and 47 percent in weak-protection states were very satisfied or somewhat satisfied with it. At the other end of the scale, the proportion of victims expressing strong dissatisfaction with the system was relatively high—more than one-fourth of the victims in the strong-protection states and more than one-third in the weak-protection states.

WHAT EXPLAINS VICTIMS' SATISFACTION LEVELS

Knowing whether and to what extent crime victims are satisfied (or dissatisfied) with the criminal justice system is not the same as knowing why. To shed light on the issue, three scales were constructed, each of which comprised several questions asked of victims. The scales measured overall satisfaction with the criminal justice system, the extent to which victims thought they were informed of their rights, and victims' perceptions of the effectiveness of their impact statements. They were called, respectively, the Victim Satisfaction Scale, the Informed Victim Scale, and the Victims' Impact Scale.

As measured by the Victim Satisfaction Scale, satisfaction with the criminal justice system was greater among female than male victims, among white

Exhibit 5
Victims' satisfaction with the criminal justice system—
percentage who are very or somewhat satisfied

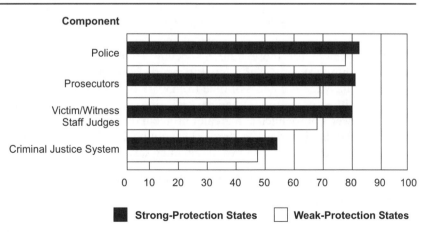

Note: All figures are statistically significant at the 0.05 level or less.

than African-American victims, and among higher income than lower income victims. Age made no difference. As expected, in the strong-protection states the Victim Satisfaction Scale scores were higher than in the weak-protection states, and this was true after controlling for the effects of gender, race, and income level.

Are victims more satisfied if they are informed of their rights? And are they more satisfied if they believe their participation in the system has had an impact on the decision process? To answer the first question, Victim Satisfaction Scale scores were analyzed in relation to the Informed Victim Scale scores, with the results revealing a strong correlation between the two: victims who were informed of their rights were more satisfied with the justice system than those who were not. To answer the second question, the Victim Satisfaction Scales were again analyzed, this time in relation to the Victims' Impact Scale scores. Again, the analysis revealed a strong correlation, indicating that victims who thought their participation had an impact on their cases were more satisfied with the system.

CRIME-RELATED PHYSICAL, FINANCIAL, AND MENTAL HEALTH PROBLEMS

Crime victims experience a variety of losses relating to the crime. They may sustain physical or psychological injuries, with some victims requiring counseling. They may lose money or suffer property destruction, loss, or damage. Victims may lose time from work or school as a result of their injuries or as a consequence of time spent consulting with law enforcement or prosecutors, or attendance at court proceedings.

Whether they were from weak- or strong-protection states, victims reported several major crime-related losses. For certain kinds of losses—property damage or destruction, property or monetary loss, time away from work or school to consult with the police, and canceled insurance coverage or increased premiums—strong legal protection made no difference, because victims in both weak- and strong-protection states were equally affected. (See exhibit 6.) For other kinds of problems resulting from the crime—time lost from work or school because of injuries and receiving medical treatment for those injuries—victims from the weak-protection states were more likely to be affected. But victims in strong-protection states were more likely to note a loss of time from work or school because of consultations with prosecutors, attending trial, or receiving counseling. This could be viewed not so much as a greater problem than as a greater opportunity: Although the time these victims lost cannot be discounted, they spent it participating in the justice system and obtaining services.

HOW THE CRIMINAL JUSTICE SYSTEM VIEWS CRIME VICTIMS' RIGHTS

This study also included a survey of criminal justice and victim assistance professionals at the state and local levels. There were two reasons for their inclusion. The first is that those professionals can affect crime victims' ability to recover and to cope with the aftermath of the offense and the stress of par-

Exhibit 6
Victims' crime-related problems—
percentage who experienced problems

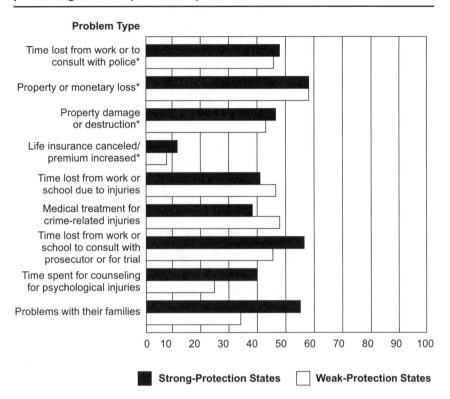

Problem Type

Time lost from work or to consult with police*
Property or monetary loss*
Property damage or destruction*
Life insurance canceled/ premium increased*
Time lost from work or school due to injuries
Medical treatment for crime-related injuries
Time lost from work or school to consult with prosecutor or for trial
Time spent for counseling for psychological injuries
Problems with their families

0 10 20 30 40 50 60 70 80 90 100

■ Strong-Protection States   □ Weak-Protection States

*Difference not statistically significant.

ticipation in the criminal justice system. The average citizen, newly thrust into the criminal justice system as a victim of crime, often has little understanding of the basic workings of the system. Representatives of the various components of the criminal justice system and victim assistance professionals can play key roles in helping facilitate access and understanding as cases progress.

There was another important rationale for surveying such professionals. The survey of crime victims produced a wealth of data on whether the strength of victims' rights laws influenced the rate at which victims received their rights and on victims' satisfaction with the criminal justice system. However, it could not suggest reasons that laws might or might not produce such an effect. Local and state professionals were surveyed to begin to explore such reasons.[12] The data produced by these surveys inform the discussion of influences on the implementation of victims' rights, and suggest additional avenues for research.

Thus, state and local officials and advocates were surveyed to determine the extent to which they were aware of the legal rights of victims, their views of how victims' rights are ensured, and their thinking about what further steps may be necessary to strengthen the protection of victims' rights. The interviews with such officials revealed much the same pattern as the interviews with victims: strong legal protection tended to translate in practice as greater implementation of those rights, but in many cases did not guarantee the provision of such rights.

Views of local criminal justice and victim service professionals. If the local officials came from strong-protection states, they were more likely than those from weak-protection states to say they "always" or "usually" provide crime victims with their rights to notification of events in the case, to be present at the various stages of the criminal justice process, and to be heard. These local officials were also about one-third more likely than their counterparts in weak-protection states to believe that victims' rights are "adequate."

Yet, large proportions of local criminal justice officials, even from states where legal protection is strong, were not aware of many victims' rights and how they are being provided. For example, only 39 percent of the local professionals in the strong-protection states knew that their state had a constitutional amendment enumerating victims' rights. For a majority of questions about victims' rights, a substantial number of officials incorrectly identified the source of the victims' right as a policy or practice, rather than a statute or state constitutional amendment. Many officials were also unclear about which agency had the duty to provide victims a given right.

State leaders' views. The opinions of state leaders indicate the extent to which crime victims' rights have achieved understanding and acceptability at high levels of government. At the state level, awareness of legal mandated victims' rights tends to be higher than it is locally. Such leaders as governors, attorneys general, heads of state criminal justice agencies, and heads of state crime victims' organizations generally were aware of the status of victims' rights and the challenges of implementing them.

At the state level, as at the local level, strong legal protection made a difference, though not in all respects. Leaders from the strong states were more likely to believe their criminal justice system was performing well, particularly in protecting victims' rights. However, even where legal protection was strong, a large majority also indicated they were aware of problems victims are experiencing in obtaining benefits and services. The problems most frequently cited had to do with victim notification.

BARRIERS TO IMPLEMENTATION

Criminal justice and victim advocate professionals at the state and local levels were asked for their suggestions for improving the provision of victims' rights. Their responses basically fell into three groups: increased funding, increased training, and increased enforcement of victims' rights.

Resource limitations were cited by officials as the most common reason for being unable to fulfill their responsibilities. Local officials from the strong-protection states were more likely than those from weak-protection states to believe that funding for the implementation of victims' rights was adequate. (In the strong-protection states, 55 percent of local officials, in contrast to 34 percent in the weak-protection states, felt funding for victim services was adequate; 39 percent in the strong-protection states, but only 27 percent in the weak-protection states, felt funding for implementation of victims' rights was adequate.) At the same time, a considerable percentage of these local leaders, even those from the strong-protection states, believed funding for victim services was very inadequate (15 percent, and 35 percent of those in the weak-protection states).

When asked if their office had funding for use in victim services programs or for implementing victims' rights, only about one-third of all officials at the local level said it had (and there was little difference between the weak- and the strong-protection states). What is more, very few of those without funding said they had actively sought it in the previous year.

At the state level, officials offered a similar assessment of funding; that is, those from strong-protection states were more likely to believe that funding was adequate than were those from weak-protection states. (Half the state leaders in strong-protection states, in contrast to 31 percent in the weak-protection states, believed funding for implementation of victims' rights was adequate.) The state leaders also cited increased funding—specifically for additional staff (victim/witness coordinators and criminal justice staff)—more often than any other need. And whether they were from states with weak or strong legal protection, these leaders most often cited increased funding or staffing when they were asked how they would minimize problems in providing victims' services.

In prioritizing suggestions to improve the treatment of crime victims in their criminal justice systems, leaders in weak-protection states most frequently named the establishment, enhancement, and/or enforcement of victims rights laws as their top priority; increased funding was a secondary priority. By contrast, among leaders in the strong-protection states, the largest percentage of responses dealt with issues of increased funding and resources for victim-related services and programs, followed by the need for better education of criminal justice officials regarding victims' rights.

WHAT MORE NEEDS TO BE DONE

The findings offer support for the position of those who advocate strengthening legal protection of crime victims' rights. Where legal protection is strong, victims are more likely to be aware of their rights, to participate in the criminal justice system, to view criminal justice system officials favorably, and to express more overall satisfaction with the system. Moreover, the levels of overall satisfaction in strong-protection states are higher. Strong legal protection produces greater victim involvement and better experiences with the justice system. A more favorable perception of the agents of the system—police, prosecutors, victim/witness staff, and judges—is another benefit. Because strong legal protection at the state level is associated with victim awareness, participation, and satisfaction, some have advocated a federal constitutional amendment to protect victims' rights.

On the other hand, legal protections per se, regardless of their relative strength in state law or state constitutions, are not always enough to ensure victims' rights. As the study revealed, even in states where victims' rights were protected strongly by law, many victims were not notified about key hearings and proceedings, many were not given the opportunity to be heard, and few received restitution. In the strong-protection states examined in this study, more than one in four victims were very dissatisfied with the criminal justice system as a whole.

Mediating factors. Several mediating factors were identified as influencing the provision of victims' rights, beyond the strength of the statute or state constitutional amendment. The first among these is knowledge of victims' rights. The survey of local criminal justice officials and victim service professionals revealed a lack of awareness of victims' rights and how those rights are implemented. The level of criminal justice officials' and victims' knowledge of victims' rights influences their conduct with respect to those rights. Criminal justice officials are not likely to enforce victims' rights laws if they are unaware they exist. They may be less likely to seek funding for services they do not know they have a duty to provide. Victims are unlikely to attempt to assert rights they do not know they have.

Even when criminal justice officials know what the law requires of them, they may not have the means to carry out their duties. Victims' rights can be ensured only if resources are sufficient, and resource limitations were cited by officials as the most common reason for being unable to fulfill their duties under the law. It can be assumed that there is a relationship between the strength of legal mandates and the provision of funding to implement those mandates. In other words, it is reasonable to assume that states with stronger legal mandates for the provision of victims' rights tend to provide more funds for implementation than states with weaker mandates. While this study did not attempt to measure the actual levels of funding, officials in the states with strong legal protections of victims' rights were more likely to believe that funding was adequate.

Finally, even where strong laws exist and are fully understood, and where resources are adequate, there may be a need for additional enforcement mechanisms to ensure that victims are given their rights. While some enforcement mechanisms may involve giving victims the power to assert their legal rights, others might involve procedures that better allow criminal justice agencies to monitor their own compliance with victims' rights laws.

Strengthening victim protection. In view of these considerations, the states and/or the criminal justice system can take several steps, on a variety of fronts, to strengthen victim protection:[13]

- Keep victims informed, provide them with opportunities for input, and consider that input carefully for, as the study revealed, informed victims, and those who thought their input had influenced criminal justice decisions, were more likely to be satisfied with the criminal justice system.

- Make changes to ensure that restitution is ordered, monitored, paid, and received.[14]
- Offer criminal justice officials and crime victims additional education about victims' rights and their legal mandates.
- Take steps to seek and ensure adequate funding for victims' services and the implementation of victims' rights.
- Institute mechanisms to monitor the provision of victims' rights by criminal justice officials whose duty is to implement the law, and provide a means by which victims who are denied their rights can enforce those rights.[15]

NOTES

[1] *President's Task Force on Victims of Crime Final Report*, Washington, DC: President's Task Force on Victims of Crime, December 1982:114.

[2] For current information about the status of crime victims' rights laws, contact the National Center for Victims of Crime at 2111 Wilson Boulevard, Suite 300, Arlington, VA 22201 (703–276–2880).

[3] For a recent review of research, see Kelly, D. P., and Erez, E., "Victim Participation in the Criminal Justice System," in R. C. Davis, A. J. Lurigio, and W. G. Skogan, eds., *Victims of Crime* (second edition), Thousand Oaks, California: Sage, 1997. Currently under way is a survey, conducted by the Council of State Governments, Eastern Regional Conference, of the attitudes of citizens, including crime victims, toward the criminal justice system. The survey, which will cover 10 Northeastern states, will cover the extent and nature of victimization, perceptions of victims' rights and victims' services, and victims' experiences in reporting crime.

[4] Formerly the National Victim Center.

[5] Unless stated otherwise, chi-square analyses were used to test differences between the groups of states. In addition, unless otherwise indicated, all findings are significant at the 0.05 level or less. Percentages were rounded to whole numbers. Because not all victims progressed equally far in the criminal justice process, percentages are based on the number of victims who had each type of relevant experience.

[6] Failure of crime victims who have reported crimes to the police to disclose the crime when contacted by victimization survey interviewers is consistent with the results of reverse records check studies (e.g., Reiss, A. J., Jr., and J. A. Roth, eds., *Understanding and Preventing Violence*, Washington, DC: National Academy Press, 1993: appendix B).

[7] Because the distribution of types of crime victims differed among the four states, interview data were weighted by state, using the proportion of victims in the entire sample as case weights. Thus, the distribution of crime types in strong and weak protection states was identical. The weighted number of crime victims in the sample was 1,312.

[8] All interviews were conducted by SRBI, a New York based survey research firm, using a computer-assisted telephone interview procedure.

[9] The term "victim services" refers to a wide range of programs and policies (such as crisis counseling, transportation, and employer intercession) that provide assistance directly to crime victims.

[10] The rights are listed in descending order of their rating.

[11] Restitution-eligible cases are those in which the victims sustained economic losses and the defendants pleaded guilty or were convicted. Findings are significant at the .05 level or less.

[12] Because in this part of the analysis the sample size for each type of state was relatively small, the data were not subjected to the same type of statistical analysis as were the data from victims.

[13] The Council of State Governments—Eastern Regional Conference (see note 3) is currently planning a regional conference that will address such issues as identifying victim issues that could be addressed through legislation, modifying existing victims' rights legislation, and developing model legislation that could meet crime victims' needs.

[14] There is a useful discussion of restitution issues in "Making Victims Whole Again," by B. E. Smith and S. W. Hillenbrand, in R. C. Davis, A. J. Lurigio, and W. G. Skogan, eds., *Victims of Crime*.

[15] A recent report by the Office for Victims of Crime presents recommendations from crime victims, victim advocates, criminal justice practitioners, health professionals, and researchers. See *New Directions from the Field: Victims' Rights and Services for the 21st Century*, Washington, DC: U.S. Department of Justice, Office for Victims of Crime, 1998. NCJ 170600.

Chapter Seventeen

The Evolution of
the Law of Victims' Rights
Is There a Conflict with
Criminal Defendants' Due Process Rights?

Gregory P. Orvis

Introduction

There is no question that crime and the damage it does to society is one of the most important questions facing the United States in the twenty-first century. Tabulations of the National Crime Victimization Survey's 1993 data revealed crime rates in the United States of 52 violent victimizations per one thousand people and 322 property crimes per one thousand households (Bastian, 1995). Furthermore, the tangible costs of crime victimizations are $105 billion a year, which include property losses, productivity losses, and medical expense outlays. By far, the greater costs are intangible, such as pain, long-term emotional trauma, disability, and risk of death, and have been estimated to be as great as $450 billion a year (National Institute of Justice, 1996).

However, the greatest damage of crime victimization this century may have been done to the judicial system. Slowly but surely, the victims' rights movement and its accompanying lobbying groups have pressured the American judicial system to apply civil-like remedies to criminal cases, despite the fact that over two hundred years of common law experience in this country alone proved that this was rather like putting a square peg in a round hole. Whereas the original purpose of the criminal courts in the United States was

Paper presented at the Academy of Criminal Justice Sciences' Annual Meeting, Louisville, Kentucky, March 14, 1997. Reprinted by permission of the author.

to protect *society* from criminal deviance, the criminal court system, to its detriment, has been increasingly altered during the last three decades to serve *individual* citizen's interests, which have been traditionally protected under the common law by the civil courts. These alterations have led to longer and more costly criminal proceedings and a confusion as to the boundary between "private law," which deals with relationships between individual citizens and in which government has only an indirect interest, and "public law," wherein the government has specific responsibilities (Gardner & Anderson, 1992).

The Common Law Tradition

During the Renaissance, all of Europe but England embraced the rediscovered "Roman" law and its tradition of codification which greatly restricted judicial discretion. England rejected the new legal trend in favor or retaining the common law system that had developed its own "peculiar features of substance, structure and culture," and, in particular, its reliance on case law and the doctrine of precedent (Friedman, 1984, at p. 16). During Henry II's reign in the late tenth century, English law recognized that crimes were more than personal disputes between criminals and victims, but were acts against society and should not be left to personal vengeance (Gardner & Anderson, 1992).

The need to preserve law and order in society created a criminal justice system that evolved under the common law separate from the "private" law that protected individuals' interests and precluded "private" vengeance for crimes. As one legal scholar notes, "Criminal justice is *public* justice; it requires *public* litigation. The plaintiff is 'the people' or 'the commonwealth' or 'the state'; the state sets the process in motion and the state pays the bills" (Friedman, 1984, at pp. 158–9). Criminal law evolved to deal "with activities that have been formally forbidden by a society's government" whereas civil law was created to govern "the relationships between individuals in the course of their private affairs," although a tort action may lead to violations of both (Calvi & Coleman, 1989, pp. 8–9). As England created colonies in the "New World," the English brought their common law traditions with them as well as their ideas about criminal justice.

This distinction leads to a great many procedural differences between criminal justice systems vested in the common law and those of counties that followed the "Roman" or codified law, often referred to as in the "Romano-Germanic" tradition, wherein criminal and civil suits could sometimes be pursued in the same proceeding (Terrill, 1992). Criminal law prosecution under the common law is an adversary system with a more partisan prosecutor and a more impartial judge than the inquisitorial, or nonadversary, system of the Romano-Germanic law, where the victim in some countries can intervene in this cooperative venture and have his civil suit tried along with the criminal suit. However, in these Romano-Germanic counties there is complete discovery of each "side's" case and the judge often leads the examination of the witnesses and the defendant (Glendon, Gordon, & Osakwe, 1985).

In the United States, due process and the protection of the defendant's rights under the Bill of Rights is better served under the common laws' adversarial tradition because the Bill of Rights' very existence draws a dividing line between the government and those accused of crimes. In the seventeenth century under King Charles I, the royal Court of the Star Chamber had abandoned such procedural protection to the detriment of those accused of crimes, usually those in the lower and middle classes, and including those in the colonies. After the American Revolution and despite the failed Articles of Confederation, the Bill of Rights "reflects deep suspicion, even hostility, to government power" (Samaha, 1996). It is not surprising that the adversary system was nurtured under such an atmosphere, with no room left for a third-party dispute in the American criminal justice process, even that of a crime victim.

Even before the American Bill of Rights, the common law had a greater quantum of proof to find a person guilty under the criminal law—the state had to prove the accused guilty of the crime beyond a reasonable doubt. This quantum of proof is very important, because under the civil law, an individual needs only a preponderance of the evidence to prove his/her case against a person who has wronged him/her. Furthermore, the rules of evidence in general are much more exacting in the criminal justice process than in the civil justice process under the common law as evolved in the United States (Torgia, 1972).

The Incremental Merging of Criminal and Civil Justice Processes in the United States

The merging of the criminal and civil justice processes in the United States began in the early eighties with the advent of the victims' rights movement. In 1982, California voters adopted "Proposition Eight," which adopted a victims' bill of rights and restricted plea bargaining, and this is sometimes thought to be the beginning of the victims' rights reform movement (Friedman, 1984). The restriction of plea bargaining is especially surprising since supporters of plea bargaining often argue the fact that 90 percent of criminal cases are settled is good for crime victims and their families because it spares them the stress and possible public humiliation of a trial, particularly in rape, murder, and child molestation cases where demonstrative evidence is often graphic and cross-examination is brutal (Glick, 1983).

Offender restitution, or the concept of transferring money or services from the criminal to the victim as damages, predates formal criminal justice systems and dates to the 1960s in the United States. However, it was the recommendations of the 1982 President's Task Force on Victims of Crime that began the trend of making it a norm to grant restitution as part of the criminal sentence, and that trend extends to restitution legislation in forty-eight states today. There are many reasons to question the efficacy of restitution, not the least of which is the inability of the criminal courts to administer restitution programs and the inability of these courts to quantify damages from violent crimes and victimless

crimes (Doerner & Lab, 1995). There has even been some dispute among federal lower courts about the constitutionality of the restitution provisions of the
Victim and Witness Protection Act of 1982, in that the Seventh Amendment
guarantees the right of a jury trial in controversies over twenty dollars in despute
between individual citizens (Reid, 1985). There are more pragmatic problems
with restitution of crime victims by criminals through the criminal courts:

> First, suitable jobs for offenders are difficult to find. Second, judges
> remain reluctant to impose restitution unless agreements are likely to be
> enforced. Third, probation and parole officials resent being relegated to
> the status of "bill collection" agencies. Finally, many appropriate cases
> slip through the cracks in the system, through a process called "shrink-
> age" or "funneling," because of unreported crime, unsolved cases,
> dropped counts, and dismissed charges. (Sheley, 1995, at p. 158)

Another recommendation of the President's Task Force on Victims of
Crime in 1982 was the establishment of a federally financed victim compensation fund. Soon after their recommendation, thirty-six states established at
least token victim compensation funds, almost all of which came quickly into
financial difficulty. As one observer noted, "Some contain so little money that
state officials try to keep them a secret" (Vetter & Territo, 1984. at p. 532).
Today, the victim compensation funds of forty-four states are subsidized by
federal funds, compensate the victims of only the most violent and injurious
crimes, and have complex rules and regulations that *must* be strictly adhered to
by the victim applying for the funds, (Karmen, 1990).

Many advocates of victims' rights believe that crime victims should play a
greater role during the pretrial proceedings, the trial, and the sentencing stage
of the criminal justice process. The greatest advances for victims have been in
legally prescribed notifications. Forty-one states require advance notification of
all court appearances, even ones where the victim is not a witness, and
twenty-seven states require that a victim be notified if the defendant is released
on bail. Twenty-seven states give crime victims consultive roles in plea bargaining, and twenty-eight states require that the state notify victims when plea bargains are agreed to by the state and the defense (Karmen, 1990). Although there
are no statistics on the costs of this additional paperwork, considering that the
criminal justice system is one of scarce resources, these costs must be significant.

The federal and many state systems require that prior to sentencing the
trial judge read a victim impact statement, in which the victim describes how
the crime affected his/her financial, physical, and mental health as well as that
of his/her family. Some jurisdictions even allow the victims to make public
statements in the courtroom (Holman & Quinn, 1996). One might remember
the New York case of a few years ago where a gunman went on shooting ram-
page on a commuter train. He was found guilty after a lengthy trial in which
the defendant represented himself, and the victims' oral statements took over
a week of the court's time and a great deal of taxpayers' money. One study
even found that victim impact statements correlated with a greater chance

that the defendant would be incarcerated (Erez & Tontodonato, 1990), although another study found no correlation between victim impact statements and harsher sentences (Davis & Smith, 1994). As it stands today, recent United States Supreme Court decisions have upheld victim impact statements as constitutional and not contrary to the Eighth Amendment, even if potentially inflammatory and used in a death penalty case (Doerner & Lab, 1995).

Victims' Rights and the Federal Court System

The federal courts have been slow in their acceptance of victims' rights and often were divided in their resolve as to whether to accept them or not. The earliest federal court cases on victims' rights were not in agreement even as to a victims' right we now consider fairly basic, restitution to the victim. Whereas one federal court rejected the restitution provisions of the Victim and Witness Protection Act of 1982 based on the jury requirements of the Seventh Amendment (*U.S. v. Welde*, 1983), another federal court upheld its constitutionality (*U.S. v. Brown*, 1984).

The United States Supreme Court itself was divided over the constitutionality of victim impact statements in the sentencing of death penalty cases. The court in a 5–4 decision decided that such statements created a risk that the death penalty would be imposed in an "arbitrary and capricious" manner (*Booth v. Maryland*, 1987). The Supreme Court does not usually overturn precedent lightly nor soon after its made, but in the case of victim impact statements, they did just that in *Payne v. Tennessee* (1991). The Supreme Court denied that the Eighth Amendment created a bar to victim impact statements without a showing that the statements were so prejudicial as to make the process fundamentally unfair and allowed the states to decide whether such statements should be used or not in criminal cases. At least forty-eight states had already taken the initiative with some form of victim participation in sentencing by that date (McLeod, 1988).

The Danger of Merging Criminal and Civil Justice Processes

The greatest danger of merging criminal and civil justice processes is that doing so diminishes the purpose of both. The philosophy of the American criminal justice system is undermined when the focus is taken from society and put on the individual victim, with "society no longer appeased or vindicated" (Doerner & Lab, 1995, at p. 67). Similarly, the public faith in the civil justice system is further shaken when insisting that the civil system cannot protect crime victims' rights except by excluding them from having to enforce their individual rights in the civil courts. Furthermore, the logic and wisdom of hundreds of years of common law precedent governing private wrongs are ignored and thus wasted when crime victims' cases are taken from the civil court arena.

Another danger is that victims' rights as advocated by the victim's rights movement in many states infringe on the rights of those accused of crimes as protected by the Bill of Rights (Reid, 1985). The victim's rights movement has been successful in lobbying forty-four state legislatures so that a victims' bill of rights is included in some format as part of those states' constitutions (Karmen, 1990). The danger of victims' rights and crime defendants' rights conflicting does not exist in the civil courts, because the constitutional rights of the accused do not apply to civil actions, and thus the constitutional dilemma is avoided completely. Still many victims' rights advocates argue that victims' rights *should* be gained at the expense of crime defendants' rights and that too much time and energy is wasted protecting the criminal. Critics of this victims' rights argument raise several objections:

> First, they argue that making convicts suffer more does not make victims suffer any less. . . . Second, they charge that many of these measures do not really empower victims but rather strengthen the government's ability to control its citizens. . . . Finally critics point out that these opportunities to press for institutionalized revenge benefit only a small portion of all victims—only those fortunate ones whose reported cases are solved and are prosecuted vigorously and successfully. (Karmen, 1990, at pp. 332–3)

The criminal courts' procedures and their rules of evidence are very different from and more complex than those in the civil courts, often because of the Bill of Rights and the due process clause of the Fourteenth Amendment. As witnessed in the aftermath of the O. J. Simpson case, public sympathy for crime victims and their families has caused many to question the criminal rules of evidence and procedure—even the presumption of innocence that is the foundation of our criminal courts. Such short-term public fervor could cause elected legislators to again second-guess hundreds of years of common law in the name of victims' rights, with possible disastrous results in the long term.

Conclusion

A defendant's due process is not specified in either the Fifth or the Fourteenth Amendments but has had almost two hundred years of precedent to establish it, albeit the majority of the precedent has been in the last four decades. Due process is therefore founded on the logic of countless legal and political scholars. Victims' rights, however, only dates to the 1980s and is based on current public fervor.

Although both claim to be based on fairness, a defendant's due process is based on the carefully constructed federal Constitution and the concept of equity that has evolved over centuries of common law. Victims' rights are based on the public's current fear of crime and state legislators' desire to curry their voters' favor. . . . James Madison warned us to avoid a "tyranny of the masses." It makes no sense to abandon common and constitutional law with hastily made decisions, thus deserting a logic of separating the criminal and the civil cases that has evolved over the centuries.

REFERENCES

Bastian, L. (1995). "Crime Victimization 1993," *Bureau of Justice Statistics Bulletin.* May 1995 (NCJ-151658). Washington, DC: U.S. Department of Justice.

Booth v. Maryland 482 U.S. 496 (1987).

Bureau of Justice Statistics. (1994). *Crime Victimization in the United States, 1992.* March 1994 (NCJ-145125). Washington, DC: U.S. Department of Justice.

Bureau of Justice Statistics. (1992). *Crime Victimization in the United States: 1973–90 Trends.* December 1992 (NCJ-139564). Washington DC: U.S. Department of Justice.

Calvi, J. V. & Coleman, S. (1989). *American Law and Legal Systems.* Englewood Cliffs, NJ: Prentice Hall.

Davis, R. C. & Smith, B. E. (1994), "The Effects of Victim Impact Statements on Sentencing Decisions: A Test in an Urban Setting," *Justice Quarterly* 11: 453–469.

Doerner, W. G. & Lab, S. P. (1995). *Victimology.* Cincinnati, OH: Anderson.

Erez, E. & Tontodonato, P. (1990). "The Effect of Victim Participation in Sentencing on Sentence Outcome," *Criminology* 28:451–74.

Friedman, L. M. (1984). *American Law.* New York: W. W. Norton.

Gardner, T. J. & Anderson, T. M. (1992). *Criminal Law: Principles and Cases* (5th ed.). St. Paul, MN: West.

Glendon, M. A., Gordon, M. W. & Osakwe, C. (1985). *Comparative Legal Traditions.* St. Paul, MN: West.

Glick, H. R. (1983). *Courts, Politics, and Justice.* New York: McGraw-Hill.

Holman, J. E. & Quinn, J. F. (1996). *Criminal Justice: Principles and Perspectives.* St. Paul, MN: West.

Karmen, A. (1990). *Crime Victims: An Introduction to Victimology* (2nd ed.). Belmont, CA: Wadsworth.

Lusk, H. F., Hewitt, C. M., Donnell, J. D. & Barnes, A. J. (1978). *Business Law: Principles and Cases* (4th ed.). Homewood, IL: Richard D. Irwin.

McLeod, M. (1988). *The Authorization and Implementation of Victim Impact Statements.* Washington, DC: National Institute of Justice.

National Institute of Justice. (1996). "The Extent and Costs of Crime Victimization: A New Look." *National Institute of Justice Research Preview.* January 1996 (NCJ-155281). Washington, DC: U.S. Department of Justice.

Payne v. Tennessee, 111 S.Ct. 2597, 115 L.Ed. 2d. 720 (1991).

Reid, S. T. (1985. *Crime and Criminology* (4th ed.). New York: Holt, Rinehart, and Winston.

Samaha, J. (1996). *Criminal Procedure* (3rd ed.). St. Paul, MN: West.

Sheley, J. F. (1995). *Criminology* (2nd ed.). Belmont, CA: Wadsworth.

Smith, C. E. (1991). *Courts and the Poor.* Chicago, IL: Nelson-Hall.

Terrill, W. (1992). *World Criminal Justice Systems* (2nd ed.). Chicago, IL: Office of International Justice.

Torgia, C. E. (1972). *Wharton's Criminal Evidence: Volume I* (13th ed.). Rochester, NY: The Lawyers Co-operative Publishing Company.

United States v. Brown, Crim No. 83-372, 7/10/84 (E.D. Pa.).

United States v. Welden, 568 F. Supp. 516 (N.D. Ala., 1983).

Vetter, H. J. & Territo, L. (1984). *Crime and Justice in America.* St. Paul, MN: West.

Victim and Witness Protection Act of 1982, 18 U.S. Code 3579.

Chapter Eighteen

The Effects of Victim Impact Statements on Sentencing Decisions
A Test in an Urban Setting

Robert C. Davis
Barbara E. Smith

The victim movement, begun two decades ago, has matured. More than 5,000 programs now provide services to victims in crisis and victims involved in the criminal justice system (Davis and Henley 1990). The great majority of these programs are no longer tenuously funded demonstration projects, but entities with established places in local, state, and federal government budgets. As part of this maturation process, victim supporters have advocated not only that victims in the criminal justice system be treated well and kept informed, but also that they receive rights to participate in the court process (e.g., DuBow and Becker 1976; Goldstein 1982).

Early attempts to allow greater participation to victims were implemented without supporting legislation. Reformers persuaded criminal court officials to listen to victims' statements or to inform them of key decisions. Often these efforts were implemented as limited-term experiments (see, for example, Clark et al. 1984; Kerstetter and Heinz 1979). As time passed, however, victim advocates became more and more strongly convinced of the need for legislation mandating that officials listen to victims and/or inform them of court actions (e.g., Davis, Kunreuther, and Connick 1984).

From *Justice Quarterly*, 11(3) (1994): 453–470. Reprinted with permission of the Academy of Criminal Justice Sciences.

Victims' Rights Legislation and Victim Impact Statements

During the 1980s, state and federal governments implemented a vast array of legislation guaranteeing rights to victims in the criminal justice process. In 1981 the federal government took the initiative by declaring a Victims' Rights Week, to focus national attention on victim issues. Soon after that time, provisions were made to inform victims of proceedings in their cases and, in some instances, to consult them about the course of prosecution.

In 1982 the federal government established a Presidential Task Force on Victims of Crime. The Task Force recommended that victim impact statements—assessments of the physical, financial, and psychological effects of crime on individual victims—be taken and distributed to judges before sentencing. That recommendation was implemented when the 1982 Omnibus Victim and Witness Protection Act became law; it mandated that victim impact statements be provided at sentencing in federal cases.

By the mid-1980s, victim impact statements had become a popular vehicle for increased participation by victims. Victims' involvement at sentencing had been endorsed by the American Bar Association and the National Judicial College (Kelly 1990). By 1982, 12 states had passed impact statement laws (Hudson 1984). By 1984 the number had climbed to 22 (Davis, Fischer, and Paykin 1985); as of August 1987, 48 states had provisions authorizing some form of victim participation in conjunction with imposition of sentence (McLeod 1988:3).

Victim impact statements offer victims the opportunity to relate the harm done to them by the crime and (in some states) to express their concerns, in the expectation that this information will be considered in sentencing decisions. Supporters of victim impact statements have argued that the introduction of such statements will improve the sentencing process by making decisions conform more closely to the community's interests (Henderson 1985), by reminding officials of the human costs of crime (Kelly 1987), and by making sentences more proportional to the actual harm done by the offender (Rubel 1986).

Victim impact statements have met with criticism on several fronts, however. Some writers have expressed fear that allowing victims to participate may reduce judges' ability to withstand unreasonable public pressure (Rubel 1986). Others have been concerned about the potential for adding costs to the justice system or contributing to delay (Carrington and Younger 1979).

The most significant concern about victim impact statements and about victims' participation generally—is that gains for victims will result in costs for defendants. Some legal scholars have expressed fear that victim impact statements may reduce uniformity in sentencing and may introduce a greater degree of arbitrariness (Abramovsky 1986; Henderson 1985; Talbert 1988), or that they will result in harsher treatment of convicted offenders across the board (American Bar Association 1981). These issues have formed the basis of court challenges to the constitutionality of victim impact statements. In June

1987 the United States Supreme Court ruled in a 5–4 decision (*Booth v. Maryland* 1987) that victim impact statements are unconstitutional in capital cases. The court contended that "such information is irrelevant to a capital sentencing decision, and its admission creates a constitutionally unacceptable risk the jury may impose the death penalty in an arbitrary and capricious manner."

In June 1989, in a further development, the United States Supreme Court upheld a ruling by the South Carolina Supreme Court, overturning a death sentence for the murderer of a "self-styled" minister. Although *South Carolina v. Gathers* (1989) did not directly involve victim impact statements, the court's decision extended and reaffirmed the *Booth v. Maryland* decision by reiterating that "a sentence of death must be related to the moral culpability of the defendant." The Supreme Court upheld the lower court ruling, which maintained that the prosecution's description of the religious articles found near the minister's body constituted information about the victim's personal character, and as such was irrelevant to the sentencing decision.

Most recently, the Court revised itself and upheld state's rights to allow victim impact statements. In *Payne v. Tennessee* (1991) the Court decided that the Eighth Amendment erects no bar to victim impact evidence per se. The decision, however, still left open the possibility of excluding victim impact evidence if the evidence "is so unduly prejudicial that it tenders the trial fundamentally unfair."

Clearly, the arguments against victim impact statements are not frivolous, and public debate on their appropriateness is useful. That debate, however, underscores the need for a fuller understanding of whether and how such statements affect sentences. The concerns raised by opponents of victim impact statements—that they may result in more disparate or harsher sentences—can be subjected to empirical scrutiny by using social research methods.

To date we know of two attempts to bring empirical evidence to bear in examining how victim impact statements affect sentencing patterns. An earlier study by our research group (Davis 1985) attempted to look at the effect of these statements on sentences by using a quasi-experimental design. An impact statement procedure was introduced by the District Attorney's office in one of two felony court parts in Brooklyn that handled essentially identical cases. (Assignment of cases to one part or the other alternated, depending on the week when the cases were arraigned.) Comparison of the effects of victim impact statements on sentencing was thwarted, however, because of prosecutors' resistance to the program. Statements reached the judge in only one of the 10 cases designated to include impact statements. In the other nine cases, either prosecutors failed to obtain an impact statement or the statements never were forwarded to the presiding judge.

More significant is a correlational study by Erez and Tontodonato (1990). These authors looked at 500 Ohio felony cases; victim impact statements were taken in some of these but not in others, according to prosecutors' files. (The authors state that impact statements were solicited only when prosecutors expected a case to be tried.) Erez and Tontodonato compared sentencing in cases with and cases without impact statements after controlling for a number of potential confounding variables (e.g., seriousness of charge, defendant's record). They found that cases in which a victim impact statement was taken were more likely than those without a statement to result in a prison sentence than in probation. A second analysis showed no association between length of sentence, among those incarcerated, and whether a victim impact statement was taken.

The correlational approach used by Erez and Tontodonato makes the results of their study difficult to interpret. These researchers found large differences in offense seriousness and in many other measures between cases that had impact statements taken and cases without statements. Although the study controlled for many observed differences between the two groups of cases, the authors acknowledged that "[T]o completely control for such bias, it would be necessary to accurately model all previous selection decisions" (1990:462).

THE CURRENT STUDY

The only way to be confident that treatments are not confounded with outcomes is to assign cases randomly to treatments (Boruch and Wothke 1985). That approach was used in the current research. In this study, implemented in the Bronx County, New York Supreme (Felony) Court, cases were assigned randomly[1] to one of three treatments: (1) impact statements were taken and distributed to officials; (2) impact statement interviews were conducted, but no statement was prepared; and (3) no interview was conducted.

The most obvious approach to examining how victim impact statements affect sentences is by comparing sentences in cases in which court officials had access to victim impact statements with cases in which they did not have access. By framing the question in this way (as did Erez and Tontodonato), one addresses the defense issue of whether impact statements may lead officials to make harsher sentencing decisions generally.

Upon reflection, however, we thought it unlikely that cases with victim impact statements would routinely receive more severe sentences than those without. In the cases with impact statements, court officials should know more about the effect of crime on the victims. Sometimes that effect will be major, and officials will become more aware of the luridness of crimes, as Henderson (1985) suggests. Experience has shown, however (e.g., Davis 1985), that for many victims the impact of crime is relatively slight and short-lived; this is reflected in impact statements. Thus impact statements can either intensify or detract from officials' perceptions of the seriousness of a crime. (Erez & Tontodonato 1990 similarly point out that impact statements may increase proportionality in sentencing.) Impact statements, *on average*, could induce officials to impose harsher sentences only if officials normally assumed—in the absence of impact statements—that the effect of crime on victims was minimal. In other words, sentences would be harsher only if impact statements awakened officials to the fact that the cases they had been sentencing actually were considerably more heinous than they had imagined.

We thought this only a remote possibility. We believe that if victim impact statements affect sentences, their influence is likely to be more subtle. We think these statements have the potential to produce sentences that are more congruent with the harm done to victims. That is, the effect of crime on victims ought to be a more accurate predictor of sentences when impact statements are available to officials than when they are not. In cases in which the effect of crime on victims is serious, impact statements may induce officials to impose stiffer sentences than they would have imposed otherwise. (In particular we expected that restitution awards might be affected by victim impact information; this point was suggested by our earlier work. See Davis et al. 1984.) Conversely, in cases in which the effect of crime on victims is slight, impact statements may induce officials to impose lesser sentences than they would otherwise have imposed. Thus the net effect of impact statements on the overall harshness of sentences may be nil; at the same time, impact statements may result in sentences that reflect more accurately the harm done to victims, whether large or small.

With these thoughts in mind, we decided to examine whether impact statements altered the distribution of sentences—how many offenders were sentenced to conditional discharges versus probation versus short or long terms of incarceration. We then investigated whether impact statements result in sentences that reflect more accurately the harm done to victims.

Method

We conducted the experiment in the Bronx (New York) Supreme Court. Between July 1988 and April 1989, 293 victims of robbery, nonsexual assault, and burglary went through the intake procedure. We chose these crimes rather than homicides or rapes in order to obtain the sample size we needed for analysis.

Sixty-nine percent of the sample were victims of robbery, 21 percent were victims of physical assault or attempted homicide, and 10 percent were victims of burglary. Twenty percent of the victims knew the offender before the crime was committed. Only one in two of the victims had completed high school; 52 percent had household incomes of less than $15,000 per year. The median age of the sample was 25 years.

TREATMENTS

Each victim was assigned to one of three treatments as follows: (1) the victim was interviewed, and a victim impact statement was written and distributed (104 victims); (2) the victim was interviewed, but no statement was written (100 victims); (3) only the victim's name and address were recorded (89 victims).

Victims interviewed, statement written

Victims who received victim impact statements were told by a caseworker (hired by the research project specifically to prepare impact statements) that they would be interviewed and that a statement, based on the answers they gave to the questions in the interview, would be written up and distributed to the judge, the defense attorney, and the prosecutor. It was explained to these victims that because an impact statement would be prepared for them, court officials might have more information about how they were affected by the crime. Victims also were told that judges would have this information during sentencing. In addition, they were informed that someone would try to contact them by phone or letter in about one month in order to update the information in their statement.

The victim impact interview typically took 5 to 10 minutes. Victims were asked about the impact the of crime in five areas of their lives: physical impact, property loss or damage that occurred as a direct result of the crime, any subsequent financial loss (such as hospital bills or pay lost from time missed from work), psychological impact, and behavioral impact (any changes in routines or habits as a result of the crime—for example, whether they now had trouble sleeping, or took a different route to work). The victims' responses to the interview questions were rated on a scale of 1 to 3 according to the magnitude of the impact of the crime (from no impact to much impact in each category of response).

Victims in the impact statement group (like all the victims, regardless of their treatment group) were given a pamphlet from the victim assistance unit located in the Bronx Criminal Court. They were told that they could go to the victim assistance office if they needed information, referrals, or counseling.

The impact interview, containing the ratings of harm to the victim, was copied immediately, and a copy was turned over to the prosecutor assigned to the case. The caseworker then wrote a victim impact statement based on the victim's responses to the interview questions and distributed it to the prosecutor and the defense attorney through the head of the Supreme Court Bureau. Copies of the statement also were forwarded to the appropriate judge for each case. One copy was mailed out as soon as a judge was assigned to the case. Another copy was delivered to the chief clerk of the Supreme Court Bureau, who enclosed the statement with the file containing the presentence report and delivered it to the judge just before sentencing.

Victims interviewed, no statement written

This treatment provided a comparison group for determining whether the impact statement procedure resulted in sentences that reflected more accurately the harm done to the victim. The victims in this treatment group were administered the same interview as the victims for whom statements were written. The caseworker explained to them that she was conducting research to learn more about the experiences of crime victims and that she would like some background information about the effects of the crime on their lives. The interview questions were asked, but none of the descriptive responses were written down; victims' responses were rated on the same scale as was used for victims who went through the impact statement procedure.

These victims, like those in the first group, were given a victim assistance pamphlet. The prosecutor received a copy of a form that reflected only the victim's and the defendant's name, the charge, the docket number, and the ratings of harm to the victim. The prosecutors required this form, which defined the victim's role in the study, to document the fact that the victim had not disclosed discoverable information to the research project caseworker.

Victims in the control group

Only the names and addresses of these victims were recorded. The prosecutor received a memo saying that each of these victims was a control in our study, and that only his or her name and address were recorded. Like the victims in the other two groups, these victims received a victim assistance pamphlet.

PROCEDURES

Intake

All victims were brought by the prosecutor assigned to their case to the research project office after their grand jury testimony. Victims were assigned to treatments according to a log sheet that was prenumbered with victims' ID numbers and a corresponding treatment group for each number. The treatments were preassigned on the basis of a table of random numbers.

The random assignment was not begun, however, until after the first 32 victims were interviewed. These initial victims, all of whom gave impact statements, were intended originally to be a pretest group. We were forced to include them in the experiment, however, when intake proved to be far slower than anticipated. Analyses revealed no significant differences between these 32 victims and later victims assigned to the impact statement group in terms of type of charge (chi-square $= 2.43$, df $= 3$, n.s.), severity of charge (t [981 $= 0.09$, n.s.), victims education (t [72] $= 0.75$, n.s.), income (t [30] $= -1.13$, n.s.), or age (t [75] $= -1.26$, n.s.).

Rating system

As explained above, we developed a rating system to rank the severity of the various effects of the crime. This system included five categories for which the victim received a rating (physical injury, immediate property loss or damage, subsequent financial loss, psychological impact, and behavioral change). Victims in the impact statement and interview-only groups were rated in these five categories on a scale of 1 to 3: 1 represented no impact or not applicable, 2 represented some impact, and 3 represented, major impact. For example, a victim who reported having suffered no physical injury received a rating of 1 for the injury category, a victim with minor injuries received a 2, and a victim who had been hospitalized received a 3.

After much debate about how to rank psychological distress, we decided to ask the victims to rate themselves. As part of the interview we asked victims whether they had been feeling upset since the crime. If they said no, they received 1 on the rating scale. If they said, yes, we asked them to say whether they would describe themselves as "somewhat" or "very" upset, and subsequently gave them a 2 or a 3 on the scale, depending on their answer.

From these five individual measures of harm to the victim—physical harm, short-term financial impact, long-term financial impact, psychological harm, and behavioral changes—we created a composite harm measure. This summary variable was produced by summing the scores for the five component items.

Follow-up

Approximately one month after case intake, we attempted to contact victims from whom victim impact statements had been taken, in order to update the information in their statements. When new information was discovered, the impact statements were revised and an updated version was given to the judge at the time of sentencing. We tracked cases; when they had been disposed, we gathered information on sentences from files of the district attorney's office.

SUBGROUP DIFFERENCES

We examined the three treatment groups to ensure that they were comparable before undergoing the experimental manipulation. We found no differences between the three conditions in terms of type of charge (dichotomized as personal crimes, attempted murder and assault, versus property crimes, robbery and burglary: chi-square = 8.10, df = 6, n.s.); severity of charge (coded from 1 to 5, corresponding to the felony class of the charge, A through E: $F = 0.78$, df = 2,283, n.s.); victim/offender relationship (dichotomized as strangers versus acquaintances: chi-square = 0.26, df = 2, n.s.); offender's prior record (number of felony convictions: $F = 0.29$, df = 2,286, n.s.); victim's age ($F = 0.13$, df = 2,212, n.s.); victim's years of education ($F = 1.66$, df = 2,209, n.s.); or victim's annual household income ($F = 0.67$, df = 2,103, n.s.).

We further compared the impact statement group with the interview-only group on ratings of crime impact, based on information provided by victims during the interview. We found no differences between the two groups on the overall measure of crime impact ($F = 1.96$, df = 1,200, n.s.); behavioral impact ($F = 0.48$, df = 1,201, n.s.); immediate financial impact ($F = 0.09$, df = 1,201, n.s.); subsequent financial impact ($F = 0.05$, df = 1,201, n.s.); or psychological impact ($F = 1,26$, df = 1,200, n.s.). The differences between the two groups on physical impact fell just short of statistical significance ($F = 3.59$, df = 1,201, .05 < p < .10).

INTERVIEWS WITH CRIMINAL JUSTICE OFFICIALS

We asked assistant district attorneys to complete a 10-item survey concerning their experiences with and opinions of victim impact statements. Surveys were completed and returned by 22 of the 24 assistants in the unit. We also conducted semistructured interviews face-to-face with all seven judges who had received victim impact statements in at least three of their cases. Interviews averaged 20 to 30 minutes in length.

Results

Case dispositions for the 293 cases in the sample were as follows: 3 percent ended in bench warrants, 14 percent were dismissed, 3 percent were acquitted, 10 percent were sentenced to probation, 14 percent were sentenced to less than one year in jail, 7 percent were sentenced to one to three years in state prison, 32 percent were sentenced to three to six years in prison, and 14 percent were sentenced to more than six years in prison. Each of the analyses described below on the effects of victim impact statements uses the 229 cases in the sample in which convictions were won and sentences imposed.

EFFECTS ON OVERALL SENTENCING PATTERNS OF VICTIM IMPACT STATEMENTS

Table 1 compares sentences for cases in the three treatment groups. The table shows only minor variations between the groups in the frequencies of conditional discharges, sentences of probation, and various lengths of prison terms. The differences in the distribution of sentences between the groups did not approach statistical significance (chi-square = 10.86, df = 8, n.s.).[2,3]

As a further check on the effects of impact statements on sentence patterns, we conducted a multivariate logistic regression analysis. We dichotomized the sentence variable as "incarcerated" and "not incarcerated" and the treatment variable as "impact statement present in file" and "impact

Table 1
Effects of Treatments on Sentencing Patterns[a]

	Victim Impact Statement	Interview Only	Control	
Conditional Discharge	2%	1%	8%	
	(2)	(1)	(5)	n = 8
Probation	15%	11%	12%	
	(13)	(8)	(8)	n = 29
0–1 Years' Incarceration	20%	22%	10%	
	(17)	(17)	(7)	n = 41
1–3 Years' Incarceration	12%	7%	6%	
	(10)	(5)	(4)	n = 19
3–6 Years' Incarceration	41%	37%	42%	
	(35)	(28)	(28)	n = 91
6+ Years' Prison	11%	22%	22%	
	(9)	(17)	(15)	n = 41
	100%	100%	100%	
	(n = 86)	(n = 76)	(n = 67)	N = 229

[a]Excludes open cases, bench warrants, dismissals, and acquittals.

statement not present in file." (We combined cases in which no impact interview was held with cases in which aid interview was held, but an impact statement was not produced.)

We introduced into the analysis extraneous variables that were likely to influence the decision to incarcerate, including seriousness of the charge, type of charge, offender's prior record (number of convictions), and overall harm to the victim (the sum of the five individual impact measures—physical, psychological, behavioral, short-term financial, and long-term financial—each measured on a three-point scale).

The results of the logit analysis are displayed in table 2. Type of charge, severity of charge, and prior convictions all exerted significant influences on the decision to incarcerate. Yet neither the presence of an impact statement in the court file (the treatment variable) nor the overall victim harm measure approached statistical significance in the analysis.

Finally, we found no indications that victim impact statements increased the use of special conditions in sentencing. Restitution was not ordered in any case in our sample. We encountered only two judicial admonishments to offenders to keep away from victims, and one order for an offender to undergo drug rehabilitation.

Table 2
Multivariate Analysis of the Effects of Treatments on the Decision to Incarceration[a]

Effect	Estimated Coefficient	SE	Significance
Charge Type	−1.39	0.61	.02
Charge Severity	−0.50	0.25	.05
Convictions	0.43	0.21	.04
Victim Impact	0.16	0.14	.26
Treatment	0.68	0.56	.22

[a]Model chi-square = 16.12, df = 5, $p < .01$

EFFECTS OF VICTIM IMPACT STATEMENTS (VIS) ON THE CONGRUENCE BETWEEN VICTIM HARM AND SENTENCE SEVERITY

To determine whether impact statements result in sentences that reflect harm to victims more clearly, we compared treatment groups in terms of the relationship between harm to the victim and sentence severity, after controlling for other factors related to sentencing. If impact statements affected sentencing, we would expect to see a stronger relationship between harm to the victim and sentence severity in the group in which impact statements were taken than in the other two treatments, in which statements were not taken or distributed to officials.

Table 3
Effects of Victim Impact on Sentence Severity, by Treatment Group

Standardized Regression Coefficients	Regression Coefficients for VIS Cases	Regression Coefficients for Interview Only Cases
Step 1		
Prior convictions	0.10	0.09
Seriousness of charge	0.32*	0.56*
Nature of charge	0.21*	0.05
Step 2		
Victim impact	0.09	0.07
Increase in Variance Explained by Adding Victim Impact to Model	<2%	<1%
	F (1,77) = 1.64, ns	F (1,66) = 1.00, ns

*p < .01

To determine whether victim impact exerted a significant effect on sentence severity, we conducted a hierarchical regression analysis. In this case we were interested in differences, according to treatment group, in the effects of harm to the victim on severity of sentence (a six-point ordinal variable, coded as displayed in table 1). Again, we controlled statistically for the effects of extraneous variables likely to influence sentence severity, including seriousness of the charge, type of charge, and number of convictions. On the first step of the analysis, we entered nature of the charge, seriousness of the charge, and offender's prior record. On the next step, we entered the overall measure of harm to the victim.

The results are displayed in table 3. This table shows that seriousness of the charge and (for VIS cases only) nature of the charge are associated with sentence severity: sentences were more severe when charges were more serious and (for VIS cases only) when the charge involved an assault or attempted murder rather than a robbery or burglary. Harm to the victim, however, played little role in sentencing decisions after charge and criminal history were taken into account. Adding victim impact to the regression model increased the model's explanatory power by less than 2 percent. This was true for the victim impact statement group (F [1,77] = 1.64, n.s.) as well as for cases where no impact statement was taken or forwarded to officials F [1,66] = 1.00, n.s.).

We conducted the same type of analyses using the separate indicators of victim impact (representing physical, psychological, behavioral, and short- and long-term financial impact), and achieved essentially the same results: victim impact measures bore no consistent relationship to sentencing decisions, either for cases with or cases without victim impact statements.

Court Officials' Reactions to Victim Impact Statements

Interviews with prosecutors revealed that 15 of the 22 thought it appropriate to consider the impact of crime on victims in negotiating dispositions, but they did not think that victim impact statements added substantially to their knowledge of impact on the victim: only three prosecutors believed that impact statements usually contained more accurate or more detailed information than they would have obtained from their files on personal interviews with victims. Moreover, 13 of the 22 prosecutors thought that procedures for taking victim impact statements were problematic (some were worried that the defense could use the statements to point up inconsistencies in victims' testimony) or inconvenient (some expressed concern about subjecting victims to "yet another interview").

Interviews with the seven judges suggested that they had received and read our victim impact statements. All of the seven believed it was helpful to learn through the statements how victims were affected by crime. Unlike prosecutors, the judges stated that they did not normally receive information on victim impact through other channels, either from prosecutors or from victims themselves.

Yet prosecutors expressed skepticism about judges' interest in the impact of crime on victims. Only three of the 22 prosecutors believed that judges usually considered victim impact in sentencing decisions.

We inspected files from the district attorney's office to determine whether the copies of impact statements given to prosecutors had been placed in the files, and whether the envelopes containing the statements had been opened. We found that impact statements were missing in 37 percent of the files where they ought to have been included. In the files that contained impact statements, 53 percent of the statements had never been opened.

Conclusions

We began this study to address some of the controversial issues surrounding the use of victim impact statements. Do impact statements result in harsher sentences? In sentences that reflect more accurately the harm done to victims?

In one important respect, our results back up the advocates of victim impact statements: we found no support for those who argue against these statements on the grounds that their use places defendants in jeopardy and may result in harsher sentences. In this respect, our data stand in contrast to the findings reported by Erez and Tontodonato (1990), who found that victim impact statements were associated with an increased likelihood of incarceration. The discrepancy between the two studies may reflect differences between courts in receptivity to such statements. Again, it may exist because Erez and Tontodonato used a weaker, correlational research design: their study gives no guarantee that cases in which victim impact statements were taken were equivalent in other respects to cases without impact statements, even after the researchers controlled for some potential confounding variables.

Our data, however, also may give advocates of victim impact statements cause for concern. These statements did not produce sentencing decisions that reflected more clearly the effects of crime on victims. Nor did we find much evidence that—with or without impact statements—sentencing decisions were influenced by our measures of the effects of crime on victims, once the charge and the defendant's prior record were taken into account. (This finding replicates the results of a study by Hernon and Forst 1983, which concluded that harm to the victim had little effect on sentencing decisions.) Yet it is also true that the impact of crime on victims is incorporated into charging decisions: more serious charges tend to reflect greater harm to victims, and our analysis found severity of charge to be highly predictive of sentences.

Interviews conducted with officials helped to explain why impact statements had no discernible effect on sentencing. Although judges professed to be interested in the impact of crime on victims, prosecutors thought, at best, that judges considered such information only occasionally. Also, although most of the prosecutors interviewed said that victim impact ought to be considered regularly, judges reported that prosecutors rarely related such information to them. Moreover, prosecutors clearly believed that information contained in victim impact statements was not especially useful to them, as evidenced by their frequent failure to incorporate the statements into their case files and their failure to open the statements that had been placed in case files.[4]

Probably the truth is that officials have established ways of making decisions which do not call for explicit information about the impact of crime on victims. They make sentencing decisions according to established norms based on the nature of the charge and the defendant's character (Rosett and Cressey 1976): in this process, officials may believe that the charge itself often conveys enough information about harm to the victim to meet the purposes of sentencing. Inducing officials to consider specific measures of victim impact entails changing well-established habits, and a brief experiment is not likely to do that.

Our conclusions about the effects of impact statements on sentencing are limited by the fact that we conducted the research on a new rather than a well-established program. Possibly it takes a long time for officials to accept and incorporate impact statements into the sentencing process—not the few short months available to us in this experiment. Moreover, the results we obtained in the Bronx may not apply equally well to lower-volume suburban or rural courts. Thus replications of our experiment are needed at other sites. Moreover, we examined common felony crimes—robbery, assault, and burglary—so that we could generate a sample large enough to permit tests of statistical inference. It may be that impact statements have greater effects for the most serious crimes—homicides, rapes, and aggravated assaults.

Pending additional research, our experiment raises troubling questions about the viability of impact statements as a vehicle for victims' participation in the court process. These statements have become the preferred method for allowing victims greater participation. They are less controversial than other means of victim participation might be, and they are relatively inexpensive to administer. For these reasons, victim advocates have pushed hard for statutes to mandate their use. But if impact statements do not give victims a meaningful voice, what gains have victims really made over the past 20 years in having their concerns represented to the court? This question deserves to be considered carefully by those interested in making the justice process responsive to the concerns of victims and other citizens.

NOTES

[1] In fact, we began the random assignment process after the first 32 cases had been taken into the sample. As described . . . , all of the first 32 cases were assigned to one of the treatment conditions.

[2] In calculating the chi-square value, we combined conditional discharges and probation sentences (the first two rows of table 1) in order to avoid expected cell frequencies less than 5.

[3] Our thanks to an anonymous reviewer who pointed out that at least one partitioning of the data would lead to an alternate conclusion. If sentences are dichotomized into six or fewer years in prison versus more than six years and if the two control groups are combined, sentences involving victim impact statements are less likely to be long-term than sentencing decisions reached without victim impact statements (chi-square = 5.1, df = 1, p = .05).

[4] One could argue that the experiment is invalidated by the fact that many impact statements were not read by prosecutors. We disagree for several reasons. First, judges also received copies of the statements, and judges are the officials who directly pass sentence on convicted offenders. Second, even if statements had been present and opened in prosecutors' files in all cases in the experiment, one still could question whether prosecutors gave them serious attention. (Indeed, prosecutors' or judges' apathy toward impact statements is an important factor that would have gone undetected in earlier studies of the effects of victim impact statements on sentencing.) In our opinion, our finding that prosecutors often did not attend to statements when they were available is a legitimate and interesting outcome of the intervention we designed.

REFERENCES

Abramovsky, A. (1986) "Crime Victims' Rights." *New York Law Journal*, February 3, pp. 1 and 3.

American Bar Association (1981) *Victim/Witness Legislation.* Report of the Victim Witness Assistance Project, Criminal Justice Section. Washington, DC: American Bar Association.

Boruch, R. F. and W. Wothke (1985) "Seven Kinds of Randomization Plans for Designing Field Experiments." In R. F. Boruch and W. Wothke (eds.), *Randomization and Field Experimentation*, pp. 95–113. San Francisco: Jossey-Bass.

Carrington, F., and E. E. Younger (1979) "Victims of Crime Deserve More Than Pity." *Human Rights* 8:10–15.

Clark, T., J. Housner, J. Hernon, E. Wish and C. Zelinski (1984) "Evaluation of the Structured Plea Negotiation Project." Report of the Institute for Law and Social Research to the National Institute of Justice.

Davis, R. C. (1985) "First Year Evaluation of the Victim Impact Demonstration Project." Unpublished report, Victim Services Agency, New York.

Davis, R. C., P. Fischer, A. Paykin (1985) "Victim Impact Statements: The Experience of State Probation Officers." *Journal of Probation and Parole* 16:18–20.

Davis, R. C. and M. Henley (1990) "Victim Service Programs." In A. Lurigio, W. Skogap, and R. Davis (eds.), *Victims in the Criminal Justice System*, pp. 157–171. Beverly Hills: Sage.

Davis, R. C., F. Kunreuther, and E. Connick (1984) "Expanding the Victim's Role in the Criminal Court Dispositional Process: The Results of an Experiment." *Journal of Criminal Law and Criminology* 2:491–505.

Dubow, F. and T. Becker (1976) "Patterns of Victim Advocacy." In W. F. McDonald (ed.), *Criminal Justice and the Victim*, pp. 147–164. Beverly Hills: Sage.

Erez, E. and P. Tontodonato (1990) "The Effect of Victim Participation in Sentencing on Sentence Outcome." *Criminology* 28:451–74.

Goldstein, A. S. (1982) "Defining the Role of the Victim in Criminal Prosecution." *Mississippi Law Journal* 52:515–61.

Henderson, L. N. (1985) "The Wrongs of Victims' Rights." *Stanford Law Review* 37:937–1021.

Hernon, J. C. and B. Forst (1984) "The Criminal Justice Response to Victim Harm." Report of the Institute for Law and Social Research to the National Institute of Justice.

Hudson, P. S. (1984) "The Crime Victim and the Criminal Justice System: Time for a Change." *Pepperdine Law Review* 11:23.

Kelly, D. P. (1987) "Victims." *Wayne Law Review* 34(1): 69–86.

———. (1990) "Victim Participation in the Criminal Justice System." In A. Lurigio, W. Skogan, and R. Davis (eds.), *Victims and the Criminal Justice System*, pp. 172–187. Beverly Hills: Sage.

Kerstetter, W. A. and A. M. Heinz (1979) "Pretrial Settlement Conference: An Evaluation." Report of the University of Chicago Law School to the National Institute of Justice.

McLeod, M. (1988) *The Authorization and Implementation of Victim Impact Statements.* Washington, DC: National Institute of Justice.

Rosett, A. and D. Cressey (1976) *Justice by Consent: Plea Bargains in the American Courthouse.* New York: Lippincott.

Rubel, M. C. (1986) "Victim Participation in Sentencing Proceedings." *Criminal Law Quarterly* 28:226–50.

Talbert, P. (1988) "The Relevance of Victim Impact Statements to the Criminal Sentencing Decision." *UCLA Law Review* 36:199–202.

CASES CITED

Booth v. Maryland, 482 U.S. 496 (1987).
Payne v. Tennessee, 111 S. Ct. 2597, 115 L. Ed. 2d 720 (1991).
S. Carolina v. Gathers, 490 U.S. 805 (1989).

Stereotyping and Prejudice
Crime Victims and the Criminal Justice System

Emilio C. Viano

Victimization as a Challenge for Change

For the purposes of our discussion, a victim is any individual harmed or damaged by another or by others, who perceives him- or herself as harmed, who makes this experience public and seeks assistance and redress, who is recognized as harmed and therefore is eligible for assistance by public, private, or community agencies. Institutions, corporations, commercial establishments, and groups of people can also be victimized and legitimately claim victim status.

The impact of stereotypical beliefs about the victim is felt at the very beginning of the victimization experience by the very victim as he or she makes the transition from suffering harm to seeing him- or herself as a victim. One of the major obstacles to recognizing victimization, even on the part of the victim, is the silent public tolerance of the phenomenon resulting from a system of values, beliefs, mores, and laws that actively support, justify, and legitimize victimization. At times, this silent tolerance is enshrined into a formal code of honor and behavior. The tacit acceptance of victimization can be the result of a "nonconscious ideology," a system of beliefs and attitudes that are implicitly accepted but remain outside conscious awareness because of prevailing stereotypes. It can also be due to the fact that alternatives are sometimes not available, possible, or even imaginable. In order to avoid the surfacing of troubling cognitive dissonance, the awareness of injustices and

From *Studies on Crime and Crime Prevention*, 5(2) (1996): 182–202. Copyright © Scandanavian University Press. Used with permission.

prevarications is blotted out and an apparent normalcy is restored by legitimizing and incorporating the victimization into the accepted values, mores, and ways of life of a particular society (Viano, 1989).

Victims themselves are brought up to accept and internalize such patterns as the way things are, at times even supporting them and opposing reforms that would be to their benefit because of intricate social and psychological dynamics stemming from, and in turn strengthening, societal archetypes (see, e.g., LaFree, 1989:28, 29, 51, 65). The few who become aware of the abnormal situation and speak up are ignored, ridiculed, silenced, crushed, cast away, declared insane, or driven to insanity. It often takes drastic social changes to shake the status quo and bring relevant issues into the open. This in turn educates the victims about their victimization, heightens their awareness, encourages their quest for change and, most of all, leads them to see themselves as victims of an unjust system.

The realization that "this should not have happened to me: I did not deserve it or cause it" constitutes the key psychological dynamic in this complex process. A major reason why people have difficulty in seeing themselves as victims is the novel, threatening, and shattering nature of the experience of being victimized. Normally, an atmosphere of safety and social harmony supports our activities. Being victimized is the dawning of a new configuration of meaning which occurs in a lived experience through a developmental process (Wertz, 1985). The disbelief expressed in victims' reports indicates that it is still a relatively empty sort of quasi-reality. It has not been fully articulated, realized, and understood.

Victimization strikes the victim's sphere of "ownness." Involved here are not indifferent or trivial matters but the victim's personal world whose center is the victim and others intimately related to the victim. The ability to overcome stereotypes, seeing oneself as a victim, and accepting one's victimization is important for another crucial reason: it is a prerequisite for the recovery process to begin. Understanding dissipates shock and confusion and opens the way for the struggle to overcome (Viano, 1989).

Cultural values also influence which forms of harm are readily and clearly accepted as being injurious so that people can see themselves as having been victimized. For example, throughout history, crimes against property have by and large been considered more detrimental to victims than crimes of violence or physical harm. The reason is that being the victim of a crime against property requires one to be part of the propertied class which in turn yields considerable political influence. On the contrary, anyone, and particularly those at the bottom of the social ladder with little, if any, political clout, can be the victim of a violent crime. Psychological harm is even more difficult to identify, attribute, label, and validate. How do we take into account individual variations in the perceptions and evaluation of seriousness and harm? How can we reach a consensus on a general continuum of victimization that will ultimately govern society's recognition and intervention in a standardized and agreed manner? Harms affecting a large number of people and harms caused by impersonal entities are similarly difficult.

The implications for social policy are clear. Approaching victims as individuals involved in discrete situations leads to interventions that are meant to alleviate the discomfort and suffering of victims but do not challenge or attempt to change (1) the system that is producing and will continue to produce more victims and that will even revictimize again and again those who are healed, and (2) the underlying values that support such a system.

There might even be collusion between the healer and the victimizer in perpetuating the cycle of victimization. The healer might, without challenging the inequity of the system, (1) mold the victim so that he or she accepts the unjust situation and (2) change the victim's behavior accordingly so that the victim can escape harm at the individual level. This process of acceptance and accommodation ultimately recognizes, legitimizes, and increases the victimizer's power and grip.

Still from a policy perspective, one could question whether it is always desirable to make people aware of their status as victims if they are not aware of it and have adapted to injustice and oppression. Are there circumstances when this may cause more harm than good? How should this process be conducted to minimize additional trauma? What if there are no available remedies, so that the awareness of victimization is useless or, worse, only fuels rage and actually inflicts additional pain? What if it leads to isolated and fruitless attempts at changing the situation, attempts that will result only in more repression by the victimizer and hopelessness in the victim? Is it right to cause dissatisfaction and raise false hopes when one cannot effectively introduce change or guarantee some success? (Viano, 1989).

After an individual has recognized an experience as victimization, he or she must still decide what to do about it. Several formal and informal avenues are open to the victim. Victims often validate their experience and their conclusions with someone they trust, a family member, friend, spouse, neighbor, doctor, or priest more often than one would think. Such validation strongly influences whether they will ultimately notify official agencies of society such as the police. Stereotypical perceptions of how society will react to the news of the victimization will determine how people respond to the victim's revelation and whether or not they will encourage him or her to seek official validation and assistance (Viano, 1994).

Many variables affect the victim's decision to publicly report the victimization such as, for example, the perceived response the victim will receive from the police, the damage or harm suffered, the relationship with the victimizer, the obstacles, expense and time involved in reporting, and the fear of being ridiculed or of suffering retaliation and revenge. Thus, social, psychological, and cultural factors and perceptions may stop a victim from publicly claiming the status of victim. At times, this can lead to continued victimization with the victimizer taking advantage of the lack of action on the part of the victim which, in turn, is often based on the victim's perception of society's reluctance, unwillingness, or inability to intervene on his or her behalf. Domestic violence is a clear case in point.

Cultural Stereotypes and Victimization

Commonly held beliefs and stereotypes about shared responsibility deeply influence public attitudes, beliefs, and policies toward crime victims. Popular images and public opinion that stress the difference between innocent and deserving victims versus those considered culpable and undeserving influence the formulation of priorities in the criminal justice and social service systems and thus that of policies, laws, and interventions (Karmen, 1990:106; Viano, 1990:7–8).

A basic factor militating against victims is the cultural value placed on winning and on being successful and in control in today's society. In the eyes of many, a victim is a loser, albeit an innocent one.

Moreover, the criminal justice process has been aptly described as a series of "status degradation ceremonies" (Garfinckel, 1956). While it has generally been assumed that this degradation applies only to the offender, it can also have an impact on the victim. As a result, the victim may have to pay a price when acknowledging and reporting victimization. This theme has been richly and originally explored by Kristin Bumiller in her study of anti-discrimination law entitled *The Civil Rights Society* (1988). Bumiller was intrigued by research showing that people who perceive themselves as being discriminated against are less likely than others who feel harmed to complain or seek legal redress (Miller & Sarat, 1980–81). In her analysis of victims' motivation to use or not use antidiscriminatory statutes, she argues that there are powerful psychological obstacles preventing discrimination victims from perceiving acts of discrimination as violating legally recognizable rights and from asserting such rights if they do. Bumiller (1988:99) points out that to become a plaintiff in an antidiscrimination case, a person must acknowledge and state that he has been victimized. In other words, the very act of utilizing the law requires that one assume the label of "victim" of a prohibited action. However, many factors deter people from taking on the "mask of the victim" (Bumiller, 1988:62–64).

One such factor is that the identity of the people for whom antidiscriminatory laws were written is already threatened or attacked by racism, sexism, "ageism," homophobia, and other forms of hostility. To face and deal with these threats, these people develop an "ethic of survival" which centers on their ability to cope on their own with unfair situations (Bumiller, 1988:78–97). Claiming publicly the status and role of victim, as the law requires, threatens their sense of mastery and control over adversity (Bumiller, 1988:93–95).

Another reason is their fear and mistrust of the law and of the power and influence of the organizations against which they must assert their claims. The law appears alien and uncertain; and their adversaries seem powerful and well connected. Since their odds of winning are low, regardless of how strongly they believe themselves to have been victimized, the price to be paid in order to use the law for redress is too high. Thus, the law and the justice system, instead of being seen as positive forces for redress, are seen as threatening the dignity of the complainant and involving a high risk of losing one's autonomy and control. Even if the complaint is successful, the law and justice system is unable to deliver. Clearly, the impact that these views can have on crime victims seeking justice can be negative and discouraging.

Procedural Reforms Not Sufficient

Given the basic nature of these attitudes, procedural reforms and other victim and witness services facilitating access to the justice system alone may not have much positive impact. Procedural reform, which is often what much legal reform consists of, is insufficient to address the needs and dilemmas of many victims. What is needed is substantive reform addressing the fundamental flaws that effectively bar victims from seeking justice. For example, in societies where setting the limits of sexual activity is the woman's responsibility, fornication a serious crime, and rape no excuse, one can readily understand a victim's reluctance to report her sexual victimization. Reporting it could be the equivalent of passing a death sentence on herself or at least seriously jeopardizing her own social status, respectability, desirability, and marriageability in the community, and the social status of her family (Viano, 1989:10; Cairney, 1995:310–13). In other words, where blaming the victim is prevalent and even internalized by the victims themselves, the psychological and social price to be paid for reporting may be too high and the gain uncertain or lacking.

Similarly, the victims' perception or realization that they will not be believed can effectively close avenues for reporting and seeking redress and possibly lead to their prolonged victimization. Moreover, the social devaluation stemming from reporting may make the victim an easy target for harassment and continued victimization by the original victimizer or others. Examples of this situation include incest, sexual harassment or assault, domestic violence, and elder abuse (Viano, 1995).

The reluctance to claim the status and role of victim is not confined to individuals. Corporations, businesses, even governments may not report being victimized in order to maintain a certain image or for other practical reasons. The acquiescence of small and even large businesses to the extortionist demands of organized crime or of corrupt customs, government, or police officials also reflects many of the same dynamics affecting the willingness of individual victims to acknowledge and claim their role as victim and seek redress (Viano, 1989:10–11).

The "Second Victimization" by the Justice System

The negative impact which the justice system has on the victim of crime seeking redress has often been described as a "second victimization" (Newburn, 1995:146, 155; Madigan & Gamble, 1991; Williams & Holmes, 1981). This victimization is particularly poignant when it is based on personal characteristics of the victim which should have no relevance whatever on legal decisions. With few exceptions (e.g., sexual assault, claims of self-defense), the character and behavior of the victim are supposed to be legally irrelevant to the question of whether or not the accused broke the law. However, research indicates that they have a definite psychological impact (see, for example, Landy & Aronson, 1969). Studies have shown that the physical attractiveness of the defendant can have an impact on mock jurors' verdicts (e.g., Mitchell & Byrne, 1973; Brooks et al., 1975; Sigall & Ostrove, 1975; Solomon & Schopler, 1978). These findings support the general punishment principle stating that the more attractive the rule-transgressor is to the victim (and to society), the weaker the punishment response will be (Heider, 1958; Byrne, 1971; Vidmar & Miller, 1980).

As to the effect of the attractiveness of the victim, the findings of Landy and Aronson (1969) suggest greater punitiveness against an accused whose victim is attractive. There is also abundant anecdotal evidence that a victim's characteristics and behavior have an effect on jurors' deliberations. A type of reasoning often mentioned is that if the victim had been more careful, the crime would never have occurred. These comments indicate that jurors feel that the responsibility for a crime should be shared by both the defendant and the victim. In other words, jurors deciding criminal cases actually use the civil law concept of contributory negligence.

Kalven and Zeisel's (1966) study of judges showed that a victim's general character, negligence, carelessness, or disreputable behavior often influence juries' verdicts, even when clearly excluded by the judge's instructions. Kerr (1978) explored the effects of a victim's physical attractiveness and responsibility on mock jurors' verdicts. Responsibility was operationalized in terms of the victim taking precautions to avoid victimization. Victim attractiveness was manipulated using facial photographs of a female victim. Kerr (1978:481) found that when the blameless victim was beautiful (and therefore well-liked by the mock jurors) less evidence of guilt was needed for conviction than when she was unattractive. However, when the victim was clearly careless and therefore at least facilitated the crime, conviction was not affected by the victim's attractiveness. Female mock jurors required less evidence to convict when the victim was blameless, regardless of her appearance (see also LaFree, 1989:108, 217, 227).

One of the classic stereotypes well established in popular belief, anecdotes, and jokes that influences negatively the reaction of the public and of the justice system toward the victim, is that of the absentminded victim of car theft who facilitated the commission of the crime by leaving the keys in the car's ignition. This stereotypical view continues to thrive even though today the neighborhood youth "borrowing" the unattended and easily available car for joyriding has long been supplanted by professional, commercial, and organized auto thieves. Car owners now may be blamed for parking costly cars on the public streets instead of using attended lots and garages and for not purchasing and installing expensive antitheft devices, even though police and experts agree that their effectiveness is limited or quickly defeated. It is actually the automobile industry that could make cars less attractive for the lucrative used car parts market, for example, by stamping the car's serial number on more sections of the car than just the dashboard. Instead, the manufacturers often blame the supposedly careless car owners perhaps to deflect attention away from themselves that design, build, and sell cars that are easily stolen (Karmen, 1981).

━━━━

The Impact of Stereotypes on Criminal Procedure

The state and its many agencies are rarely seen as a gendered milieu. Yet research . . . indicates that gender is a major characteristic of the state and a principal area for its activities (Burstyn, 1983; Ursel, 1986; MacKinnon, 1989; Smart, 1989; Franzway, Court & Connell, 1989; Connell, 1990). Indeed, when one examines personnel, style, and function, the state, and particularly its coercive apparatus, the military and the criminal justice system, are masculine-dominated institutions (Messerschmidt, 1993:155). In recent years the criminal justice system has come under repeated criticism for its failure to protect women against physical violence, sexual abuse and harassment and for its own poor, clumsy, and even hostile treatment of the victims (Gelsthorpe & Morris, 1990; Newburn, 1995:146, 155, 157). These shortcomings are rarely the outcome of deficiencies in the substantive law, with the exception of marital rape. Instead, they derive primarily from the discriminatory impact that stereotypical assumptions and beliefs have on the discretionary decision making of police and prosecutors (see LaFree, 1989:79). In the case of domestic violence, for example, the police reluctance to intervene is explained by the perception, mostly unsupported by research, that the threat to the officers' personal safety is very high and by the widespread belief that such work is not "real" police work (Parnas, 1972; Pahl, 1982; Smith, 1989; Sherman, 1992; Newburn, 1995).

It is not surprising therefore that several studies of sexual assault and wife battering have connected the high rate of attrition in these cases with the deeply rooted, institutionalized sexism of the justice system (Parnas, 1973; Russell, 1983, 1984; Freeman, 1984; Wright, 1984; Walker, 1989). Research has also studied the processes used in making judgments of responsibility for rape (Abbey, 1987). Assignment of responsibility and blame can powerfully affect the incident itself through the victim's and the rapist's understanding of each other's intentions beforehand, their subsequent views of their own and each other's blameworthiness, of their social backing or stigma, and the impressions of the jurors about all those implicated.

Various stereotypes are reflected in law enforcement's approach to the victims of rape and in the victims' response to police intervention. It is often said that police officers are insensitive and judgmental in dealing with victims. Anecdotal literature on police attitudes and response to victims of rape generally states that victims are regularly met with hostile, callous, and uncaring treatment by the police. Susan Brownmiller in *Against Our Will* (1975:352) wrote that "despite their knowledge of the law they are supposed to enforce, the male police mentality is often identical to the stereotypical views of rape that are shared with the rest of the male culture. The tragedy for the rape victim is that the police officer is the person who validates her victimization" (see also Germaine Greer, 1975:382; Hurst, 1977:116; Katz & Mazur, 1979; Chambers & Millar, 1983; Feinman, 1994).

The empirical research literature depicts a more positive view of police behavior, even though the data indicate that some officers are influenced by the circumstances of the victim, the attacker, and the act itself. Galton (1975) studied the criteria used by police investigators in Texas to evaluate rape complaints. He found that investigators hold rape victims to a higher standard of behavior than is required by the law. Gottesman (1977) evaluated the effect that training may have on police attitudes toward rape. She reported that most officers (95%) responded positively to the training which, for instance, increased their understanding of rape victims. However, she also found that the belief that victims are partially responsible for the attack because of their dress or behavior remained basically unchanged by the training.

Feild (1978) studied attitudes towards rape among police (254 agents), citizens, and rape counselors. A factor analysis of the data collected identified the following major elements: woman's responsibility in rape prevention; sex as motivation for rape; severe punishment for rape; victim precipitation of rape; normality of rapists; power as motivation for rape; favorable perception of a woman after rape; and resistance as woman's role during rape. After analyzing data collected by means of a questionnaire from 54 criminal justice system workers in the Seattle, Washington area, Feldman, Summers and Palmer (1980:38) concluded that the unsympathetic treatment that rape victims often complain about is connected with "beliefs held by the criminal justice system members which tend to place blame and responsibility on the victim." They also found that police, judges, and prosecutors had similar beliefs about causes of rape and ways to reduce its frequency. Social service personnel held significantly different beliefs.

LeDoux and Hazelwood (1991) analyzed questionnaires returned by 2,170 county and municipal law enforcement officers from a representative sample of police departments throughout the United States. Their analysis of the data showed that police are not typically insensitive to the suffering of rape victims. However, they are suspicious of victims who show certain behaviors like previous and willing sex with the defendant, or who "provoke" rape through their appearance or actions. What partly affects police acceptance of reports of rape is their construction of "good" and "bad" rapes. Moreover, officers as a group were confused as to whether rape is a sex crime. Significantly, the study showed that there is still a small but persistent number of police officers who strongly agree with statements like "Nice women do not get raped," or "Most charges are unfounded. "At times, these stereotypes are reinforced when the police are trained to recognize the crime. The content and approach of this training seems more focused on discrediting sexual assault victims than on bringing their attackers to justice. Reportedly, a senior U.S. Air Force investigator responsible for training other criminal investigators, told them at a seminar in Alaska that "50–60 percent of all sexual assault reports are false." He also shared with the trainees a rape victim "checklist . . . to aid in establishing the falsity of the report." (*Washington Post,* October 2, 1992). Clearly, these police officers are prejudiced against rape victims. Fundamentally, the root of all of this may very well be that police see little harm in most rapes as long as there is no overt physical injury. The consequence is that police declare many rape reports to be false complaints and minimize their impact on the victims. This way, police culture simply mirrors the attitudes, beliefs, and wishes of the larger society which also depends on myths to deal with sexual assault (see also LaFree, 1989:26, 73, 76, 87). Efforts have been undertaken to fashion analytical models to give structure to the varying number of cues that can affect rape judgments (Pugh, 1983; Shotland & Goodstein, 1983; Wiener and Vodanovich, 1986). Langley et al. (1991:356) asked 177 undergraduate volunteers to read one of six randomly distributed scenarios describing a situation of forced sexual intercourse in a dating situation and then to complete a questionnaire assessing date rape attribution. The findings show that the victim was blamed more and judged as desiring sexual intercourse with later onset of protest, when her attacker used less force, and in general by male respondents. Female respondents were more likely than male respondents to rate the incident as violent, regardless of the actual violent content.

The precariousness of the victim's position in the justice system also stems from the application of evidentiary and procedural law requirements in court. For example, even though the corroboration requirement in cases of sexual offenses applies equally to both genders, its effect is much bigger on women since they are more vulnerable to sexual assaults. It is where the law is susceptible to wide judicial discretion that the problem of legal bias is most serious—to the point, at times, of subverting the legislative intent. Provisions of the "rapeshield" laws that limit the admissibility of evidence related to the sexual history of the victim in rape cases are at times effectively annulled by adverse judicial interpretations of the law (Adler, 1985). Implicit in the judges' and prosecutors' behavior is the belief that a victim must demonstrate "moral worthiness" before she can lodge a complaint about this type of criminal assault. That the same is not expected of victims of other offenses against the person, like armed robbery, or that there is no suggestion in those cases that they "asked for it" indicates the depth of bias against victims of rape (Nixon, 1992:41).

The decision "not to enforce" often made by police and by prosecutors probably affects the largest number of victims. It is often overlooked for various reasons. Among them are our society's emphasis on commission rather than omission, the "grayness" of the area which makes detection and research on it difficult and time consuming, and resistance by the system that considers any scrutiny of its operations a violation of its operational freedom and an unwelcome meddling by people who do not understand the realities of law enforcement.

Reasons for not enforcing the law vary greatly, thus reflecting the vast discretionary powers of police and prosecutors (Goldstein, 1960). For example, a decision may be made to trade enforcement for information, or not to investigate felonious assaults unless the victim signs a complaint, something that then the victim is discouraged from doing in order to reduce the pressures of police and prosecutorial work. At times, it may simply be a matter of timing and convenience as when police do not make an arrest because it would delay their getting off work or require a court appearance on their day off.

Most importantly, the private value systems of police officers can greatly influence policy- and decision-making as when, for example, police assume that violence is an acceptable means of solving interpersonal disputes and maintaining domestic "tranquility" among certain groups, most often immigrants from different cultures, . . . [people of color], and the very poor. Many police officers dichotomize a community into normal and deviant populations. Lower working class and racial minorities are more likely than middle-class whites to be lumped into the deviant category. Thus, sexual assault, wife beating, and other types of victimization among the former are taken less seriously by police than those happening among the latter (Ferraro, 1989). As a matter of fact, the police have often and long been accused of a lesser response to complaints made by lower-working class and racial minorities, especially black women (Young, 1986; MacLean and Milovanovic, 1991). Thus, arrest policies are mediated by class and race police stereotypes.

Police and/or the prosecutor may also anticipate on the basis of their own perceptions and prejudices that the victim will not cooperate with the investigation and prosecution of the case and thus dismiss or decide to *nolle prosequi* the crime. The influence of stereotypical values held by the police in cases of domestic violence, leading to nonenforcement and deprivation of protection for the victims, at times with fatal consequences, has been well documented in various jurisdictions. Studies in Canada (Burris & Jaffe, 1983; Ursel & Farough, 1985; Jaffe et al., 1986), England (Edwards, 1986a & b; Shapland & Hobbs, 1987), Australia (Hatty & Sutton, 1986a & b), and Ireland (Casey, 1987) have all criticized police response to domestic violence which is still not considered by many to be a "real" crime. Police neglect and indifference have led to a number of successful lawsuits in various jurisdictions in the United States mandating the police to follow a full enforcement policy and arrest those accused of family violence (see, for example, *Bruno v. Codd* 90 Misc. 2d 1047, 396 N.Y. S. 2d 974, Sup. Ct. 1977 and *Tracey Thurman et al. v. the City of Torrington CT* 595 F. Supp. 1521, Dist. Conn., 1984).

A vicious cycle thus develops as a consequence of the police and prosecutor's beliefs and behavior. Anticipating rejection or worse at the hand of the system, victims often do not report their victimization. This, in turn, not only makes them more vulnerable to predators but is used to justify adverse justice policies because of the paucity of cases and the perceived lack of cooperation.

Sentencing is another phase of criminal procedure in which judges have traditionally enjoyed wide discretionary power. While sentencing guidelines and minimum mandatory sentences are now being introduced in the United States at the federal and some states' levels to curtail such discretion, judges still enjoy considerable freedom. Often, judges have imposed minor penalties on men for serious crimes against women (Jeffreys & Radford, 1984; Radford, 1984). Generally, the clemency of judges is frequently legitimized by downplaying the harm done or by blaming the victim for "contributory negligence" or "provocative behavior" (Newburn,1995:155–56). This approach reflects an underlying set of beliefs about female sexuality that is pervasive in the legal field and in judicial thinking. It is most apparent in cases of domestic violence where women have found to their cost that the law does not always deliver the protection it promises (Dobash & Dobash, 1980; Edwards, 1984; Pahl, 1985; Gelles & Fedrick-Cornell, 1985). It is also found in cases of incest where the victims are either denied access to legal redress because of restrictive statutes of limitation or find such recourse difficult or routinely unsuccessful. Even when the crime is prosecuted, the court may ultimately provide little or no protection to the victim if the perpetrator is not imprisoned, possibly on the grounds that the family needs him as a financial provider. Then, it is the victim who has to leave the home or accept to live under the same roof with her victimizer. It should come as no surprise that under such circumstances, there are women victims who do not seek the protection of the justice system. Rodabaugh and Austin (1981) state that more education will be necessary to change police officers' behavior so that inappropriate remarks will not be made during police-victim interactions. Nelson (1981) maintains that sensitivity training and proper interviewing techniques for police personnel are the key to effective investigations. His research shows that officers have difficulty and are uncomfortable when interviewing a rape victim. Many officers feel that it is the most difficult job that they encounter. Bruckman (1977) connects the discomfort police feel to the perception by rape victims that the officer is insensitive and does not want to be there. He states that one reason why women do not report rape to the police is primarily because of attitudes and expectations about police behavior.

One of the remedies often mentioned is to have female police officers investigate sexual assault cases. McCahill et al. (1979) found that 40 percent of the victims studied preferred a policewoman. However, male police attitudes toward women as victims often resurface in their attitudes to women as police officers. On the one hand, male police perceptions of themselves as tough crime fighters facing hardened criminals devalue rape investigations as a task for women police. On the other, while women police have been allowed to take statements and accompany the victims to the hospital or to court, the real investigation and any arrest stemming from it have been reserved for the male police (for these trends in Australia, see Nixon, 1992:44).

Problems Impacting Male Victims

Male victims of sexual assault face considerable difficulties too.

Ambiguity in defining the sexual victimization of male minors, particularly when it comes to coercion and the ability to give consent, mirrors societal values that are gender-biased. Most laws on sexual crimes involving male victims are chiefly concerned with controlling homosexual behavior. The overall presumption is that males, including children, are rarely victimized in a heterosexual situation with predictable consequences when it comes to reporting and convictions. The stereotype of women as nurturing, protecting, and wanting to take care of children makes it difficult for society to accept the possibility of women as sexual predators, even though it has been suggested that they may actually constitute a considerable number of abusers of boys (Fritz, Stoll & Wagner, 1981; Urquiza, 1988). This role is easily assigned, however, to homosexual adults while the female sexual offender has been and remains virtually invisible. Moreover, there are people, including male victims, who consider sexual relations between younger males and older females as not being abuse. The victim is deemed "lucky" to receive this sexual "training." Thus, the recorded rate of male sexual victimization is much lower than the equivalent one for females.

Criminologists have generally taken a relaxed view of this deviant behavior. Browne and Finkelhor (1986) note the paucity of empirical work on the incidence and emotional consequences of sexual abuse among males. For instance, West (1987) considers homosexual offenses as matters of immorality or indecency with the young rather than true assaults. The main reason he gives for this position is that such crimes rarely involve violence and are often consensual. Finkelhor (1984) found that Boston families rated male perpetrator–male victim abuse as less harmful than male perpetrator–female victim abuse, in part because they presumed that the sexual contact was initiated by the younger person. A report by the Howard League (1985) similarly states that "boys are more likely to be active collaborators . . . because reported incidents occur when they are older and in situations in which they could escape." West also reflects the traditional view that the only context where males are really at risk for sexual victimization is in prison or in similar institutions. This, consequently, puts male sexual victimization in a context that is quite different from the daily experience of most males and of people in general and depicts this type of victimization as being rare and extraordinary. It is important to recall that this view of male victimization is quite similar to that of female sexual victimization many people had some 20 years ago.

Male sexual victimization outside of prison has begun to be studied in the United States (Goyer & Eddleman, 1984; Kaufman et al., 1980; Groth & Burgess, 1980). There has also been a number of clinical reports that describe specific cases of sexual victimization of boys (Rogers & Terry, 1984;

Barton & Marshall, 1986; Krug, 1989) and gender-based differences in the sexual victimization of children (Urquiza, 1986; Pierce & Pierce, 1985). It has also been shown that in nonincest cases, child molesters target boys much more frequently than they do girls (Abel et al., 1987). Along the same lines, in the United Kingdom, McMullen (1990) declares it a mistake to assume that sexual victimization of males is rare only because few examples are known or reported. He also states that a frequent consequence of this type of attack is to stigmatize the male rape victim as a homosexual. Thus, males not only can be expected to suffer the same distress and crisis as females in the aftermath of rape but to have additional burdens stemming from the feeling of homosexual contamination and loss of masculinity (Urquiza & Capra, 1990:114–26; Olson, 1990:137–38, 148–50).

Currently, laws and legal practices on sexual crimes are beginning to embody a more realistic understanding of what sexual victimization is and to recognize more adequately its negative impact when the victim is female although this is less true when the victim is male. Ironically, this may be due to the fact that it was the women's movement which originally spurred research and legal reform on sexual assault. As a consequence, the nomenclature and practice in the field have a strong female orientation. This has also skewed research and data on the frequency, types, and gender preferences of offenders (Hunter & Gerber, 1990:80). In addition, powerful cultural double-standards that romanticize younger male–older female relationships and consider men as dominant and in control of sexual relationships make it hard for researchers, therapists, the legal and justice systems and public opinion to realize the extent and the impact of the sexual, victimization of males and to respond appropriately. There is no legitimate reason for the law to discriminate between male and female victims in this situation. Yet, the law does discriminate; so do legal practices and the perception of what should be written into the law. Thus, one could argue that the low rates of reporting by male victims stem more from the law's inability or unwillingness to protect male adults and children from sexual assault than from the presumed rare occurrence of these crimes. Transferring to male victims most, if not all, of what has been learned about female victims would definitely contribute to eliminate harmful stereotypes, correct existing injustices, and facilitate reporting and recording (Adler, 1992).

Stereotypical Role and Semantics Affecting the Victim

The basic tendency in criminal cases is to consider the victim in general as just another piece of evidence. The role of the victim is seen simply as helping to establish a legal case against the suspect. In other words, victims are seen not as injured individuals but rather as "symbols of [an] injured order" (Phipps, 1988:180) whose primary concern and interest are in crime and offenders. In the vernacular of the criminal court personnel, victims are only "witnesses," even though most witnesses in criminal court are also the victims of the crime being tried. Davis et al. (1980:294) found that 94 percent of a representative sample of prosecution "witnesses" in the Brooklyn, New York, Criminal Court were also crime victims. To depict victims as only "witnesses" has negative consequences for the manner in which court officers see them, think about them, and make crucial decisions.

"Witnesses" can easily be considered as having no personal interest in the end result of a case. They are not thought of as those who were victimized. Thus, they are not considered to be truly parties to the case. Victims, on the other hand, are those who took the direct impact of the crime and consequently have a strong personal stake in the result of the case and very definite attitudes about what they want the court to do (Davis, 1983). Thus, the criminal court parlance distorts who the victims really are, what their interests might be, and how they are or are not taken into account by court officers. The behavior and decisions that are bound to follow will easily be perceived by the victims as unpleasant, unfair, and distressing and will, in turn, color their perceptions of the justice system as inequitable, ungrateful and unresponsive to them (Walster et al., 1973:173).

In the case of a victim of rape, there is still at times no consideration shown for her struggle to come to terms with the assault, for the reactions of loved ones and peers, or for the attitudes she faces when interacting with the justice system. It is reported in the literature that victims find their contacts with the police, the prosecutor, and court personnel quite traumatic, at times more than the incident itself (Newburn, 1995:146).

The general expectation in our society is that, even though many justice professionals exhibit negative attitudes and predispositions toward rape victims, the judge will counteract them and redress any inequity. Judges project themselves and are seen as the objective source of authority and oversight in the courtroom that will act to balance the interests and the actions of the highly charged, success-oriented prosecution and defense. People believe and expect that the judge's role is to ensure that even-handed justice will triumph, serving the best interests of society by punishing the offender and protecting the victim. On the contrary, it has been shown that the attitudes of judges toward rape victims are much less impartial than it is usually thought. The importance of this type of research is that judicial attitudes correlate with judicial behavior and are a key element in affecting the experience of the rape victim in the courtroom. A judge can influence the conduct and substance of a case both directly through his rulings on evidentiary issues and indirectly through his conduct toward the parties in the trial. Bohmer (1974) was one of the first researchers to interview judges to ascertain their attitudes toward deciding rape cases. She selected and interviewed 38 judges of the Philadelphia, Pennsylvania, courts who had tried rape cases. She found a high level of judicial skepticism toward those who allege a rape. The judges divided victims into three types: "genuine victims" who elicited considerable judicial sympathy toward themselves and punitiveness against their attackers; "consensual intercourse" cases where the defendant was consequently treated with leniency; and "female vindictiveness" cases where judges believed the accused to be innocent. The importance of the judges' attitudes toward the victim is underlined by the great weight that the judges gave to circumstantial evidence. Thus, for example, reluctance to testify or to cooperate on the part of the victim, even though the system may have given her reasons to, was seen as a clear indication that she had started to doubt her own accusation of rape (Bohmer, 1974:304–305). The "rape victim checklist" used for awhile in U.S. Air Force investigations contains a series of questions that confirm the pervasiveness of similar attitudes toward victims. It implies that women who do not act like the stereotypical "good victim" are lying (*Washington Post*, October 2, 1992).

These attitudes are so deeply rooted among justice personnel that they impact not only victims belonging to the general public but female police officers as well. For example, a woman police officer in a suburb of Washington, D.C., accused her superiors of purposely failing to investigate her allegations that she had been "date-raped" by a fellow police officer. The police department countered that it was she who had not cooperated in an appropriate manner. The victim in turn criticized the intrusive demands made on her by her own superiors as a condition for investigating the case (*Washington Post*, November 23, 1992).

Research on incest reveals the same pattern (Garbarino & Stocking, 1980; Kocen & Bulkley, 1984; Melton, 1984; American Bar Association, 1985; Finkelhor, 1986). Mitra (1987) studied the decisions of the Court of Appeal in the United Kingdom in cases of father-daughter incest. Her sample consists of 63 appeals against a conviction in incest cases heard by the Court of Appeal (Criminal Division) between 1970 and 1980. Sixty-two of the appellants were male. Mitra focused first on the presence of violence and found that the Court either did not take it into account or did not give it great weight in sentencing, except in cases of severe violence. Secondly, she found that the court was very inclined to accept such mitigating factors as the victim's "promiscuity" or "seductiveness." When the daughter was not a virgin, the Court basically held her responsible for the sexual abuse. The effects of the attitude of the judges were, directly, to acquit the father and, indirectly, to control female sexuality by reasserting the traditional model of the family which emphasizes male dominance and female dependence.

Wives who cooperated with the system, blamed themselves for their husbands' transgressions and generally supported them, were compensated with the return home of the breadwinner who was spared imprisonment or ordered early release. Thus, the system worked effectively in reinstating the man to his position of power within the family, which had made his offense possible in the first place (Mitra,1987:144–45).

In the United States Saunders (1986) surveyed judicial beliefs about children's culpability and credibility in sexual assault cases. Fully 75 percent of the judges strongly agreed or agreed with statements that children cannot be held accountable for their sexual abuse. However, the rest, 25 percent, were not sure or felt that the children may have contributed to their victimization. Some judges stated that children are somewhat responsible for the assaults carried out against them; others found children's statements doubtful; and quite a few gave the impression that they did not take seriously the danger of child sexual abuse in today's society (Saunders, 1986: 96–98). The fact that many states in the United States and many other jurisdictions in the world, still have laws that presume young children to be incompetent witnesses and require that a judicial hearing be held to determine whether or not a child is competent before allowing him or her to testify indicates an institutionalized stereotype about the lack of credibility of child witnesses. This favors adults who have the law on their side in discounting a child's account of sexual or physical abuse or neglect from the very beginning (Dziech & Schudson, 1991:1–40).

Even recent reforms in the justice system have been influenced by stereotypes that impact the victim adversely. As Rock (1990:88) states:

> [Victims] were to become a working projection of the politics of penal reform, a figment of the reforming imagination, shaped by the concerns and purposes of their creators. Their character never seemed to be . . . [something] to be . . . considered. It was invented and bestowed and the result was a contradictory creature.

Special Burdens for Minority Victims and the Disabled

Some victims involved with the justice system face racial prejudice and discrimination. Racism is the systemic oppression of and violence against groups of people identified by the color of their skin, their culture, nationality, ethnic and/or religious beliefs. In most societies, racism is perpetuated by a system that is based on privilege and power for the few at the expense of many, represented by people of color, immigrants, Aboriginal people, and refugees.

In Western countries, when it comes to sexual assault, society generally focuses on the white victim, especially when the rapist is . . . [a person of color], and ignores the . . . victim [of color], particularly when the attacker is white. One major societal myth related to rape is that it is almost always committed by a black man against a white woman, even though research and published crime data show that in the U.S. almost 90 percent of all rapes are intraracial (U.S. Government Printing Office, 1993). This mythology and prejudice have serious and negative ramifications for black or minority women. For instance, often samples used in research on rape do not have adequate minority representation. Studies on rape have not paid enough attention to multiethnic differences in rape. Black women, expecting a negative and blaming response from the police and perceiving themselves devalued by society, are less likely than white women to report an incident (Wyatt, 1993; Gillespie, 1992). Societal indifference to black-on-black crime and the stereotype that black women are easily aroused and therefore sexually available or promiscuous (D'Emilio & Freedman, 1988:46) have kept the sexual assault of black women from being recognized and punished as the crime that it is (LaFree, 1989:219).

Mock jury trials have demonstrated that when the victim of rape is a black female, it is often difficult to convince jurors that the victimization has taken place (O'Brien, 1989; LaFree, 1989:217). In these cases, jurors easily depend on the "just world theory" stereotype (Lerner et al., 1976:137–140) to reach the conclusion that good women do not get raped and that consequently most black women who are raped are not good women. Anticipating this bias, prosecutors are reluctant to pursue rape cases involving a . . . woman [of color] and a great injustice is done.

Similar obstacles and reactions also await people with a disability who are victimized. A person's physical appearance can have a profound effect on the police's course of action (Wertlieb, 1991:333). Even the recognition of a disability may not be sufficient to preclude problems in interaction. It has been shown that police automatically and unfairly discount statements made by persons perceived to be mentally . . . [challenged]. It is also true that, for example, a deaf person's signing skills may be poor (Wertlieb, 1991:334). The vulnerability of the disabled is increased by society's failure to accept that they are also sexual beings, preferring instead to think of them as perennial children or "Peter Pan" figures. Society, and that includes the families of the disabled, finds it difficult to affirm the disabled in their search for companionship, marriage, and sexual intimacy (Schwier, 1994). Disabled persons are at a much higher risk of sexual abuse than others. Though society tends to ignore this problem, it is a serious one. Over 99 percent of the victims know their assailant (Lidke & Cole, 1988:46–47). At the same time, the opposite myth is also widely believed, that the disabled are more easily aroused. This belief has often justified the sterilization of females and false accusation of sex crimes and perversions against males. During the . . . wave of accusations of widespread child sexual abuse in Wenatchee, a rural community in the state of Washington, quite a few of the adults eventually convicted were at least mildly retarded (Chretien, 1995). When the disabled report rape, justice is often denied them as they are accused of provocation, depicted as obsessed with sexuality, or dismissed because the act is thought to be impossible (Carmody & Bratel, 1992:212–13). Some steps are fortunately being taken to assist the disabled victim and witness. For example, a . . . California state law could allow disabled victims to testify outside the courtroom, possibly through closed circuit television, to spare them the turmoil of facing their assailants (Lozano,1995).

Conclusion

The adverse impact that stereotypes can have even at the basic stage of perceiving oneself as victimized highlights the importance of public education and consciousness raising so that people can transcend particular explanations and justifications of victimization and grasp the systemic and widespread nature of the harm impacting victims. This is essential for developing a sense of outrage and for realizing that something must be done to change the situation not just for a particular case but for an entire class of actual or potential victims.

Basically, any system of criminal justice ultimately depends on its credibility and integrity. We cannot disregard with impunity the fact that laws will be recognized as valid only if they are made reliable through impartial enforcement. In its turn, such dependability is based on the willingness of victims to report. And victims will not approach the justice system if they conclude that the system will brush them aside or revictimize them. The objective is not merely to make the victim feel better but to ensure the full protection of the law for victims at all stages of the justice system and to secure full consideration, attention to accuracy, fairness, and legality for their cases when there is a danger that they will be ignored or downgraded because of bureaucratic, political, and plea bargaining pressures.

The importance of improving education and raising consciousness is far-reaching. This will certainly minimize victim-blaming and other negative behaviors and altitudes of police, prosecutors, and judges. Informed and sensitive police, prosecutors, and judges will be in the best possible position to make correct decisions that reflect a balanced approach to the competing interests and rights of the victim and of the accused.

In most Western systems of justice, it is the jury that determines guilt or innocence. If the public has not been reached and educated, the likelihood is small that the jury will be able to understand the dynamics of victimization and agree with the victim's vision of him- or herself and of the events. While considerable efforts should be undertaken to educate people in the criminal justice system about the plight of victims, if the public from which juries are selected is overlooked, all these efforts will be ultimately fruitless.

Will more attention and consideration of the victim in the end put more pressure on the already burdened justice system? Not necessarily. Increased victims' cooperation should make it easier to prevent crimes and enable them to be more speedily solved.

Seriously implementing alternatives to imprisonment like restitution and community service should help reduce the burden on corrections. As to the more serious crimes, if more respect for victims' rights will generate more convictions, we should welcome the outcome and be prepared to meet the cost.

The justice ideal demands a balanced approach to both victim and defendant, respecting the rights and dignity of both. This can only be achieved if society makes a determined effort to confront and eliminate existing stereotypes about victims as it has attempted to do with those having an impact on defendants.

REFERENCES

Abel, G. G., Becker, J. V., Mittelman, M., Cunningham-Rathner, J., Rouleau, J. L. & Murphy, W. D. (1987). Self-reported sex crimes of non-incarcerated paraphiliacs. *Journal of Interpersonal Violence* 1: 3–25.

Adler, Z. (1985). The relevance of sexual history evidence in rape: Problems of subjective interpretation. *Criminal Law Review*: 769–780.

American Bar Association (1985). *National policy conference on legal reforms in child sexual abuse cases.* Washington, DC: National Legal Resource Center for Child Advocacy and Protection.

Bohmer, C. (1974). Judicial attitudes toward rape victims. *Judicature* 57: 303–307.

Browne, A. & Finkelhor, D. (1986). Impact of child sexual abuse: A review of the research. *Psychological Bulletin* 99: 66–77.

Brownmiller, S. (1975). *Against our will.* New York: Simon & Schuster.

Brooks, W. N., Doob, A. & Kirshenbaum, H. M. (1975). *Character of the victim in the trial of a case of rape.* (Unpublished manuscript). Toronto: University of Toronto.

Bumiller, K. (1988). *The civil rights society.* Baltimore MD: Johns Hopkins University Press.

Burris, C. A. & Jaffe, P. (1983). Wife abuse as a crime: The impact of police laying charges. *Canadian Journal of Criminology* 25:309–318.

Burstyn, V. (1983). Masculine dominance and the state. In: Miliband, R. & Saville, J. *The Socialist Reader.* London: Merlin Press, 45–89.

Byrne, D. (1971). *The attraction paradigm.* New York: Academic Press.

Cairney, K. F. (1995). Recognizing acquaintance rape in potentially consensual situations: A re-examination of Thomas Hardy's *Tess of the D'Urbervilles. Journal of Gender and the Law* 3, Spring: 301–331.

Carmody, M. & Bratel, J. (1992). Vulnerability and denial: Sexual assault of people with disabilities. In: Breckenridge, J. & Carmody, M. *Crime of violence: Australian responses to rape and child sexual assault.* Sydney: Allen und Unwin, 207–218.

Casey, M. (1987). *Domestic violence against women.* Dublin: Social Organisational Psychology Research Unit, UCD, Dublin, Ireland.

Connell, R. W. (1990). The state, gender, and sexual politics: Theory and appraisal. *Theory and Society* 19: 507–544.

Chretien, P. N. (1995). Rule of law: What the Wenatchee prosecutors should remember. *Wall Street Journal,* November 29, A, 15:3.

Davis, R., Russell, V. & Kunreuther, F. (1980). *The role of the complaining witness in an urban criminal court.* New York: Vera Institute of Justice.

Davis, R. (1983). Victim/witness noncooperation: A second look at a persistent phenomenon. *Journal of Criminal Justice* 11:287–299.

D'Emilio, J. & Freedman, E. B. (1988). *Intimate matters: A history of sexuality in America.* New York: Harper and Row.

Dobash, R. E. & Dobash, R. (1980). *Violence against wives: A case against patriarchy* (especially ch. 11). London: Open Books.

Dziech, B. W. & Schudson, J. C. B. (1991). *On trial: America's courts and their treatment of sexually abused children.* Boston MA: Beacon Press.

Edwards, S. M. (1984). *Women on trial.* Manchester: University Press.

Edwards, S. M. (1986a). Police attitudes and dispositions in domestic disputes: The London study. *Police Journal* 130–141.

Edwards, S. M. (1986b). *The police response to domestic violence in London.* London: Polytechnic of Central London.

Feinman, C. (1994). *Women in the criminal justice system.* Westport CT: Praeger.

Feldman-Summers, S. & Palmer, G. (1980). Rape. A view from judges, prosecutors, and police officers. *Criminal Justice and Behavior* 7: 19–40.

Ferraro, K. J. (1989). An existential approach to battering. In: Hanmer, J., Radford, J. & Stanko, E. A. *Women, policing, and male violence* New York: Routledge, 155–184.

Finkelhor, D. (1984). *Child sexual abuse: New theory and research.* New York: Free Press.

Finkelhor, D. (1986). *A sourcebook on child sexual abuse.* Beverly Hills, CA: Sage.

Franzway, S., Court, D. & Connell, R. W. (1989). *Staking a claim: Feminism, bureaucracy, and the state*. Boston: Allen and Unwin.

Freeman, M. D. A. (1984). Legal ideologies, patriarchal precedents, and domestic violence. In: Freeman, M. D. A., ed. *State, law and the family* (ch. 4). London & New York: Tavistock.

Fritz, G. S., Stoll, K. & Wagner, N. A. (1981). A comparison of males and females who were sexually molested as children. *Journal of Sex and Marital Therapy* 7: 54–59.

Galton, E. R. (1975). Police processing of rape complaints: A case history. *American Journal of Criminal Law* 4: 15–30.

Garbarino, J. & Stocking, S. H. (1980). *Protecting children from abuse and neglect*. San Francisco, CA: Jossey-Bass.

Gelles, R. J. & Fedrick-Cornell, C. (1985). *Intimate violence in families*. Beverly Hills, CA: Sage.

Gelsthorpe, L. & Morris, A. (1994). *Feminist perspectives in criminology*. Milton Keynes: Open University Press.

Goldstein, J. (1960). Police discretion not to invoke the criminal process: Low-visibility decisions in the administration of justice. *The Yale Law Journal* 69: 543–592.

Goyer, P. E. & Eddleman, H. C. (1984). Same sex rape of non-incarcerated men. *American Journal of Psychiatry* 137: 576–579.

Greer, G. (1975). Seduction is a four-letter word. In: Schultz, L. G., ed. *Rape victimology*. Springfield IL: C. C. Thomas.

Groth, N. & Burgess, A. W. (1980). Male rape—offenders and victims. *American Journal of Psychiatry* 137: 806–810.

Hatty, S. E. & Sutton, J. E. (1986a). Policing violence against women. In: Hatty, S. E. *National conference on domestic violence*. Canberra: Australian Institute of Criminology.

Hatty, S. E. (1986b). *Children of battered women: Attitudes of intervening police officers*. Unpublished paper.

Heider, F. (1958). *The psychology of interpersonal relations*. New York: Wiley.

Howard League Working Party (1985). *Unlawful sex*. London: Waterlow Publishers.

Hunter, Mic & Gerber, Paul N. (1990). Use of the term "victim" and "survivor" in the grief stages commonly seen during recovery from sexual abuse. In: Hunter, M., ed. *The sexually abused male*, Vol. 2. Lexington MA: Lexington Books, 79–90.

Hurst, C. J. (1977). *The trouble with rape*. Chicago IL: Nelson Hall.

Jaffe, P., Wolfe, P., Telford, A. & Austin, G. (1986). The impact of police charges in incidents of wife abuse. *Journal of Family Violence* 1: 43.

Jeffreys, S. & Radford, J. (1984). Contributory negligence or being a woman. In: Scraton, P. & Gordon, P., eds. *Causes for concern* (ch. 7). Harmondsworth: Penguin Books.

Kalven, H. & Zeisel, H. (1966). *The American jury*. Boston: Little, Brown.

Karmen, A. (1981). Auto theft and corporate irresponsibility. *Corporate Crises* 5: 63–81.

Karmen, A. (1990). *Crime victims: An introduction to victimology*. Belmont CA: Wadsworth.

Katz, S. & Mazur, M. (1979). *Understanding the rape victim*. New York: John Wiley and Sons.

Kaufman, A., DiVasto, P., Jackson, R., Voorhees, H. & Christy, J. (1980). Male rape victims: Non-institutionalized assault. *American Journal of Psychiatry* 137.

Kerr, N. L. (1978). Beautiful and blameless: Effects of victim attractiveness and responsibility on mock jurors' verdicts. *Personality and Social Psychology Bulletin* 4: 479–482.

Kocen, L. & Bulkley, J. (1984). Analysis of criminal child sex offense statutes. In: Bulkley, J., ed. *Child sexual abuse and the law*. Washington DC: American Bar Association.

Krug, R. (1989). Adult male report of childhood sexual abuse by mothers: Case descriptions, motivations, and long-term consequences. *Child Abuse and Neglect* 13: 111–119.

LaFree, G. (1989). *Rape and criminal justice: The social construction of sexual assault.* Belmont CA: Wadsworth.

Landy, D. & Aronson, E. (1969). The influence of the character of the criminal and his victim on the decision of simulated jurors. *Journal of Experimental Social Psychology* 5: 141–152.

Langley, T., Beatty, G., Yost, E., O'Neal, E. C., Faucett, J. M., Levi Taylor, S., Frankel, P. & Craig, K. (1991). How behavioral cues in a date rape scenario influence judgments regarding victim and perpetrator. *Forensic Reports* 4: 355–358.

LeDoux, J. C. & Hazelwood, R. R. (1991). Police attitudes and beliefs toward rape. In: U.S. Department of Justice, ed. *Deviant and criminal sexuality.* Quantico VA: FBI Academy.

Lerner, M. J., Miller, D. T. & Holmes, J. G. (1976). Deserving and the emergence of forms of justice. In: Lerner, M. J., ed. *Advances in experimental social psychology* vol. 9. New York: Academic Press.

Lidke, K. & Cole, S. (1988). A conspiracy of silence: Sexual abuse of the disabled. *USA Today*, May, vol. 116: 46–47.

Lozano, C. V. (1995). Law to erase trauma of testifying for disabled. *Los Angeles Times*, November 1, A, 3:1.

McCahill, T., Meyer, L. & Fischman, A. (1979). *The aftermath of rape.* Lexington MA: Lexington Books.

MacKinnon, C. (1989). *Toward a feminist theory of the state.* Cambridge MA: Harvard University Press.

MacLean, B. D. & Milovanovic, D. (1991). *New direction in critical criminology.* Vancouver BC: Collective Press.

McMullen, R. J. (1990). *Mate rape—breaking the silence on the last taboo.* London: GMP Publishers.

Madigan, L. & Gamble, N. C. (1991). *The second rape: Society's continued betrayal of rape victims.* New York: Lexington Books.

Melton, G. B. (1984). Procedural reforms to protect child victim/witnesses in sex offense proceedings. In: Bulkley, J. ed. *Child sexual abuse and the law.* Washington DC: American Bar Association.

Messerschmidt, J. W. (1993). *Masculinities and crime: Critique and reconceptualization of theory.* Lanham MD: Rowman and Littlefield.

Miller, R. E. & Sarat, A. (1980–81). Grievances, claims, and disputes: Assessing the adversary culture. *Law & Society Review* 15: 3–4, 525–566.

Mitra, C. L. (1987). Judicial discourse in father-daughter incest appeal cases. *International Journal of the Sociology of Law* 15:121–148.

Mitchell, H. & Byrne, D. (1973). The defendant's dilemma: Effects of jurors' attitudes and authoritarianism on judicial decisions. *Journal of Personality and Social Psychology* 25: 123.

Nelson, R. (1981). Establishing rapport with victims. *Police Chief* 48: 130–136.

Newburn, Tim (1995). *Crime and criminal justice policy.* London: Longman.

Nixon, C. (1992). A climate of change: Police responses to rape. In: Breckenridge, J. & Carmody, M. *Crimes of violence: Australian responses to rape and child sexual assault.* Sydney: Allen und Unwin.

O'Brien, E. M. (1989). Black women additionally victimized by myths, stereotypes; Scholars say. *Black Issues in Higher Education*, December 7, 8–9.

Olson, Peter E. (1990). The sexual abuse of boys: A study of the long-term psychological effects. In: Hunter, M., ed. *The sexually abused male*. Lexington MA: Lexington Books, 1990.

Pahl, J. (1982). Police response to battered women. *Journal of Social Welfare Law*, November.

Pahl, J. (1985). *Private violence and public policy* (especially ch. 6). London: Routledge & Kegan Paul.

Parnas, R. I. (1972). The police response to domestic disturbance. In: Radnowitz, L. & Wolfgang, M. E. eds. *The criminal in the arms of the law*. New York: Basic Books.

Parnas, R. I. (1973). Prosecutorial and judicial handling of family violence. *Criminal Law Bulletin* 9: 733–769.

Phipps, A. (1988). Ideologies, political parties, and victims of rape. In: Maguire, M. & Pointing, J., eds. *Victims of crime: A new deal?* Milton Keynes: Open University Press.

Pierce, R. & Pierce, L. H. (1985). The sexually abused child: A comparison of male and female victims. *Child Abuse and Neglect* 9: 191–199.

Pugh, M. D. (1983). Contributory fault and rape convictions: Loglinear models for blaming the victim. *Social Psychology Quarterly* 46: 233–242.

Radford, J. (1984). 'Women-slaughter': A licence to kill? In: Scraton, P. & Gordon, P., eds., *Causes for Concern* (ch. 9). Harmondsworth: Penguin Books.

Rock, P. (1990). *Helping victims of crime*. Oxford: Clarendon Press.

Rodabaugh, B. J. & Austin, M. (1981). *Sexual assault: A guide for community action*. New York: Garland STPM Press.

Rogers, C. & Terry, T. (1984). Clinical interventions with boy victims of sexual abuse. In: Steward, I. & Greer, J., eds. *Victims of sexual aggression*. New York: Van Nostrand Reinhold, 91–104.

Russell, D. E. H. (1983). The prevalence and incidence of forcible rape and attempted rape of females. *Victimology* 7: 81–93.

Russell, D. E. H. (1984). *Sexual exploitation: Rape, child sexual abuse, and sexual harassment*. Beverly Hills CA: Sage.

Saunders, E. J. (1986). judicial attitudes toward child sexual abuse: A preliminary investigation. *Judicature* 70, 2: 95–98.

Schwier, F. M. (1994). *Couples with intellectual disabilities talk*. Bethesda MD: Woodbine House.

Shapland, J. & Hobbs, D. (1987). *Policing on the ground in Highland*. Oxford: Centre for Criminological Research.

Sherman, L. W., Schmidt, J. D. & Rogan, D. P. (1992). *Policing domestic violence: Experiments and dilemmas*. New York: Free Press.

Shotland, R. S. & Goodstein, L. (I 983). Just because she doesn't want to doesn't mean it's rape: An experimentally based causal model of the perception of rape in a dating situation. *Social Psychology Quarterly* 46: 233–242.

Sigall, H. & Ostrove, N. (1975). Beautiful but dangerous: Effects of offender attractiveness and nature of the crime on juridic judgment. *Journal of Personality & Social Psychology* 31: 410–414.

Smart, C. (1989). *Feminism and the power of law*. New York: Routledge.

Smith, L. J. F. (1989). *Domestic violence: An overview of the literature*. London: HMSO.

Solomon, M. R. & Schopler, J. (1978). The relationship of physical attractiveness and punitiveness: Is the linearity assumption out of line? *Personality & Social Psychology Bulletin* 4, 3, 483–486.

Ursel, E. J. & Farough, D. (1985). *The legal and public response to the new wife abuse directive in Manitoba.* Winnipeg area study, report no. 4, Department of Sociology, University of Manitoba.

Ursel, E. J. (1986). The state and the maintenance of patriarchy: A case study of family, labour, and welfare legislation in Canada. In: Dickinson, J. & Russell, B. *Family, economy, and the state.* New York: St. Martin's Press.

Urquiza, A. J. (1986). *Behavior problems in child victims of sexual abuse: An empirical investigation.* Unpublished master's thesis. University of Washington, Seattle.

Urquiza, A. J. (1988). *The effects of childhood sexual abuse in an adult male population.* Doctoral dissertation. University of Washington, Seattle.

Urquiza, A. J. & Capra, M. (1990). The impact of sexual abuse: Initial and long-term effects. In: Hunter, M., ed. *The sexually abused male.* Lexington MA: Lexington Books, 1990.

U.S. Government Printing Office (1993). *Criminal victimization, 1992.* Washington DC: Bureau of Justice Statistics.

Viano, E. (1989). Victimology today: Major issues in research and public policy. In: Viano, E., ed. *Crime and its victims.* Washington DC & New York: Hemisphere.

Viano, E. (1990). The victimology handbook. New York & London: Garland Publishing.

Viano, E. (1994). The protection of victims: Socio-political considerations and a plan for action. *Quad. Psich. Forense* III: 34–57.

Viano, E. (1995). Victims, crime and the media: Competing interests in the electronic society. *Communications and the Law* 17: 41–65.

Vidmar, N. & Miller, D. T. (1980). Social-psychological processes underlying attitudes toward legal punishment. *Law Society Review* 14: 545–602.

Walker, L. (1989). When the battered woman becomes the defendant. In: Viano, E. *Crime and its victims.* Washington DC & New York: Hemisphere, 57–70.

Walster, E., Berscheid, E. & Walster, G. W. (1973). New directions in equity research. *Journal of Personality and Social Psychology* 25:151–176.

Wertlieb, E. C. (1991). Individuals with disabilities in the criminal justice system: A review of the literature. *Criminal Justice & Behavior,* September, 18: 332–350.

Wertz, F. J. (1985). Methods and findings in a phenomenological psychological study of a complex life-event: Being criminally victimized. In: Giorgi, A., ed. *Phenomenology and psychological research.* Pittsburgh PA: Duquesne University Press.

West, D. J. (1987). *Sexual crimes and confrontations.* Aldershot: Gower.

Wiener, R. L. & Vodanovich, S. J. (1986). The evaluation of culpability for rape: A model of legal decision making. *Journal of Psychology* 120: 489–500.

Williams, J. E. & Holmes, K. A. (1981). *The second assault: Rape and public attitudes.* Westport CT: Greenwood.

Wright, R. (1984). A note on the attrition of rape cases. *The British Journal of Criminology* 24: 399–400.

Wyatt, G. E., Newcomb, M. D. & Riederle, M. H. (1993). *Sexual abuse and consensual sex: Women's developmental patterns and outcomes.* Newbury Park CA: Sage.

Young, Y. (1986). Gender expectations and their impact on black female offenders and victims. *Justice Quarterly* 3: 305–327.

Chapter Twenty

A Role for Victims in Offender Reentry

Susan Herman
Cressida Wasserman

In recent years, the number of offenders under criminal justice supervision has grown dramatically. The 1990 to 1999 increase in the number of prisoners under federal or state jurisdiction averaged 4.2% annually, with a 44.6% gain overall during the entire 9-year period (Bureau of Justice Statistics [BJS], 2000). Corresponding to the dramatic increase in incarceration rates, nearly 600,000 inmates are expected to be released from prison in 2001 (BJS, 1999).

These trends have prompted new approaches to one of the oldest questions in the criminal justice field, namely, how best to ensure the successful reintegration of offenders into the community. The process of reintegration for returning offenders who have few prospects and multiple handicaps—often made worse by long separations from families and communities—is inevitably difficult and hazardous. But for the victims of crimes committed by these offenders, it may also be a time of great need and challenge. For many who have already struggled to overcome the consequences of their victimization, the release of offenders may revive trauma, renew fears, heighten tensions, and threaten personal safety.

Over the same period that Americans have seen the buildup of prisons and criminal justice supervision, America has also witnessed another important change, namely, the development of fundamental changes in the relationship between victims of crime and the criminal justice system. Victims' relatively new rights to attend and participate in many critical stages of the criminal justice process have direct impact on prisoner reintegration.

Largely due to stereotyping of victims and victims organizations, a common perception exists that the increase in victim involvement in the criminal justice system results in damaging outcomes for offenders (Shapiro, 1997; Staples,

From *Crime & Delinquency*, 47(3): 428–445, copyright © 2001 by Sage Publications, Inc. Reprinted by permission of Sage Publications, Inc.

1997). Yet victims, their relationships to offenders, and their views about appropriate criminal justice outcomes resist generalization. Indeed, we will argue that victim involvement, rather than impeding the interests of returning offenders, can contribute to reentry successes in significant ways. Victims and victims organizations can positively assist in the reintegration of offenders by providing decision makers with important and relevant information; offering experience and expertise; encouraging offender accountability; and furthering the goals of victim empowerment, safety, restitution, and reintegration.

The purpose of this article is to develop a framework for defining the roles of victims and victims organizations in reentry programs and processes and to suggest the value of their involvement.

Victims and Offenders

Contrary to a popular perception of victims as people with no relationship to offenders, removed from the world of offenders generally, and without sympathy for offenders, closer examination reveals that victims of crime are highly diverse, with experiences of enormous range and variety. Sometimes victims themselves have histories as offenders or direct experience of offenders (as family members, neighbors, peers, or partners), and victims often do not share a common view of the appropriate outcomes of the criminal justice system.

THE DIVERSITY OF VICTIMS OF CRIME

Each year, nearly 30 million people in America become victims of crime (Rennison, 2000). They represent all ages, ethnicities, races, sexes, sexual orientations, regions, neighborhoods, and categories of victimization. A recent survey found that nearly half of the public (47%) in a region that covered nine northeastern states had been victims of violent crime or had a family member killed or seriously injured in a crime (Boyle, 1999). Yet, crime does not affect all members of society equally. For example, a young, single, poor, African American man living in an urban area is at greatest risk of becoming a victim of violent crime. Persons in households with annual incomes of less than $7,500 experience the highest rate of violence of all income categories. Hispanics are more likely to become victims of robbery and aggravated assault than non-Hispanics. Those in low-income households, or who are Black or Hispanic, are at greater risk of burglary (BJS, 2001b). In addition, whereas some victims experience crime as a frequent occurrence, either personally or indirectly through someone they know, for others it is a single traumatic event. Any reentry initiative that seeks to address victims' needs must take their diversity into account.

VICTIMS' RELATIONSHIPS TO OFFENDERS

Victims also have a variety of different relationships to offenders. In many instances, victims know their offenders well. Violence against women is primarily partner violence committed by a current or former husband, cohabiting partner, or date (Tjaden & Thoennes, 1998). In 1999, almost 7 out of 10 rapes or sexual assaults were committed by an intimate, relative, friend, or acquaintance. About 40% of the victims of nonfatal violence in the workplace reported that they knew their offender (BJS, 2001b). Statistics on violent crime against juveniles show that in 80% of cases, victims know their perpetrators because the offender is a family member or an acquaintance (Finkelhor & Ormrod, 2000).

Furthermore, in many crimes, the line between victim and offender is not easily drawn. It is widely accepted that childhood maltreatment is associated with a significantly increased risk for numerous adolescent problem behaviors, serious and violent delinquency, drug use, and poor school performance. For example, abused and neglected girls are nearly twice as likely to be arrested as juveniles, twice as likely to be arrested as adults, and more than twice as likely to be arrested for violent crimes compared with girls who have not been abused and neglected (Widom, 2000). Looking at state prison populations, 19% of inmates and 16% of jail inmates or offenders on active probation told interviewers they had been physically or sexually abused before their current sentence. Women experienced abuse as juveniles and adults, whereas males were most often abused at age 17 or younger. A third of women in state prison and a quarter in jail said they had been raped before their incarceration (Harlow, 1999).

Finally, decision makers must understand that often the environments in which victims and offenders live are not separate and unrelated. Many victims have direct personal knowledge about the treatment of offenders. Family members may have been involved with the criminal justice system, or they may live in communities so ravaged by crime that their friends or neighbors, or children of their friends and neighbors, have been arrested, convicted, or imprisoned. These realities underscore the complicated relationship between many victims of crime and the criminal justice system and the way the lives of crime victims and offenders often overlap.

VICTIMS AND REENTRY

For some communities, typically in the poorest and most deprived urban neighborhoods, a correlation has been shown between increases in the number of newly released inmates and increases in crime (Butterfield, 2000). According to John DiIulio, it has become the administrative norm in many cities for community corrections officers never to see their probationers except on paper. "Probation has simply lost track of about 350,000 probationers, including thousands of violent felons. Most 'intensive' supervision probation programs remain shams" (DiJulio, 2000). New Jersey may be a case in point. It has 452 probation officers to supervise about 67,000 adult offenders and 200 officers to oversee the cases of about 14,000 juveniles (Kinney, 2001). It is not surprising that at least half of those on probation commit new crimes or that victims are apprehensive about the return of offenders to their communities (Manhattan Institute, 1999).

For individual victims, however, the precise repercussions of offender reentry depend on many factors. These include the nature and seriousness of the crime; the length of time that has passed since the crime was committed; the personal and economic circumstances of the victim; the victim's relationship, if any, to the offender; the chance of undesired encounters; any specific dangers posed by the offender's return; the strength of family and social networks; and the extent and quality of community-based support services and resources. Every victim's experience is different: the traumatized rape victim who learns the perpetrator is back or who is surprised to meet him in the neighborhood, because she did not know he had been released; the domestic violence victim afraid her abuser will return, homeless and jobless, to seek revenge; the victim of burglary who discovers that the offenders that invaded his home are back on the streets; or victims of gang violence who hear the gang leaders are out of prison.

Whereas crime victims may fear the release of their offender or of offenders in general, they have a common interest in initiatives designed to prevent recidivism. With this in mind, it is fruitful to explore how the experience of victims and victims organizations can contribute to the policies and decisions that guide offender reintegration.

Framework of Victim Involvement in Prisoner Reentry

There are several ways to delineate victim involvement in prisoner reentry. First, victims can exercise their rights to participate at key stages of the criminal justice process, particularly the sentencing and parole decisions and community supervision. Second, they can become involved by participating in programs that seek to educate offenders, either before or after their release from custody, about the impact of crime. Third, victims organizations can assume roles in the development and implementation phases of reentry initiatives, particularly educational programs and systems designed to improve the effectiveness of community supervision.

Victim Impact Statements[1]

The initial terms and conditions of offender reentry are determined at sentencing, and every state now allows some kind of victim impact information to be submitted at this stage. A majority allow oral and/or written statements and require the information to be included in presentence reports. Sometimes, victims are allowed to use videotapes, audiotapes, or other electronic means to convey the information, and child victims are able to submit drawings in place of written or oral statements. A victim impact statement typically describes the harm caused by the offense, including its financial, physical, psychological, and emotional impacts; medical and psychological treatments required by the victim or the victim's family; the harm to family relationships; and the need for restitution. Many states also allow victims to express their opinion on an appropriate sentence. The right to present victim impact information in court occasionally depends on the discretion of the judge but is generally guaranteed by statutes and state constitutions. Approximately one third of states specifically require the court to consider victim impact statements. Even though notification to victims varies considerably across the country, we do know that when victims are actually notified of their right to make a statement at sentencing, more than 90% of them do (Kilpatrick, Beatty, & Howley, 1998).

Opponents of victims' involvement in the sentencing phase of the criminal justice system predicted increased severity in sentencing outcomes, but available evidence does not support this (Tobolowsky, 1999). Studies in the United States and Australia have shown that the opportunity to present victim impact statements does not correlate with harsher sentences and that their absence does not correlate with more lenient sentences. In fact, in the majority of cases victim impact statements have not been shown to affect sentencing patterns or outcomes at all (Erez, 1999). This is not as surprising as it may first appear, because the information from victims is only one factor among many that determine sentencing outcomes. Furthermore, the court may infer the harm to the victim from other sources. However, qualitative research (involving interviews with judges, prosecutors, and defense lawyers in Australia) indicates that in the few cases where impact statements did influence sentencing, such statements were as likely to result in greater leniency as in greater harshness. In these cases, in the opinion of those interviewed, justice was enhanced because, otherwise, the sentences would have been too heavy or too light (Erez, 1999). For example, when a statement indicated that the victim had made a good recovery from the effects of the crime, a more lenient sentence was considered in order. When it disclosed the offense was perpetrated in an especially ruthless or cruel manner, a harsher sentence was more appropriate.

Therefore, in principle, by providing additional, relevant information that allows for better informed sentencing decisions, victim impact statements appear to make a contribution to proportionality, not to the severity of sentencing (Erez, 1999). Victim impact statements can also help tailor restitution awards, orders of protection, or other conditions of release relevant to the offender's eventual return to the community (National Center for Victims of Crime, 1999).

Victims and Parole Decisions

Parole hearings provide another opportunity to determine the length of incarceration and/or set conditions of release. Over the past two decades, victims have also been granted rights to participate in these decisions. This participation has taken on greater importance as the number of cases resolved by guilty pleas, including agreements regarding sentencing, continues to increase. In these situations, the "right" of the victim to make a statement at sentencing may be hollow. Consequently, a parole hearing may be one of the few opportunities a victim has to tell his or her story and explain specific concerns (Petersilia, 2000).

Victims' rights relating to parole fall into four main categories: (a) the right to be informed or notified about parole-related events and proceedings, (b) the right to be heard on matters relating to the offender's parole and related incidents, (c) the right to be present at parole proceedings, and (d) the right to an order for restitution as a condition of parole. These rights are designed to ensure that the views of victims can be taken into account before decisions about parole are made and to help victims prepare themselves for the offender's release. Depending on the provisions of individual state laws, the right of victims to be informed may apply to a wide variety of parole-related hearings and events. These include the earliest estimated date an offender is eligible for parole, the date of a parole application or hearing, the right to attend the parole hearing, the right to submit a victim impact statement, a parole decision or parole conditions, a parolee's proposed release date or actual release, a parolee's violation of parole conditions (and the date of any subsequent hearing on the violation), revocation of parole or any hearing to determine whether parole should be revoked, discharge or termination of parole or any hearing related thereto, and the escape of a convicted offender from a correctional setting.

Most states let victims comment on offender requests for parole. Forty-six states allow statements to be submitted in person; 42 states allow written statements. A few states allow statements to be made through a representative, teleconferencing, audiotapes, or videotapes. Victims can ask the court to attach special conditions to parole orders for safety reasons, such as requiring the parolee to live a minimum distance from the victim's residence or to refrain from contact with the victim. In most states, victims can comment on the offender's suitability for parole, and in many they can attend the proceedings. In some states, victims can also attend hearings on parole violations, revocation, and final discharge. Payment of restitution as a condition of parole may be automatic or left to the discretion of the parole authority.

Cases involving mentally ill offenders pose a distinct subset of reentry issues for victims. When mentally ill offenders remain under the jurisdiction of criminal justice authorities, the rights of their victims will be the same as other victims'. When jurisdiction transfers to mental health authorities, victims generally have fewer rights. For example, only a few states provide victims with notice of hearings on an offender's mental competency or release, and only about half of all states require notification when mentally ill offenders are released from mental health facilities. Very few states have incorporated victim impact statements into commitment processes or notify victims when incarcerated offenders become mentally ill and are transferred for mental health treatment. It is particularly interesting that only 21 states have provisions for victims to be notified when an offender escapes from a mental health facility.

Parole-related rights are highly relevant to the reentry process. Victim input can highlight the need for strict supervision or special conditions such as restitution orders, orders of protection, mandated treatment to address substance abuse or violent behavior, and restrictions on where offenders can work or live. Subject to provision of appropriate resources for offender programs, stipulations such as these can contribute to successful reentry by creating conditions that can discourage reoffending and encourage reintegration. At the same time, it is also empowering for victims to have a voice in the process that determines when, and on what conditions, offenders are to be released.

However, the potential contribution victims can make to reentry successes through the exercise of parole-related rights depends on parole boards' retaining discretionary powers of release. Yet, the policy trend has been in the opposite direction. In 1998, parole boards retained full powers of release in only 15 states and had only limited powers in 21 others (Petersilia, 2000). The more recent "truth-in-sentencing" movement has promoted the idea that offenders, particularly violent offenders, should serve a fixed amount of time in prison, with release being virtually automatic (Ditton & Wilson, 1999). Consequently, many states are witnessing a rise in mandatory release once offenders have served the requisite portion of their sentences, regardless of whether their release poses a danger. Ironically, the victim of an offender who "maxes out" (and for that matter, the public at large) may end up less protected than the victim of an offender granted parole ("Prisons Release Record Numbers," 2001). Parole-related victim participation can help the criminal justice system take advantage of victims' critical knowledge about offenders, provided parole boards retain their discretionary powers and victim input is encouraged.

VICTIM AND COMMUNITY SUPERVISION OF OFFENDERS

In addition to victims' formal parole-related rights, informal communication between victims and probation or parole officers may contribute to reentry goals. Many victims will know, often sooner than anyone else, whether the offender has complied with probation/parole conditions. They may be able to tell probation or parole officers whether offenders have contacted them without permission, paid restitution on time, attended mandated treatment or classes, or told the truth about any other condition of release. Encouraging victims to volunteer relevant information may contribute to the effectiveness of supervision, especially in stalking or domestic violence cases in which offenders are particularly likely to deny or minimize their behavior (American Probation and Parole Association [APPA], 1999).

VICTIM IMPACT AND RESTORATIVE JUSTICE PROGRAMS

Individual victims can also become involved in reentry by interacting with offenders directly in a range of programs that promote victim-offender communication. These programs seek to foster reintegration by educating offenders about the impact of crime on its victims and generating remorse that will change offender behavior in the future (Bazemore & Umbreit, 1998). Many of these programs reflect restorative and community justice theories (Kurki, 1999).

Some programs such as victim impact panels have fairly narrow educational goals. These are forums in which victims of different types of crime talk about the crime's impact on their lives. The aim is to convey to offenders (the consequences of their actions in terms of the victims' pain and suffering. For victims, these panels may be a way to promote recovery by helping them regain control over their lives. Victim impact panels take place in diversion, probation, parole, or in-custody programs, and offender participation may be part of the sentence imposed by the court (APPA, 1999).

Other programs, such as victim-offender mediation, family group conferencing, reparative boards, and circle sentencing have broader, more ambitious aims. They seek to supplement or replace traditional retributive justice and move the focus away from punishment of the offender toward repairing community relationships and the harm caused by the crime. These programs differ in many respects, including form, procedure, the number of participants, the function of the mediators or facilitators, and even program goals (Bazemore & Umbreit, 1998). In all cases, however, victim participation is integral to their philosophy and design.

In victim–offender mediation programs, victim and offender meet with a mediator to discuss what happened. Offenders get the opportunity to understand the consequences of their actions and take responsibility, whereas victims are able to question the offender directly and participate in a process structured to produce an agreement on what the offender will do to ameliorate the harm. Agreements commonly involve payment of restitution and an apology (Bazemore & Umbreit, 1998; Greenwood & Umbreit, 1998).

Family group conferences, like mediations, generally target young offenders charged with minor offenses. One Australian model that has attracted attention in the United States is the police-facilitated conference, founded on the theory of "reintegrative shaming," a process designed to avoid renewed feelings of rejection and alienation that foster criminal behavior (McCold, 1999). Here, the primary participants, the victim and the offender, attend conferences with their respective "supporters": family members and/or friends. Reduced recidivism is one of several conference objectives that also include enhancing victims' satisfaction, repairing harm, educating juvenile offenders, providing alternatives to punishment, increasing community satisfaction, and reducing court workloads (McCold & Stahr, 1996).

Vermont's reparative probation boards are explicitly based on restorative justice ideals. They consist of small groups of specially trained volunteers who conduct public face-to-face meetings with nonviolent adult and juvenile probationers. Victim involvement is encouraged but not essential. Board members discuss the nature of the offense and its negative consequences, then enter into a contract with the offender that stipulates appropriate restorative sanctions (Bazemore & Umbreit, 1998). Volunteers contact victims to inform them about the hearings, offer support, and encourage their participation in the process. If victims attend the hearing, they can tell their story and seek accountability and restitution from the offender. If victims decline to attend, a volunteer surrogate will speak on their behalf and request appropriate reparative sanctions (Vermont Reparative Probation Program, 2001). Participating probationers' sentences are suspended on the condition that no more crimes are committed and the contracts—often community service—are fulfilled.

In a number of jurisdictions, a variety of restorative justice programs operate side by side. In Minnesota, for example, there is not only victim-offender mediation and family group conferencing but also neighborhood conferencing, sentencing circles, merchant accountability boards (where representatives from local businesses adjudicate minor shoplifting cases), and reparative community service projects (Kurki, 1999).

Opinions on the merits of restorative justice interventions vary. Some believe each model has strengths and weaknesses, and all contribute to innovative solutions to problems of offender reintegration (Bazemore & Umbreit, 1998). Others conclude that the lack of rigorous empirical research makes it hard to gauge the real effects on victims, offenders, or communities (Bonta, Wallace-Capretta, & Rooney, 1998; Schiff, 1998). There is some evidence that restorative justice initiatives provide greater satisfaction to offenders than the traditional system, and victims come away less afraid that they will be victimized again by the same offender (McCold & Wachtel, 1998; Schiff, 1998; Strang & Sherman, 1997; Umbreit, 1997). Police-facilitated family group conferencing also appears to reduce recidivism among certain types of young offenders (Sherman, Strang, & Woods, 2000). Although it is clear that victim input is a key element of all these programs, it is less clear whether victims benefit from their participation as much as offenders. Some of the caution or even suspicion with which victims and victims organizations sometimes view such programs may be justified and need to be addressed (Achilles, 1999; Bazemore & Umbreit, 1998).

Roles of Victims Organization in Reentry Planning and Implementation

Victims' voices in reentry initiatives may also be heard through organizations that serve and advocate on their behalf. These organizations can generalize about victim needs and offender behavior, provide information about the problems victims of particular crimes are likely to encounter when offenders are released, and identify measures that can best protect them. Furthermore, because only 36% of victims report the crimes to police (BJS, 2001a), and victims of certain crimes (e.g., sexual assault) are more likely to report to service providers than the police (Kilpatrick, Edmunds, & Seymour, 1992), these organizations can often give a more accurate picture of the nature and prevalence of crime in a particular locality. Victims organizations may therefore be especially helpful in designing reentry initiatives.

New approaches to reentry are emphasizing the need for planning and continuity between in-custody and postrelease programs—mirror support systems that allow offenders to "move from one to the other seamlessly on release" (Nelson & Trone, 2000; see also Travis, 2000). Some recent efforts involving victims organizations have focused narrowly on education and treatment programs, but others are broader, including victims organizations in criminal justice or community partnerships. The following sections illustrate the range of roles victims organizations can play and demonstrate the benefits of their participation.

IMPACT OF CRIME CLASSES

Impact of Crime on Victims (IOC) classes aim to educate violent and non-violent adult and juvenile offenders. They exist at the federal level and in about

20 states and, like victim impact panels, take place in a wide variety of settings. However, IOC classes have broader educational purposes and cover property offenses, domestic violence, sexual assault, homicide, robbery, child abuse, and victims' rights. They may explore views of other people's rights, how childhood experiences of victimization influence offenders' behaviors, and how to develop nonabusive relationships (APPA, 1999). As experts on victimization, victims organizations enrich IOC classes by helping design curricula, training the teachers, identifying victims to participate, and participating themselves.

JAIL-BASED VIOLENCE PREVENTION PROGRAMS

In keeping with newer approaches to reentry, jail-based violence prevention programs often link in-custody and postrelease efforts. For example, the Resolve to Stop the Violence Program (RSVP) created by the San Francisco Sheriff's Department espouses restorative justice principles; includes education, drama, therapy, life skills training, and group learning; and emphasizes victim empathy. The in-custody curriculum is intensive—14 hours a day, 6 days a week, for a minimum of 60 days. The postrelease program reinforces what has been taught in the jail program. Participants are required to attend violence-prevention men's groups, take advantage of education and job placement services, and participate in community and victims organizations' violence prevention services. RSVP also works directly with the victims of offenders in the program, helping them with immediate financial and other practical needs (San Francisco Sheriff's Department, 1999). Other jail-based programs focus on preventing particular categories of crime such as domestic violence or sexual assault (Schuster, 2001). As planners, trainers, and participants, victim advocates make an important contribution to decisions about in-custody and postcustody programs.

REENTRY COURTS, REENTRY PARTNERSHIPS

Reentry courts and reentry partnership initiatives are designed to make justice processes more effective by developing new roles for judges, victims, and community-based organizations, including victims organizations. First proposed by the U.S. Department of Justice and now funded by Congress, reentry courts will involve judges in overseeing and monitoring offender reentry. Mechanisms for holding offenders accountable to victims and victims organizations include citizen advisory boards, restitution orders, offender participation in victim impact panels, and active involvement of crime victims and victims organizations in the reentry processes (Office of Justice Programs, 1999).

The Justice Department's Reentry Partnerships Initiative also represents a new collaborative strategy to improve risk management of released offenders through prerelease reentry planning, effective surveillance and monitoring in the community, repairing the harm done to victims, and strengthening individual and community support systems. All of the proposed partners—state corrections agencies, local law enforcement, and community-based organizations—are charged with developing offender reentry plans together and overseeing their implementation. Core elements of the strategy include strong interagency collaboration including victims organizations, individual victim involvement and support, and structured postrelease reintegration of offenders based on a reentry plan the offender has helped design (Office of Justice Programs, 2000).

VICTIMS ORGANIZATIONS AND SEX OFFENDER MANAGEMENT

Sex offender reentry programs provide one of the most instructive examples of how victims organizations can enhance policy making and day-to-day reentry management decisions. Sex offenders present especially challenging reentry issues, because 68% of rapes and sexual assaults are not committed by strangers (Rand, 1998). In fact, family members are offenders in 27% of sexual assaults involving children and, where victims are aged 6 through 11, this percentage rises to 42% and for children younger than 6, to 49% (Snyder, 2000). In many cases involving juvenile victims, the offenders are older juveniles (Snyder & Sickmund, 1999). In addition, those who victimize children "differ in terms of their choice of victims, their criminal backgrounds, their sexual arousal patterns, their social functioning, and their risk of re-offending" (Grubin, 1998).

To control the manipulative behavior of sex offenders and ensure appropriate treatment based on shared information, the Center for Sex Offender Management has recommended collaborative networks that go well beyond traditional cooperation (Center for Sex Offender Management, 2000a). In these networks, victims organizations not only assist victims but provide information that can affect the offender's supervision and treatment, thereby enhancing safety for individual victims and the public (Center for Sex Offender Management, 2000b). Connecticut is one of the few states that has translated these ideas into practice by creating a full-time victim advocate position in its corrections-based intensive sex offender supervision unit. In addition to serving victims, the advocate's role is to work with offenders' families to help them understand the dynamics of sex offending, make unannounced field visits with probation and treatment providers to help identify problems, and assist treatment providers with group therapy sessions and weekly case reviews. Sometimes, they also assist law enforcement with door-to-door notification of the presence of an offender in the neighborhood (Center for Sex Offender Management, 2000b).

AN OVERLOOKED RESOURCE

Given that there will be many missed opportunities to prevent recidivism without victim involvement to ground ideas in relevant facts, we must ask ourselves why victims and victims organizations are so rarely "at the table." There are several reasons. First, despite the proliferation of laws designed to promote victims' participation in the criminal justice system, a recent survey showed that even in states with strong legal protections, nearly two thirds of victims were not informed of the pretrial release of the accused, half of all victims in cases resulting in plea agreements were not given an opportunity to consult with the prosecutor prior to the agreement, and nearly half were never notified of the sentencing hearing at all (Kilpatrick et al., 1998). If victims do not know how and when to participate, they are not likely to exercise their rights.

Another reason is that many victims organizations focus on the needs of individual victims and do not have the resources to engage in broader problem-solving endeavors. Without additional support to participate in reentry initiatives, the core work of these organizations could suffer. Furthermore, many victims organizations do not realize the value their knowledge could bring to the process, so they may not propose their own participation.

There is another overarching reason. Many victim advocates do not participate because they believe that reentry initiatives, like the criminal justice system in general, are not primarily designed to address victims' needs. Whereas positive reentry outcomes no doubt benefit victims, the education, counseling, job training, housing, and community support systems created to enhance offender reintegration do very little to address similar reintegration needs of victims. Even the most victim-sensitive reentry programs will probably not fully undo the consequences of victimization. They are not likely to reduce the trauma of violent crime significantly or provide meaningful restitution for grievous losses. They cannot cure the emotional problems and substance abuse many victims subsequently suffer. They cannot help intimidated victims relocate. However appropriate and desirable, the new policy interest in offender reintegration only highlights an acute lack of attention to crime victims' need to be reintegrated into healthy, safe, and productive lives.

Conclusion

The increase in prison populations and the general expansion of criminal justice supervision have substantially increased the extent of criminal justice involvement in the lives of Americans. One consequence has been increased levels of prisoners' reentry. For victims and victims organizations, the new focus on reentry issues is generally welcome as good crime prevention, and participating in the reentry process can help some individual victims regain a sense of control in their lives and enhance their safety.

The 25-year history of victims' increased participation in the criminal justice system has demonstrated that victims can be constructively involved in reentry decisions such as sentencing and parole. Innovations in the mediation, restorative justice, and community justice movements have also demonstrated the value of specific victim-offender interactions. More recent collaborative initiatives such as reentry partnerships, victim impact classes, and sex offender management teams underscore the specific contributions that victims organizations can make to reentry planning and implementation.

The larger lesson from this typology of roles of victims in offender reentry, however, is that victims' voices and victims' participation should be welcomed and not feared or discouraged. The complexity of victims' experiences and of victim/offender relationships provides valuable richness and reality to the reintegrative functions of the criminal justice system.

NOTE

1. The information about victims' rights in the criminal justice system is drawn from information collected by the National Center for Victims of Crime, most of which is available on the World Wide Web: *www.ncvc.org*.

REFERENCES

Achilles, M. (1999). *Working together: Victim services and victim–offender mediation programs*. Retrieved October 15, 2000, http://sites.state.pa.us/PA_Exec/ova/working.htm

American Probation and Parole Association. (1999, July). *Promising victim-related practices and strategies in probation and parole* (U.S. Department of Justice Publication No. NCJ 166606). Washington, DC: U.S. Department of Justice, Office for Victims of Crime.

Bazemore, G., & Umbreit, M. (1998). *Circles, board, and mediations: Restorative justice and citizen involvement in the response to youth crime*. Washington, DC: U.S. Department of Justice, Office of Juvenile Justice and Delinquence Prevention.

Bonta J., Wallace-Capretta, S., & Rooney, J. (1998). Restorative justice: An evaluation of the restorative resolutions project (Rep. No. 1998-05). Retrieved January 6, 2001, http://www.sgc.gc.ca/epub/coss/e 199810b/e199810b.htm

Boyle, J. M. (1999). *Crime issues in the Northeast: Statewide surveys of the public and crime victims in CT, DE, ME, MA, VT, NH, NJ, NY and RI*. Lexington, KY: Council of State Governments.

Bureau of Justice Statistics. (1999, August 22). *U.S. correctional population reaches 5.9 million offenders* [Press release]. Washington, DC: U.S. Department of Justice. Retrieved December 16, 2000, http://www.ojp.usdoj.gov/bjs/pub/press/ppus98.pr

Bureau of Justice Statistics. (2000, July 23). *U.S. correctional population reaches 6.3 million men and women, represents 3.1 percent of the adult U.S. population* [Press release]. Washington. DC: U.S. Department of Justice. Retrieved January 9, 2001, http://www.ojp.usdoj.gov/bjs/pub/pdf/pp99pr.pdf

Bureau of Justice Statistics. (2001a, January). *Criminal victimization in United States, 1999 statistical tables*. Washington, DC: U.S. Department of Justice. Retrieved February 5, 2001, http://www.ojp.usdoj.gov/bjs/pub/pdf/cvus99.pdf

Bureau of Justice Statistics. (200lb, January 24). *Victim characteristics*. Retrieved January 26, 2001, http://www.ojp.usdoj.gov/bjs/cvict_v.htm

Butterfield, F. (2000, November 29). Often, parole is one stop on the way back to prison. *New York Times*. Retrieved November 29, 2000, http://www.Nytimes.com/ 2000/11/29

Center for Sex Offender Management. (2000a, January). *Community supervision of the sex offender: An overview of current and promising practices*. Retrieved January 16, 2001, http://www.csom.org/pubs/supervision2.pdf

Center for Sex Offender Management (2000b, March). *Engaging advocates and other victim service providers in the community management of sex offenders*. Retrieved January 10, 2001, http://www.csom.org/pubs/advocacy.pdf

DiIulio, J., Jr. (2000, September 1). Keeping crime on the run. *Blueprint Magazine*. Retrieved December 4, 2000, http://www.ndol.org/blueprint/fall2000

Ditton, P., & Wilson, D. (1999). *Truth in sentencing in state prisons* (U.S. Department of Justice Publication No. NCJ 170032). Washington, DC: U.S. Department of Justice, Bureau of Justice Statistics.

Erez, E. (1999, July). Who's afraid of the big bad victim? Victim impact statements as victim empowerment and enhancement of justice. *Criminal Law Review*, 545–556.

Finkelhor, D., & Ormrod, R. (2000, June). Characteristics of crime against juveniles. *Juvenile Justice Bulletin* (U.S. Department of Justice Publication No. NCJ

179034). Washington, DC: U.S. Department of Justice, Office of Justice Programs, Office of Juvenile Justice and Delinquency Prevention.

Greenwood, J., & Umbreit, M. (1998). National survey of victim offender mediation programs in the U.S. *VOMA Connections,* Winter 1998, 1.

Grubin, D. (1998). Sex offending against children: Understanding the risk (Police Research Series, Paper 99). London: Home Office, Research Development and Statistics Directorate.

Harlow, C. W. (1999). *Selected findings, prior abuse reported by inmates and probationers* (U.S. Department of Justice Publication No. NCJ 172879). Washington, DC: U.S. Department of Justice, Bureau of Justice Statistics.

Kilpatrick, D., Edmunds, C., & Seymour, A. (1992, April). *Rape in America: A report to the nation.* Arlington, VA: National Center for Victims of Crime.

Kilpatrick, D. G., Beatty, D., & Howley, S. (1998, December). The rights of crime victims—Does legal protection make a difference. In *Research in brief,* (U.S. Department of Justice Publication No. NCJ 172837). Washington, DC: U.S. Department of Justice, National Institute of Justice.

Kinney, D. (2001, January 30). N.J. courts seek 150 more parole officers. *The Star-Ledger.* Retrieved January 30, 2001, http://www.nj.com/news/ledger/index.ssf?/jersey/ledger/1232375.html

Kurki, L. (1999, September). Incorporating restorative and community justice into American sentencing and corrections. In *Sentencing and Corrections, Issues for the 21st Century, 3.* Retrieved December 16, 2000, http://www.ncjrs.org/pdffilesl/nij/175723.pdf

Manhattan Institute. (1999). *Transforming probation through leadership: The "broken windows" model.* Retrieved January 9, 2001, http://www.Manhattan-institute.org/html/broken_windows.htm

McCold, P. (1999). Restorative justice practice—The state of the field 1999. *Real Justice.* Retrieved December 12, 2000, http://www.realjustice.org/Pages/vt99papers/vt_mccold.html

McCold, P., Stahr, J., Lt. (1996). Bethlehem police family group conferencing project. *Real Justice.* Retrieved December 17, 2000, http://www.realjustice.org/Pages/bethlehem.html

McCold, P., & Wachtel, B. (1998). *Restorative policing experiment, the Bethlehem Pennsylvania police family group conferencing project.* Retrieved December 8, 1999, http://www.realjustice.org/Pages/summary.htm

Murray, R. (1999, June 16). Trying to fit sex offenders back into society. *The Free Press*, pp. 1A, 8A.

National Center for Victims of Crime. (1999). *Promising practices & strategies for victim services in corrections, a training and resource manual.* Washington, DC: U.S. Department of Justice, Office for Victims of Crime.

Nelson, M., & Trone, J. (2000). Why planning for release matters. In *Issues in Brief.* New York: Vera Institute of Justice.

Office of Justice Programs. (1999). *Reentry courts: Managing the transition from prison to community, a call for concept papers.* Washington, DC: U.S. Department of Justice. Office of Justice Programs.

Office of Justice Programs. (2000). Request for applications for reentry partnerships process evaluation. http://www.ojp.usdoj.gov/nij/pdf/reentrymain.pdf

Petersilia, J. (2000, November). When prisoners return to the community: Political, economic, and social consequences. In *Sentencing and Corrections Issues for the 21st Century, 9.* Retrieved December 16, 2000, http://www.ncjrs.org/pdffiles1/nij/184253.pdf

Prisons release record numbers of ex-convicts. Communities are scrambling. (2001, January 3). *USA Today.* Retrieved January 4, 2001, http://www.allsoul.com/allsoul/articles/122700/index_05.htm

Rand, M. (1998). *Criminal victimization 1997: Changes 1996–97 with trends 1993–97.* Washington, DC: U.S. Department of Justice, Bureau of Justice Statistics.

Rennison, C. (2000). *Criminal victimization 1999: Changes 1998–99 with trends 1993–99* (U.S. Department of Justice Publication No. NCJ 182734). Washington, DC: U.S. Department of Justice, Bureau or Justice Statistics.

San Francisco Sheriff's Department. (1999, June 22). *Jail programs. RSVP: Resolve to Stop the Violence Project.* Retrieved January 19, 2001, http://www.ci.sf.ca.us/sheriff/ rsvp.htm

Schiff, M. (1998). Restorative justice interventions for juvenile offenders: A research agenda for the next decade. *Western Criminology Review, 1.* Retrieved December 19, 2001, http://www.wcr.sonoma.edu/vlnl/schiff.html

Schuster, B. (2001, January 8). Jailhouse rehabilitation for batterers. *Los Angeles Times*, p. A1.

Shapiro, B. (1997, February 10). Victims & vengeance: Why the victims' rights amendment is a bad idea. *The Nation, 264*, 11. Retrieved February 5, 2001, from Lexis/Nexis.

Sherman, L., Strang, H., & Woods, D. (2000). *Recidivism patterns in the Canberra reintegrative shaming experiments.* Canberra: Australian Institute of Criminology. Retrieved January 6, 2001, http://www.aic.gov.au/rjustice/rise/recidivism/conclusion.html

Snyder, H. (2000). *Sexual assault of young children as reported to law enforcement: Victim, incident, and offender characteristics* (U.S. Department of Justice Publication No. 182990). Washington, DC: U.S. Department of Justice, National Center for Juvenile Justice.

Snyder, H. N., & Sickmund, M. (1999). *Juvenile offenders and victims: National report.* Washington, DC: National Center for Juvenile Justice.

Staples, B. (1997, September 22). When grieving "victims" can sway the courts. *New York Times*, p. A26.

Strang, H., & Sherman, L. (1997). *The victim's perspective.* Canberra: Australian Institute of Criminology. Retrieved January 9, 2001, http://www.aic.gov.au/rjustice/rise/working/risepap2.html

Tjaden, P., & Thoennes, N. (1998). *Prevalence, incidence, and consequences of violence against women: Findings from the national violence against women survey.* Washington, DC: National Institute of Justice and Centers for Disease Control and Prevention.

Tobolowsky, P. M. (1999). Victim participation in the criminal justice process: Fifteen years after the president's task force on victims of crime. Retrieved February 5, 2001. from the *International Victimology* Web site: http://www.victimology.nl

Travis, J. (2000). But they all come back: Rethinking prisoner reentry. In *Sentencing & Corrections Issues for the 21st Century, 7.* Washington, DC: U.S. Department of Justice, National Institute of Justice.

Umbreit, M. (1997). *Fact sheet: Victim offender mediation.* St. Paul, MN: University of Minnesota, Center for Restorative Justice and Peacemaking.

Vermont Reparative Probation Program, Vermont Department of Corrections (2001). *Restorative justice panels and the reparative probation program.* Retrieved January 3, 2001, http://www.communityjusticeburlvt.org/reparative.html

Widom, C. S. (2000). Childhood victimization and the derailment of girls and women to the criminal justice system, research on women and girls in the justice system. In *1999 Conference on Criminal Justice Research and Evaluation-Enhancing Policy and Practice Through Research Vol. 3.* Washington, DC: U.S. Department of Justice, National Institute of Justice.

Chapter Twenty-One

A Preliminary Study of a Large Victim/Offender Reconciliation Program

Mike Niemeyer
David Shichor

Crime and juvenile delinquency are of major concern in the United States and in many other countries. There is a growing recognition that the prevailing approach of criminal and juvenile justice, which focuses on the behavior of and the subsequent punishment of individual offenders, is an ineffective and outdated approach that provides little or no opportunity for the victims to participate actively in the justice process. In the current system, which is an outgrowth of the historical emergence of the state as the dominant power in modern times, crime is perceived as an act against the state. This approach has led to the gross neglect of individual victims, who have been seen as passive entities, have been almost completely locked out from any decision making in the justice proceedings, and often have not been compensated for the harm that occurred to them.

A different approach to providing justice, often referred to as "restorative justice," is gaining ground (Zehr, 1990). As Umbreit explains: "Rather than defining 'the state' as the victim, restorative justice theory postulates that criminal behavior is first a conflict between individuals. This person who was violated is the primary victim, and the state is a secondary victim" (1994, p. 2). Both victims and offenders assume active problem-solving roles aimed at restoring the material and psychological losses that accrued to the individual victims and to the community (Umbreit, 1994). Thus, restorative justice relies "on informal resolution of underlying problems, conflict reduction through dialogue and mediation, and efforts to achieve satisfactory agreements" (Bazemore & Umbreit, 1995, p. 14). The clearest operationalization of restorative justice is expressed in the form of victim-offender mediation programs (see Galaway & Hudson, 1990).

Source: *Federal Probation*, 60(3) (September 1996): 30–34.

One of the most popular models of this kind of community program is the Victim/Offender Reconciliation Program (VORP), a sentencing alternative whereby offenders agree to meet their victims in order to negotiate over the severity of harm caused by the offense and, with the help of a mediator, to decide on a mutually agreed upon amount and type of restitution (Dittenhoffer & Ericson, 1992). VORP is a process where victims and offenders are given a chance to meet with each other and "make things right." This program is frequently an alternative to the court process. The concept of victims and offenders meeting with each other in a mediation setting has been described in numerous articles. It was first implemented in Canada. On May 28, 1974, two boys from Elmira, Ontario, pleaded guilty to vandalizing 22 properties. At the prompting of the probation officer and a Mennonite volunteer, the judge ordered the two boys to meet the victims and work out restitution directly with them (Dittenhoffer & Ericson, 1992).

During the last few years, several studies have been conducted to evaluate various VORP projects. In one study of the effectiveness of victim-offender mediation by Coates and Gehm (1989), 83 percent of offenders and 59 percent of victims were satisfied with the experience. The researchers also found that when the victim and the offender met, an agreement was reached 98 percent of the time. Victims generally reported a high level of satisfaction, and most victims and offenders said that they would participate in the process again if given the choice (Umbreit, 1992). The American Bar Association (ABA, 1994) has recommended that local, state, and federal agencies take steps to incorporate these programs in their criminal justice process. The ABA recommendation included the use of this process for violent as well as nonviolent crimes, under the proper conditions.

Recidivism also has been examined and showed mixed results. Umbreit and Coates (1992) found that participation in victim-offender mediation had a small but not statistically significant effect (18 percent versus 27 percent for nonmediated cases) on offenders' recidivism. In another study Umbreit (1992) found no significant reductions in a four-state survey and noted that this was consistent with earlier studies (Dignan, 1990; Marshall & Merry, 1990) but also noted that one study by Schneider (1986) had shown a significant decrease in recidivism due to mediation. Nugent and Paddock (1995) found that VORP participants were less likely to reoffend and that their offenses were less severe than those of juveniles who had gone through more traditional treatment.

This article is an exploratory evaluation of one of the largest VORPs dealing with juvenile delinquents in the United States, the Orange County, California, program sponsored by the St. Vincent De Paul Center.

Program Development and Resource Management

VORPs or VOMPs (Victim/Offender Mediation Programs) are almost exclusively organized at a county level with one program serving one urban or several rural counties. The Orange County program handles both juvenile and adult criminal cases and is sponsored by the St. Vincent De Paul Society. Based on the volume of cases handled, more than 1,000 in the first 8 months of 1995, this is one of largest programs of its kind in the United States. Program development has involved the management of three critical resources: funding, cases, and volunteers.

FUNDING

Substantial program funding comes through the California Dispute Resolution Programs Act (1991), which assesses an $8 surcharge on civil court filing fees and disburses that money through a county administrator to local nonprofit agencies. In Orange County that surcharge generates a little more than $900,000 annually for five different alternative dispute resolution (ADR) programs of which VORP receives $282,000.

REFERRALS TO VORP

The first referrals to VORP came from the Orange County Probation Department in August 1989. As with most new programs, some time was needed for the referral agencies to use it. While upper management embraced the idea early on, it took years for probation staff members to use the program in any significant numbers. Probation, police, and juvenile courts expressed concerns that the program was optional for offenders and doubted that victims would want to meet with their offenders. There was also concern that an unsophisticated victim would be manipulated by a clever offender. With experience these concerns were overcome, and, as table 1 shows, between 1989 and 1995 a total of 2,496 juvenile offenders were referred to the program by the probation department and the various law enforcement agencies. These cases included pretrial diversions and post sentencing formal probation cases.

Table 1
Number of Cases Referred to VORP by Year, Budget, and Cost per Case

Year	Number of Cases	Total Budget	Cost Per Case
1989	5	14,540	2,908.00
1990	24	14,540	605.83
1991	12	15,083	1,256.92
1992	167	15,083	90.32
1993	550	107,000	194.55
1994	538	107,000	198.88
1995 (estimated)	1,200	300,000	250.00

VOLUNTEERS

Most VORPs rely heavily on trained volunteer mediators. Some programs use a single mediator, with 8 to 10 hours of training and no mentoring, while others, including the Orange County program, require 30 to 40 hours of classroom training and an apprenticeship with a comediator. Central to the philosophy of VORP is the belief that trained volunteers are best able to mediate between the victims and offenders and to provide the time, energy, and cultural sensitivity required for this process. VORP staff support the volunteers by assisting with recruiting and training and the clerical and administrative aspects of case management.

VORP volunteers invested 5,814.5 hours in victim-offender mediation cases since the inception of the program. Under the California Dispute Resolution Programs Act of 1991, trained mediators can be valued at $25 per hour for the purpose of matching grant funds. This is equivalent to $145,000 in in-kind donations to the program. The study found that the most time-consuming mediations seem to be those involving "serious personal" crimes. In addition to significant staff time, these cases required an average of 12.6 volunteer hours each.

The ratio of paid staff to volunteers remained fairly constant throughout the first 6 years of the program. A paid, full-time case manager supported about 50 to 75 volunteers, who in turn handled about eight cases each per year. When the annual program budget was divided by the number of cases processed each year, the cost per case went from almost $3,000 in the first year to around $250 in 1995, as table 2 indicates.

STATUTORY AUTHORITY

The Orange County program and other VORPs in California developed under the broad authority that allowed law enforcement agencies to divert cases (California Welfare and Institutions code section 654) rather than under any specific statutory authority. Since 1992 several bills have been introduced in the state legislature to promote the VORP process directly or mediation in general. In its third year of operation, the Orange County program benefited from funding available in the California Dispute Resolution Programs Act of 1991. This legislation also encouraged numerous mediation programs in California and the training of hundreds of mediators. Many of the mediators in the Orange County VORP had come from other mediation programs in search of a different type of experience. Other legislation attempted to make VORP mandatory, a policy which the VORPs found onerous. Concerns over how VORP could be legislated prompted a special meeting of the California VORPs in 1994 to discuss public policy issues and develop a definition of VORPs.

Some Outcomes of the Victim/Offender Mediation Process

Our examination of the Orange County victim-offender mediation process included a study of client participation rates, mediation rates, agreement compliance rates, and timelines. For purposes of the study, the cases were placed into 6 groups based on the nature of the offense (see table 2).

THE PROCESS

In the Orange County program the case is assigned by a case manager to a pair of volunteer mediators. The mediators make the initial phone call to the offender and then meet with that person and his or her parents. If they are willing to participate, the mediators contact the victim to arrange a meeting with him or her. If the

Table 2

Types of Juvenile Cases Referred to VORP

Type of offense	Percent of the total
Serious personal	24
Minor personal	15
Serious property	16
Minor property	9
Sex-related	1
Graffiti/tagging	35
	100

victim is interested in participating, the mediators arrange a joint meeting between the offender and the victim. During this meeting, both sides tell their story, express their feelings, and discuss what might be done to make things right. Where an agreement is reached, a contract is written up. Once mediated the case is returned to the VORP office, where a staff person follows up on the execution of the restitution agreement.

On average it took 27 days from the day of intake to the date of the first meeting between the VORP mediator and the offender and 35 days to meet with the victim. The process averaged 45 days between intake and the joint meeting or mediation. An average of 164 days was needed to complete a restitution agreement and close the case.

CLIENT PARTICIPATION

Client participation was of interest because, as explained, this program is based on victim-offender participation in the justice process. It was important to see how many and what kind of offenders would agree to this process. Offenders were given the opportunity to take part in the program, although they likely faced other sanctions if they chose not to participate in VORP.

The study found that most victims and offenders chose to meet face to face with the other party. Victims were most likely to agree to meet their offender in minor personal crimes (disturbing the peace, trespassing, annoying telephone calls, and malicious mischief) (79 percent). Almost the same percent (74 percent) of victims of serious property crimes and victims of minor property crimes (also 74 percent) agreed to meet with the perpetrators of the crimes, while the least likely to agree to such a meeting were victims of serious personal crimes such as assault with a deadly weapon, murder, and assault and battery (58 percent).

When victims chose not to meet with the offender, they most often indicated that the case was not important enough to warrant participation (75 of 215 responses or 35 percent). Thirteen percent reported that they had already worked out some arrangement with the offender on their own. Lack of confidence in the offender's goodwill, fear, or anger were given as reasons in only 9 percent of the cases.

Offenders were least likely to agree to meet the victim in minor personal crimes (69 percent) and were most likely to agree in property offenses (more than 80 percent). In serious personal crimes offenders agreed to a meeting in 77 percent of the cases. When offenders articulated a reason for refusal to participate in the VORP process, they most often indicated that they did not feel that they had done anything wrong (64 percent). In 33 percent of the cases the parents did not want the offender to participate.

The extent of participation was not the same in all offense categories. The highest level of participation was reported among offenders who were involved in sex-related charges including sodomy, sexual battery, and rape; in this group 86 percent of the cases were mediated. However, it is hard to make generalizations based on these data because the number of juveniles who had these charges was only 12.

Among the cases involving graffiti (usually turf marking by gang members) and tagging (wall painting to express personal or collective style), which had the largest number of referrals—495—the participation was extensive; 333 (67 percent) reached mediation. Another high category was the one for "serious property offenses" (burglary, grand theft, hit and run, and arson). Quite unexpectedly, in this category 54 percent of the referred cases (120 out of 222) reached mediation in spite of the seriousness of the offenses. Common sense would, suggest that both victims and offenders in this category would be more reluctant to participate in mediation than would the parties in "minor property/ motor vehicle-related" offenses, but in the latter only 32 percent went to mediation.

AGREEMENT RATE AND CONTENT OF CONTRACTS

Of all juvenile cases referred to VORP, 48 percent reached a written agreement through mediation, 40 percent were closed without having reached an agreement (because the parties opted out or could not be located), and 19 percent were still in the process of being mediated. Where there was a joint meeting, an agreement was reached in 99 percent of the cases. Community service was specified in 49 percent of the cases and 54 percent called for monetary compensation. The average amount of community service was 93 hours, and monetary restitution averaged $234 per case.

Community service is used more frequently in European countries than in the United States, but it is an integral part of VORP. This disposition was most frequently applied in the graffiti cases. In this category the majority of offenders—62 percent (208 out of 333)—agreed to participate in cleaning graffiti and tagging from the walls and fences in the community.

In the City of Santa Ana all first-time graffiti vandals are referred to VORP. Of 409 total juvenile arrests for tagging, 97 were referred for criminal prosecution and 134 were diverted to VORP. The police department noted that graffiti decreased from 691,000 square feet per month to 243,000 in the months following the introduction of the program.

In only one other category was community service agreed upon in the majority of cases, in "minor personal" offenses (disturbing the peace, trespassing, and annoying telephone calls). Sixty-five percent of mediation agreements involved community service in this category. In addition, there were two more offense groups that used community service agreements in a substantial number of cases: "serious property" offenses (25 percent) and "minor property and motor vehicle-related" offenses (20 percent). A total of 3,1319.3 hours was completed in community service. These hours, when translated to the prevailing minimum wage of $4.25, add up to $133,107, a sum which was in a sense put back into the community.

The most significant and visible community service was dedicated to cleaning the graffiti and tagging. Juveniles charged with this offense agreed to 27,699 hours in graffiti abatement activities. The importance of this service is considerable not only because of its visibility, but also because many people relate to graffiti as a sign of "incivility" and as a serious threat to the "quality of life" in the community. In a letter to VORP dated January 24, 1994, Santa Ana Police Chief Paul Walters stated that, because of the resulting reduction in graffiti and impact of offender restitution and community service,

> These funds and community service hours have been used not only to offset city costs expended to combat this form of urban blight, but also to relieve city personnel from graffiti removal duties. This program has permitted us to redirect city labor to other, more valuable projects benefiting our community and has resulted in a salary savings of approximately $212,000.

Monetary restitution also became a part of the mediation agreements; 19 percent of them included this option. The total sum of monetary restitution collected was $86,973.63. This is a sizable amount of money, especially if one takes into consideration that most of the juveniles in the program are from low income families. The average sum per juvenile who was involved in the restitution agreement was $256.04.

As expected, the use of monetary restitution was not evenly distributed among the various offenses. It was most often used among juveniles involved in "minor personal" offenses, which include primarily "nuisance" behavior; 84 percent in this category made some restitution. However, the average sum paid by these violators was only $75.65. Restitution also was applied frequently (59 percent) for "serious property" offenders. In this category the average amount was $506.93. More than half (51 percent) of the graffiti-tagging agreements involved monetary restitution as well. In 43 percent of "minor property" offense cases restitution was agreed upon. The lowest level of use of this alternative was, not unexpectedly, with offenders who committed "serious personal" crimes (13 percent) and in "sex-related" offenses (8 percent).

AGREEMENT COMPLIANCE

Of all cases in which agreement was reached, 96.8 percent of the contracts were completed or were current; only 3 percent failed to be fulfilled. Interestingly, the failures came almost exclusively from property offenses. So while it was harder to get the parties to a mediation session in personal crime cases, once they did meet, the agreements were at least as durable as, or maybe even more durable than, those in property offense cases.

RECIDIVISM

Recidivism is often used as one of the main indications of effectiveness of corrections programs. Our evaluation examined official statistics of reoffending of VORP "graduates" and a comparison group of juveniles. Because of the large number of individuals involved in the Orange County VORP since its inception in 1989, we selected for the study a systematic random sample of every fifth from the list of participants, providing a random sample of 131.

The comparison group was comprised of all juveniles who were referred to VORP but did not participate in the program for various reasons (mainly because they had moved and could not be contacted by the program staff, their address was not correct, they did not have a telephone to be reached, or they refused to participate in the program). The total number of juveniles in this group was 152.

Reoffending was operationalized as an official contact with any Orange County law enforcement agency. In the VORP sample the number of juveniles that had a known contact after completing the program was 37 (28 percent). They accounted for 64 contacts, an average of 1.7 contacts for each recidivist. In the comparison group 36 juveniles (23 percent) had a subsequent contact with law enforcement agencies after the initial referral. The total number of offenses in subsequent contacts was 59, an average of 1.6 offenses for each known recidivist. The differences between the two groups were not statistically significant.

These results do not show that participation in VORP leads to better results in terms of further contacts with law enforcement, i.e., in less future delinquent involvement. In fact, VORP participants showed a somewhat higher level of recidivism than juveniles in the comparison group. We also note that participation in VORP costs money while comparison group members did not cost any money beyond the initial efforts to contact them. However, since the comparison group consists of a less stable population (as mentioned, most of them could not be reached by the VORP staff), it is possible that many of them moved away from Orange County or were moving back and forth from one place to another, and therefore their subsequent delinquent involvements were harder to detect.

Usually, recidivist behavior starts during the first year after the juvenile was handled by the authorities and/or finished some kind of intervention program. That was the case in this project as well. Among the VORP recidivists 58 percent had at least one police contact during the first year after completing the mediation program, and an additional 36 percent had a contact in the second year. In the comparison group a significantly higher per-centage, 80 percent, had a law enforcement contact in the first year. This pattern may indicate that participation in VORP slows down the subsequent involvement in delinquency even though later this involvement increases.

The most likely juveniles to have had agency contact after their gradua-tion from VORP were the ones who were referred to the program for minor offenses against the person, probation violations, and vehicle violations (58 percent), but the total number of juveniles in this group was only eight. None of the minor property offenders (eight in total) had any additional law enforcement contacts. In the comparison group the highest recidivism rate was among minor property offenders (33 percent—5 out of 15 cases). Thus it seems that although it is risky to generalize on the basis of relatively small numbers, participation in VORP has the highest benefit for juveniles referred for minor property offenses. On the other hand, the unique experi-ment of mediation that the Orange County VORP initiated in graffiti cases did not seem to make a difference since 16 juveniles (28 percent) out of a total of 57 recidivated. At the same time, in the comparison group 11 young-sters (29 percent) out of 38 graffiti offenders did so.

Conclusion

Crime victims' high participation rate in VORP indicates that there are some victim needs which are best met through victims' direct contact with offenders. The fact that 49 percent of the cases resulted in a written agree-ment between the victim and offender without monetary restitution shows that not all the victims were participating in VORP simply to recover restitu-tion. Ideally, the process resulted in a better understanding between the vic-tims and the offenders—a less tenable but not less important aim of this program. The program's ability to help victims and offenders to reach dura-ble agreements counts also as a plus. The study failed to show a significant difference in recidivism rates between the program participants and a com-parison group of nonparticipants. Further studies will have to be conducted before we are able to reach more definitive conclusions about the effective-ness of the Orange County VORP.

REFERENCES

American Bar Association. (1994). *Report to the House of Delegates* (Report #101B). Chicago: American Bar Association.

Bazemore, G., & Umbreit, M. (1995). Rethinking the sanctioning function in juvenile court: Retributive or restorative response to juvenile crime. *Crime and Delin-quency*, 41(3), 296–316.

Coates, R., & Gehm, J. (1989). *Mediation and criminal justice*. London: Sage.

Dignan, J. (1990). *Repairing the damage: An evaluation of an experimental adult repara-tion scheme in Kettering, Northamptonshire*. Sheffield: University of Sheffield, Centre of Criminological and Legal Research.

Dittenhoffer, T., & Ericson, R.V. (1992). The victim/offender reconciliation programme: A message to the correctional reformers. In E. A. Fattah (Ed.), *Toward a critical victimology*. New York: St. Martins Press.

Galaway, B., & Hudson, J. (1990). (Eds.). *Criminal justice restitution and reconciliation*. Monsey, NY. Criminal Justice Press.

Marshall, T., & Merry, S. (1990). *Crime and accountability: Victim/offender mediation in practice*. London: HMSO.

Nugent, M. R., & Paddock, J. B. (1995). The effect of victim offender mediation on severity of re-offense. *Mediation Quarterly*, 12(4), 353–367.

Schneider, A. L. (1986). Restitution and recidivism rates of juvenile offenders: Results from four experimental studies. *Criminology*, 24(3), 533–552.

Umbreit, M. (1994). Issues to be faced in starting a local program. In *Victim meets offender: The impact of restorative justice and mediation*. Monsey, NY: Criminal Justice Press.

Umbreit, M., & Coates, R. (1992). *Victim offender mediation: An analysis of programs in four states of the U.S.* Minneapolis, MN: Minnesota Citizens Council on Crime and Justice.

Zehr, H. (1990). *Changing lenses: A new focus for crime and justice*. Scottsdale, PA: Herald Press.